THE ANATOMY OF

DR SHIRLEY ROBIN LETW̶ [...]
on political philosophy. Afteɪ graduate study at
the London School of Economics, she received
the degree of Doctor of Philosophy from the University of Chicago. Apart from her books, she has
published numerous essays in scholarly journals
and has contributed political commentaries to
periodicals and newspapers. She has taught at
Cambridge University, the London School of
Economics, Harvard, Brandeis, Cornell, and the
University of Chicago. She has been a Gug-
genheim Fellow and a Fellow of the Radcliffe
Institute. She has been awarded research grants
by the Rockefeller Foundation, the American
Council of Learned Societies, and the Earhart
Foundation. She is currently President of the
Institut International de Philosophie Politique. As
a Director of the Centre for Policy Studies
(founded by Margaret Thatcher and Keith
Joseph), and through her long association with the
Institute of Economic Affairs, and as a member of
the Tory Philosophy Group, she has been personally acquainted with many of the leading figures
in the story of Thatcherism.

The Anatomy of
Thatcherism

Shirley Robin Letwin

Fontana
An Imprint of HarperCollins*Publishers*

Fontana
An Imprint of HarperCollins*Publishers*
77–85 Fulham Palace Road
Hammersmith, London W6 8JB

A Fontana Original
First published 1992
9 8 7 6 5 4 3 2 1

ISBN 0-00-686243 8

Phototypeset by Intype, London

Printed and bound in Great Britain by
HarperCollins Manufacturing, Glasgow.

CONTENTS

ACKNOWLEDGEMENTS

In writing this book, I received considerable and substantial assistance from Oliver Letwin. In particular, I owe to his knowledge of recent British politics, his ability to point out the heart of the matter, and his facility in communicating his insights the solution to the riddle of Thatcherism, and especially the theme of the 'vigorous virtues', offered here. But as the use made of assistance is not always what was intended, the responsibility for what appears in the book is entirely mine.

For help with meeting the cost of research and typing, I am grateful to the Institute for Policy Research and especially to Lord Joseph for arranging it. I greatly appreciate the immense trouble taken by Alistair Cooke to make available and direct me to the relevant material at the Conservative Political Centre. For having generously taken time to clarify matters which would otherwise have remained obscure, I am indebted to: Lord Annan, Kenneth Baker, Sir Paul Beresford, Sir Rhodes Boyson, Sir Keith Bright, Professor Tim Congdon, Lord Harris of High Cross, Lord Joseph, Professor Elie Kedourie, Tony Kerpel, Dr Sheila Lawlor, John O'Sullivan, Enoch Powell, Professor Sig Prais, Nicholas Ridley, Professor Ben Roberts, Marjorie Seldon, Arthur Seldon, Stuart Sexton, Eric Sorensen, David Willetts, John Wood.

The onus of having suggested this project to me rests with John O'Sullivan. I would like to thank Stuart Proffitt and Philip Gwyn Jones for their discerning and helpful editorial suggestions; Anthea Zeman for her very painstaking and ingenious ordering of an unruly mass of documents; Andrew Best for his interest and encouragement throughout, and Peter Robinson for his expeditious help with the final arrangements; Caroline Boon, for her accommodating and skilful typing of complicated manuscripts, repeatedly revised.

My debt to my husband, William Letwin, is even more pervasive than usual.

for M.H.S.

PROLOGUE

The strangest thing that happened in Britain in the 1980s was the attachment of a prime minister's name to an 'ism'. The French, of course, are used to such things and have their Pétainisme and Gaullisme among others, but the British never dreamt of anything like Churchillism. What rendered the appearance in Britain of this bizarre 'ism' even stranger was that after winning three elections, with almost embarrassing majorities, in the third year of her third term, that very same prime minister felt obliged to resign.

On the morning of her resignation, rumours that it would soon be announced were everywhere. The rumours also kept being denied. By midday the resignation was definitely confirmed, but no one found it easy to believe. People spoke about her departure as if a comet had been sighted off course.

The astonishment was almost as peculiar as the event itself. True, Mrs Thatcher had talked of going 'on and on', and even those who did not want her to do so rather expected that she would. But it was also true that her resignation had long been foretold. Indeed predictions that Mrs Thatcher's downfall was imminent began almost from the moment she set foot in 10 Downing Street. For the first eighteen months, pundits like Peter Jenkins, then the *Guardian*'s political columnist, were assuring everyone that the talk was not of her consenting to a Heath-like U-turn but of her resigning.

Not long after the 1983 election, in which, contrary to the predictions of the *cognoscenti*, Mrs Thatcher had won a stunning victory, the voices of doom were gabbling again. On almost any Sunday the *Observer* might be found informing its readers that it was now obvious that their Prime Minister was suitable only for fighting General Galtieri and that the Tories were beginning to realize that the fish had begun rotting from the head. For the moment, the *Observer* did not believe that Mrs Thatcher's position was in danger, but it was very ominous that the criticisms had begun to be directed at No 10.

By 1984, rumblings began coming from the 'Right' of the Tory Party itself. She was accused of 'converting herself rather clumsily, into a time-serving trimmer on the model of all of her most mediocre predecessors', a charge that T. E. Utley dismissed by arguing that she had never been as 'tough as people supposed and was no different now'.[1] Nevertheless, talk of 'banana skins' was all the rage, so much so that W. F. Deedes, the *Daily Telegraph* columnist and friend of Denis Thatcher, admonished Conservatives to stop picking on Mrs Thatcher: 'Jokes about banana skins, rough headlines, bad polls and even a handful of tendentious journalists' meant only that the 'art of protest' now attracted more attention than 'the art of governing'. He advised Mrs Thatcher to ignore the snipers and continue to stay well away from the bog of 'consensus politics'.[2]

The 'wet' side of her party was basking in the certainty that her time was up. John O'Sullivan, a loyal Thatcherite, reported receiving assurances from a leading 'wet' that, 'It's all over, dear boy. First the Iron Lady melts towards the Soviet Union. Then she announces her reliance on economic growth for any prospect of tax cuts . . . No rolling back of the State.' In such quarters, the end of the Thatcherite revolution was being 'trumpeted widely, sometimes gleefully, sometimes to the tune of the 'Last Post'.[3]

By 1985, anti-Tory columnists like Alan Watkins in the *Observer* became more guarded in their pronouncements that Thatcherism had 'probably been proved false'. When the 1987 election brought another resounding victory for Margaret Thatcher, she seemed to be unstoppable. It was generally agreed that she could go to her next party conference 'with a degree of confidence that is remarkable for a Prime Minister in the middle of a third term in office'.[4] Indeed her speech at the 1988 Party Conference was acclaimed as one of the most remarkable displays of self-confidence in modern British politics. Even the *Independent* was now sure that she was no longer struggling to retain the leadership of the party, nor inhibited by fear of a financial crisis, and that the worst thing about her government was that there was no alternative to it.

But by 1989, Mrs Thatcher's downfall was again being sighted by the watch. The very poor Tory showing in the European elections in June of 1989 brought new forecasts of disaster for Mrs Thatcher. The Tory campaign was admitted to be a 'shambles' and Mrs Thatcher was blamed for making it negative and 'anti-European'. It was the party's first defeat in a national election since 1974. Mrs Thatcher no longer seemed to be invincible.

After the Cabinet reshuffle which removed Sir Geoffrey Howe from the Foreign Office and replaced him with John Major, complaints about the Prime Minister from MPs going off for the summer recess were well aired in the newspapers: 'Weary Tory MPs warn Thatcher she could be isolated,' ran *The Times* headline.[5] There was even greater consternation in the ranks of the Tories when, at the celebrations of the French Revolution in Paris, Mrs Thatcher chose to remind the French, as no one else had dared, of some nasty truths about that glorious event and was booed for her pains.

Reports of an anti-Thatcher mood were confirmed by Mrs Thatcher's favourite friendly interviewer, Brian Walden, who detected an 'almost universal loathing in which Mrs Thatcher is now held in her own party and throughout the upper reaches of the country'. He himself was finding that he could no longer offer a drink to a friend without receiving a tirade against the Prime Minister: 'If I request that someone pass me the mustard, I do not get it until I have been told how obnoxious the Thatcher woman is. Hatred of Mrs Thatcher seems to have become obsessively implanted in the minds of the chattering classes and provides their principle source of conversation.'[6]

At the Party Conference of 1989, it was felt that Mrs Thatcher did not exude the self-confidence of the previous year. And the *Telegraph*'s reception of her speech was short of enthusiastic. She seemed too eager 'to escape into uncontentious abstractions about liberty and the need for adequate defence' rather than to argue on contentious policies.[7] The *Spectator*'s political columnist, Noel Malcolm, agreed and warned the Government that it would 'remain beached unless it can get the economy running smoothly again. Inflation and high interest rates are the Tories' fundamental problems.' Of course, the 'signs of failure' were really the product of 'Lawsonism, not Thatcherism'; but that could not help Mrs Thatcher because 'the public will not bother to make the distinction'.[8]

The 1989 Party Conference also marked the public emergence of Sir Geoffrey Howe as a centre of Conservative opposition to Mrs Thatcher. Not having been invited to address the Conference, he spoke at a fringe meeting to the Bow Group where he dwelt on the importance of moving more power to cabinet committees and away from the prime ministers. His supporters were relying on him to 'act as a focus for widespread disquiet about Thatcher's leadership' and 'to form a close working alliance with the Home Secretary, Douglas Hurd, and the Chancellor, Nigel Lawson'. 'Informed sources' revealed that Howe was nursing resentment at having been moved out of the Foreign Office, and especially at the manner in which it was done. It was the job he had coveted after his successful period as Chancellor, and with the job he had lost the house, Chevening, he had much enjoyed. He was not expected to challenge Mrs Thatcher immediately, but it was believed that he would not 'stay silent if a show of independence is needed'. He was ready to do 'a real job'.[9]

On 26 October, as it seemed 'out of the blue', the Chancellor, Nigel Lawson, resigned, ostensibly because he resented the interference of Mrs Thatcher's personal adviser, the distinguished economist, Sir Alan Walters. The *Telegraph* declared that it was 'the most serious crisis of Mrs Thatcher's administration since the Falklands War, perhaps even since 1979'. Never before had a 'resignation or sacking caused such a turmoil'. It indicated 'a wider malaise in the conduct of Cabinet business'.[10] In the explanations that both Lawson and Mrs Thatcher gave at different times on television, it was generally thought that the Prime Minister had the worst of it. More agitation was stirred up by Mrs Thatcher's statement in an interview in the *Sunday Correspondent* that she was unlikely to fight a fifth election. That would make her, the pundits predicted, a lame duck leader for the next election. 'In effect,' said *The Times*, 'by placing a limit on her term of service she tempts would-be successors to throw their hats in the ring.'[11]

'In the twinkling of an eye', Brian Walden concluded, the

Government had become 'transformed into a bickering, accident-prone gang, falling over its own feet while exciting public mockery'. He advised Mrs Thatcher to cease relying so much on her strength of will: 'Not will-power, but cold critical analysis is what Mrs Thatcher needs to turn the position round.'[12] Like Auberon Waugh, registered Thatcher-haters were certain that her doom was at hand: 'Our opportunity [that of "intelligent, liberally educated" people] will come when Thatcher and her yobbish new generation of Conservative MPs are trounced and humiliated at the next election, as they certainly will be if she survives that long. Practically none of the nine million voters in the 18–28 age group will vote for her because they detest her . . . Thatcher desperately needs the yobs' vote of Murdoch's *Sun* readers, but Murdoch can't deliver them . . . '[13]

At the end of a year that saw enthusiastic celebrations of her tenth anniversary, for the first time in her fifteen years of leadership, Mrs Thatcher was officially challenged by Sir Anthony Meyer. The languid MP for Clwyd North-West described himself as 'a sloppy Tory Wet';[14] and gave as his reasons for the challenge his belief that 'Mrs Thatcher will find it much harder to win the next election than would another Conservative leader . . . that her policies are out of tune with the feelings of the British people, that her European policy is disastrous . . . '[15] Everyone regarded him as a stalking horse. But no one else joined him.

The Times took the view that the challenge from Sir Anthony Meyer was not a sign of change. There had always been 'Meyerites' in the Cabinet as well as on the back-benches. They were noisier now 'only because the Government is in rough water over the return of inflation and high interest rates, discontent about some public services and dislike of . . . the poll tax and privatization of water and electricity.' Mrs Thatcher should 'have come to grips earlier with her differences with Mr Lawson even if it had meant his earlier departure', and she might have been more tactful in moving Sir Geoffrey Howe out of the Foreign Office. But every politician made mistakes and they were not necessarily fatal.[16]

In the end only sixty MPs withheld their votes from the Prime Minister. 'She'll be pleased with that, and right,' said one rebel.

'But it gives her something to think about'. Her supporters rejoiced that if she could take eighty-four per cent of the votes when the government was doing so badly, she need not fear.[17] Nevertheless, it was the first challenge to her leadership, and the fact that she had been 'shilly-shallying' about how long she intended to go 'on and on' further diminished her aura of invincibility. Conservatives were beginning to ask more seriously whether they would do better at the next election with or without her. But the weight of opinion was against taking the risk of dumping a prime minister. And besides, it was assumed that Mrs Thatcher 'would be certain to fight any such attempt to the last ditch'.[18]

Everyone knew that there was a prince over the water waiting to be called. Michael Heseltine had been discreetly but assiduously cultivating friends throughout the country ever since he had stalked out of the Cabinet during the Westland affair in 1986. He had ample resources, energy, and determination and he had been appearing regularly and effectively on the television screen. But he always declared his loyalty to the Prime Minister and firmly refused to be drawn by impertinent interviewers into intimating a challenge to her leadership.

From early in 1990, the Cassandras had no end of material for their dire prophecies. On 29 February 1990, the *Sunday Times* reported that 'the Prime Minister's popularity is plunging towards the lowest ratings of her decade in power . . . Her leadership image has rarely looked more vulnerable.' According to the MORI poll, sixty-two per cent of the people questioned thought that she was 'out of touch' with ordinary people, and fifty-five per cent that she 'talks down to people'. The Tories were trailing a record seventeen points behind Labour in the same poll and Labour was ahead of the Tories in all regions, including the south of England and in rural areas as well as towns and cities.

In the *Spectator*, Noel Malcolm felt obliged to state the 'unpalatable truth' that 'it is not Mrs Thatcher's style of leadership that has gone out of fashion, but Mrs Thatcher herself.' It was believed that Mr Heseltine had now been promised support by a group of MPs on the Right of the Party. Nevertheless, Tory MPs would probably hang on to Mrs Thatcher for a while longer. Their line seemed to be: 'If she's still a liability with the public once inflation and mortgage rates have come down again, there'll still be time to get rid of her in 1991.'[19]

By October 1990, doubts about Mrs Thatcher's survival were evident everywhere. *The Times* found that her government was in danger of running onto the rocks and had no more rope and beeswax. More of those who had once been vigorous and influential Thatcherites were now singing tunes out of the pre-Thatcher hymn-book. From the Party Conference at Bournemouth, in October, came reports that the 'Tory faithful were for the most part subdued, at times even glum', although Mrs Thatcher gave one of her most adroit conference performances. Nevertheless, the *Sunday Times* predicted that the party was no longer consumed with debilitating leadership speculation and that Mrs Thatcher would lead the Tories into the next election and on her own terms.

Such streaks of optimism were brought to an end by the Eastbourne by-election, on 18 October. In a safe Tory seat, the Tories lost resoundingly to the Liberal Democrats. Three of the five serious Sunday papers advised Margaret Thatcher to start considering how she could depart 'with honour and dignity before the voters told her she had outstayed her time'. The *Independent on Sunday* told her that she was a source of division rather than unity: 'She is growing old. And she is making mistakes. The final service she could give her party is the decision to resign gracefully and allow her successor time to prepare for the election.'

Nevertheless, *The Times* carried an encouraging word – that the tactical voting in the Eastbourne election was not likely to be repeated in a national election. And the *Telegraph* dismissed any attempt to unseat Mrs Thatcher – it would only 'leave the Tories standing for nothing at all'.[20] But elsewhere, the emphasis went the other way. Doubts about Mrs Thatcher's leadership kept appearing in newspapers throughout the country. Was she responding adequately to the challenge of the new, credible Labour Party? To the *Yorkshire Post*, the Eastbourne election suggested that millions of natural Tory supporters had been alienated. The *Birmingham Post* lamented that the Tory party was stuck with the image, however unfair, of an uncaring party serving the haves and failing the have-nots.[21] To all this, the socialist, Ian Aitken of the *Guardian*, who had been around Westminster a long time, observed with a yawn that it looked as if we were in for another ' "Maggie Must Go" scenario'.[22]

There were still those who remained Tory because of Mrs Thatcher. Charles Moore, Deputy Editor of the *Telegraph*, firmly declared that: 'The commander-in-chief does still think that for her there is still a purpose in being at the top other than just being at the top. She has been the only person in the government making noises that one could recognize as Tory.' The alternative was 'government too tired by the struggle to survive to think beyond the next week, too used to office to imagine what it is like to be the governed rather than the governor, and too harassed by its past acts to be able to think about new ones.'[23]

But at the same time, the team of Cassandras on the *Independent* ceaselessly stirred the pot. William Rees-Mogg reported that in the Far East Mrs Thatcher was already regarded as a museum exhibit and Britain 'as a population of idlers governed by an activist; we would be better off as a population of activists governed by an idler.' Peter Jenkins discovered that on the Continent the Iron Lady had become the Tin Lady.[24] Speculation about who would replace Mrs Thatcher appeared regularly.

It became more noticeable that former admirers were abandoning the ship. The judicious *Times* columnist, Ronald Butt, who had once been considered a staunch Thatcherite, became openly hostile by the beginning of 1990. The Thatcher Government, he said, had 'fallen into two possibly fatal political traps'. It had begun to feel invincible and had become doctrinaire: 'There had developed an unwillingness to read the writing on the wall or even to take public opinion seriously.' The public was now blaming all the troubles on Mrs Thatcher herself, while she persisted in dismissing 'warnings from those who most value its great achievements' as 'wimpishness'.[25]

All the while, Mr Heseltine was much in evidence. When the Tories in Parliament cheered a speech by him on the Bank of England's independence, a poll of MPs in the *Independent*, which had asked them why they had cheered, concluded that Heseltine was 'becoming a useful sort of chap for a panicking party to have on board' – he was the Tories' 'secret insurance policy'. He was delivering an average of six speeches a week, a record equal to that of a candidate for the American Presidency, and the message was always that there is a Tory alternative to Thatcherism. His biographer and school chum, Julian Critchley, reported Heseltine's speaking of 'that bloody woman' and her 'lunatic' economic policy, but to interviewers, Heseltine still expressed unwavering loyalty to the leader of his party.

The final act began when Sir Geoffrey Howe, who had been the twin pillar of Thatcherism, resigned as Deputy Prime Minister and leader of the House of Commons on 1 November, a week before the new session of Parliament opened. The prologue had been prepared at the Rome summit where, led by the Italian, Signor Andreotti, the other members contrived to make Mrs Thatcher look 'isolated', which greatly disturbed many of her colleagues at home. Her virtuoso performance in the House of Commons when, on 30 October, she reported on the meeting, made matters worse. Far from calming the turbulence, she was belligerent and attacked notions of Euro-federalism with gusto: in her sharpest tones she said 'No, no, no!' The three negatives were much taken amiss and talked about incessantly.

Sir Geoffrey's resignation rang no alarm bells because he was supposed to have assured the Prime Minister that he would not stand against her in the coming leadership election. But when the hostile contents of his lengthy resignation letter became known, it was clear that 'the knives were out'. Michael Heseltine quickly served notice on Downing Street that Mrs Thatcher's fitness to lead the Tories into Europe was in doubt. On 2 November, he wrote to his constituency chairman, declaring himself an ally of Howe's in the campaign against Mrs Thatcher's style of leadership, her attitude to Europe, and her ability to lead the Party in the next election. An abridgement of the letter was published in the *Sunday Times* of 4 November. When Mr Heseltine flew off to Hamburg to speak on Europe, his refusal to tell the press whether he would challenge Mrs Thatcher was taken as a sure sign that he had decided to run.

The stage was set for Sir Geoffrey Howe to make his much-awaited resignation speech at 3.15pm, on Tuesday 13 November. The voice and manner were as quiet as always; the words were hardly oratorical gems; but the message was clear and sharp. He denounced the Prime Minister for obstructing European unity; he attacked her personal style as well as her politics. And he concluded with: 'The time has come for others to consider their own response to the tragic conflict of loyalties with which I have myself wrestled for perhaps too long.' The Labour benches cheered and the Conservatives looked stunned. The next day, Wednesday 14 November, Michael Heseltine declared that he would stand in the leadership contest.

The voting on the first ballot took place on Tuesday 20 November 1990. After the ballot box in Committee Room 12 closed at 5.50pm, few MPs admitted to voting for the challenger because, as one of them explained, 'This is murder being done and no one wants their fingerprints on the dagger.'[26] When the result was announced, although Mrs Thatcher had won a clear majority – fifty-five per cent of the votes cast, she had missed victory – according to the contorted rules which had been devised in the 1970s – by four votes. If two more MPs had voted for her instead of Heseltine, she would have been home and dry. A second ballot was now required. Even before all the MPs had left the committee room, it became known that Mrs Thatcher had told reporters outside the British Embassy in Paris that 'it is my intention to allow my name to go forward.'

Early the next morning, on the *Today* programme, Michael Heseltine assured listeners that his bandwagon was gathering pace and he was just eighteen votes short of the simple majority needed for victory. Mrs Thatcher was still in Paris, attending the final session of the European security conference and taking part in the treaty signing ceremony. When, by midday, 21 November, she was back in Downing Street, Westminster corridors were filled with rumours that the grandees were reporting fatal defections from Mrs Thatcher's camp. One ex-Cabinet minister who had campaigned for her in the first ballot but had now lost hope, said, 'It's a great tragedy; the day after she's gone she'll be a national heroine again.' But from the strongly Thatcherite No Turning Back Group came: 'I hope she will roll up her sleeves and really fight like we know she can.' And indeed, when the Prime Minister left Downing Street at 3.10pm to make her report to the Commons, she told reporters: 'I fight on. I fight to win.' When she finished her report on the summit to the Commons, Labour's Peter Shore declared: 'What a paradox! This is the best statement on international affairs to be made in forty-five years.' Even Labour's most embarrassing extremist, Tony Benn, acknowledged that: 'She believes in something. It's an old-fashioned idea.' And Hugo Young, too, said in the *Guardian* that she had shown herself to be 'no puny leader, shaking a derisory fist as her enemies gather for the kill. Her self-image gives her a mighty stature, and she conveys this with every word of defiance she utters.'[27]

At 5pm, the Prime Minister, accompanied by her campaign team, was in the Commons tea-room, where she had not been much seen before, encouraging supporters. Her campaign management had been changed – John Wakeham, the Energy Secretary, had replaced George Younger who, everyone agreed, had run a far from effective campaign on the first ballot. At 5.25pm, the Foreign Secretary, Douglas Hurd, and John Major, the Chancellor, ended speculation about whether they would support Mrs Thatcher by proposing and seconding her nomination for the second ballot. When at 6pm Mrs Thatcher prepared for her weekly audience with the Queen, her supporter Gerald Howarth advised: 'Tell her you're staying.' And the Chief Whip, Tim Renton, was reported to be annoyed at stories in the evening papers saying that he had told the Prime Minister that she could not win.[28]

The pundits were certain that she would fight on. The *Guardian* leader writer rejoiced over the chaos that would follow in what was once the 'great pragmatist of British political life', the Conservative Party. Mrs Thatcher's spirit was magnificent but her decision to fight on was a disaster: 'She will pull the temples down with her. She will actively precipitate the election of her most reviled enemy rather than try to pass the succession to a third runner; and from the backbenches, later, she will make Ted Heath look a good loser.'[29] Many others were as sure as Hugo Young that, given her character, she could not stand down: 'Would the leader who saw off Galtieri and Scargill seriously be expected to fall on the sword proferred to her by Brutus Howe and his fellow conspirators in the Commons?' What made her great made it impossible for her to do what the circumstances demanded and save her party from electoral disaster.

Mrs Thatcher spent the evening conferring with her Ministers, one by one. They all, it was said, brought a similar message – that she risked defeat on the second ballot, and that if she stood down, the contest could be widened to include others besides Mr Heseltine. Some said that they would support her if she decided to carry on. Some suggested that even if she won, she would be leading a divided and demoralized party. A deputation of MPs led by Mr George Gardiner, an early supporter of her election as leader fifteen years ago, came to urge her not to stand down; they believed the talk of defections by her supporters was 'black propaganda' by her opponents. Norman Tebbit called in to urge her to stand firm. Members of the No Turning Back Group – Michael Portillo, Michael Forsyth, and Michael Fallon came to see her. She worked on her speech for the next day's Commons debate on the censure motion until 1am.

The following morning, few reporters were there to see Mr Peter Morrison, the Prime Minister's parliamentary private secretary, arrive to be informed of Mrs Thatcher's decision to resign. At 9am the members of the Cabinet assembled at Downing Street, all except Mr Major, who was still recovering from his wisdom tooth operation, and Mr Hunt, the Welsh Secretary, who was in Korea. At 9.33am the Prime Minister's deputy press secretary opened the door of 10 Downing Street and handed the waiting reporters a press release. In her resignation statement, Mrs Thatcher said: 'Having consulted widely, I have concluded that the unity of the Party and the prospect of victory in a General Election would be better served if I stood down to enable Cabinet colleagues to enter the ballot for the leadership.' Noel Malcolm suggested that when her colleagues had advised her to save herself from humiliation on the second ballot, they were really asking her to save them from Heseltine.

In the meantime the Cabinet was trying to carry on with its usual business. When the officials left, the ministers discussed the next steps and it became clear that both Mr Hurd and Mr Major would stand on the second ballot.

That afternoon, in response to Neil Kinnock's No Confidence Motion, for which none of his own party later thanked him, Mrs Thatcher gave the greatest performance yet. Enemies and friends alike said that she was Marlene Dietrich and La Passionara wrapped in one. With her usual forcefulness, she reviewed what she thought had been achieved in the past eleven years to save Britain from becoming a banana republic. She reiterated her stand on Europe and her belief in the fundamental principles of Thatcherism. Somewhere in the middle she suddenly stopped to say, 'I'm rather enjoying this!' The *Telegraph* commented: 'How dare she . . . It was like Charles I waving breezily from the scaffold . . . '[30] After she ended, the motion of no confidence in the Government turned into a celebration of Margaret Thatcher. One Conservative backbencher pleaded with her to reconsider her decision to step down: 'You'd wipe the floor with this lot,' he shouted, pointing to Messrs Heseltine, Major and Hurd. Both when she entered the Chamber and at the end of her speech, the Conservative MPs rose to their feet and waved their order papers in what struck seasoned members of the gallery as an unprecedented display of enthusiasm. It was said on all sides that if the vote had been taken then, she would have been swept to victory.

I

Identifying Thatcherism

1

A Bundle of Attributes

Although the term 'Thatcherism' had been introduced by her opponents to suggest that Mrs Thatcher had imposed by force of will a dogma rejected by most people in Britain, the term was taken up and used even more persistently by her supporters. After her resignation it became, if anything, still more difficult to discuss politics in Britain without talking about Thatcherism. Academics no less than journalists and politicians, however much they disliked coining 'isms', came to speak of Thatcherism and Thatcherites because they had no other name for what they regarded as an important, and readily discernible, new feature of British politics.

Those who talk about Thatcherism appear to have in mind a clear definition. But that is hardly the impression that one gets from the dozens of books, essays, and incidental discussions devoted to explaining Thatcherism that have poured from the presses since 1979. In all these commentaries and studies, there is no agreement whatever about what is meant by Thatcherism. That, perhaps, is less remarkable than that, generally, the commentators cannot escape either being incoherent or fastening incoherence on Thatcherism, and often they do both.

It is, of course, possible that what happened after 1979 had no distinctive pattern and that Thatcherism is a meaningless label. That indeed is what some have suggested.[1] They believe that although the Thatcher Governments had altered and achieved much, there was nothing new about the aims pursued; they had been 'twinkles in Tory eyes for decades'.[2] Or else Thatcherism is said to signify merely that old ideas had recaptured political power 'after a century of retreat'.[3] Others assert that Thatcherism was of a piece with what was going on everywhere else: all governments 'were becoming more conservative' and were 'cutting public borrowing, deregulating the private sector, reducing income taxes, and pursuing financial prudence before every other goal'. Parties of 'the welfare left' were everywhere 'losing their traditional political base'. Even the Labour Government that had preceded Mrs Thatcher's first administration had been following the same course. In short, the notion that the Thatcher governments were 'engaged on a project that was unique' should be dismissed as a fantasy. Thatcherism, according to such commentators, was just the 'British response to a global phenomenon'.[4]

The significance of Thatcherism is dismissed in still another way by those who describe it as a mere 'ragbag of ideas'. Margaret Thatcher, they say, 'made much of her big ideas, the need for radical change and the possibility of a new world'. But in fact she had no clear notion, either in public or in private, of what she really meant to do. She offered nothing more than 'a uniquely seductive package of nostrums and prejudices'. There were plenty of plans, but no 'Big Plan'. She loved to talk of her 'philosophy' and hobnob with Conservative dons, but what she garnered from them was a hodgepodge from which she drew whatever came to hand.[5]

Nevertheless, as we *do* speak of Thatcherism and everyone seems to assume, even in the course of denying it, that the term has some meaning, there is good reason for persisting in the search for that meaning. Moreover, the jumble of conflicting explanations is not quite a Tower of Babel. Certain attributes reappear regularly and they can be arranged under four headings: 1) an enterprise shaped by economic concerns; 2) a drive for power; 3) a moral crusade; 4) an intrinsically self-contradictory undertaking.

Any interpretation of Thatcherism which sees it as essentially an economic enterprise attaches to it one or more of three different characteristics: a project to make the rich richer; a clearly focused programme to increase economic efficiency; a determined effort to put into practice an economic dogma.

Seeing Thatcherism as a drive to make the rich richer has the virtue of being simple and coherent. Those who take this view describe the essence of Thatcherism and indeed of all Conservatism as 'greed'.[6] Thatcherites, they say, are supremely selfish to the exclusion of all other concerns. They are inspired by a bleak and harsh vision of a world in which lonely buyers and sellers try to do one another down in an impersonal, heartless marketplace. Amassing more money is the fount of virtue and fighting to acquire wealth is the only activity that Thatcherites value. For the poor at whose expense fortunes are accumulated they feel no pity. Besides, the idolization of wealth and the ascendancy of finance over industry has profoundly debased British culture. 'The conspicuous consumption shamelessly favoured by the *parvenues* who made their fortunes in the City' produced 'the bourgeois triumphalism'[8] that distinguished Thatcherite Britain. As 'yuppies' had been encouraged 'to shed all inhibitions about enjoying the spoils of the class war', 'vulgarism rules O.K.'[9] and Britain has ceased to be 'a nation of decency'.[10]

Who the fortunate beneficiaries of the Thatcherite bonanza are intended to be remains obscure. Some hold that it is 'commercial interests' or the City, and that manufacturing industries are the main victims. Other candidates are the 'big corporations', 'country landowners', 'industrial polluters', and 'transport interests'. But conclusive evidence for believing that Thatcherism is out to make the rich richer, they all say, is provided by the Thatcherite devotion to reducing taxes. For that, it is assumed, benefits only the rich. And all other policies are explained as means for making it easier to reduce taxes. The aim of privatization could not have been to promote economic efficiency because, according to this view, there is no 'incontrovertible evidence' that privatized industries run better than nationalized ones. The real reason for privatization is the sordid desire for cash which dominates all Thatcherite thinking. It not only enriched the City institutions that organized the sales and the executives who now run the privatized companies, but chiefly, by bringing in funds to the exchequer, privatization made it possible to reduce taxes and so to feed Thatcherites' greed.

A more favourable view of Thatcherism as an economic project is taken by those who describe it as a drive for economic efficiency, motivated by the desire to rescue capitalism. This view rests on the neo-Marxist argument that, as the old mass-producing industries have ceased to be viable, the rising importance of new kinds of industry has rendered obsolete the old social democratic policies which were aimed at supporting manufacturing workers. Thatcherism responded to that change by recognizing that in order to 'relaunch Britain as a successful capitalist economy',[11] the 'shibboleths of social democracy' had to be abandoned. That is why Thatcher Governments undertook to wage war on the unions. They found monetarist policies better suited to 'the logic of the growing financial and commercial integration of the world economy'.[12] By widening share ownership, they tried to nurture the values and attitudes needed to maintain capitalism in the new circumstances.

Even those who do not follow the neo-Marxist line agree that the drive for economic efficiency made reducing the role of government one of 'the prime objectives of the Thatcher Government, repeated from a thousand platforms and rehearsed in scores of policy documents', along with endless eulogies of business, profits, the balance sheet and the bottom line.[13] Thatcherism is accordingly considered synonymous with 'market liberalism' of which 'the axiomatic principle' is that 'state intervention in what markets did to the economy should be held to a minimum.'[14]

Whereas the preceding interpretation of Thatcherism as an economic enterprise gives it a highly pragmatic character, a third version treats Thatcherism as a dogmatic economic doctrine. Some who trace the ancestry of the doctrine to Adam Smith conclude that Thatcherism is wedded to 'nostrums devised for an older simpler world of unspoiled markets, a golden age that probably never was', which makes it incapable of solving the problems of the late twentieth century.[15] Others, who emphasize the influence of the American economist Milton Friedman, equate Thatcherism with monetarism and regard strict control of the money supply as the defining objective of Thatcherism. Some charge that the adherence to monetarism prevented Thatcherites from responding flexibly to practical problems, while others argue that the abandonment of monetarism, which had produced the economic miracles of the early eighties, gave rise to the difficulties of the late eighties. Although some of those who equate Thatcherism with an economic doctrine are its most stalwart admirers, others conclude that Thatcherism thus introduced right-wing ideological politics into Britain.

A more colourful, and wholly different because irrational, character is assigned to Thatcherism by those who see it as a drive for
power. In one version, the emphasis falls on Margaret Thatcher's
personal ambition. She is portrayed as a 'ruthless crusading leader
who knew she was right and had a supreme duty to remain in
power'. According to this view, Thatcherism is nothing like an
ideology or any other 'system of ideas'. It is rather driven and
shaped by ambition of 'the small town variety' than which 'there
is none more ardent'. The ambition is allied to certain instincts
which, being 'narrow in range' and 'dogmatically voiced', created
the illusion of a doctrine. But it was not because she was a 'conviction politician' or an 'ideologue engaged on some lifelong crusade'
that Mrs Thatcher set out 'to kill socialism'. She was really moved
by the 'natural antagonism' of the lower middle class to the working
classes and their allies, the upper middle class intelligentsia.[16]

In other words, here Thatcherism is the creed of an extremely
ambitious small-town girl, a workaholic with lower-middle-class
prejudices, who found an outlet for her formidable energies in the
war on socialism.[17] Her gift for appealing to the people over the
heads of her colleagues and her charisma gave her pursuit of power
an aura of respectability. The weapons for her assault were ready
to hand in the stockpile assembled by her recent predecessors
– Healey's monetarism, Wilson's and Heath's anti-traditionalism,
Callaghan's attack on the decline of educational standards, Eden's
property-owning democracy. When Mrs Thatcher threw this
arsenal into a well-articulated campaign to 'kill socialism' and to
eradicate all its appurtenances, she created Thatcherism.

A grander version of the 'dash for power' view of Thatcherism
equates it with a drive to enhance the glory of Britain. Thatcherism
is described as a Gaullist project, out to demonstrate that Britain
no longer suffered from 'a crisis of governability and legitimacy'.
Strengthening the power of the state was part of a grand mission
to restore Britain's standing among the great nations.[18] Critics of
Thatcherism-as-Gaullism add that, under the pretence of protecting itself against its enemies, the state curtailed the freedom of the
press and television to an extent not known before in Britain. And
others attribute Mrs Thatcher's Gaullism to her provincialism, her

disdain for foreigners, and describe it as 'Little Englandism'.

In another disparaging variation on the power theme, Thatcherism is seen as a project for enhancing the might of the central government by destroying the autonomy of local authorities and of all powerful interest groups. The Thatcherite assault on the financial independence of local authorities is said to have culminated in the poll tax, which ensured that more of local spending 'would henceforth be determined from Whitehall'. The sale of council houses and flats to tenants, the reforms allowing schools to run themselves on money provided by the government, the 'smashing' of the trade unions were all dictated by the Thatcherite programme for 'seizing control over more and more'. Rivals to the central state were systematically 'emasculated or dismantled' because the idea of genuine independence, even of competing sources of wisdom and advice, became increasingly uncongenial to a government which was hardly ever obliged to make concessions to opponents. We are therefore assured that whatever else Thatcherism might be, 'it was not an exercise in reducing the power of the central state.'[19]

Both power and money are dismissed as Thatcherite objectives by those who regard Thatcherism as a moral crusade. The object of the crusade, according to one version, is to restore old-fashioned discipline in Britain. Here, too, Mrs Thatcher's upbringing is emphasized. She is supposed to have been taught at her father's knee to elevate the 'economics of sound housekeeping above the merely political to the moral level', and to regard spending no more than you earn as a matter of moral rectitude. Indeed 'the appeal to righteousness', this thesis runs, 'went far beyond economic management and can account for Mrs Thatcher's determined insistence, in the early years, on fiscal rigour'.[20] Her antipathy to inflation rested on her naive belief that 'if the value of money was allowed to decline, so would other values.'[21] And more broadly, Thatcherism aimed to restore traditional values such as respect for authority, hierarchy, discipline and order, that is to say, 'the military virtues'.[22] It establishes Thatcherism as the implacable enemy of the permissive society.

But the very opposite character is bestowed on Thatcherism in another version of the moral crusade thesis. Here its object is to enlarge the freedom of individuals and to uproot traditional ways. In this role, Thatcherism becomes the instrument for enabling the permissive society to survive. Its appeal is to 'yesterday's hippies who are now today's yuppies' and to the 'raw, uncouth, socially and psychologically insecure new elites, or rather would-be elites'. That explains why Mrs Thatcher found her natural constituency among the 'rough, hard, no nonsense new men', who resented as she did the temporarily defeated but not yet extinguished Establishment – the metropolitan cliques such as the BBC and the 'toffee-nosed south-eastern establishment' of Oxford and Cambridge, the Foreign Office and the Athenaeum.[24] The 'new men' profited from the Thatcherite effort to make the British 'individualistic rather than collectivist, preferring private to state ownership, putting the rights of the members before the interests of the trade union'. In the new Britain, shaped by Thatcherism, people were to be moved by a desire to own their own homes, to possess 'a stake in things' and to provide 'a better chance for their children'. A subtler version of this view emphasizes that Thatcherism aimed to free people from feeling guilty for pursuing wealth, for seeking to better themselves by earning or owning more, and more generally to rid British culture of a disposition to 'collective guilt' for past and present evils, regardless of any direct responsibilty for them.[25] In short, Thatcherism should be understood as a libertarian project bent on destroying the 'liberal consensus'.

When the various interpretations of Thatcherism are set out in this fashion, their incompatibility becomes obvious enough. It is all the more striking because the conflict does not always arise from differences of opinion among writers. Quite often, several conflicting interpretations are offered by the same writer. Some commentators, having noticed this difficulty, try to deal with it by characterizing Thatcherism as an inherently self-contradictory project. But there is no agreement on what produced the incoherence.

One suggestion is that Thatcherism could increase the scope for individual capitalist endeavour and reduce state interference in the economy only by using the state's authority in ever more autocratic ways. In other words, in order to roll back the state, the government had to become highly interventionist and centralizing. This committed Thatcherism to policies that were by turns libertarian and 'authoritarian', and gave rise to considerable division and confusion among its followers. According to another diagnosis, Thatcherism suffers from a tension between its Gaullist project of reversing national decline and its 'neo-liberal view of the world market' because the former is supposed to require protectionism while the latter is devoted to free trade. A third conflict within Thatcherism is attributed to its being a movement that is 'both revolutionary and counter-revolutionary', appealing on the one hand to new aspirations but on the other hand reasserting old values, promising both freedom and order, choice and discipline.[26]

We cannot, of course, expect an account of the coherence of Thatcherism from the thesis that it is inherently self-contradictory. But that thesis has the merit not only of recognizing the conflicts among the various interpretations but also of acknowledging, implicitly, that no one of the available interpretations can, by itself, identify Thatcherism.

The shortcomings are more obvious in some interpretations than in others. Although the view that Thatcherism is out to promote greed is especially popular among its more eminent critics, it is the least plausible. For even if we grant that Thatcherism has encouraged greed, is it likely that Mrs Thatcher and her associates sat down and said to themselves, Now, how can we best go about promoting greed? We might as well conclude that because envy had increased under socialism, the object of socialism is to promote envy. There must at least have been some heroic mis-description on the part of Thatcherites which enabled them to suppose that they were doing something which a reasonable person might wish to promote. Moreover, some of the policies for which Thatcherism is criticized by those who equate it with greed are blatantly incompatible with that aim. Why, for instance, should the Thatcher Government have tightened immigration laws if its aim was to make the rich richer?[27] It should have done the opposite – eased immigration in order to enlarge the workforce and so drive down wages.

A more serious effort to account for Thatcherism has been made by those who see it as a project to revive capitalism. It is not an implausible view. But it cannot explain why an enterprise of that sort should have been something so special as to be worthy of a name and dignified, by friend and foe alike, as an 'ism'. The belief that Thatcher governments were concerned with encouraging efficiency and were influenced by certain economic doctrines also cannot be lightly dismissed. But none of the interpretations of Thatcherism as an economic enterprise can offer any insight into why others should have seen it as a crusade to revive 'the military virtues', a dash for power, or a patriotic enterprise to restore the glory of Britain.

We are left with not so much an identifiable political outlook as a bundle of attributes, held together only by time and place. Thatcherism appears to have something to do with greed, ambition, hatred of socialism, patriotism, a lust for power, moral certainties, hostility to the permissive society, rugged individualism, increasing liberty, promoting efficiency, an ideology, cutting taxes, enlarging and reducing the power of the central government. Far from having acquired a clear identity, which explains why it is worthy of being an 'ism', Thatcherism becomes an impenetrable mystery.

Nevertheless, the medley serves a useful purpose. It provides a survey of the attributes which have been associated with Thatcherism, and must somehow be accounted for by an adequate interpretation. In what follows, it will be shown that these attributes can be explained by a coherent definition, both simpler and more surprising than anything offered hitherto.

2

The Vigorous Virtues

There is a great danger that the definition of Thatcherism offered here, simple though it is, may be misunderstood. That is because this definition has such an unfamiliar character.

We are disposed nowadays to see every assertion about political affairs (as well as other matters) as an attack or a defence. We are not accustomed to distinguishing between a defence of a political phenomenon and an explanation of it. Least of all are we accustomed to distinguishing between an account that describes events and one that abstracts an identity from them. All this might dispose readers grossly to misinterpret the thesis of this book.

To avoid such misinterpretation the reader needs to remember two things: that this chapter is devoted to defining Thatcherism, and that this definition does not – indeed could not because it is a definition – *describe* what Thatcher governments or Thatcherite politicians have said and done. It is rather an *abstraction* from such sayings and doings. Being an abstraction, it can no more tell us what 'plans' Thatcherites made or whether what they did was good or bad than the chemical formula for water – H_2O – can tell us whether the sea at Brighton is cold or polluted. What the definition of Thatcherism offered here can do is to expose the thread that unites all the various manifestations of Thatcherism. In this sense it can explain what the phenomenon that we call Thatcherism *is*.

The thread that identifies Thatcherism has been so difficult to discover because Thatcherism is a political undertaking concerned with specific political problems. The assertions of other great isms, whether Aristotelianism, Kantianism, Marxism, or Fascism, were in principle eternal truths. Not so Thatcherism. It is a historical phenomenon, addressed to the concerns of a particular time and place. As a matter of essence, Thatcherism is rooted in history. Its

content was shaped by the response of its founders, above all of
Mrs Thatcher herself, to the condition of Britain as they saw it.
In short, Thatcherism is anything but timeless.

Neither is it a theory. The point here is not the banal one that
Thatcherism goes beyond theory, but rather that it has not ever
been, or been based on, a theory. A theory requires theoreticians
to articulate it. Mrs Thatcher herself never had the time, aptitude
or inclination to act as her own theorist. And although many genuine theoreticians (especially F. A. Hayek and Milton Friedman)
and their theories influenced Mrs Thatcher and her supporters or
were admired by them, none of them has ever seen himself or
been seen by Thatcherites as the theorist of Thatcherism. This is
no accident. Political theory moves from analysis to judgement by
means of argument. Thatcherism, by contrast, never pretended to
consist in an academic analysis of politics at any level of abstraction.
Its concern has been with action. Thatcherism has not got what it
takes to be a theory.

The description of Thatcherism as a theory also misses attributes
which Thatcherism does have and which theories do not possess.
In the first place, a theory cannot offer concrete guidance on the
appropriate response to concrete practical circumstances at a given
place and time. Even Marxism (which pretends to be a theory
that prescribes action) offered Lenin what he himself regarded as
insufficient practical guidance on how to deal with the Russian
situation at the beginning of this century. Lenin had therefore to
translate Marxist theory into a series of more practical handbooks.
Thatcherism, not being a theory, has had no difficulty accommodating itself to the concrete realities of a particular time and place.
Instead of offering general principles which might be difficult to
translate or make applicable to the situation of Britain at the end
of the twentieth century, Thatcherism, by eschewing theoretical
argument and concentrating solely on practical prescriptions, was
able to avoid any problems of translation.

The absence of a theory in Thatcherism also avoided what is
for a practical political party a particularly corrosive form of internal
dissension: argument about which of any two propositions represents 'the truth' as perceived by the orthodox doctrine. There

has been no room for such disputes since the concern of Thatcherism has not been with analysis, theory or 'the truth', but with finding the right course of action under particular political circumstances.

Finally, because it was never a theory, Thatcherism has necessarily been flexible in its response to changing circumstance. Whereas a theoretician must re-examine circumstances as they alter – to check, first, whether his analysis still holds good in the light of the changed evidence and, second, how his theoretical propositions should be translated into practical actions that might deal with the changed circumstance – Thatcherism carries none of this burden. As circumstances change, Thatcherism has provided remedies and prescriptions with an immediacy belonging to the cabinet room or even the war room, and wholly unlike the slow gyrations of the university common room. Given that Britain at the end of the twentieth century is a representative democracy, in which governments have at best a five-year life, this is just as well. Government by theory can proceed in a monastery, the Communist Kremlin, or in any other place where rulers can afford, through lack of opposition, to think in decades and centuries. A government in modern Britain, for better or worse, cannot afford such luxuries.

To deny that Thatcherism has never been a theory is not, however, by any means to suggest that Thatcherism has simply been a random collection of ideas and actions. The thesis that Thatcherism amounts to no more than a 'ragbag' fails to explain not only the attitudes of Thatcherism's adherents but also of its opponents. On both sides of the divide (and it is a commonly remarked feature that there *is* to an unprecedented degree, a divide) the adherents and the opponents agree that Thatcherism has constituted a *direction* in politics. Whether it be the opponents repeatedly suggesting that the Thatcher government was about to do a 'U-turn' or a group of Thatcherite MPs styling themselves the 'No Turning Back' group, the metaphor of movement and direction has been a consistent theme.

An equally consistent theme has been the recognition of Mrs Thatcher herself, by opponents and by supporters, as a 'conviction politician'. In part, this phrase may be a description of political *manner* rather than political substance. But here the description conveys something more. It suggests a politician who has some form of *mission*, a term whose etymology aptly links the notion of conviction with the metaphor of movement and direction. The sense that Thatcherism was always *about* something is reinforced not only by the very existence of the term 'Thatcherism' (to be contrasted with the absence of Churchillism or Macmillanism) but also by the repeated cries of Mrs Thatcher herself and of her adherents that there is 'much more to be done'. Clearly, she and they, along with the commentators who so readily use and discuss the term, have agreed that Thatcherism amounts to *something* and that it has been going somewhere, or at any rate trying to go somewhere. In place of a Conservative Party conceived as a party of consolidation, consensus and accumulation, a party which genuinely entertains a 'ragbag of ideas', Thatcherism is distinguished, as even its opponents have admitted, by direction, movement, and purpose.

Here, then, is an apparent paradox. On the one hand, Thatcherism is not in itself, and does not advocate or adhere to, a theory. On the other hand, Mrs Thatcher, her adherents and her opponents have all discerned in Thatcherism something more coherent than a mere ragbag of ideas. Those whose view of politics allows of only two possibilities, politicians that do and politicians that do not pursue a theory, find this paradoxical. If coherence in politics can be granted only at the theoretical level, then it cannot be explained how Thatcherism, unmistakably lacking a theory, is nevertheless widely commended and damned for its coherence.

The paradox can be resolved only by abandoning the supposed dichotomy between theory and incoherence. In practice, it is perfectly possible to be coherent without having a theory. The sculptor fashioning his statue out of marble has a coherent aim, and realizes this aim in an object which manifests and embodies that coherence, but he need not be, and generally is not, guided by any theory. So, too, a politician, working to fashion concrete results out of concrete circumstances may have, and manifest in his achievements, a coherent aim without ever being guided by theory. Nor does he have to be wholly successful in the execution of his ideas to achieve such coherence. Just as Michelangelo's prisoners struggling for existence in their incomplete liberation from formless stone display a purpose only partly realized, so a politician can display coherent purposes even when those purposes are unfulfilled or only partly fulfilled by the policies and practical results in which they are embodied. It should not, therefore, be surprising to find that Thatcherism is at once both coherent and non-theoretical.

Whether right or wrong, lovable or objectionable, Thatcherism has offered a coherent political attitude; it has provided a coherent set of responses to things as they are, or were seen to be, in Britain at the end of the twentieth century. And it has translated these responses into action in a coherent and distinctive manner.

What is not peculiar to Thatcherism is its conception of government. Nevertheless, that conception is both a necessary postulate of those aspects of Thatcherism that are distinctive and a marked break from what had preceded it, and has therefore to be considered first.

For a Thatcherite the purpose of governing is 'to do the right thing'. In this respect, Thatcherites bear a resemblance to full-blooded socialists and are wholly unlike the Conservatives who had earlier dominated the party. For the latter wanted to do not what is in some objective sense 'right', but rather whatever would best reconcile the demands of the more troublesome barons in the land, whether trade unions, business, or others. Thatcherites do not think of governing as an activity of satisfying 'interests' or encouraging 'partnerships' with industry or labour (what is euphemistically described as 'pragmatism') but as serving the *public* good'. And that is why Thatcherites are not preoccupied with achieving 'consensus' or 'balance'. They have convictions about what ought to be done and seek to fulfil them on grounds not only of their rectitude but also of their feasibility without, however, worrying unduly about whether their policies will meet with the immediate approval of this or that interest. In other words, they make a sharp distinction between the responsibility of government and the demands of pressure groups.

This explains why Thatcherites are sometimes accused of having a lust for power and described as 'authoritarian'. But the term fits only if derived (as it generally is not) from the strict sense of 'authority' – the *right* (as opposed to the power or strength) to take certain decisions. Because according to the constitutional procedures of Britain, the *right* to take certain decisions belongs to the elected government, Thatcherites regard the handing over of such decisions to 'partnerships' with non-governmental groups as a dereliction of duty. In their conception of government, the authority of the Prime Minister, other Ministers and officials is given to them by the electorate and can be removed only by the electorate. And this conviction that the electorate as a whole and not any one part of it ought to decide whether the government has done the right thing is what makes Thatcherites averse to letting governmental decisions be shaped by whatever interest makes the loudest noise or threatens the most trouble. The Thatcherite insistence on doing 'the right thing' is thus the very opposite of a lust for power because it follows from a strong sense for the distinction between *right* and *might* and a lively awareness of whom the law has authorized to do what.

Although the Thatcherite view of government is entirely in keeping with what was until this century generally accepted in Britain, its rejection of pressure group politics has given rise to the belief that Thatcherism is an 'ideology'. For it is commonly supposed that there are only two ways of conducting politics – either to follow some abstract blueprint or to satisfy the demands of interest groups. Given this assumption, if Thatcherism rejects the latter, it must be doing the former, which makes it an ideology. But that conclusion is wrong because Thatcherism is in essence a practical response to a historical state of affairs. Thatcherism cannot be an ideology because it is neither a theory nor concerned with establishing an eternally correct programme of action.

But if Thatcherism is nothing like an 'ideology', it does produce a similar impression of movement, direction, and purpose. This quality is much amplified by the fact that Thatcherites have had not only a will to do 'the right thing' but also a fairly definite idea of what that 'right thing' was. It had to be a response to the condition of Britain at the end of the twentieth century. And that response falls into three distinct parts, relating respectively to individuals, families and the state.

It has frequently been said that, for a Thatcherite, 'there is no such thing as society'. This otherwise profoundly mysterious remark – which Mrs Thatcher once made – makes sense only when the tri-partite character of the Thatcherite view of Britain is exposed, and the movement of ideas from one category to the next is understood. Thatcherism starts with a conception of the individual, moves to a conception of the family suited to foster the individual characteristics which it favours, and regards the proper society as one in which the favoured characteristics of individuals and families can flourish and be manifested. 'Society' is therefore seen not as something which exists in its own right or which ought to have a certain form for its own sake, but rather as an arrangement of relationships among individuals which enables them to live a certain form of life. It is in this sense, and in this sense only, that 'there is no such thing as society' for a Thatcherite.

The Thatcherite conception of the individual is the most important and at the same time the least understood element of Thatcherism. The mere fact of *having* a conception of the individual is in itself something quite out of the ordinary in modern politics. If one were, for example, to ask what conception of the individual was held by Socialists, Christian Democrats, Gaullists, Liberals, Tory supporters of the 'middle way', or by the Institute of Economic Affairs (IEA) one would draw an enormous blank. Modern politics has focused so extensively on the *relationships* among individuals that it has almost entirely abstained from taking a view on the individual himself. So true is this, that commentators on Thatcherism have tended either wholly to ignore Thatcherism's central preoccupation with the nature of the individual or have dismissed this preoccupation as a trivial obsession with 'Victorian values'. The idea of a politics founded upon a conception of individual character is wholly alien to the modern liberal consciousness.

Although the Thatcherite conception of the individual has never been announced in a single soliloquy at centre stage, or indeed ever articulated, it has been the clear, though implicit, theme of a series of speeches, policies and acts. After fifteen years of the rhetoric and practice of Thatcherism, its outlines are clear. The individual preferred by Thatcherism is, to begin with a simple list: upright, self-sufficient, energetic, adventurous, independent-minded, loyal to friends, and robust against enemies. A preference for this sort of individual, though far from universal, is not exclusive to Thatcherism, but what matters here is the role it plays in Thatcherism.

The first important point about the list is the *kind* of trait that it contains. There is nothing substantive, that is to say, no description of the individual's profession, level of education, achievements, wealth or poverty, position in society, marital status, proficiency in particular skills, political views, aesthetic sensibilities, religion, likes or dislikes. It is, in other words, possible for a person to conform to the Thatcherite conception and yet *be* any one of an infinite number of different kinds of person. This is because the list contains *virtues* or, in other words, attributes which qualify all the acts of a person, and which can be displayed in an infinite variety of particular, substantive lives.

To say that the list contains no prescriptions for particular substantive lives does not mean that it is mere pious waffle. On the contrary, the qualities described in the list are of a very marked stamp. Broadly, they can be described as the *vigorous* virtues. They are to be contrasted with the 'softer' virtues such as kindness, humility, gentleness, sympathy, cheerfulness. The softer virtues are, of course, to a great degree compatible with the 'vigorous' virtues. A person may be both upright and cheerful, both self-sufficient and kindly, both energetic and gentle. But there is a question of emphasis. Thatcherism has always been a 'vigorous' creed in the sense not that it wishes to abolish the softer virtues but that it emphasizes the vigorous virtues, and if necessary, where conflicts arise, at the expense of the softer virtues.

Being a creature of its location in space and time, Thatcherism has seen Britain at the end of the twentieth century as a place in which the softer virtues have been too much stressed and the vigorous virtues insufficiently regarded, whether by official moralists in the churches and lecture theatres or by the unofficial moralists of the media, the arts and the charity world. This is not a universal prescription but a point of crucial significance for understanding that Thatcherism is a view about what is needed in Britain at the end of the twentieth century. Thatcherites assume that these virtues have been neglected in recent British history and that the leading evil to be combated by an individual in Britain at this time is, by and large, the decadence that comes from an insufficiency of the vigorous virtues rather than the harshness that comes from an insufficiency of the softer virtues.

Whether Thatcherism has been right to identify an insufficiency of the vigorous virtues as the main danger in Britain at the end of the twentieth century is, for the purposes of this book, not at issue. For understanding Thatcherism, the important point is that a view about character, about the characters of individuals, is at the heart of it. That view takes the form of a belief that certain qualities have been underrated in Britain at the end of the twentieth century. And the importance of this point lies not merely in the fact that many of the substantive policies of Thatcherism have sprung from the belief that the vigorous virtues need to be reinforced but also in the fact that this belief has moulded Thatcherite rhetoric. Because of their concern with the vigorous virtues, Thatcherites have been at pains to emphasize the unrealized potentialities of the ordinary, robust British citizen rather than the irremediable disabilities of the least favoured members of society. They have, in other words, drawn attention to the healthy and vibrant, rather than the sick, the halt and the blind. Indeed Thatcherites have been willing, on numerous occasions, to sound harsh in order to avoid the rhetoric of socialism (as of liberalism and 'middle way' Conservatism) which – by emphasizing the need for public support of those who cannot look after themselves – may all too easily, in a Thatcherite's view, suggest that *everybody* is in some way sick or incapacitated, and thus discourage if not enervate people who could well stand on their own feet.

Whereas socialists and liberals tend to regard the individual members of a society as objects of 'care', as if they were all invalids who have to be 'looked after', while regarding government (if benign) as the agency that does the looking after, Thatcherites think of people as eager and on the whole able to care for themselves. By their reckoning, people look to government not for 'care' as a child looks to a parent or a patient to a doctor but for something quite different – for maintaining a set of arrangements that will allow each person to pursue his projects, whether alone or in co-operation with others, in security and without conflict. They look to government as the agency which, apart from protecting them against internal and external aggression, makes possible and enforces the contractual relationships which they arrange for themselves. Because contractual relationships cannot exist without the rule of law (as Eastern Europe is painfully discovering), regard for the rule of law has all along been emphasized by Thatcherism. It is important to notice that the Thatcherite emphasis on law is inspired not by the 'hanging and flogging' lobby in the Conservative party but by a vision of the British as people distinguished by vigorous virtues, who are offended by attempts to treat them as children or invalids, who want to pursue their own projects in their own way, within the framework established by the law of the land.

None of this means that Thatcherites do not or cannot consistently recognize that there are people who need to be 'looked after'. What it does mean is that the image which dominates Thatcherite thinking is not that of invalids but of people being energetic and self-sufficient. And it means furthermore that in devising measures for looking after those who cannot help themselves, Thatcherites are concerned to shape those measures in a fashion that will discourage dependency and emphasize the importance not just of administering aid and comfort but of taking pains to bolster, rather than to destroy, the self-respect and striving for independence even of incurable invalids.

Associated with the Thatcherite emphasis on vigorous virtues has been a set of views about the nature of a family. Whilst these views about the family are not in a strict sense entailed by the emphasis on the vigorous virtues, they are strongly linked. For a Thatcherite, the family is of critical significance because it is the means whereby the moral qualities, and in particular the vigorous virtues, of one generation are instilled in the next. Its centrality is assured by the fact (or, at any rate, by what the Thatcherite supposes to be the fact) that qualities so intangible, so subtle and so difficult to instil as uprightness, self-sufficiency, energy, independent mindedness, adventurousness, loyalty and robustness cannot possibly be taught out of a textbook but must rather be communicated by example and constant individual exhortation in an atmosphere of trust and love. It has always been, to the Thatcherite, inconceivable that the vigorous virtues will be acquired on a broad scale across society unless they are transmitted by the family from one generation to the next. This, in turn, generates a certain conception of what the family needs to be if it is to fulfil this role. First, it must be close, attentive, preoccupied with the task in hand. Second, it must have the confidence of its convictions: far from 'letting anything go', the adults in the family must insist with all the patience and care at their disposal on the cultivation of the vigorous virtues. Finally, it must persist across time. Days or months being quite insufficient for the purpose of transmitting virtues, the inculcation requires years or decades.

Allied to this conception of a family as nature's patient mentor, passing on virtue from one generation to the next, is a broadening of the Thatcherite notion of the 'self'. Because the Thatcherite believes in the family as the transmitter of virtue, the notion of 'self-sufficiency' (itself one of the cardinal vigorous virtues) is extended to include the self-sufficiency of the family as an entity. Far from thinking of the individual as an isolated atom, the Thatcherite sees the family as a band of individuals brought together in their common task of transmission, acting to support one another across time. Hence, for the Thatcherite, it is a matter of intense regret that, in the Britain of the late twentieth century, even the nuclear family is under threat. For the Thatcherite, the undoubted ideal has been a family stretching over many generations, a family extended to become a mutual support, both within and across the generations.

The special feature of Thatcherism, the feature that marks it out as different not merely in detail but in kind from other forms of late twentieth-century liberal politics, is its conception of the individual and family. But, in line with other forms of politics, Thatcherism also has a conception of the nation. This conception is as rooted in time and place as the Thatcherite emphasis on the vigorous virtues and on the family. There has not been any general Thatcherite theory of the nation or of society as grand abstractions.

There is no identifiably Thatcherite analysis of the relationship between abstract items such as 'state' and 'civil society'. There is no underlying thesis about the historic or future development of states or societies. There has, however, been a conception of what Britain as a nation ought to be like at the end of the twentieth century. In part, this conception follows directly from Thatcherite views on the individual and the family – Britain should be a place filled with individuals who exhibit the vigorous virtues, and with families that transmit, encourage and sustain such virtues from one generation to the next. But the Thatcherite notion of Britain goes beyond this. For the Thatcherite, British society should be organized in such a way that individuals who do practise the vigorous virtues have room to flourish; and it should be a country which, as a result, is rich, powerful, culturally dynamic and universally respected by the other nations of the globe.

It is a vision of Britain as a country of dynamism, wealth and power, but unencumbered by either the trappings of a great empire, or the Victorian *angst* associated with a world half of which is coloured red. For the fifty years before Thatcherism, the Conservative Party struggled with Britain's imperial heritage, never quite shaking off a belief in or at least a nostalgia for empire. Thatcherism, in its post-imperial modernity, has suffered no such hangups. It has concentrated instead on the revival of Britain as an independent island power, a country in which the interplay of vigorous individuality is supposed to form the basis of a self-sufficient and respected island power.

This positive Thatcherite vision – of individuals imbued with the vigorous virtues, nurtured in families that sustain such virtues and together composing a vigorous, independent and powerful Britain – has been attractive to some and repulsive to others. It is no purpose of this book either to defend or to attack this vision, but simply to understand how it has been embodied in the rhetoric and practical action of Thatcherite politics. Such an understanding, however, requires a further adjustment in the thinking of those accustomed to the ideas of modern liberal politics. For, in addition to its unusual emphasis on individual and familial virtues, Thatcherism is surprising in its political *method*.

The paradigm for political action for at least a century has been extremely simple: first identify what is wrong, then get the government to do something about it. To the Thatcherite, this paradigm has in itself seemed part of the problem. It has had to be replaced with a different paradigm: first, identify the problem; second, discover whether the problem is caused by government action or government inaction; third, if the problem is caused by government action, put an end to that action; and fourth, only if the problem is caused by government inaction, get the government to do something about it.

No one would be more surprised than Mrs Thatcher herself, or those most closely associated with her in the execution of her policies, to discover that they had been responsible for a 'paradigm shift' in the conduct of modern politics. Just as Thatcherites have not imagined themselves to be cultivating the 'vigorous virtues', so they have not consciously sought to change the nature of thinking about political action. This would have been far too abstract and theoretical a proposition to have been taken seriously in the Cabinet Room or in the Conservative Party. But Thatcherites have deliberately and constantly reiterated the need not to think of government as the solution to all ills; and, in joining that theme to their positive vision of the individual, the family and Britain, they have created a new political method of which they have themselves never been aware at the theoretical level.

This paradigm shift or change of method arises necessarily from the nature of the positive vision of individuals, families and Britain in Thatcherism. Inspecting Britain at the end of the twentieth century, Thatcherites have seen problems everywhere because so many aspects of the positive vision are so far from being fulfilled. To take the most obvious examples: in relation to the individual, Thatcherites have seen criminality (in place of uprightness), a sense of dependency on the state (in place of self-sufficiency), defeatism in relation to self and country (in place of energy), sloppy adherence to passing fashion (in place of independent-mindedness), a feeling that 'the world owes one a living' and that 'someone will look after things' (in place of adventurousness) and an overwhelming celebration of 'compassion' (in place of loyalty and robustness). In relation to families, Thatcherites have seen the disintegration of the extended family, the growing disrepute even of the nuclear family, widespread lack of concern for the moral upbringing of children, and an enormous lack of self-confidence in the rectitude of one generation passing on its morality to the next, in short, the antithesis of the Thatcherite conception of what the family should be. And, in relation to Britain as a country, Thatcherites have seen declining wealth compared to neighbours, lack of intellectual and cultural dynamism, dirt, ugliness, complacency and powerlessness.

Having identified these conditions as 'the problem', Thatcherites were bound not to accept the usual paradigm for political action. For 'the government' cannot be expected 'to do something' about the condition of individuals and families in a modern liberal state. And if, as Thatcherites believe, Britain itself can attain the desired condition only if individuals and families are so reformed, then the government cannot 'do' what is required for Britain either. The paradigm must therefore shift. Hence, as a matter of practice rather than theory, Thatcherites abandoned the automatic assumption that a problem, once identified, can be resolved by government for the view that government must identify which aspects of the problem are themselves caused by government action and which by government inaction, and take steps accordingly. In so doing, Thatcherites of course implicitly accepted that many aspects of a problem might be caused not by anything that the government did or failed to do but rather by deep intellectual and cultural inheritances and would remain troublesome. For Thatcherites, as Conservatives, this is not in the least remarkable. Thatcherism is Tory and not millennial or revolutionary precisely because it has never contained anywhere in it the presumption that the vision of Britain as it ought to be at the end of the twentieth century can be realized in its entirety by any form of political action.

These observations about the Thatcherite vision and method together constitute the central thesis of this book. The essential features of Thatcherism are that it is a form of practical politics devoted to achieving certain concrete results in Britain at the end of the twentieth century. Its aim has been to emphasize and promote the vigorous virtues in individuals, promote the family as the organization in which those virtues are transmitted and nurtured, and make Britain a flourishing island power through the liberation of the vigorous virtues. And, unlike other modern political enterprises, it has never expected positive government action fully to achieve its aims.

This thesis gains plausibility from four general and widely recognized features of Thatcherism in practice: the offence it has given to the 'establishment'; the remarkable style of government adopted by Mrs Thatcher herself; the strong divergence both from the proponents of the 'middle way' within the Tory party and from '*laissez-faire*' liberals; and the puzzlement and incomprehension of the serious commentators.

The talent of Thatcherism for offending the establishment is legendary. That much-reviled phrase, 'one of us', suggests a small band of devoted followers battling against the world, and there is certainly much of the established world against which Thatcherism has battled in its day. From the inception of the first Thatcher administration in 1979, the civil service was 'taken on'; a body of men and women which had grown ever larger since the war was cut back to the point where it became the smallest civil service since the war. The number of peerages and knighthoods given to the most senior civil servants markedly declined; relations between ministers and their officials were – to quote one senior official off the record – 'absolutely awful'. In the wake of the civil servants came the doom of the heads of nationalized industries. A host of new recruits – MacGregor in British Steel and later in British Coal, Day in British Shipbuilders, Edwardes (and later Day) in British Leyland, Bright at London Transport, Reid in British Rail, King and Marshall at British Airways – were sent in to shake up the management. The big business lobby, above all represented by the CBI, was displaced from the position of grandeur it once occupied. Instead, the upstart Institute of Directors (IOD), speaking for the smaller businessmen, and the new entrepreneurs – the Murdochs, Goldsmiths, and Hansons – found the sun of Thatcherite rhetoric shining upon them. Bankers were described as 'overpaid and underworked'. Following them, the professional establishments have been attacked one by one: academics found their tenure disappearing; teachers found salary structures altered; doctors have been subjected to new contracts; barristers have lost their monopoly. Attention was turned to that establishment of establishments, the BBC, with a sustained attack from the arch Thatcherite, Norman Tebbit. In its wake, came attacks upon various 'improprieties' of the press, to the outrage of editors. Most notoriously, those two great English institutions, the unions and local government, have been subjected to repeated waves of new regulation.

Why should a government, while so clearly wishing to remain in power, have taken on so many establishments in a democracy where 'opinion' is so much formed by those establishments? The only plausible explanation is that Thatcherism conceived these establishments as somehow 'part of the problem', as agencies which were formally or informally responsible for the decline of the vigorous virtues, the failure of the family and the state of Britain. In each case, what was being 'taken on' was an establishment which was thought to constitute a 'cosy cartel', a source of complacency, a centre of defeatism, an obstacle to vigour, an instigator of dependency, a cause of poverty or powerlessness. The attacks were so numerous precisely because of the 'paradigm shift' of Thatcherism. The Government did not believe that it could by direct action 'do something' to release the vigorous virtues. Instead it had to concentrate its firepower on those institutions which it believed were responsible for denigrating those virtues or holding them in check.

The moral and national purposes of Thatcherism, combined with the paradigm shift, also explain the remarkable **style** of government which the Thatcher administrations pursued. Because the efforts of government were concentrated upon removing what were seen as the obstacles to the flourishing of the vigorous virtues, Mrs Thatcher acted, and allowed herself to be portrayed, as the leader of a crusade, of a 'continuous revolution'. There was throughout an almost unprecedented sense of a peacetime prime minister 'leading from the front', pushing forward to keep up the momentum, persuaded that there was 'so much more to be done'. Because the entire enterprise of government was conceived by

Thatcherism as an attempt to overturn a decadent establishment, the government itself was frequently seen as 'part of the problem': there was a constant fear that ministers had been or might be captured by the establishments with which they were meant to be battling in the cause of liberating the vigorous virtues. Hence, Mrs Thatcher's notable affection for 'kitchen cabinets' and for personal advisers who were thought to share the moral vision and sense of urgency and who were regarded by others with considerable suspicion. Hence, too, the frequent reshuffles in succeeding attempts to find ministers capable of rooting out the obstacles to the vigorous virtues, and hence also the intense desire of Mrs Thatcher herself to take part in the councils of the world.

Finally, it is the moral vision and the paradigm shift in government which explain the almost obsessive attention paid by Mrs Thatcher to administrative detail. The discouragement of dependency and the encouragement of vigour were seen so frequently to rest on administrative details that these could not be ignored. A minister who believes that Britain can be literally rebuilt by government in a dash for growth, as Macmillan did, need not attend to the precise details of the administrative means by which government brings forth this result, any more than a general in the field need concern himself with the activities of every platoon. But a minister who wishes to liberate vigorous virtues by forcing councils to let tenants become home owners must attend to every last detail if he is to prevent his scheme from being thwarted by the establishment (in this case the council itself) which is at once the direct object of the attack and the body which must carry out his policy. In other words, because Thatcherism consists of taking on the establishment in order to bring about a set of moral effects, the establishment had to be taken on with its own weapons, above all, by the mastery of administrative detail. That is one reason why Thatcherism has been seen by some as the promotion of 'intrusive' government, centralization, and the concentration of unprecedented powers in the Prime Minister.

The fact that Thatcherism was a crusade against obstacles to the realization of a moral and national vision also explains the extent of its divergence from both the old 'middle way' Tories and true '*laissez-faire*' liberals. The 'middle way' Tory is, sometimes by origin and always by culture, by his attitude to the poor and by his view of business, what is now thought of as 'aristocratic'. He displays a love of empire and disdain for concentration on the pursuit of wealth, along with a predilection for the 'softer' virtues which associate him in current popular thinking with the 'aristocracy'. Thatcherism, with its emphasis on the vigorous virtues, its fear of decadence, its modernity and absence of nostalgia for empire, displays a very different temperament. But this does not mean, as some suppose, that Thatcherism is distinguished by a prejudice against certain classes such as the squirearchy or Etonians. It is true, however, that the qualities admired by Thatcherism are the ones usually (and wrongly) not associated with these classes. And this puts Thatcherism at odds with the 'middle way' Tory who, in pursuit of consensus and calm, seeks compromise on all sides – with socialists, the CBI, the TUC, the BBC, in short, with every establishment that Thatcherism has 'taken on' in the course of its crusade to liberate and promote the vigorous virtues. The 'middle way' Tory has no belief in the paradigm shift of political action; he is indeed a believer in the old paradigm. For him, government can achieve miracles through planning, economic controls, investment in industry, spending on welfare in order to foster wealth without 'the sting of selfishness'. To a Thatcherite, the proponent of the 'middle way' is therefore wrong not merely in his failure to see the appropriate aim of politics but also, as a result, in his view of the mechanics of political action.

Perhaps less obviously, but equally importantly, the fact that Thatcherism has been a crusade to free the vigorous virtues from the grip of the establishments explains its profound differences from '*laissez-faire* liberalism'. The caricature liberal or 'libertarian', as such theorists are now commonly called, who departs considerably from Adam Smith's doctrine, favours a completely free market in drugs as much as in cars; he distrusts the police and the army; he favours freedom of information at all costs; he is not sure that there should be compulsory education and he is certain that the welfare state should be dismantled at a stroke. He is willing to make no concessions on public expenditure; his goal is the absence

of public expenditure, and, to the extent possible, the absence of
government itself. Superficially, his similarity to the Thatcherite is
considerable. He and the Thatcherite share a dislike of the various
establishments that have created and fostered dependency; he is,
indeed, an extreme proponent of the paradigm shift, since – far
from wishing government to 'do something' – he wishes to see
government practically or even actually non-existent. But the profound divergence between his views and those of the Thatcherite
become apparent when one understands Thatcherism as aimed at
a specific moral result for the individual, the revivification of the
family, and the recreation of a rich, powerful and culturally dynamic
Britain. These are aims which make the Thatcherite an opponent
of some free markets (what could be more deleterious to the more
vigorous virtues than free markets in drugs?), a friend to the police
who enforce uprightness and to the army who manifest Britain's
power, and a believer in ensuring that each child receives the
education that would effectively initiate him into his civilized inheritance and equip him to sustain himself. Above all, these concrete
aims of Thatcherism make concession and compromise inevitable
in many cases, in relation to the welfare state, to public expenditure,
to political circumstance as it arises. Whereas Thatcherism has
been a historically located and dedicatedly practical form of politics,
the libertarian is an armchair theorist and a lover of liberty in the
abstract. He cannot share and has no sympathy with either the
practicality or the moral aims of what he regards as the jingoistic
nationalism of Thatcherism. In the last resort, Thatcherism has
always been Tory; the libertarian is not.

As well as explaining the tendency of Thatcherism to attack so
many establishments, the remarkable personal method of government and the strong divergences of Thatcherism from both 'middle
way' Toryism and *laissez-faire* liberalism, the thesis that Thatcherism has been a crusade to liberate the vigorous virtues can explain
the many puzzling things that have been said about Thatcherism
by the serious commentators. Those who call Thatcherism a
'ragbag of ideas' are complaining, in the first place, that Thatcherism is not a theory, hence a 'ragbag'. And they are right because
Thatcherism is not a general political theory, but a historically

specific and ruthlessly practical project. When commentators look for first principles, for analysis, for argument, they do not find any because it is not there. They wrongly leap to the conclusion that there is no coherence. It is as if they spotted that Thatcherism was a practical, moral vision and then discarded this understanding as something too implausible to be believed. The lack of analysis and argument merely indicates that the coherence of Thatcherism lies in its concrete vision of how Britain should be at the end of the twentieth century rather than in a theoretical construction. And it is this practicality, too, this dominance of a moral vision, that explains the 'narrowness' and 'dogmatism' so often deplored by opponents. Thatcherism is 'narrow' and 'dogmatic' in the sense that it is one simple vision of how things should be in one place at one time with no analytic pretensions and no capacity to illuminate the nature of politics or civilization. And it also becomes clear why Mrs Thatcher should be called a 'Little Englander' and why Thatcherism is described as 'British Gaullism'. Thatcherism is 'Little Englandism' and a form of 'British Gaullism' in the sense that it is a vision of England as an independent island power.

When Mrs Thatcher is accused of 'plundering ideas', that charge too is right: the Thatcherite vision of Britain has no more claim to be 'original' than the emphasis on the vigorous virtues. Thatcherism is meant to *happen*, not to win prizes for originality. Nor is there any difficulty in understanding why Thatcherism should be seen as a project to 'kill socialism', or described as 'revenge for . . . the cultural revolution of the 1960s'. In its effort to promote and liberate the vigorous virtues, and to create a Britain made rich, powerful and culturally dynamic by the interplay of those virtues, Thatcherism has 'taken on' as its two greatest enemies socialism and 'the cultural revolution of the 1960s'. These two phenomena are, to the Thatcherite way of thinking, the great agents of dependency, the causes of Britain's decadence and decline. To the Thatcherite, given the paradigm shift, the belief that government cannot by itself 'do something' to realize either the individual moral character or the vision for Britain that he hoped to promote, political action necessarily became above all the task of 'killing socialism', undoing 'the cultural revolution of the 1960s' and ridding Britain

of the other obstacles to the flourishing of the vigorous virtues
which these twin phenomena had created. Those who equate Thatcherism with opposition to socialism and to the culture of the
sixties correctly identify what was being attacked but fail to discern
the positive vision which inspired the attack.

At the same time, it is possible to resolve what strikes the
commentators as a paradox – the fact that Thatcherism, though
seemingly committed to the 'paradigm shift', has been in many
ways strongly interventionist, displaying a tendency towards 'seizing
control' and leaving establishments other than the state itself 'emasculated' or 'dismantled'. These phenomena are puzzling only if
and to the extent that Thatcherism is confused with *laissez-faire*
liberalism. Once Thatcherism is understood as a crusade to liberate
the vigorous virtues the fact of its strong and consistent attack on
the many entrenched interest groups can be seen not as an
irrational bid for centralized authority but as an attempt to 'emascu-
late and dismantle' those institutions which, rightly or wrongly,
have been seen by Thatcherites as the obstacles to the cultivation
of the vigorous virtues. It is also why Thatcherism should seem to
have espoused a 'supreme duty to remain in power': not being a
theory and aiming at concrete moral results for Britain at the end
of the twentieth century, Thatcherism, whilst moving towards its
objectives with unceasing energy, felt obliged to take all the turns
and twists that would be used by any practical politician. The
commentators find it difficult to reconcile the 'conviction politics'
with the willingness to make concessions and strong efforts to retain
power because they fail to identify the *practicality* and *historicity* of
Thatcherite convictions.

Last, but by no means least, the thesis that Thatcherism has
been a crusade to liberate the vigorous virtues makes it possible to
understand why Thatcherism should be accused of being a license
for greed, and for 'bourgeois triumphalism', or of being a form of
'acquisitive individualism', and identified with the wish to 'sell off
every cathedral close to Tesco's in the name of the free market'.
The key lies in the fact that the vigorous virtues are what we might
expect to find in the entrepreneur, and it is the entrepreneur who
has been chosen repeatedly by Thatcherites to exemplify them. In

reality, of course, the vigorous virtues are also those of Dr Johnson and Edward Elgar, of Baden-Powell and of Edith Cavell. But it is easy to see why those whose constant fear is the onset of a commercial philistinism should rapidly identify Thatcherism's predilection for the vigorous virtues as a predilection for entrepreneurs and nothing else. When the entrepreneurial head fits the cap, it requires a certain subtlety to see that there are other kinds of heads which could fit the same cap.

The thesis – that Thatcherism was concerned with restoring the vigorous virtues and achieving a paradigm shift in the relation between government and the governed – is an abstraction from what Thatcherites did and said. Because it is an abstraction, it does not imply – and should not be interpreted as implying – that any Thatcherite ever spoke of the vigorous virtues, had a plan for promoting them, or articulated the definition of Thatcherism given here. Neither does it imply that all Thatcherites were at all times in perfect agreement, disinterested, and high-minded. Nor can this thesis, by itself, establish that what Thatcher governments believed and did was right or good.

Those readers who share the Thatcherite preoccupations might assume that a book which identifies Thatcherism with their own preoccupations must be designed to defend it. On the other hand, those who interpret Thatcherism in one or another of the conventional ways – as a drive to make the rich richer, a project inspired by the values of a Grantham grocer, *ad hoc* responses to the demands of party politics, a crusade to impose an economic dogma – might find it difficult to understand how such a very different, indeed strange, way of defining Thatcherism could be anything but a defence. Nevertheless, nothing could be wider of the mark than the supposition that this way of understanding Thatcherism constitutes a defence.

On the contrary, it can provide ammunition for either opponents or supporters because it is designed to explain rather than to make a case for or against Thatcherism. In order to defend Thatcherism or to attack it, one must present an *argument* to demonstrate why what Thatcherism is should be considered good or bad. For both arguments, the identification of Thatcherism presented here can serve as a minor premise. None of this, of course, need prevent either a defender or an opponent of Thatcherism from challenging the validity of the thesis here on the grounds that it fails to account adequately for the attributes of Thatcherism, or rests on faulty evidence. But that challenge, however successful, like the thesis, cannot by itself determine whether Thatcherism is good or bad. Whether a particular understanding of Thatcherism is adequate has to be established on grounds very different from those for deciding whether Thatcherism deserves commendation or opprobrium.

What this identification of Thatcherism can do is to account for the many conflicting attributes imputed to Thatcherism. It explains why adherents no less than opponents believe that it makes sense to speak of 'Thatcherism' and why they have nevertheless described Thatcherism as both a jumble of off-the-peg ideas and a narrow dogma. It can account not only for the confusion in the commentaries but also for the divergence of Thatcherism from both 'middle way' Toryism and libertarianism, as well as for the peculiarity of Mrs Thatcher's style of governing. But the thesis that Thatcherism has a coherent identity cannot tell us how that identity was acquired, whether it grew up as an unintended consequence or was imposed by the will of Mrs Thatcher, or appeared in some other way. Nor does it follow that Thatcherism acquired this identity on the day that Mrs Thatcher entered 10 Downing Street. It is an identity that has been discovered by looking back from beyond Mrs Thatcher's resignation. How Thatcherism acquired this character can be ascertained only by engaging in a very different kind of inquiry from that pursued in this book.

It remains to assemble the evidence that supports the validity and explanatory power of this identification of Thatcherism. That evidence is to be found in the history of Thatcherite policies. But the significance of those policies emerges only within the historical setting of Thatcherism, and in particular the evolution of the Conservative Party and the condition of Britain since the Second World War.

3

The Historical Setting: The Conservative Party and the State of Britain

Thatcherite policies did not spring out of nothing. The way was prepared for them by the confluence of a variety of ideas, activities, and circumstances. Two aspects of the historical context of Thatcherism are crucial for understanding how Thatcherite policies developed – the state of the Conservative Party and the state of Britain. They can explain why Thatcherism has been both dismissed as old wine in new bottles and accused of (or commended for) making a revolution, and why neither is correct.

The State of the Conservative Party

i. THE MYTH OF LAISSEZ-FAIRE

The greatest obstacle to seeing how Thatcherism fits into the British political scene as a whole and is related to the Conservative Party in particular is a misunderstanding of British political history. It is the belief that the issue that divided Conservatives from their liberal opponents in the nineteenth century was *laissez-faire*. Liberals were supposed to have advocated it and Conservatives to have opposed it. That issue, it is assumed, continued to dominate British politics throughout the nineteenth century to our own time, but with a reversal in the positions of the parties. Conservatives who supported Margaret Thatcher are now regarded as advocates of *laissez-faire*, against opposition from 'liberals' and 'socialists'.

What *laissez-faire* means is obviously crucial to the story. It is taken to be a description of the kind of political order defended by Adam Smith in the *Wealth of Nations* and put into practice in Britain in the nineteenth century. The phrase itself, however, was never used by Adam Smith. It was invented by French writers, the physiocrats, and imported into England to be used as a term of abuse in the 1880s, more than a century after the *Wealth of Nations* was published.

The meaning usually ascribed to *laissez-faire* is the principle that government should not interfere with competition among individuals engaged in the making and exchanging of goods and services. *Laissez-faire* has accordingly become synonymous with wholly unfettered competition. Nothing of the sort is advocated in the *Wealth of Nations*. On the contrary, Adam Smith makes it clear that wholly unfettered competition could not be anything but an imaginary condition, a chimera. He was arguing against a particular kind of restriction, that advocated by the mercantilists, who wanted laws which would fix prices and keep out foreign goods which forced down prices of English goods. The measures advocated by mercantilists were denounced by Smith for being designed to restrict competition so as to increase the profits of merchants at the expense of the consumer. And in order to show that mercantilist policies were neither beneficial nor just, he explained how competition in the market to buy as cheaply and to sell as dearly as possible could organize the activities by which men make a living and satisfy their wants. By explaining how a market economy operates, he founded scientific economics.

Smith's explanation rests on two assumptions which are all too often forgotten, by his disciples no less than by his opponents. The first is that men may pursue their various economic projects for a great variety of motives, that they may as easily be inspired by a concern to provide for others or by a delight in the work they do, as by greed for more wealth. Although he argued that the wealth of the nation would be increased by allowing the kind of competition that mercantilists wanted to eliminate, he did not maintain or expect that those who compete in the market and seek to make a profit need or should be obsessed by a desire for wealth.

Secondly, Smith assumed that a market economy cannot function without a legal system which defines rights and duties. To maintain a market economy, the government has to make and enforce an elaborate system of laws which establish the terms on which property may be held and goods and services exchanged, and which identify and prohibit force and fraud. In addition, he expected the government to provide national defence, maintain certain public works, ensure education of the young and perhaps subsidize religious instruction. In short, even though he opposed interference with the operation of competitive controls, he assumed that competition had to be regulated by the government.

In theorizing the character of a market economy more completely than had ever been done before, Adam Smith was not inventing a new political order. He was distinguishing certain features of the arrangements for governing themselves that the people of Britain had been developing since the Middle Ages. In all that he wrote, Smith took for granted a certain understanding of government which had by his time become traditional in Britain, and was accepted as well by the mercantilists whom he opposed. This understanding was what Edmund Burke was defending in his tirades against the ideological politics of the French. It continued to prevail throughout the nineteenth century and was not repudiated by either Whigs, Tories, Peelites or Liberals, however much they differed with one another.

Their quarrels were about what emendations of established rights and duties were called for by new circumstances and about whether the proposed emendations were compatible with maintaining the established way of governing. They differed on questions such as whether certain products of agriculture or industry should be protected from foreign competition, whether the Church should be disestablished, what to do about the demand for Irish Home Rule, how far to extend the franchise. Neither those who proposed legislation to limit the hours of working men and to prohibit child labour nor those who wanted to reform the treatment of the unemployed ever dreamt of destroying either private property or the inequalities that arise from the free exchange of goods and services in a market economy. It is true that Disraeli's 'policy of sewage' in 1874–80 which brought in the Public Health Act, as well as the

Artisans' Dwellings Act, the Conspiracy Act which gave trade unions the right to strike, and the Acts regulating the sale of food and drugs were described by Lord Randolph Churchill as 'Tory Democracy' and by others as 'a drift to collectivism'. But in fact they were neither because they were not designed to change the fundamental character of government but to amend certain rules of political association in accordance with changed opinions and circumstances.

The basic ingredients of opinion were the same in all parties, only mixed in different proportions. Moving from one party to another, as Gladstone and Peel did, was accordingly no more remarkable than the fact that measures to protect workers against harsh conditions of employment or to facilitate the education of the poor found advocates in all parties. Changing one's stand on the issues of the day neither required nor signified a fundamental revolution in political outlook. Some landowners were Whig, others were Tory. If the new men, who had become prosperous through commerce and industry were less likely to vote Tory, the Radicals, who were supposed to lead opinion among the industrial classes, sat with the Tories in the House of Commons. The Conservatives first ardently defended the Corn Laws and insisted on a substantial property qualification for voting, and then repealed the Corn Laws and extended the franchise. Their readiness to adopt new stances won them an accolade for supreme opportunism from Trollope: 'no reform, no innovation – experience almost justifies us in saying, no revolution – stinks so foully in the nostrils of an English Tory as to be absolutely irreconcilable to him. When taken in the refreshing waters of office any such pill can be swallowed.'

But whether or not opportunism was the motive, there was no betrayal of fundamental convictions in such shifts because the reforming measures were designed to modify particular arrangements, not to destroy the fundamental political character of Britain. Movement between the parties was occasioned by opinions on particular issues, by personal loyalties or animosities, not by disagreements on fundamental principles. No one was startled by Trollope's account of the political division between Plantagenet Palliser and his son, when Lord Silverbridge decided to stand as a Conservative. While the father, whose family had always been Whig or Liberal, was not pleased, he saw no reason to quarrel with his son. They would sit on opposite sides of the House and he trusted that his son would do his duty as conscientiously as he himself did. Family tradition had made him a Liberal, but no deep moral or emotional division separated him from Conservatives, or made them distasteful to him. In the great debates, especially between the giants, Gladstone and Disraeli, the parties hurled anathemas at one another but that was part of the game of politics, not a matter for enduring agitation.

It is true that the seeds of another kind of quarrel were already present. They appeared in wholly unmatured form in the writings of Jeremy Bentham and in the activities of his disciples. Riper seeds were planted by Coleridge, Carlyle, John Stuart Mill, under the inspiration of German and French writers, and later in the century by the evolutionary theory of Darwin and the 'Social' Darwinians. And by the 1890s a full-blown alternative understanding of the political order had emerged and was being propagated by Beatrice and Sidney Webb at ascetic lunches for important people and in monumental histories of trade unionism and local government. Although the Labour Party contained some whom the Webbs regarded as faint-hearted adherents to the new truth, the success of Labour in the 1922 election, which made it the head of a coalition with the Liberals, signalled the debut into British politics of a fundamentally different outlook, which had had no place in Britain before then.

The new element was recognized as 'socialism'. Then as now, most people supposed that socialism was about promoting the interests of the poor or the working class against the interests of the rich, and about using the government to restrain greed by redistributing property and wealth. Beatrice and Sidney Webb knew that something more profound was at stake but they were happy to let the fundamental change that they wanted be introduced in conventional dress without alarming people. They pinned their hopes on the benign effects of war. Habits acquired during the First World War, when the State managed the whole of life, would, they believed, make the transition to a truly socialist commonwealth inevitable. But events did not justify their optimism. The Labour Party neither took power nor developed into more than a rough amalgam of trades unions, Fabians, assorted radicals and do-gooders.

As even the trade unions were regarded by them as 'paper tigers', Conservatives saw nothing very ominous in the appearance of the new party beyond the obvious and simple danger arising from the ability of a third party to destroy majorities in elections. Their leading worries were not about general principles or doctrines, but about practical questions requiring an immediate answer: how to ward off the Liberal Party; whether British industry could be protected by tariffs without alienating working-class voters; what was the best way to defend the Empire; how to deal with unemployment; how to balance the claims of Church of England schools against those of the Roman Catholic ones; what to do about the iniquities of the Rating and Valuation Act. In the thirties, there were more serious anxieties about the depression and unemployment. And these gave way to preoccupation with Hitler, rearmament and war. Only after the Second World War did Socialism become a central concern of the Conservative Party.

But even when they became seriously concerned about socialism, the Conservatives were far from clear about the reasons for their quarrel with it or indeed whether they had a quarrel. The only undisputed point was that Labour had become the leading opposition party and that the Conservatives had to address themselves to changing their reputation as the party of depression and unemployment to something more benign. They set out to repudiate *laissez-faire*.

It was the socialists who had popularized the anarchistic principle of *laissez-faire* and attached it to their opponents. But the Conservatives unselfconsciously accepted the socialist invention and learned to see themselves as a party that had in the past been taken over by 'Whigs' and 'money barons'. Even before the Second World War had ended, Rab Butler launched a campaign to cleanse the Conservative Party of the beliefs that it had never held.

ii. THE BUTLER 'REFORMS'

Under Butler's competent guidance, the Tory Reform Group produced pamphlets with titles, which became familiar enough in the eighties, but with a rather different content. In a publication called *Full Speed Ahead – Essays in Tory Reform*, the leader of the Tory Reform Committee, Lord Hinchinbroke, denounced Tory alignment with big business and commercial interests and called upon Tories to give up their allegiance to *laissez-faire*. He advocated that the state should take control of aircraft manufacturing, coal mines, agriculture, finance and investments. To accept management of the economy by the government was the only way to bring the 'old tug of war between capital and labour'[1] to 'a happy draw'. A Tory revival depended on a commitment to a programme for national unity, full employment, and social reform.

The same message came from many others, who filled the Tory magazine, the *Onlooker*, with denunciations of *laissez-faire* and the Whig tendency in the party. Disraeli was adopted as the mascot by the advocates of 'One Nation politics'. Quintin Hogg (later Lord Hailsham and Lord Chancellor under Margaret Thatcher) warned Conservatives that 'if you do not give the people social reform, they are going to give you social revolution.' And the reforms had better not be milk-and-water measures but full-blooded planning and public ownership. Instead of fearing 'schemes for social security', the Conservatives had to recognize that such schemes were the only basis for the 'social stability necessary to the restoration of industry'. The Conservatives had to aim for a 'classless democracy', in which differences of education and technical skill were the only distinctions 'and replaced privileges based on birth and wealth.'[2]

Far from being criticized for accepting socialism, Hogg's call was greeted as the quintessence of Conservativism. The *Onlooker* could hardly praise him enough for being 'entirely in accord with the progressive Conservativism of today' and vehemently denied that he was 'meeting socialist policies half way'. David Eccles welcomed Hogg's suggestions as the answer to the great question that had been worrying the Tories, 'How to reconcile the necessities of the two-party system . . . with the mechanics of planned unemployment and a just distribution of the resulting national income.'[3]

The Conservative Manifesto of 1945 did not go quite so far in the direction of 'reform' as the Right Progressive wing wanted. But to an uncommitted observer, the difference between the Conservative and the Labour programmes in 1945 was hardly sensational. If the Conservatives did not unequivocally endorse nationalization, they still advocated a massive extension of state control and state spending. When the Conservatives lost the 1945 election, the defeat, which caught most Conservatives by surprise, was blamed on the party's failure to commit itself wholeheartedly to truly radical changes. Macmillan concluded that since there were at the time so many economic and financial difficulties, 'it may well be that by a sound instinct the British people felt that it would be wiser for a Government of the Left to be in control.'[4]

What followed was the reorganization directed by Butler to shake 'the Conservative Party out of its lethargy' and 'to rethink its philosophy and reform its ranks with a thoroughness unmatched for a century'.[5] By 1947, the party conference approved the Industrial Charter which unequivocally committed the Tories to maintaining full employment and the Welfare State, to lavish spending of public money and generally to expanding the power of the state, and which accepted nationalization as irreversible, and sold 2.5 million copies in six months. The programme was nevertheless described by Butler as an alternative to socialism, and was seen as such by its enthusiastic supporters. Macmillan rejoiced that the 'progressive element in the party' had at last 'seized control' without resort to 'force or a palace revolution, but by the vigour of its intellectual and spiritual power'. It had thus restored the Conservative Party to 'the tradition of Disraeli, Randolph Churchill and Joseph Chamberlain',[6] who had by now become indistinguishable from socialists in the imagination of Conservatives like Macmillan.

Dissident voices were occasionally heard, but not to great effect. The drive for reforming conservatism was not seriously impeded by attacks such as that of A. G. Erskine-Hill on Hinchinbroke's pamphlet, *Full Speed Ahead*. 'Full speed to where?' asked Erskine-Hill. Reforms should not be made, he argued, at 'the expense of the personality, dignity, and character of the individual, however humble'.[7] Together with others, he organized the Progress Trust to oppose the party's new direction and to propagate their views in the *Signpost Booklets*. But such dissident views did not worry the party leadership for they were generally dismissed as the eccentricities of die-hards.

The dominant view was that expressed by T. E. Utley, who later became a highly valued supporter of the Thatcher reforms and a speech writer for the Prime Minister. But in 1949, he held that the hopes of the 'Whig tendency' in the Conservative Party were doomed to be disappointed because socialism would not fail and the Conservatives would not be invited to replace it with good old capitalism: 'The present, or some future, Socialist Government may fail, but the Socialist economic system which it has created will remain, and the public will demand not a government of Liberal revolutionaries to restore the economic system of the nineteenth century, but a competent technocracy to apply the ultra-revolutionary and coercive measures necessary to rescue a Socialist economy from disaster.'[8] In the same vein, the Tory MP, Christopher Hollis, warned that there was 'no future' for rolling back the state and encouraging free enterprise – 'not because we are necessarily better or more humane than our ancestors, but because the conditions for the restoration of such a society do not exist'.[9]

Of course, some deny that there ever was anything like a 'post-war consensus'. Peter Jenkins argues that the consensus, which Margaret Thatcher 'believed herself to be smashing was founded more in myth than in reality'. It is far from true, according to Jenkins, that the 'parties had had more in common than the differences between them and that government, and especially the management of the economy, had proceeded according to a broad agreement. They did no such thing. Indeed Britain suffered unduly compared with some other, more successful countries from sharp and usually ideologically-inspired changes in direction – enactments and repeals, nationalizations, and denationalizations.'[10] Nevertheless, Jenkins grants that all three parties, Conservative, Labour and Liberal, fought the 1945 election on the same commitment to use the state for economic reconstruction and redistribution.

Those were the years when one of Labour's star candidates, Denis Healey, felt free to welcome the Communist takeover in Eastern Europe, to denounce the 'selfish, depraved, dissolute and decadent' upper classes and to declare that 'the socialist revolution has already begun in Europe and is already firmly established in many countries in eastern and southern Europe. The crucial principle of our foreign policy should be to protect, assist, encourage, and aid in every way the socialist revolution wherever it appears.' He urged the Labour Party to be 'prepared to understand' the point of view of labour movements in Europe who found it 'necessary to introduce a greater degree of police supervision and more immediate and drastic punishment for their opponents than we in this country would be prepared to tolerate'. Even in 1947 when Mr Healey had become head of Labour's international department, he took the trouble to write in the left-wing weekly, *Tribune*, to denounce Cardinal Mindszenty in the same fashion as the Communist government of Hungary did a year later when they arrested and imprisoned the Cardinal.

None of these statements caused a scandal. Both socialists and Conservatives were bent on understanding and tolerating the new enlightenment. But the Conservatives prided themselves on being the most reasonable of the lot because they had discovered the 'middle way' which would restore the politics of 'One Nation'.

iii. THE 'MIDDLE WAY'

The 'middle way' was a phrase used in 1938 by Harold Macmillan as the title for his book advocating not just the redistribution of wealth and use of inflation to combat recession, but also public control of the utilities, nationalization of the coal mines, legal enforcement of a minimum wage, public works, trade union participation in state planning boards, and a National Nutrition Board which would act 'as an expression of the organized consumers' needs' and run National Bakeries so as to produce a standard loaf. To young Tories at Oxford, such as Hugh Fraser and Edward Heath, the 'middle way' provided a light to live by. That the socialist journal, the *New Statesman*, applauded it as the road to socialism did not worry followers of the 'middle way'. Indeed it shocked no one other than the Macmillan nanny who declared that 'Mr Harold is a dangerous Pink.'[11] His intent had been, Macmillan explained later, to devise 'some coherent system, lying in between unadulterated private enterprise and collectivism . . . an industrial structure with the broad strategic control in the hands of the state and the tactical operation in the hands of private management, with public and private ownership operating side by side'.[12]

Having embarked on the 'middle way', the Conservative Party claimed that it had rediscovered its true self. The myth of *laissez-faire* and the misinterpretations of the nineteenth century had by now become entrenched in Conservative thought and rhetoric, and were enrolled in the service of electoral victory. In the past, to temper the excesses of Liberals, the line went, Conservatives had advocated Factory Acts, legalized trade unions, and generally promoted constraints on capitalism. Now, against the socialists, they were opposing wholesale collectivism and the loss of individual freedom while preserving the benefits of moderate collectivism.

The 'middle way' tendency acquired a 'think-tank' when the Bow Group appeared in 1951. It saw itself as the Conservative answer to Labour's Fabian Society, whose task it was to sponsor research groups and publish pamphlets with policy recommendations. In 1957, they began a quarterly journal, *Crossbow*, the first issue of which declared that, like its sponsors, it was a sign of the change in British politics since the war. Formerly the number of people willing to give time and energy to promoting ideas from the Right was remarkably few, but now the pendulum was swinging the other way. The two leading aims of *Crossbow* were to oppose the 'die-hards' (who were still devoted to maintaining the imperial character of Britain) and to promote economic growth: 'An expanding economy is no idle slogan; growth makes all policies easier, both at home and abroad.' The arguments between free enterprise and socialism were beside the point. The only real issue was how best to promote economic growth. Of course, dedication to economic growth took for granted direction and control of the economy by the state. To rid the party of any inhibitions inherited from the past, the Bow Group renounced conservatism as the mark of the Tory party. Conservatism was an 'obsession with problems of the past' which polluted trade unions, the Civil Service, and the Labour party far more than the Conservative party.[13]

By the 1959 election, it had become 'a truism', according to *Crossbow*, 'that the Tories are the progressive party and that the Socialists are stuck in the past'. Labour's prospects were hopeless because 'the people of this country are not interested in social revolution but in prosperity and freedom.' Indeed if Labour was to survive it must become more like the Conservative Party, as Roy Jenkins had recognized in his book, *The Labour Case*, which the *Crossbow* reviewer described as 'more like a series of Bow Group pamphlets than a statement of Labour policy'. But the same reviewer in *Crossbow* took a much less charitable view of a revised edition of Quintin Hogg's *Conservative Case* because it 'allowed only six pages' to the 'central problem of the future of the Welfare State'.[14]

Throughout the fifties, Conservatives remained confident that the 'middle way' would bring prosperity and contentment. The 1955 slogan was, 'Invest in Success', and in 1959 the electorate were told that 'Conservatives give you a better standard of living – Don't let Labour ruin it.' The Manifesto of 1959 declared that 'Eight years ago was a turning point in British history. The Labour Government had failed in grappling with the problems of the post-war world. Under Conservative leadership this country set out upon a new path. It is leading to prosperity and opportunity for all.'[15] Quintin Hogg was certain that socialism had been defeated by 'the fantastic growth of the economy, the spectacular rise in the standard of living, the substantial redistribution of wealth, the generous development of social welfare and the admitted humanizing of private industry.'[16] The new strategy had not only brought prosperity, R. A. Butler told a CPC Summer School in 1960, but also restored national unity. To Macmillan, Conservative victories – three in a row since 1951 – demonstrated the rightness of the 'middle way'. It showed that 'The class war is over and we have won it.' The British did not want 'to allow themselves to be divided into warring classes or tribes filled with hereditary animosity against each other'.[17] The journalistic and academic pundits agreed with the politicians that the nation had chosen to stay on 'the middle ground of politics'.

But where the 'middle way' lay was not so easy to discover. It turned out to be a winding, sinuous, intricate trail. The name implies of course the mean between two extremes, and what the extremes are is easy to guess – socialism on the one hand, and *laissez-faire* on the other. But examined more closely, the 'middle way' turns out to have a more self-sufficient character. Its doctrine is spelt out most clearly in the documents produced by the Conservative Party between 1945 and 1950 – the *Industrial Charter*, the *Workers' Charter*, the *Agricultural Charter*, the *Right Road for Britain*, and the speeches and essays collected and published by the Conservative Political Centre in *Conservatism 1945–50*. What one finds in these documents are two quite discordant themes.

One is a commitment to individualism expressed in statements which describe 'the highest development of the individual personality' as the aim of Conservative policies, and private property as 'a means of self-expression'. The Labour belief that 'the majority of people wish to become tenants of council houses' and their nostrum that owning one forty-eighth-millionth part of every shop and factory in the country, thanks to nationalization, can replace home ownership is dismissed as nonsense. Only the man with 'his own house and garden' can call his soul his own because he can 'exercise his creative faculties' and take pride in the home he creates. In short, a 'property-owning democracy', the slogan adopted at the 1947 Party Conference, is what Conservatives promise.

The same themes appeared in the election campaigns of 1950 and 1951 when the Conservative Party promised to 'set the people free' and to 'roll back' the state. Returning the nationalized industries to private enterprise was declared a necessity by Churchill. At the end of the Second World War, he had been anxious to maintain the collectivized state of affairs developed by the coalition government to deal with the war, but now he warned Britons that they could be neither free nor prosperous unless industry were removed from state control: 'The choice is between two ways of life; between individual liberty and state domination; between concentration of ownership in the hands of the state and the extension of ownership over the widest number of individuals; between the dead hand of monopoly and the stimulus of competition; between a policy of increasing restraint and a policy of liberating energy and ingenuity; between a policy of levelling down and a policy of opportunity for all to rise upwards from a basic standard.'[18]

To restore freedom and promote material progress, by giving rein to flexibility and initiative, there had to be a bonfire of the controls imposed by Labour. They were justified during the war when everything had to be subordinated to one purpose, but 'in peace, industry must meet that individual choice of millions of individuals which is an important demonstration of personality.' Rationing had continued only because of the Government's incompetence. Once embarked on controls, it is difficult to stop because controls breed like rabbits: 'The very fact of rationing one article, like bread, makes it all the more likely that substitutes for that article, like potatoes, will become scarcer and be rationed in turn.' Some of the controls are dangerously impertinent as well as ludicrous, such as the measure prohibiting the private householder from making repairs on his own house with his own labour. As the controls are unnecessary and impossible to enforce, the people disregard them with impunity, which brings the law into disrepute by crowding the statute books with rules which cannot be enforced.[19]

Profit was defended as 'a legitimate and worthy motive' no different in kind from salaries and wages: 'It is the reward for a different type of service to industry . . . no less essential than the service of labour. Every Government through its borrowing policy acknowledges that the fruits of abstaining from current expenditure are entitled to a rate of interest.' In risky trades justice requires that there should be a higher rate of return, just as special abilities and exceptional qualifications receive a higher wage or salary. In order that Britain should prosper, there had to be incentives to make greater effort worthwhile, and incentives were 'in danger of suffocation' by nationalization and the controls imposed both on economic and other activities. There was even a promise to reduce taxation by reducing Government expenditure.[20]

In this vein, too, the Conservatives insisted that the collective provision of social security must be 'a springboard and not a sofa' so as not to discourage the self-reliance of individuals. They emphasized the importance of a variety of voluntary associations, lamented the destruction of voluntary hospitals by the National Health Service, promised to remove the closed shop and declared a determination to protect the family. The rule of law was not a prominent subject but praised as a protection against arbitrary administrative decisions. The practice of invoking special tribunals which excluded those trained in the law from the hearings was condemned for placing justice in the hands of administrators: 'Ministers and their servants become judges and even judges in their own cause. They are not bound to give justice in open court' or 'give reasons for their judgements.' To protect administrative decisions against review by the judiciary was an invitation to tyranny.[21]

What is startling about this set of Conservative professions is the context in which they appear, for mixed in with the defence of individualism, private property and the rule of law, sometimes within the same paragraph, is quite another theme. It appears in talk about a balanced society, organic unity, a great common enterprise, a partnership between government, industry and labour, a strategic plan for national recovery, efficient use of the resources of the nation.

In this mood, often immediately after declaring their opposition to nationalization, conservatives discover 'that there is no clear-cut division between nationalization and other forms of industrial organization' and take pride in having done more than any other party to promote an industrial partnership between state and industry. Opposition to nationalization 'in principle' does not prevent Conservatives from recognizing that a state monopoly is only one form of monopoly, and that all 'large undertakings tend by their very nature to be bureaucratic whatever their ownership.' They see the public utility as an advanced form of state control and when that becomes unacceptable, they conclude that 'complete nationalization might represent a freeing of endeavour.' Municipal ownership of public utilities is also welcomed. Indeed no form of organization is intrinsically good or bad to Conservatives taking the 'middle way'. What matters is 'that the form of organization should make possible the greatest endeavour to raise the well-being of the nation by enabling each man to put forward his best'.[22]

Using taxation to reduce inequality of wealth is accepted, with the qualification that it might be better to refine the taxation of property by taking into account not only the level of wealth but also the obligations attached to the property. But 'no Conservative would deny that collective action involves some redistribution of wealth.' That there are '300,000 more civil servants today than there were before the war, apart from a similar increase in local government officials', is pointed out not in order to suggest cuts but to promise that the burden of the senior civil servants, charged to supervise a huge mass of juniors, should be reduced.[23]

All this was in keeping with the central message of the Industrial Charter, that a Conservative government took its task to be managing the economy so as to maintain full employment and 'make the best use of our own resources'. If that required deficit financing, the Government would not flinch. Since 'maintaining employment means keeping industry running,' Conservatives would concentrate first of all upon industries subject to fluctuations, especially 'basic industries producing for capital investment and export'. Of first importance was 'maintaining a steady rate of constructional work in housing, factories and other buildings'. To achieve this, the Government would 'concert with important industries and public authorities in plans for an even flow of investment', and where there is a special need for capital equipment, the Government would stand ready to give special help.[24]

Despite their compliments to voluntary associations, 'middle way' Conservatives boasted of having supported the Coalition schemes for a unified social security and for a national health service, adding meekly that of course 'good real wages and steady earnings are more important than the residuary measures of insurance and relief.' The Conservative emphasis on respect for authority was enlisted as a ground for recognizing that labour has 'rights' which are the 'duties of management'.[25] But there was no mention of the duties of labour.

Planning is centre-stage in the Charters. The task of the state is described as indicating the objectives and standards for industry to achieve, and guiding economic decisions 'in order to secure a high and stable level of employment'. Fixing wages and prices is part of such planning. The period between the two wars which was a 'time of active and positive Government interference' provided a precedent, and the war itself made a useful contribution by having inspired the Government to develop 'a greatly improved technique of central planning with many lessons of use in peace'. To the criticism that such a commitment to central planning is 'but thinly veiled socialism', came the firm answer that there can be no rational government policies without a plan to indicate the right policies: no one could be a warm advocate of tariffs while opposing a central plan, because 'tariffs must be built on a principle, and that principle is the conscious guidance of the national economy into pre-deter-mined channels. Conservatives were planning before the word entered the vocabulary of political jargon.'[26]

The commitment to planning is coupled with a commitment to 'a partnership' between government, industry, and labour, between government, industry, and the individual, indeed to partnerships galore between the government and every interest group to ensure that the grand plans take into account all points of view. 'Partner-ship' denotes an informal relationship, not required or regulated by legal procedures, which can take any form desired, whether beer and sandwiches in Downing Street, or the appointment of committees including representatives of every interest group. The object is to ensure 'consultation' by providing 'joint machinery' which will enable the various interest groups to meet with the government and declare their views on the proposed plans. Such arrangements, it was promised, would become a permanent feature of a Conservative government, thus enabling representatives of industry, labour, local government and other interests to give minis-ters 'the benefit of their experience and advice on all questions concerning our national resources and how they can best be used . . . ' Partnership between government and industry has to be supplemented by joint consultation within every industry so that there will be 'no sides in industry and all are working to a common purpose.' 'Co-partnership' everywhere – through schemes such as profit-sharing or employee share-holding and new variations on such schemes[27] – was the darling of those who travelled on the 'middle way'.

Far from being embarrassed by the conflict between the two themes in their declarations of intent, the 'middle way' Conservatives hailed it as the mark of their virtue. It confirmed their allegiance to the 'middle way'. It showed that they were a 'pragmatic', 'romantic', and 'evangelistic' party, committed to 'unity founded on variety' and above all to 'balance'. Indeed 'balance' became the Tory watchword. The Party announced its readiness to 'strike a balance between the claims of producer and consumer, employers and employed, landlord and tenant, nation and nation in a way that will make the greatest contribution to human progress'. For that was the way to achieve 'balance between freedom and order'.[28] Thus along with 'balance', 'freedom and order' became a Tory refrain.

The devotion to 'balance' was attributed to Conservative 'realism' which 'is essentially the striking of a balance'. Their realism, Conservatives told themselves, protected them from theories that commended 'extremes'; it kept Conservatives 'human instead of doctrinaire', ready to encourage initiative and to trust human nature instead of being deeply suspicious of it. Realism leads Conservatives to draw their inspiration from 'national unity instead of attempting to rule by division', as the socialists do. Because realism protected Conservatives against becoming bogged down in theory, they would concentrate, as the socialist government does not, 'on encouraging the building of more houses and the getting of more coal and the exercise of more forethought about the country's food supplies'. By recognizing that its tasks are more administrative than legislative 'a Conservative Government would contribute more to material well-being than does the nationalization of a dozen industries.'[29]

The realism that committed Conservatives to 'balance' enabled them, they boasted, to oppose nationalization 'as a principle on which all industries should be organized' yet without absolutely repudiating it, to recognize that 'public ownership' can take different forms and be combined with 'decentralization' and 'devolution'. Public ownership, when 'balanced', need not mean government interference 'in the detailed and daily management of industrial enterprises'; it is compatible with the confinement of the government to the making of large 'strategic plans'. Thus under Conservatives, even nationalized industries would not be run by rigid bureaucracies imposing a drab and inefficient uniformity. All good things would be secured by recognizing that the government must decide the overall strategy but can devolve the making of plans through 'a well-knit system of consultation and responsibility extending from the Cabinet room to the floor of the work-shop' and devolve the execution of plans by leaving the carrying out of the national strategy to 'the enterprise and public spirit of industry'.[30]

Their devotion to 'balance' led Conservatives to welcome the National Health Service while regretting the destruction of voluntary hospitals, to welcome more public projects in the hands of local authorities but to deplore the replacement of small local authorities by large regional ones, to hold to a 'belief in Personality' while also recognizing that its link to Christian ethics implies 'the duty to love one's neighbour as oneself'. What could be more 'balanced' and 'realistic' than to insist, as the Conservative Party did, on the importance of material welfare and at the same time to depreciate the love of gain? Continuity with the past of the Conservative Party was provided by the going misinterpretations of nineteenth-century politics. When, in the nineteenth century, the doctrine of *laissez-faire* exalted cheap goods, and man as a consumer and his individual rights, the story went, Conservatives emphasized 'man as a producer with duties to his fellow men' and invoked 'the collective power of Society to redress the social wrongs caused by economic development'. But now that Socialism unduly exalted the state, Conservatives emphasized the importance of the individual and brought in the 'traditions and values of the old world to redress the balance of the new'.[31]

The party accordingly advocated maintaining the welfare system created during the war but 'without reducing the individual to "a digit of the State", supplemented by "a code of behaviour" for industry which would "remove the sting of selfishness" and yet retain the urge which enterprise alone can give'. And far from insisting on the iniquities of socialism, they emphasized the virtue of a common approach to the 'fundamental problems of the day' in the belief that 'throughout our long and properly controversial political history, the body politic has always been healthy when there is agreement on politics.' After all, who could disagree with the objective of freeing industry from 'unnecessary controls and restrictions' and substituting 'for the present paralysis . . . a system of free enterprise, which is on terms with authority, which reconciles the need for central direction with the encouragement of individual effort, which allows the government to plan for full employment and the most efficient use of resources without interfering with the exercise of initiative and enterprise?'[32]

There was something for everyone in this brave new Conservativism: 'To the worker we offer a new charter giving assurance of steady employment . . . To the consumer we offer the ultimate restoration of freedom of choice . . . To the owner and shareholder we offer encouragement to raise the efficiency of his industry to the highest pitch . . . To the individual trader we offer fair competition, greater elasticity and less wastefulness from the operation of controls, in short, a fair reward for initiative, effort and personal service.'[33] In short, the 'middle way' was a bold exercise in eating one's cake and having it.

iv. THE CRISIS OF THE EARLY SIXTIES

The cake did not survive. By 1963, the euphoria had died down. De Gaulle's veto of Macmillan's attempt to enter the EEC was regarded as a misfortune. There were besides more obvious economic difficulties. In 1961 there was a balance of payments crisis, and the Chancellor of the Exchequer, Selwyn Lloyd, ordered what went by the euphemism 'a pay pause', along with higher taxes and restrictions on credit. Whereas all the other European economies were flourishing, Britain could not boast of anything like the same growth. It was suddenly discovered that Britain was 'the sick man of Europe'.

In the Orpington by-election of 1962, a Liberal, Eric Lubbock, won a noticeable victory over the Right Progressive Conservative, Peter Goldman, who had been a director of the Conservative

Political Centre. Opinion polls were producing discouraging signals. The electoral defeats of 1964 and 1966 confirmed the worst fears.

As always when things are going badly, some said it was because what had been done in the past had not gone far enough, while others began to canvass a change of direction. Julian Critchley, who belonged to the former party, diagnosed the trouble as a failure to keep up with the rapid movement of the times,[34] and urged the Prime Minister to strengthen the 'progressive forces' in the Cabinet. When Macmillan did so in the notorious 'night of the long knives' on 13 July 1962, the *Spectator* welcomed what they saw as the now unmistakable ascendancy of the 'new liberal wing of the party'.[35] The 'new liberal wing' which had been promoted into the Cabinet included names now firmly attached to Thatcherism: Powell and Joseph along with Maudling and Boyle. Heath, Macleod and Hogg were already in the Cabinet. The victory of the progressive tendency seemed so clear that Henry Fairlie, who provided the balance in the *Spectator* for Julian Critchley's progressivism, lamented that it was now hardly possible to discern the Right within the party.

As the condition of the 'sick man of Europe' grew worse, Conservatives began to prepare for another reassessment. The 'middle way' no longer appeared to be a radical progress in a new direction. It began to look more like an abject acquiescence to socialism. As before, Tories began to hear and believe that whereas in the past they had been conservative and averse to change, they must now become radical. Conservative leaders were compelled 'by the logic of circumstances', Angus Maude wrote in a stirring trilogy for the *Spectator*, 'to proclaim themselves the party of radical economic and social change ... ' The Party should not be surprised to find itself committed to the advocacy of some most un-Conservative measures.'[36] Although T. E. Utley agreed with part of Maude's diagnosis, he pointed out that calling for more individual enterprise and responsibility 'appears to bear surprisingly little relation to anything which the Tory Government has done since it came to power'.[37] And he laid the blame on the impossibility of achieving what the Tories had aimed to do – to reconcile 'the conflicting demands of the public for full employment, extensive social services, constant economic expansion, unrestricted trade unionism and stable prices'.[38]

Tory governments had been pushed into continuing Labour's policy of high taxes, greater public spending, genuflection to the power of the trade unions and to 'a public opinion already half-Socialist'. Whereas in 1949, Utley had declared that the advance of collectivism was inevitable, he now praised the government for its 'containing operation' against socialism and urged the party to renounce the 'middle way'. In its next manifesto, the Tory Party should declare an offensive against socialism. The dominant theme should not be 'the need to temper public planning with administrative prudence, but the need to fight it with the ideas of private opportunity and personal duty'. It was essential to cut public spending and to assure the British electorate that the Tories were prepared to make whatever changes would enable Britain 'to depend less on her Government and more on herself'.[39] In short, Utley and Maude were urging a return to the traditional market economy that the Conservative Party had so bravely abandoned since 1945.

Even the Bow Group acknowledged that the Tories had a crisis on their hands. Economic weakness, they feared, would make Britain incapable of playing her part in fighting Communism. Nevertheless, they rejected the Maude-Utley diagnosis. They attributed the crisis to the waste of energy, in both parties, on a 'doctrinal argument over more or less State control, more or less capitalism'. The Conservatives had been too concerned with containing the growth of the state: 'The aim of "Setting the People Free" has probably been followed as far as, if not further than, is possible, in many fields of policy. In other directions the pursuit of "freedom" should certainly mean an extension of the role of the state.' What was really needed was that 'the best brains in the country' should be put to 'the single task of streamlining the economic machine, so as to make capitalism work'. Britain now needed something like the French Commissariat du Plan, which would operate 'within the framework of an overall consensus of a high growth rate'.[40]

The new question, according to the Bow Group, had to be not, 'Has the State a role?' but 'What kind of role must it play?' Capitalism could work in a complex society only if the state became deeply involved in running the economy.

Once Conservatism became committed to economic growth as the only objective in politics, it would bring the prosperity that could remove the issue of 'class' from politics. Then the Tories could more realistically take up again the banner of One Nation without becoming distracted by class divisions. The advocates of 'a dash for growth' recognized that it would be resisted by interest groups in both parties who objected to the introduction of new techniques. But they believed that these groups, could be safely ignored because pursuing economic growth would appeal to a new class, 'an army of young men and women', who had risen from the working class to become 'the managers, executives and administrators of our changing society – a *parvenue elite* picked for their brains'.

V. HEATH: THE CRISIS CONTINUES

When Edward Heath became leader in 1965, he tried to revive Conservative spirits with an emphasis on three themes: the importance of private enterprise, the reform of the Welfare State, and securing Britain's entry into the Common Market. The talk of private enterprise gave the impression of a decisive shift of the Conservative Party away from the 'middle way' and One Nation politics – a victory for Maude and Utley over the Bow Group. Certainly the 'middle way' was denounced in a flurry of pamphlets. Timothy Raison and David Howell argued that there could not be an efficient economy without abandoning the policy of conciliating labour at all costs. Where there were no strikes, Howell said, industry was probably badly run: 'Strikes do at least indicate that toughness is being shown on the management side in face of unreasonable demands... The absence of strikes may well be evidence of a tacit conspiracy between management and work people to do nothing new and disturbing... and in general to preserve a cosy climate of inefficiency.'[41]. In a pamphlet called *A Bonfire of Restrictions*, Russell Lewis rejoiced that Mr Heath did not suffer from the 'One Nation psychosis', and was ready to abandon that 'turning down a blind alley', incomes policy. What the country needed now was legislation that would enable managers to refuse inflationary settlements with the unions. The proper role of the state was to arrange for 'the creative destruction of brakes on our national energies'.[42]

Nevertheless, the views of the Party's leading intellectuals had not changed all that much. The Bow Group's belief in 'growth' was still seen as the key to success. Tories should insist, Nigel Lawson wrote, 'that for them it is economic growth and economic growth alone that is the overriding objective of long term state intervention in the economy . . . '[43] David Howell went further: 'The pursuit of a national economic growth policy demands the state as an active partner, particularly in the export field, where the state's bargaining power can be decisive in backing up individual export enterprise.'[44] No one suggested that there be moves towards dismantling the nationalized industries or discouraging the government from spending on promoting industrial enterprises. Whatever contributed to economic growth was good, and if economic growth were achieved, the Tories were bound to succeed.

Those who might be tempted into making 'dogmatic claims for pure economic liberalism' or 'heartfelt appeals to the spirit of individualism' were sternly warned that such moves held no attraction for the various interest groups that normally supported the Conservative Party. The wage freeze and resale price maintenance were thought to be popular with the middle classes and this indicated, according to *Crossbow*, that the traditional Tory supporters were no longer enamoured of competition and individualism. By failing to recognize this, the Party risked becoming 'rootless' and 'boring', with no vision of what kind of society Conservativism had to offer.[45] Iain Macleod even questioned whether legislation to control the trade unions or measures to increase incentives for managers instead of measures to increase pensions would be tolerated by the mass of Conservatives.[46] Some feared that talk of competition would revive the old image of the Tory Party as the defender of big business and opponent of change and assistance to the working class.

In short, the same dedication to managerial government that had previously been called the 'middle way' continued to be the predominant theme of Conservative discourse. The only difference was in the emphasis and vocabulary. Talk of 'growth' and 'efficiency' replaced conciliation and national unity. But there was no hard opposition to the hallmarks of a Labour government – a prices and incomes policy, national plans for economic growth, national corporations for restructuring industries, subsidies to industry.

True, Heath's determination to attach Britain to the EEC was presented and interpreted at the time as a break with the past, a commitment to free trade which would expose British industry to the discipline of foreign competition. And this seemed to be confirmed by the Selsdon Park conference in 1970, when the Conservative shadow cabinet met to plan for the coming election. What emerged from the conference sounded like a commitment to a radical change which would replace managerial government with a different manner of ruling, emphasizing the role of government in maintaining law and order and generally setting the framework for an economy regulated by the market. When the Heath Government took office in 1970, it was accordingly expected to disband all the planning, restructuring and subsidizing boards, to reduce taxation, to muzzle the trade unions, to discard an incomes policy, and generally to restore a competitive economy.

But the lack of detail in the Selsdon renunciation of the bad old ways was not an oversight. Within a year of Heath's accession to office, 'middle way' policies (and 'middle way' problems) were clearly in evidence. The brief flirtation with an alternative had not produced a miracle. The Government was frightened by the growing inflation, strikes, rising wages and falling productivity. Although by 1970, the state was spending over half of the Gross National Product (GNP), there was no desire to cut public expenditure. Instead, ailing enterprises were rescued. Early in 1971, Rolls-Royce's aero-engines division was nationalized and soon after, subsidies to the Upper Clyde Shipbuilders were restored. Thanks to the Industry Act of 1972, the Department of Trade and Industry acquired important new powers to support industrial projects which found favour with the Government. Later in 1972, legislation empowered the Government to freeze pay, prices, and dividends.

Inflation rose to 13.5 per cent, and finally the miners' strike, directed at the pay policy, brought down the government.

vi. THE HERETICAL VOICE OF THE FIFTIES AND SIXTIES: ENOCH POWELL

While the leading voices in both the Party and successive Conservative governments remained addicted to the 'middle way' in one form or another, simmering in the background was a very different brew. By the 1950s members of the One Nation group – and in particular Enoch Powell – had begun to take the lead in exploring a new way of thinking. Powell admonished the Conservative Party to remember that what it valued could be preserved only by a capitalist free economy. For that alone could ensure that 'men shall be free to make their own choices, right or wrong, wise or foolish, to obey their own consciences, to follow their own initiatives.' Because it was the only system that gave everyone a say in what was produced and at what price, a free economy was the economic counterpart of democracy: 'Everyone who goes into a shop and chooses one article instead of another is casting a vote in the economic ballot box; with thousands of millions of others that choice is signalled through to production and investment and helps to mould the world just a tiny fraction nearer to people's desire. In this great and continuous general election of the free economy, nobody, not even the poorest, is disfranchised: we are all voting all the time.'[47]

Instead of trying to reconcile divergent points of view and move the Party gently to another place on the 'middle ground', Powell declared bluntly that the issue was whether a free society was to survive in Britain or be destroyed by socialism. He emphasized moreover that it was not an economic issue. How we answered the question, whether the state ought to decide what the nation shall produce and consume, how its citizens shall apply their effort, their income and their savings had consequences that went far beyond the management of the economy. Liberty could not survive where the state owned or controlled all the resources on which the material life of the nation depended. For Powell, what distinguished capitalism from socialism was not so much its efficiency at producing wealth as its indispensability to freedom.

To persuade his audience to accept this view, Powell unwrapped the abstractions that dominated public discourse. What did the socialists mean when they argued that without socialism there could only be chaos? They meant that nothing is well managed unless a little group of men 'somewhere in the centre' managed it, that 'the people and the nation can be trusted to decide nothing unless the Government supplies the answer.' And what was this 'august abstraction "the state"?' It was just 'a little group of fallible men in Whitehall, making guesses about the future, influenced by political pressures and partisan prejudices and working on projections drawn from the past by a staff of economists'.[48] And they were invariably wrong, 'crashingly wrong', and necessarily wrong because they could not possibly have the information needed to make their 'plans' and set their 'targets'.[49]

By contrast, a free economy is run by the 'most wonderful computer the world has ever known', which is constantly being fed with millions of facts from all over the world and tells us what can be produced 'economically and competitively and in what quantity and where'. This computer, which is the market, is what socialists want to replace by 'the pathetic figure of a President of the Board of Trade going through the old Trade Returns with his officials'. A minister and his civil servants, committees and councils trying to determine the 'ideally right imports and exports' are like 'a hippopotamus trying to catch fleas . . . ' As the governmental apparatus lacks both 'the quickness and sensitivity needed for the job', it 'neither knows where the fleas are nor could catch them if it did'.[50]

This inescapable rigidity of socialism was repeatedly contrasted by Powell to the flexibility of the market: 'How different from the ceaseless revision to which firms and industries and individuals are all the time subjecting their plans and their intentions. Thus change comes naturally, quietly and swiftly, before the economists have got around to noticing.' Moreover, when the government makes a mistake, it has enormous consequences because it is nationwide. The planners have thus made catastrophic mistakes about the building industry, steel, the demand for coal, the dollar shortage, the pattern of Britain's export trade, that were to last a generation.[51] The biggest successes occurred in the directions where the planners never looked.

For the same reason, Powell opposed fixed exchange rates. They imposed a rigidity which could not be maintained: 'If the rudder of a ship is lashed in one position it takes a deuce of a lot of rowing to steer the ship between the rocks.' When the price mechanism which would automatically adjust the supply and demand for sterling is put out of action by the fixed exchange rate there are bound to be balance of payment troubles every few years 'simply because there is nothing to keep exports and imports in balance.' Thus the Bretton Woods agreement of 1944 met the same fate as 'befalls all similar attempts at mass self-deception. It keeps breaking down. And we call the inroad of reality a deficit in the balance of payments of a particular country'.[52]

The rigidity of incomes policy was another regular target of Powell's phillipics. Here too he argued that given the many different factors that entered into the movements of profits and wages, how much they varied from one industry, place, or time to another, 'the plain fact' was that no government could have the foreknowledge needed to make an incomes policy sensible. Incomes policy was therefore 'a nonsense, a silly nonsense, a transparent nonsense'. And it was also a dangerous nonsense because it invited the nation 'to drug itself, as with a narcotic, with the idea that just round the corner', some wonder worker would discover 'a device which would make the economy more efficient, more progressive and more competitive'.[53]

The rigidities introduced by regional planning and programmes of public works were blamed by Powell for the sharp differences in levels of employment between different parts of the country. Not too much freedom but too little caused the trouble. The government's proper task is to remove obstacles to the free movement of labour. Our attitude should not be, Powell said, 'Somebody ought to do something so that we do not have to move or change', but rather, 'Come on, let's get out of here and beat the other bounders to it.'[54]

One function of government that Powell did not dispute but emphasized was the responsibility for the sound working of the money system. He was arguing for 'monetarism' without using the word. He appealed not to American or Austrian economists, but to a fourteenth-century treatise which said that every change in money involved forgery and deceit, and could not be the right of the prince. The complexities of modern finance made it easier to conceal the facts, but governments which allowed inflation defrauded their subjects just as surely as the princes who clipped the coinage.

Of course, the government had also to decide on behalf of the nation as a whole about foreign affairs and defence, about the public services and social welfare. But that was 'all the more reason to guard, and not throw away, the ability of the nation to shape its economic future through the free choice of its citizens.'[55]

Restrictions imposed without the authority of law were even worse to Powell's way of thinking. He attacked the trade unions for their restrictive practices. Collective bargaining was denounced as nothing other than price fixing enforced by coercing the individual into withholding or restricting his labour against his own judgement, and compelling him to join associations to which he did not wish to belong. The usual defence of the price-fixing by unions, that it is an exercise of the right of free association, Powell dismissed because it 'means nothing unless there is an equal right of non-association'. But since the unions had the power to deprive an individual of his livelihood if he disobeyed their orders, they constituted a state within a state. Allowing such powers, which belong only to a 'public authority acting under the law and enforced by due process of the law', to be exercised by trade unions was not 'compatible with the Rule of Law'.[56]

The corporatist version of collectivism was treated with even more scorn. Powell did not venerate 'responsible businessmen'. Once two or more businessmen or industrialists are put on a committee and set to manage other people's businesses or industries, he said, they become just like any other committee men, administrators, or politicians. For they have been severed from 'the umbilical cord of self-interest which attached them to the nourishing forces of profit and competition'. Bodies given the right to spend capital provided by the taxpayer will be no better at discovering 'desirable regroupings' or opportunities for industry than any other body of men who are spending other people's money: 'It is an ancient but pathetic delusion that those who are unaffected by the consequences of economic decisions are most likely to take them wisely.' An economic policy based on this principle is literally one of 'irresponsibility – of putting in charge of economic decisions and influence those who will bear no responsibility for the outcome.'[57]

It was just as nonsensical to talk of 'responsible' trade union leaders: 'Who appointed these trade union leaders, these restrictionists, to be "responsible"? And responsible for what and to whom . . . I am not aware that you or I or Parliament have entrusted such a responsibility to anybody, still less indicated to them the principles in accordance with which we want them to fix prices at non-market levels.' Contracting with unions to deliver a certain performance is an evil arrangement. For the unions can deliver their contract only by being 'endowed with disciplinary powers over their members', which means that their members are subjected to a private law or code. A trade union then ceases to be a voluntary association: 'The idea would carry us far down the road to the fascist, corporate state, where the economic life and decisions of the individual are regulated by corporations of employers and unions. It would endow the private combinations of employers and employees with the authority of organs of the state.'[58]

Powell was not prepared 'to trust anyone, however decent and nice a chap he may be, with the function of rigging prices by restricting supply'. He found the mere offer to do so arrogant and presumptuous. Nor would he countenance efforts of the government to avoid the inconvenience of passing legislation through Parliament by coaxing or bribing, or to threaten people into complying with their views of what prices or wages should be or what should be exported or imported. If the nation wished to fix prices and wages at particular levels regardless of supply and demand, then the right way to do so was to get Parliament 'to make laws to that effect . . . and we will have the courts to administer those laws, so that we shall know where we stand and what we may do, and what we may not do, after the manner of true-born Englishmen.'[59]

What emerged from Powell's teaching was not an economic lesson but rather a way of thinking about Britain. At the heart of it was a fierce resentment against the 'enormous and steadily increasing dead weight of organization and constraint', the 'great and growing host of organizations advising, exhorting, cajoling, planning, interfering', all endeavouring to promote uniformity, to 'eliminate all scope for choice and initiative',[60] and to evade the Rule of Law.

vii. HERETICAL VOICES OF THE SEVENTIES: THE IEA

By the end of the sixties, the conclusions advocated by Powell were receiving strong support from the Institute of Economic Affairs, an eccentric institution, with a marked personality. The Institute began as a gleam in the eye of Antony Fisher, whose fears about the way things were going were confirmed by reading a summary of Hayek's *Road to Serfdom*. On meeting Hayek himself, he was persuaded that there was a need for a research organization 'to influence intellectual economic opinion'. As the Buxted Chicken business that Fisher had started after the war flourished, he became able to assist such an organization. He and Sir Robert (later Lord) Renwick contributed £1000 jointly in 1957. In time, though not without periods of financial difficulty, donors became numerous and the diversity of contributions – which were never allowed to be earmarked – became a protection of the IEA's independence.

The association of the trio who ran the Institute in its heyday – Ralph (now Lord) Harris, Arthur Seldon and John Wood – came about fortuitously. Fisher met Ralph Harris in 1949 at East Grinstead, where Harris, then a don at St Andrews, was giving a lecture; by 1957, Harris had taken up the post of General Director of the IEA. Soon afterwards Arthur Seldon was suggested as an author for a book on pensions by Lord Grantchester, who had met him through the Liberal Party. Seldon became an unofficial editorial adviser, and Editorial Director in 1961. John Wood (who had been supervised in economics at Cambridge by Stanley Dennison at the same time as Ralph Harris, and was working in the Research Department of the Conservative Party in 1948 when Harris was an education officer there) was an early Trustee and came to work full-time at the Institute in 1969.

Although at the outset the IEA had no definite programme, by the late sixties publishing was established as its central activity. The publications were odd in form as well as matter. Both academics and politicians of all persuasions came to rely on them but they were neither political arguments nor purely theoretical discussions. They were designed to meet academic standards yet be accessible to the common reader – Arthur Seldon managed to everyone's surprise to persuade economists to write English prose. Classical economic theory was used not as a doctrine but as a method for analysing economic issues. And instead of considering the economy as a whole, as it was then fashionable to do, the IEA papers studied specific aspects of economic life.

There was no resemblance either to a coterie like Bloomsbury or to a political pressure group like the Fabian Society in the atmosphere of the seminars and Hobart lunches at Lord North Street, Westminster, where the IEA made its home after 1969. It was more nearly like a common room with a highly unorthodox membership. Suits and ties, not sandals, were the norm. But Ralph Harris's ironic manner of presiding over the meetings banished earnestness together with long-windedness, and made trade unionists, social democrats, and Labour Party members as welcome as businessmen, Hayekians, and assorted cranks.

The IEA papers attacked the post-war consensus from several different directions. In their general analysis of how markets worked, they challenged the commonplaces about a market economy. They denied that competition is a war of each against all or a zero-sum game in which winners gained only at the expense of losers, describing it instead as a system of co-operation between suppliers and consumers. They argued that the supply and demand for any good, whether labour or bread, is never fixed. They explained that price is not a barrier to satisfying wants but essential information about what resources are available and what is wanted. And they tried to demonstrate that the standard of living can advance only if the information provided by prices can be readily used to transfer labour and other factors of production from the firms or industries that are declining into expanding markets, as the suppression of market-determined prices in the state-directed economies of Eastern Europe and the nationalized industries of Britain made it impossible to do.

More particular studies set out to expose fallacies in specific popular beliefs, such as that hire purchase encourages profligacy, that entrepreneurs receive profits for nothing, that 'experts' can forecast what is wanted in the future, that the restrictive practices of trade unions benefit their members, that the management of a publicly owned industry behaves better than the management of private industries. A study of advertising, for example, concluded that it was but one of many activities devoted to providing information about the choices available in a free society and therefore useful rather than parasitic. In addition, the IEA conducted a number of factual inquiries into different industries and consumer preferences, arguing against an integrated transport system run by the government, and employing questionnaires to establish that, if asked to choose between higher taxes for a National Health Service and private health insurance (which other pollsters never asked), people would choose private health.

Writers were directed to examine everything '*ab initio*' and without regard to what is 'politically possible' on the grounds that what is politically possible may change and that regard to it merely served as an excuse for lazy thinking. IEA papers accordingly advocated many policies which seemed unthinkable at the time: freeing the exchange rate and removing rent controls, charges on pollution, vouchers for education, contracting out and charging for public services. They argued that since social services provide private benefits to identifiable individuals, better services could be provided at a lower cost by replacing universal free services with charges in conjunction with income supplements.

In papers that explored how the behaviour of voters or politicians and bureaucrats and the role played by self-interest are affected by different administrative arrangements, the IEA publicized the new work in the economics of politics, for which James Buchanan received a Nobel Prize in 1986. The effects of various kinds of legal regulation on the power of special interest groups were investigated. A major part of the IEA's attention was devoted to the causes of inflation, and to demonstrating that it was produced by changes in the money supply, rather than by higher wages, and that 'fine tuning' of the monetary system was bound to aggravate the disease. But, oddly enough, the IEA never suggested privatizing nationalized industries by selling shares to the public.

Of course, the IEA was accused of the sins usually attributed to advocates of a market economy – that it was turning back the clock, promoting out-of-date, callous, hard-hearted policies, and trying to do away with government. But if support for the last was occasionally provided by Arthur Seldon's sporting a button saying, 'No government is good government', the IEA was far from a home for anarchists. Nor was it in the least charitable about businessmen and industrialists. Richard Crossman's suggestion in the *Guardian* that the IEA was out to serve commercial interests was one of several such accusations, which were retracted with firm apologies when the IEA threatened to sue.

More serious objections came from Conservatives who sympathized with the general intent but disliked the concentration on economic analysis and economic questions. They felt that the IEA ignored aspects of life and of British politics which could not be analysed by the economic method and which ought sometimes to be given priority over economic considerations. That the IEA opposed managerial government and was concerned with liberty as well as with economic efficiency was clear to everyone. But those who were worried by the economic preoccupations of the IEA, wondered how far it might carry them if it were compelled to choose between efficiency and traditional British preferences. Certainly the emphasis on a British manner of doing things in Powell's speeches did not appear in the analytical talk and writing of the IEA. Nor was attention paid to questions about the relation between economic objectives or analysis and other ends and ways of thinking. Had it done so, the IEA probably could not have done its work with such clarity and effectiveness. Nevertheless there was ground for concluding that the IEA's attack on collectivism suffered from a narrowness of interest in which affection for the village green, the cloisters of Oxford and Cambridge or the poetry and the civility that made Britain distinctive played no obvious part. Some disliked what they saw as the arid rationalism of the ahistorical economic analyses.

Others merely regretted that the high quality of the IEA's economic analysis had not been matched by moral reflection, or else deplored the IEA's political detachment and refusal to take political stands.

Such doubts inspired the creation of other groups in the late seventies to complement the IEA's work – the Centre for Policy Studies (which was launched by Margaret Thatcher and Sir Keith Joseph), the Tory Philosophy Group, the Salisbury Group and the Adam Smith Institute. But before any of these had come to prominence, the IEA had acquired an adherent occupying a central position in the Conservative Party.

viii. HERESY AT THE CURIA

It was Sir Keith (now Lord) Joseph who took the IEA's message to the Conservative Party. Unlike Enoch Powell – who became a peripheral figure, and left the Party in 1974 – Joseph was regarded in the early seventies as a mainstream figure. Between 1974 and 1979, he tirelessly went about the country explaining – to large but sometimes aggressively hostile audiences especially in the universities where his message came as a shock to many – why socialism, the 'middle way', and all other forms of collectivism had to be abandoned. His aim in these speeches was to move the Conservative Party away from the 'middle ground' to the 'common ground'. The 'middle ground' was dismissed as nothing 'but a slippery slope to socialism and state control, whose present results even socialists now disown' because it was defined simply 'by splitting the difference between Labour's position and the Conservatives'. As Labour's position was 'arrived at by splitting the difference between their left and their centre', the Labour Party kept moving left under pressure from its extremists, and by trying 'to remain on the mystical middle ground' so did the Conservatives. The middle ground 'was thus dictated by extremists of the left'.[61]

But in arguing against the drift to socialism, Joseph talked mainly about economic questions. At the centre of his concerns was the economic decline of Britain. And the remedy he proposed was summed up in the word monetarism. With his famous Preston speech of September 1974, he launched monetarism into British politics.

It was an awkward time to attack the policies that the Conservatives shared with Labour, for the Labour Government was expected at any moment to call an election. Nevertheless Sir Keith did not mince words. He blamed inflation on an 'excessive money supply' and denounced government spending to keep up full employment. *The Times* praised Joseph for continuing the argument 'once associated with Enoch Powell', only 'at a deeper level of understanding'. Some of the party were outraged because Keith Joseph seemed to be ensuring a Conservative defeat in the coming election. But to others, the Preston speech established him as the apostle of a new conservativism.

Whereas the Preston speech put Keith Joseph in the running for the leadership of the Conservative Party, his Birmingham speech on 19 October 1974 in effect brought his candidacy to an end. He denounced the 'permissive society' and called for a crusade against both socialism and libertarianism. To fight the battle of ideas, he said, intellectual as well as moral courage was needed. And as an example of such courage he cited what needed to be done to end the 'cycle of deprivation'. His argument was that the 'human stock' of Britain was being 'threatened' by the 'high and rising proportion of children . . . being born to mothers least fitted to bring children into the world and bring them up' and that to meet this threat birth control facilities had to be extended to young unmarried girls who were 'the potential young unmarried mothers'.[62] His use of the phrase 'human stock' and of numbers to grade different social classes gave his proposals a eugenicist slant. 'Sir Keith in "Stop Babies" sensation' trumpeted the *Evening Standard*.

The insinuations against Keith Joseph were ludicrous, but the idea that dominated the language of the speech – the idea of Britain as a productive enterprise – also dominated his thinking about

Britain's economic situation. He accepted the diagnosis of Britain's troubles which had become a commonplace as much among socialists and 'liberals' as among Conservatives. It was the thesis that the spirit of enterprise in Britain had been destroyed by the aristocratic ethos nurtured by the public schools who taught their pupils to disdain dirtying their hands with making money and to aspire to live as 'gentlemen' in rural retirement. That the historical foundations of this thesis were much less impressive than the corporatist prejudices of its inventors did not strike Keith Joseph. The same frame of mind, however, helped to make him peculiarly effective in persuading the supporters of the post-war consensus to abandon it. Since they also regarded Britain as a productive enterprise, he was able to argue with them from common ground, and to use phrases that proved irresistible to headline writers bred on the same prejudices.

The two themes that Sir Keith Joseph associated with the new conservatism were 'monetarism' and 'monetarism is not enough'. In connection with monetarism, he talked about the virtues of the 'social market economy', a phrase borrowed from the German Social Democrats to indicate that he was not advocating selfish neglect of those who could not help themselves. In popular, off-the-cuff lectures, Sir Keith translated the general teaching of the IEA about the virtues of competition and markets, the relation between the money supply, inflation and unemployment into language suitable for sixth-formers. Using the cause and effect language of science, he argued that spending by the government and the subsidized employment of labour divorced from its economic function might temporarily relieve 'symptoms' but could not eliminate the 'cause' of Britain's illness. The message throughout was that Britain was 'over-governed, over-spent, over-taxed, over-borrowed, and over-manned'. When he turned to 'Monetarism is not enough', he spoke of the need to rid Britain of the 'socialist anti-enterprise climate', the 'indifference, ignorance and distaste on the part of politicians, civil servants, and communicators for the processes of wealth creation and entrepreneurship'. By taxation, inflation, 'the remorseless flood of regulations and legislation', and by 'constant and arbitrary interventions', governments since the war, he said, had destroyed 'the rewards that once made risk-taking worthwhile', and driven out or discouraged the wealth creators. And he warned his audiences that without 'wealth creation' the welfare state could not be supported, that without the entrepreneur there could be no wealth creation, and that a plenitude of entrepreneurs depended on the incentive of profits and an 'enterprise culture'.[63]

ix. THE HERETICS TAKE OVER

The effect of the IEA and its political spokesman, Sir Keith Joseph, on the Conservative Party became evident in 1977 when the Conservative Political Centre published *The Right Approach to the Economy*, edited by Angus Maude and signed not only by Sir Keith Joseph himself but also by Sir Geoffrey Howe, James Prior and David Howell – all to be central figures in the next Conservative cabinet. It had been preceded the year before by *The Right Approach*, produced by the CPC with no named authors, which still used 'middle way' language and talked about 'balance' and 'partnership between government and industry'. Although a few of its proposals were repeated in the 1977 document, there was a marked difference in spirit.

The central thesis of the new document was that Britain's problems could not be 'solved by an impoverished and apathetic people in a declining economy', and that only 'another break for freedom' could solve those problems. Recognition of 'the unique importance of each individual in the scheme of things' was described as the 'instinctive outlook of Conservatives' – a recognition which led Conservatives to rely on people rather than 'corporate bodies and institutions', on individual flair and drive rather than on 'committee analyses and sector plans to provide the spearhead of industrial and commercial recovery'. Of the old infatuation with 'partnerships' there was not a sign. Although the authors did not make a firm commitment to abolish the National Economic Development Council (NEDC), they did renounce the 'industrial strategies' and 'get-togethers between businessmen and bureaucrats' associated with the 'middle way', on the grounds that such 'strategies . . . convey to ordinary people a comforting but damaging illusion that the laws of nature can be suspended by government action'. Instead of the interference, tinkering, and palliatives required by an 'industrial strategy', the authors proposed to create conditions in which 'wealth-creating' would flourish. Whereas corporatism diminished the role of Parliament, they would enlarge it. Their legislative programme would be drawn up not in accordance with the demands of trade unions or big business but in order to serve the public interest. They committed themselves as well to controlling the money supply, reducing government expenditure, removing restrictions that made business expansion difficult, ending the 'pointless community acquisition of building land' and pressing for more efficiency in the administration of local government.[64]

Another new note was the emphasis on denying that there was a 'fixed amount of work to be done by the British people' and the suggestion that new markets, which could not be identified by government, could be found not only by the manufacturing industries but also by the service industries. To suggest that banking, finance, insurance, printing, publishing, entertainment, and large-scale tourism were 'the seed-corn of future growth'[65] was to abandon the identification of industry with manufacturing learnt from Marx, which had been (and still is) an axiom among 'middle way' Conservatives no less than among socialists.

The policy of moving jobs out of London and other big cities, which had reduced them to 'industrial and commercial deserts', was renounced and blamed on over-ambitious redevelopment plans and controls that had 'discouraged job-creating new enterprises'. There were proposals to encourage more people, especially in the lower income levels, to become owners of property. The commitment to a scheme for assisting council tenants to buy their houses and to help other first-time house purchasers, that had appeared in *The Right Approach*, was repeated. Tax relief and other incentives to encourage wider share ownership were promised. So were changes in the tax system to simplify and ease the burden of taxation. Rescue operations for industries in trouble were forsworn – as they took money from the more efficient and gave it to the less efficient: 'The philosophy behind these operations is therefore the very opposite of what we need for industrial and commercial recovery.' Nationalized industries would be required to become more competitive and a scheme for requiring the consent of the workpeople before the closed shop could be enforced outlined. 'Broad price and profit controls' were opposed because they reduced 'not prices but jobs'.[66]

If it was not a shocking document, it did suggest that the Conservative Party had absorbed the teaching of Powell, the IEA, and Sir Keith Joseph.

The State of Britain

Thatcherism arose because a loosely articulated group of people close to the heart of the Tory Party, and in particular Margaret Thatcher herself, were disenchanted with the condition of Britain as they saw it in the late 1970s and were sceptical of the ability of continued 'middle way' policies to provide a remedy for that condition. Thatcherism triumphed within the Tory Party because a sufficient number of Mrs Thatcher's Parliamentary colleagues had also been impressed by the failures of 'the middle way', had begun to listen attentively to Sir Keith Joseph, wanted a 'new direction', and were prepared to struggle to steer their party on their preferred course.

Whatever may be true of works of art, the beauty or ugliness of a country certainly lies to a great degree in the eye of the beholder. And, although no country at any time is likely to appear perfect to the eye of any beholder, there is no doubt that Britain, as it presented itself to the Thatcherite gaze in 1979, was a particularly sorry mess. By gradual attrition over four decades and more, a once-great empire had dwindled to insignificance; a nation, half of whose inhabitants could remember themselves being citizens of one of the world's great powers, found itself firmly in the second rank; but there was no question of having achieved the calm simplicities of a peaceful little country. Britain was no longer a rival to the United States but had not become Switzerland: endowed with the defects of each and the virtues of neither, Britain seemed to Thatcherites to be a society in sore need of repair.

In part, the sense of need for a national renewal arose from a vague perception of vast intangibles: a lack of pride in Britain and in things made or done in Britain; tension between the parts of Britain expressed in powerful and almost-successful nationalist movements, and between the various races inhabiting Britain expressed in a continuing and heated debate about immigration; uncertainty about Britain's role in the world – reluctant leader of the Commonwealth, reluctant participant in the European Communities, a close ally of the United States but always fearful of becoming its fifty-first state. These were images and feelings, not capable of direct or conclusive documentation, but nonetheless powerful for that. Regardless of the objective facts, throughout the 1960s and 1970s Thatcherites (and many others with them) had been coming to the conclusion that there was indeed a British disease, a malignancy that needed removal, a malaise that needed a cure.

It should not, however, be imagined that these intangible feelings were without their objective correlatives. On the contrary, a survey of the concrete actualities of Britain in the late 1970s provides a clear explanation of the Thatcherite feeling that something was wrong. In every department, there were the manifestations of a decadence abhorrent to Thatcherites.

A gloomy Thatcherite in 1979 would certainly have begun such a survey by pointing out the extent to which Britain had been collectivized. Of the more than twenty-five million people employed in 1979, almost a third (some 7.45 million or 29.3 per cent) were employed in the public sector. The Civil Service alone (at 738,000) was roughly twice as large as it had been in 1939, whilst the National Health Service was employing one and a half million people – more than three times the entire number of personnel in the armed forces. The nationalized industries employed over two million people (accounting for nearly half of the total employment in manufacturing industries). And the local authorities employed a staggering three million souls.

It was not just a matter of collectivization in itself, but also the cost of collectivization. Public sector corporations in 1979 had debts of some 27 billion (equivalent to some 55 billion in 1990 money), and increased this figure by ten per cent in 1979–80 alone. The scale of the cost of the nationalized industries in 1979 can be grasped only when one realises that the total of subsidies to nationalized industries (4.6 billion in that year) added to the total borrowing by those industries (2.5 billion in that year) came very close to equalling the entire cost of servicing the national debt (8.4 billion in fiscal 1979). What was worse, from a Thatcherite perspective, these vast sums were being spent not on growing industries such as the electricity supply industry (whose volume had grown roughly tenfold between 1938 and 1979, and which was profitable) but rather on the old, declining industries such as coal (whose tonnage – despite the subsidies – had declined by a third since 1938) and rail (which, in spite of enormous subsidies, was offering roughly half as many kilometres of rail service in 1979 as it was in 1938). Nor was the collectivization confined to the nationalized industries. In the so-called 'private sector', too, not competition but two large, powerful organizations of interest groups called the tune. Industrial policy was made and unmade by those two titans of industry and labour, the Confederation of British Industry (CBI) and the Trade Unions Congress (TUC). Ever since the fifties, government had come to be conducted as a partnership with these two august institutions. The lone entrepreneur did not get a look in.

Not surprisingly, the power of the great collective bodies was reflected in their attractiveness to potential members. Union membership in 1979 reached its all time peak of 13.3 million (representing some fifty-five per cent of the total employed workforce), and roughly ninety per cent of these were to be found in trade unions with memberships of over fifty thousand, almost all affiliated to the TUC. For a Thatcherite, it did not seem surprising that this high degree of collectivization in the economy, and in particular in the manufacturing sector, was associated with the lowest growth in productivity of any major Western country, with an eight-or nine-fold increase in the number of working days lost through strikes compared to the years immediately before the Second World War. Nor did it surprise them that it had defeated successive governments, Labour and Conservative, and culminated in the destruction of Barbara Castle by the TUC and of Ted Heath by the miners. The decadence of British manufacturing as a whole was symbolized by the accelerated decline of the motor car industry, where the once-great Austin and Morris marques had combined in an ever-declining and amorphous British Leyland which was heading not so slowly towards a seemingly inevitable demise.

Allied to this picture of industrial collectivism and decline was the spectacle of an economy in which the value of money (and hence of non-speculative savings) had been allowed by successive governments to diminish with an astonishing cumulative effect. One pound sterling in 1980 had barely one twentieth of the purchasing power of a pound sterling in 1938. A loaf of bread costing the equivalent of 1.5 pence in 1938 cost some 65 pence when Mrs Thatcher came to power, an increase of over 4,200 per cent in the price of the most basic of all commodities in just forty years. With prices rising by an average of 13 per cent over 1978–9 and set to rise by another 18 per cent between 1979 and 1980, there was every sign of inflation accelerating rather than decelerating, bringing all the deplorable effects on the stability of expectation, the value of savings and the creation of tension in the workplace and society at large which such rates of inflation might be expected to have. In Thatcherite eyes, governments had not only collectivized and demoralized industry but also begun a trend towards South American levels of hyper-inflation. The entry of the International Monetary Fund (IMF) onto the scene (under Denis Healey's Chancellorship), for the first time in British history, reinforced the impression that the United Kingdom was becoming a banana republic.

A Thatcherite surveying the scene in 1979 could also have little confidence that the most able and energetic people in society would have an incentive to pull Britain out of the condition in which she then found herself. Certainly some groups of people were better off. Post-war governments prided themselves on the fact that ordinary workers had seen substantial rises in their standards of living. Even after allowing for the declining purchasing power of salaries, miners were almost five times better paid than in 1938, with agricultural workers, factory workers and railmen more than three times better paid. But, by contrast, doctors, airline pilots, teachers and solicitors had seen rises in the real value of their salaries of less than fifty per cent, and university professors and senior civil servants were actually receiving less than they had been in 1938. Meanwhile, the level of taxation for all – but particularly for the better off – had increased beyond recognition. In 1938–9, rates of income tax ranged from just over 8 per cent to 47.5 per cent, rising with income. By the mid-1970s, the rates ranged from 25 per cent to an astonishing 90 per cent. Efforts were also being made to ensure that anyone who, despite decreasing differentials in pay and increasing proportions of taxation, nevertheless wished to accumulate and pass on to the next generation a nest-egg would be strongly discouraged from so doing. By 1977, inheritance tax had reached not only the notorious 75 per cent on bequests of more than 2 million but also (if less notoriously, perhaps more importantly) 30 per cent on modest inheritances of £50–60,000.

Collectivization, demoralization, strikes, inflation and disincentives to the accumulation of wealth had all, unsurprisingly to the Thatcherite, taken their toll on Britain's comparative standing. Although Britons had seen ownership of cars multiply tenfold, airline travel a hundred fold, and TV sets, refrigerators, washing machines, telephones and central heating become the norm, the British people were nevertheless the poor men of Europe. The value of the pound had halved against the dollar and much more than halved against the Deutschmark since the war. Britain's share of world exports, still almost a fifth in the late 1950s, had declined to less than a tenth. National per capita income, which was 40 per cent above the Western European average in the late fifties, was by the late seventies below average. Our EEC partners, whose real per capita Gross Domestic Product (GDP) had more than doubled since 1958 noted with sometimes obvious derision that Britain's had increased by only 60 per cent over the same period. With postwar growth rates averaging less than 3 per cent in Britain compared to over 5 per cent for Belgium, Italy, France, Luxembourg, Germany and the Netherlands, this was hardly surprising. By every other measure, too, the UK was lagging behind: industrial production in the sixties and seventies had grown almost half as fast as production in the original six EEC countries, while the cost of living had risen one and half times faster than for the six over the same period; by 1979, only the south-east corner of the UK could compete with France, northern Italy and West Germany on anything like equal terms; the rest of Britain was an underprivileged area by European standards.

The chance for people, and especially for the less fortunate members of society, to move from the stricken areas into the more thriving parts of Britain was greatly reduced by the form of housing tenure. Nearly a third of all housing was rented from public sector agencies, and it was frequently nearly impossible to relinquish a council flat in the north and find another in the south. Successive waves of council house building, combined with the Rent Acts which had reduced private renting to 10 per cent or less of the housing market, had unintentionally locked the young and the unemployed into regions of the country where work and opportunities were scarce. Combined with heavy unionization that kept wages and unemployment in those regions high, forty post-war years had mixed what seemed to Thatcherites a lethal cocktail, capable of poisoning both the economy and society as a whole.

Health, education and social services had, of course, greatly expanded. Since the forties, the school-leaving age had been raised from fourteen to sixteen, the number of university students had multiplied more than fivefold and polytechnics accommodating 400,000 students had been built. Unemployment benefit had more than doubled and pensions more than tripled since the war, even after allowing for the effect of inflation. And a million employees had been added to the National Health Service. But numerical expansion had not been accompanied by the expected increase in the quality of either education or health or by a more rational allocation of resources. Of the 915,000 school leavers in 1979, only 121,000 could manage three A-levels and an awesome 434,000 proved unable to achieve even a single O-level, figures representing a standard of achievement shamefully below that in other Western European countries. Half the employees in the National Health Service were non-medical; a fifth of the beds were not occupied; and what had started as a service with a mission had become, to Thatcherite eyes, a bureaucracy with little sense of responsibility to the patient as a consumer.

The social patterns that had emerged over the period since the war were equally worrying for Thatcherites. Life expectancy had increased by twelve years, and as a result a declining proportion of young people were working to provide support for an increasing proportion of pensioners (those aged under fifteen had fallen from 22 per cent of the population to 19 per cent, whilst those over sixty-four had increased from under 9 per cent to over 15 per cent.) Life had become more stressful, with a 30 per cent increase in the number of people dying from heart attacks. At the same time, there were radical cultural changes. Britain had become far less homogeneous, with one person in twenty belonging to an 'ethnic' group. And the proliferation of new moral ideas was exacerbated by the predominance of television, which the average person watched for twenty-five hours per week.

Against this general background of social change, two patterns in particular provided Thatcherites with cause for worry: the family had declined in significance and crime had greatly increased. Whereas 95 per cent of births in 1938 had been inside marriage, the figure had declined to 87 per cent by the time that Mrs Thatcher came to power and was in the process of rapid further decline (with less than 75 per cent of births inside marriage by 1989). The number of divorces per year had multiplied twentyfold between 1938 and 1979 and the rate of increase in the number of divorces was still accelerating. Where 700 crimes had been recorded per 100,000 members of the population in 1938, some 7,000 were recorded in 1979; the prison population, despite efforts to keep criminals out of prison, had multiplied more than fourfold over the same period; and, most importantly, crimes of violence against the person had risen from barely over 1,500 to an alarming 50,000 per year.

It was changing this state of affairs – the collectivized economic decline, the diminished role and decreasing social responsibility of individuals – that the Thatcherites saw as their task in 1979.

II

Thatcherism in Practice

4

The Importance of Being an Owner

Privatization is generally regarded as *the* textbook case of Thatcherite policy. It therefore constitutes an important test of the thesis of this book. Can privatization – as it has been conducted in Britain over the past twelve years – accurately be portrayed as a policy that aims at the promotion of the vigorous virtues in individuals, the reinforcement of the family as a transmitter of the vigorous virtues, and an example of the paradigm shift?

There can be little doubt that privatization has been intended to contribute to Britain's wealth and economic vitality. Even before the advent of Thatcher herself as leader, the advocates of Thatcherism were making the point that privatization would bring economic advantages. As early as 1971, Dr Rhodes Boyson – later to be amongst the staunchest of Thatcherites – was writing that: 'The economic record of the nationalised industries judged by return on capital invested is about one third of that of private industry, despite the periodic and massive writing down of capital in the nationalised concerns.'[1] Twelve years later, in the heyday of Thatcherism, John Moore, the minister with special responsibility for privatization, made the economic aim of the policy even more explicit: 'The government's economic strategy is justified on economic and business criteria . . . if the present momentum is maintained, it will help provide a remedy for some of the ills that have beset UK industrial performance in recent years.'.[2]

This economic drive was clearly recognized by foreign commentators observing the Thatcherite privatization programme. In a paper presented to the UNIR conference in May 1985, the French commentator, Jean Loyrette, included amongst the principal objectives of privatization: 'Reduce the burdens of the Exchequer and reduce the State's budget deficit . . . make the economy more competitive.'[3] Similarly, a survey carried out amongst senior figures in the Turkish government suggested that the three top priorities for a privatization programme would be 'To allow market forces to stimulate the economy; to increase productivity and efficiency; to increase quality, quantity and diversity of the goods and services.'

The economic motive for privatization – the Thatcherite wish to use it as a tool for restoring vitality to the British economy – is evident not only in the rhetoric but also in the practice. In 1979–80 the nationalized industries as a whole absorbed some 3 billion of taxpayers' money – equivalent to about 15 billion in 1990 money. By 1988–9 the former annual deficit had been converted into a surplus of about 400 million. In the course of the programme, some of the world's greatest and most persistent loss-making corporations had been transferred out of the public sector and out of public subsidy. The British Steel Corporation, which lost one-sixth of its capital in the single trading year of 1978–9, was a leading example.

As well as stemming the outflow of cash to ailing nationalized industries, privatization raised vast sums for the Exchequer. This inflow, as Thatcherites intended, enabled the Government to steer a steadier financial course; the Public Sector Borrowing Requirement dropped dramatically, and was replaced in several Thatcher years by budget surpluses that were used to reduce the Public Debt. Without this improvement in the public finances it is highly doubtful whether the Thatcher Government's moves towards tax reduction would have been feasible. Privatization can therefore legitimately be regarded as a nearly indispensable part of the Thatcherite desire to release economic energies by reducing the tax disincentives to wealth creation, disincentives which Thatcherites believe to have been a major cause of Britain's economic decline.

In addition to stemming outflows from and increasing inflows into the Exchequer, privatization would, according to Thatcherites, improve the long-term performance of industries. Whether this confidence, that privatized companies would operate more efficiently than they had as nationalized industries, is justified, remains to be seen. True, a large number of privatized firms (including Amersham International, British Airports Authority,

British Airways, British Steel, British Telecom, Cable & Wireless and Rolls-Royce) showed markedly increased profitability between their privatizations and 1989. True also, increases in productivity and profits in some privatized companies (notably BAA, British Gas, British Steel and British Telecom) have been impressive. But many of these achievements were made at a time when the British economy as a whole was booming, and many of them can be paralleled by the huge increases in profitability and productivity of industries such as British Coal and British Rail, which the Thatcher governments left in their nationalized state but subjected to serious financial disciplines. Nevertheless, Thatcherites operate on the presumption that, over time, privatized industries will show significantly better results than nationalized ones because decision-making in a private-sector concern is ultimately related to its rate of return on investment and is hence intrinsically governed by economic rationality, whereas decision-making in a nationalized industry is influenced above all by the political concerns of its political masters, rather than by what the industry can sell and earn.

Another reason for supposing that the Thatcherite programme of privatization has been dominated by economic considerations is the increasing attention which it has paid to the introduction of competition. From the start, this was a major concern of Thatcherites in relation to the privatization of local government services. Thatcherites were impressed by evidence from the US, Canada and Japan that the introduction of competitive tendering into local services could bring about significant increases in efficiency and productivity. As a result, successive efforts were made by the Thatcher Government to enforce competitive tendering on local authorities in the UK.

In the headline privatizations of major nationalized industries during the early years, little was done to make the privatized industry a competitive one. The opening of the market for telephone equipment to free competition, and the introduction of Mercury as a protected competitor to BT were exceptions; but British Gas and the water authorities were left intact as monopolies. Gradually, pressure from the Thatcherite Right mounted, accompanied by a chorus of dissent from academic economists. The watershed was the privatization of the electricity supply industry – where, at the expense of hundreds of man-years of effort by officials, advisers and the industry itself, the world's first competitive spot market in electricity was set up, with provision for competition in both the generation and the delivery of electricity.

The changes introduced by the spot market in electricity are a good illustration of what economic effects Thatcherites had come to expect from privatization. Before the spot market was created, electricity had always been sold at a price that was fixed for long periods, which seldom changed as often as annually and which most certainly did not vary according to short run fluctuations in supply and demand. As a result, supply and demand were practically always unbalanced in the short run. Capacity stood idle at certain hours and on some days; at other hours and on other days, demand surged to a level that overstrained capacity. Constant prices offered users, especially industrial and commercial users, no incentive to take up more power when supply was over-plentiful or to take less when supply was overstrained. At the same time they offered the nationalized generating monopoly, EGB, little or no incentive to install plants which could cheaply alter their output in accordance with momentary fluctuations in demand. Persistent disequilibrium meant persistent waste of resources. All that has been fundamentally changed by the spot market. The National Grid Company organizes the market by announcing each day the various prices at which it will sell power during each half-hour of the twenty-four. As might be expected, it quotes low prices for half-hours during the dead of night and relatively high prices for half-hours when people wake, go to work, or retire into the comforts provided by the electric kettle and TV set. Its price-list differs according to the prevailing temperatures, the season, and various other conditions. Users are thus induced to vary their usage in accordance with potential supply, and producers are induced to vary actual supply in accordance with demand during each particular half-hour, thus making the use of electricity power more efficient throughout British industry.

There is, in short, plenty of evidence that Thatcherites have seen privatization as a means of improving Britain's economic performance, and hence contributing to the re-establishment of a flourishing and vigorous economy. But to suppose, as the commentators have all too frequently supposed, that these economic ends – stemming the outflow of subsidies, increasing the inflow of cash, improving the efficiency of industry and increasing competition – constituted the sole aim of Thatcherites in promoting privatization would be to misunderstand both Thatcherism itself and the privatization programme.

If the aims were purely economic, why would the Thatcher governments so frequently have chosen mass public offers as a method? In almost every case, the discounts necessitated by such offers yielded, as the Thatcher governments expected, receipts lower than those that would have accrued to the Exchequer from private deals with major industrial companies or financial institutions. Revenues for the Exchequer could have been increased, and very possibly the management of the privatized industries made more efficient, if the shares had been sold to major, existing, private-sector entities rather than to 'Sid' (the prototype of buyers of shares in the advertisement for privatization) and his five million friends. Why, if revenue were the sole consideration, have the Thatcher governments sold off 1.6 million council houses at a discount? How, if economic concerns were at the forefront, could Thatcher governments, with their deep faith in the economic advantages of competitive markets, have opted for privatizing British Gas and the water authorities as virtual monopolies? Why, if the entire privatization had been driven by straightforward economic rationality, has it so frequently been attacked as 'ideological'?

The answer to these questions is that the privatization programme has indeed been 'ideologically driven', in the sense that it had aims other than that of merely increasing economic rationality. The privatization programme has been specifically designed not merely to resuscitate economic vitality but also to promote the vigorous virtues in individuals, to strengthen the family, and to bring the paradigm shift to bear on industrial policy.

The Thatcherite aim to use the privatization programme as a means of promoting the vigorous virtues in individuals is in fact already well known though by a different name: popular capitalism. It is the association of privatization with popular capitalism that explains much of the willingness of Thatcher Governments to sacrifice sheer financial advantage for the sake of a different kind of objective. As early as 1985, John Moore, speaking of major privatizations, was saying that: 'Importantly, they provide a major stimulus to wider share ownership.'[4] By 1986, the emphasis on popular capitalism and the ownership of shares by the ordinary man – the underlying social effects of privatization – had become far stronger, as another speech by John Moore in that year indicates: 'Our programme, which is already succeeding beyond the dreams of the optimists, is directed towards three key areas of life: homes, work-places and the wider community. We are extending home ownership, increasing employee participation in the ownership of their companies and spreading the ownership of public companies to millions of ordinary people.'[5] There can be no doubt that Thatcherites saw privatization as a means not merely of giving people ownership but of changing the attitudes of individuals by restoring a sense of self-sufficiency, independence and vigour. As John Moore put it: 'Possession means power, the kind of power that matters to ordinary people – power to make choices, power to control their own lives. Our aim is to extend this power to as many people as we can. We are doing it by extending ownership as widely as possible.'[6]

The contribution of mass privatizations (the sale of vast public companies to millions of individual investors) to the promotion of popular capitalism and the vigorous virtues was undoubtedly a matter of discovery rather than premeditated invention for Thatcherites. The sale of British Telecom (the first of the great mass UK privatizations) to millions of small investors was, in the first instance, prompted not by a desire to promote ownership and a sense of independence in such investors but rather by the desire to find a source of UK capital greater than that which could be provided by traditional investors in Britain, and which would avoid the need to privatize BT by selling it to foreigners. However, the success of the BT sale was rapidly recognized by Thatcherites as having implications for social attitudes and for individuals going far beyond the mere transfer of ownership. In subsequent mass privatizations – notably British Gas, the water authorities and the regional electricity companies – the Thatcher Government deliberately (and at great expense) sought to maximize popular ownership on the very grounds that John Moore foreshadowed in 1986 – the desire to extend share ownership to many individuals, and by making them owners to give them an increased sense of vigour and power over their own lives.

The mass privatizations are merely part of a general pattern. The promotion of management buyouts, the involvement of employees in all major UK privatizations, the continuous efforts of succeeding Thatcherite Chancellors to promote share ownership and personal savings through Personal Equity Plans (PEPs), profit-sharing schemes in companies, and portable pensions, all these attest to the desire of Thatcherites to promote personal ownership as a matter of social policy. A classic case of this desire, of course, is the sale of council houses. Because owning one's home matters far more to most people than owning some shares, the sale of 1.6 million council dwellings to their former tenants is not merely, or even principally, an economic policy. It is a social policy designed to give erstwhile tenants a new-found sense of independence and self-sufficiency.

Whether Thatcherites are right in supposing that ownership by individuals is a key contributor to the promotion of vigorous virtues in those individuals is, and will remain for many years, a vexed question. But, for those seeking to understand Thatcherism, the logic of the Thatcherite position on ownership is clear. Ownership by an individual of assets, above all his or her own home, should make that individual more independent, and not only financially. Though financial independence might by itself be expected to have an important effect on the social attitudes of the individual, it might also have a direct effect on the individual's sense of self-sufficiency. Thatcherites would of course concede that an individual who owns little or no property *can* nevertheless be wholly independent-minded and self-sufficient. But the Thatcherite argues that being one's own master – in the sense of owning one's own home or disposing of one's own property – provides an incentive to think differently about the world. The case can most easily be understood by contrast with the diametrical opposite, an individual who owns practically nothing in the world, rents his lodgings, has no savings and no pension, depends for his earnings upon a remote impersonal employer, and is, in short, wholly at the mercy of others for all the necessities of life. Such an individual would need to be a remarkable character if he were to retain a moral sense of independence and self-sufficiency. Indeed, it is this observation which lies at the root of Marxist objections to the entire capitalist system. A Thatcherite, whilst not believing that patterns of ownership absolutely determine people's moral attitudes, nevertheless stresses that the two are connected, and sees in wider individual ownership a useful means of promoting the moral attitudes that Thatcherism seeks to cultivate.

Nor is it only independence and self-sufficiency which the Thatcherite hopes to encourage by means of wider ownership. Personal energy and adventurousness, critical components of the vigorous virtues – are also believed by the Thatcherite to be encouraged by wider ownership. Here, too, the logic is clear, regardless of whether the proposition is in fact correct. The Thatcherite argues that an 'owner' who feels that he is 'in charge' and 'secure', is more likely to be active, to take risks, to display initiative. Once again, it is the lurid negative that most vividly illustrates the plausibility of this positive claim. An individual who is wholly dependent on the will of others for his living quarters must be remarkable indeed if he is to avoid both despondency, as his fortunes change through the actions of others beyond his control, and the extreme cautiousness that is bred of fear; only a very robust personality would take the risk of offending those who have power over him. A council tenant living in dilapidated accommodation all too easily ceases to regard improvement of the situation as feasible. But a person owning his own property may quickly set about putting it to rights, and in the course of doing so, discover a spirit of energy and adventure which, so the Thatcherite hopes, may permeate the rest of his life.

Privatization, for a Thatcherite, is therefore not merely a route to extending ownership but, through the extension of ownership, a route to the promotion in ordinary individuals of at least four of the vigorous virtues: self-sufficiency, independent-mindedness, energy and adventurousness.

But the Thatcherite claim for privatization, and for the extension of ownership which privatization (pursued in the Thatcherite manner) facilitates, goes beyond its immediate effect on the individual. The Thatcherite also hopes, through the extension of ownership, to promote the family. As with the intended promotion of the vigorous virtues, the validity of the claim that wider ownership promotes the family is a matter for speculation. But, again as in the case of the vigorous virtues, the logic of the Thatcherite argument is clear.

Marx noted that the family, under capitalism, had become a 'property relationship', and accordingly poured scorn upon it. But, for a Thatcherite, the fact that the family is in part a 'property relationship' is something to be accepted and to be built upon rather than something to be scorned. The Thatcherite sees that ownership and the passing of ownership through inheritance from one generation to another can provide a strengthening of the sense of the family. Within a single generation, a family whose members have a joint stake in, a joint responsibility for, and joint power over commonly held property is, according to the Thatcherite, an entity more likely to survive than an association of individuals held together solely by affection or habit. And a family whose members have inherited from previous generations, and will pass on to successive generations, property which is associated with that family is, in Thatcherite eyes, more likely to see itself as an historical continuity than a family whose current members are associated with the past only by memories and abstract knowledge. As with the vigorous virtues, it is no part of the Thatcherite case to assert that families *cannot* exist or be strong, both within a generation and across the generations, on the basis of affection, memory and hope; indeed, a Thatcherite might well take the view that such a family is based upon the surest foundations. But the Thatcherite claim is that such sure foundations in emotion and abstraction can be built only by remarkable individuals. For most of us, the Thatcherite believes, the grounding of the family in the common holding and inheritance of property is an invaluable assistance to the strengthening of the sense of family. The Thatcherite hope – whether or not justified – is that a family provided with the artificial strengthening produced by commonly held and inherited property will tend to enhance those natural attachments which are the real essence of family life. The attempt is to convey to ordinary people the sense of family which the British aristocracy, with its great properties transmitted from one generation to the next, has undoubtedly sustained over many centuries.

Among Thatcherites, whether rich or poor, this way of thinking about the family is so much taken for granted that, although the importance of restoring the family has been a regular feature of Thatcherite rhetoric, no politician has ever spelt out the link between family sentiments and family holdings of property rights. And this is hardly surprising, because such a link was accepted as a commonplace in Britain, even amongst the poor, since medieval times. The association of family with property rights is a steady theme throughout British law, literature and public discourse, questioned only by eccentrics, and rarely even by radicals. But with the progress of socialism in the twentieth century, this way of thinking about the family came increasingly under attack. Not only was the private ownership of property in itself dismissed as sinful. Socialists like Beatrice and Sidney Webb explicitly advocated a Britain consisting of stocks of public housing estates, where tenants would be relieved of all private responsibilities and blessed instead with effective public supervision, and housing thus associated not with 'family homes' but with 'accommodation for efficient productive factors'. Above all, the Webbs pointed out, such tenants, freed from the burdens of property, would not be distracted by the frivolities of gardening from using their free time to attend political meetings, which, for the Webbs, constituted the good life. It was against this ethos that the Thatcherite drive to restore a sense of family by encouraging private ownership of homes was directed.

When opponents of Thatcherism describe privatization as a policy 'ideologically driven', they recognize these points. The opponent who accuses Thatcherite privatization of 'ideological' intent, acknowledges, albeit inarticulately, that rather than aiming merely at economic efficiency and the promotion of a richer Britain the programme is intended to achieve effects upon the moral attitudes which constitute society. Indeed, it is precisely this deeper objective of the privatization programme which causes the opponents of Thatcherism to dislike it so much. If privatization were merely a matter of economic rationality, its opponents might argue against it calmly and in technical economic terms, as some economic commentators have indeed done. The fact that privatization has been regarded by many opponents as wicked rather than as economically misconceived is an indication that those opponents have seen that the programme aims to effect moral results for the individual and the family, moral results that the opponents regard as vicious.

Still another aim of the privatization programme is even less clearly understood. This is the contribution of the privatization programme to the paradigm shift which Thatcherism has attempted to bring about in politics. It is a point far too infrequently observed that, for a Thatcherite, privatization is not merely a policy but a means of changing how policy is conceived and executed – a means of changing expectations about the nature of government and the nature of politics.

To understand the Thatcherite view of the effect of privatization on the nature of government and politics, one should begin with the Thatcherite analysis of how nationalized industries affect government and politics. This was powerfully articulated by Sir Alfred Sherman, formerly a speech writer for both Margaret Thatcher and Keith Joseph, and Director of Studies at the Centre for Policy Studies: 'On entering office, the minister is bound to be faced by a crisis in all "his" industrial undertakings, since they are by their nature in permanent crisis. He will be urged by his advisers to give more money to keep them going, "while things can be sorted out". It then transpires that losses are higher than envisaged – they always are. A new chairman is sought, who must be given a chance. His terms of reference are in essence: "Go on running it while we work out what to do, but try to do so more efficiently", whatever that may mean. But, of course, it will not be managed more efficiently, for all the reasons underlying its establishment in the first place. The choice is between hiving off and closing down, on the one hand, or facing losses which increase by their own momentum, on the other . . . It is like a bad film re-made time and time again with different actors . . . nationalization is an extension of politics by other means.'[7]

The point that Sherman is making cannot fail to appeal to any Thatcherite. Politicians and administrators are bound to feel responsible for the performance of an industry that is owned by the state. Being the people who act as its shareholders and have the duty to sit on its board, they must answer for it in Parliament and stand behind it when it needs financial assistance. Inevitably, they begin to concern themselves with its operation, its investment decisions and its financial performance. Instead of regarding themselves as custodians of the public interest over and against the industry, they naturally begin to identify with the interests of the industry, for which they themselves have over the years become increasingly responsible. Every attack comes to be seen by the minister and his officials as what it all too frequently is, an attack on them personally. A Thatcherite sees this entanglement as one which no normal human being occupying the position of a minister or an official in charge of a nationalized industry is likely to be able to resist.

The apotheosis of nationalization is embodied, according to the Thatcherite outlook, in the familiar Whitehall expression, a 'sponsoring department', that is, the particular department of government which promotes the interest of any given industry. The notion that the government should foster the special interests of any industry or all industries is the very antithesis of the kind of government that Thatcherism stands for. In its view, government should not serve any special interest at all; it cannot and should not solve all the problems or cure all the ills that from time to time beset various groups of citizens; many aspects of ordinary life will and should remain beyond government's reach. In consequence, the notion that industries need and deserve 'sponsorship' by government appears to Thatcherites both ridiculous and harmful.

Part, and indeed a great part, of the merit that Thatcherites see in privatization is that it jettisons the notion of sponsorship. It distances government and privatized industries from each other.

That is not to say that privatized companies acquire immunity from the laws. But once transferred to the private sector they cease to be wards of the state, no longer enjoying its parental protection but no longer compelled to obey its commands. And the government is, as according to Thatcherism it should be, thus relieved of the duties to protect and command industrial enterprises, duties that it should not have undertaken and could not perform well.

Even in the special case of the utility companies, which supply 'essential' telecommunications, gas, electricity, and water, privatization has distanced the government from the companies. To be sure, agencies of the government regulate the companies' prices and the quality of their products and services. But the regulatory bodies, such as OFTEL and OFGAS, are generally headed by professional economists whose sole functions are to assure that utility companies operate as efficiently as possible and that their customers are served as well as possible and at reasonable prices. Unlike the former ministerial and official 'sponsors', current regulators have neither responsibility nor power to aim at wider political or social goals. Aside from this limited degree of regulation, the privatized utility companies are free to manage their businesses as they see fit. But like any other business in a free economy, they are subject to a large variety of constraints. They must adequately satisfy their customers, employees, shareholders, creditors, neighbours, and others with whom they come into contact. They must conform to general laws – such as those concerning contracts, restrictive practices, and pollution – as well as to the specific legal requirements built into their licences or franchises. They are, at the extreme, subject to ministerial orders issued under the authority of regulatory statutes. Nevertheless, the government no longer manages or subsidizes them; it only obliges them, like everyone else, to obey the rules of the game.

For a Thatcherite the importance of this shift from government which manages industries to a government which oversees industry has wide implications for the nature of government as a whole. Privatization, by shifting the paradigm in relation to industry, helps to shift the paradigm in every other respect. If, as Thatcherism holds, government does not need – as is shown by privatization –

to intervene directly to manage industrial activity, cannot the same logic be applied in a wide variety of other areas? And it is this logic which has indeed affected Thatcherite policy making in local government, in education and in health, to name but a few examples. In the case of local government, the contracting out of local services can, of course, be regarded as a form of privatization. In this instance, the paradigm shift – from local government 'doing something' about every dirty street, to local government merely ensuring that someone else does something – can be regarded as an example of, rather than an extension of, the effect of privatization upon the nature of government. But in relation to schools and hospitals, where – as is illustrated elsewhere in this book – Thatcherism has pursued the paradigm shift by seeking to withdraw government from direct involvement in the provision of service, there has been no question of privatization itself. Schools that 'opt out' and hospitals that become 'self-governing trusts' remain, from the point of view of ownership and funding, fully 'nationalized'. And yet, opponents of Thatcherism have been successful in categorizing both opting-out and conversion to trust status as examples of 'privatization'. This is highly instructive. It illustrates, in the rhetoric of Thatcherism's opponents, the extent to which the paradigm shift in government has come to be identified with the privatization programme, and it thereby illustrates the extent to which the privatization programme has contributed to the pervasiveness of that shift.

Nor is this surprising: privatization is the natural prototype of the paradigm shift. In a privatization, the government illustrates to the world and to itself, more clearly than in any other act, its intention to distance itself and its refusal to take on the responsibility for doing something about everything. Privatization is a vivid act of disengagement. Just as Clement Attlee, in his nationalizations, signalled Labour's intent to seize all the levers, to create a social revolution by political means, to use government as a tool for the betterment of every aspect of human life, so the Thatcher Governments by selling off Attlee's legacy have signalled with unmistakable clarity their view that the government should *not* be seen as an entity capable of providing solutions for all social problems.

Given the practical rather than theoretical character of Thatcherism, it is not altogether surprising that leading Thatcherites in the Government and Conservative Central Office took relatively little trouble to explain their position on privatization in response to various broad criticisms.

The criticism that attracted most attention, because it was voiced by a former Tory prime minister, Harold Macmillan, held that privatizing the nationalized industries amounted to 'selling the family silver'. Thatcherites might have pointed out that whereas to sell a family's silver thoughtlessly betrays a crass disregard for sentimental values, neither the public nor the Government were sentimentally attached to the nationalized industries. They might have said also that selling the nationalized industries was in no way spendthrift unless the government had recklessly wasted the proceeds on idle luxuries, which nobody suggests. Moreover, given their huge demand for subsidies, far from being an asset, the nationalized industries were a constant drain on the nation's resources. So far as the proceeds were used to reduce taxes or to avoid increases in taxes, all that was being done was to transform the negative value of 'the family silver' into real property of positive value to the members of the family.

Another criticism that Thatcherites failed to rebut successfully was that selling the nationalized industries handed over to a relatively small number of private persons, the new shareholders, assets that had previously belonged to all the citizens. But Thatcherites might have replied that this, though superficially true, overlooked two facts. Whereas property can be managed and disposed of by its owners, 'all the citizens' of Britain could do neither with the nationalized industries. Secondly, the new shareholders had paid 'all the citizens' for what they bought. So the 'all' in question had participated in an exchange which gave them cash (or, more strictly, gave it to their trustee, the Treasury) in return for imaginary 'shares' in loss-making enterprises, which they had been compelled to subsidize with their taxes.

Again, critics said that privatization degraded public monopolies, which served the public, into private monopolies, which would chiefly serve their greedy owners. The Thatcherite answer is that this overlooked the fact that some privatized industries, for instance electricity, though monopolistic while nationalized, were restructured as competitive industries in the course of privatization. And it overlooked the fact also that industries that remained virtual monopolies after privatization – such as British Telecom and British Gas – were subjected to a considerable degree of regulation following privatization.

And finally, critics said that the privatization of council dwellings radically reduced the stock of dwellings available for the homeless and needy. Here the Thatcherites could have answered simply and clearly that transferring the ownership of a house from the council to its tenant could not possibly diminish the number of houses in the UK. There might well be a case for maintaining that the number of dwelling units in the UK or in parts of it is too small, but that was and is due, according to Thatcherite views on housing, to legal restrictions which prevent housing from being built on certain sites or in certain ways and prevent landlords from letting quarters at reasonable rates.

Because Thatcherites did not effectively answer those criticisms and others, opposition to privatization probably lasted longer than it might have done otherwise. But in any case the criticisms did sooner or later lose whatever influence they may have had on public thinking. So at least one must judge from the fact that none of the three main parties now calls for renationalization on a broad front.

Privatization, then, is indeed a textbook case of Thatcherism. It has, undoubtedly, an economic motive: it aims to revivify large swathes of British industry and thereby to promote the economic dynamism associated with England in the past. But, beyond this, the Thatcherite approach to privatization has attempted to use the transfer of assets from public to private sector as a means of widening share ownership and the ownership of property generally. And this transfer of assets was being made in order to promote, through ownership, the vigorous virtues of self-sufficiency, independence, energy and adventurousness in individuals and, equally, to promote the cohesion of the family as an association whose members are joint owners of common property both within a single generation and by inheritance from one generation to the next. Finally, privatization as a policy exhibits to a prime degree the tendency of Thatcherite policy in general not merely to seek the promotion of specific substantive ends but also to promote a paradigm shift in both the nature of and attitude to government. Privatization, for a Thatcherite, is not merely a means of promoting substantive economic, moral and social aims but also, and perhaps above all, of changing both the reality and the perception of the relationship between government and the governed.

5

Thatcherite Economics:
An Attitude Not a Policy

Students taking aptitude tests are sometimes asked to match one word with another off the top of their heads: tailor for tinker, sailor for soldier and so forth. If the word Thatcherism were to be included in such an aptitude test, the word most often heard with it would be the word, 'economics'. The association of Thatcherism with economics goes so deep in the public mind that it might almost be said to constitute an identification. For many people, Thatcherism *is* economics.

Adam Smith is regularly described as 'the intellectual inspiration behind Thatcherism'.[1] The commentaries on Thatcherism, insofar as they do not deal with Mrs Thatcher's biography or the quarrels among her ministers, concentrate entirely on economics. Giving an account of Thatcherism is taken to mean describing the development of economic policy and filling the pages with statistics.

But if Thatcherism were, in essence, an economic policy, it would be reduced to the status of a technical programme for mending economic malfunctions. It could not be concerned to cultivate certain virtues in individuals, a certain attitude towards the family, a certain kind of society in Britain, and a certain method of governing. Both its scope and its methods would be quite different.

Yet it is easy to see why people should so frequently have thought of Thatcherism as an economic doctrine. To begin with, the gurus of Thatcherism have tended to be economists. Professors Milton Friedman, F.A. Hayek, Alan Walters, Brian Griffiths, Patrick Minford, Tim Congdon – the list of distinguished economists who have been at the heart of Thatcherism runs on and on. In the early days, Margaret Thatcher and Keith Joseph were understood to be

Conservatives who had read Friedman and Hayek; the fact that the message of Thatcherism had been propagated by the Institute of Economic Affairs rather than an institute of social or political affairs was entirely in line with the fact that one of the first and most significant of the publications of Thatcherism's own Centre for Policy Studies was 'Monetarism is Not Enough' – a pamphlet in which Keith Joseph himself put forward what was taken to be the classical Thatcherite concern with macro-economic policy.

When Mrs Thatcher came to power in 1979, it was the economist, Adam Ridley, who first came to Downing Street to assist her and then, after his speedy migration to the Treasury, was replaced by John Hoskins, a businessman concerned with macro-economic management who made his mark in the 1981 budget. From that time until almost the last days of the Thatcher administrations, the presence of Professor Alan Walters in Downing Street was never forgotten by Whitehall or by the media. It was he, and his economic advice, that became the prime focus of attention for Thatcherites and their opponents in 1989. In the earlier part of his tenure, the economist and columnist for the *Financial Times*, Sam Brittan, was regularly in evidence both in the Treasury and in the penumbra of Downing Street; in the later years, the macro-economist, Professor Brian Griffiths took his place – first as an unofficial adviser and then as the official head of the Downing Street Policy Unit – in the pantheon of Thatcherite economists. From start to finish, the group of economists inhabiting the advisory committees and writing the pamphlets of the IEA were to be seen and heard as, ostensibly at least, the living embodiments of Thatcherism. When Professor Patrick Minford or Professor Tim Congdon wrote about the money supply, inflation, unemployment and the free market, they were taken to be Thatcherites preaching Thatcherism.

Nor was it a matter merely of being surrounded by economic gurus. Thatcherism was associated, or indeed identified, not only with the concern for economics but with a particular view of economics. In the crudest accounts, Thatcherism was regarded as synonymous with 'monetarism'; so much so and so effectively that, during the first few years of the Thatcher administrations, the talk was constantly of how and when Thatcher would do a 'U-turn' away from monetarist policies. Control of the money supply, and through it control of inflation, was portrayed as the great cause for which Thatcher stood.

Even in subtler accounts, monetarism was conceived as the cornerstone of Thatcherism. In Keith Joseph's own words: 'Let me emphasize, to say that 'monetarism is not enough' is not in any sense to retreat from monetarism. On the contrary it is to advance from monetarism. It is to recognize that our argument has gone a long way towards winning, but it will not be enough to have reduced inflation if we do not enable the private sector to revive when we have won the battle . . . That is why, by itself, the strict and unflinching control of the money supply though essential is not enough. We must also have substantial cuts in tax and public spending and bold incentives and encouragements to the wealth creators, without whose renewed efforts we shall all grow poorer.'[2]

In this subtler view, Thatcherism was identified not simply with monetarism but with 'free market' economics as a whole – the abolition of controls on prices and wages, dividends and exchange rates; reductions in taxation and in public expenditure; fiscal purity; the provision, wherever possible, of goods and services by the private sector. The achievement of a free market economy was widely proclaimed as such by Thatcherites themselves.

This was not merely a matter of talk or of advisers. The identification of Thatcherism with free-market economics was made more plausible by the shape of Mrs Thatcher's Cabinets. Plenty of the leading ministers, of course, were by no means economists; one does not associate Whitelaw, Carrington, Hailsham, Biffen and Hurd with a set of economic policies, free-market or otherwise. But these ministers – perhaps for that very reason – are also not associated with full-blooded Thatcherism. The great Thatcherite stars of the Thatcher Cabinets – Joseph, Howe, and Lawson were economic ministers and ministers with an economic message. One did not expect to hear Thatcherism from the mouths of Ministers for the Arts – St John Stevas, Gowrie, Luce – but rather from aspiring financial and economic Secretaries to the Treasury – Lawson, Moore, Lamont, Lilley, Maude.

Disillusioned Tories – Macmillan and Heath prominent amongst them – attacked Thatcherism as the remorseless pursuit of free-market economics and hence a diversion of the Party from the true Tory tradition of concern for the creation and sustenance of 'one nation'. From the Left, Scargill and Benn or, more moderately, Shirley Williams and Bryan Gould, attacked Thatcherism as a form of materialism, an obsession with the market and with market economics at the expense of people, jobs and compassion.

Within the Thatcherite camp, too, the great controversies were about economics. The battle over the 1981 budget, now chronicled extensively by Walters, Hoskins and others, was a set piece encounter between the 'Treasury view' and Thatcherite concerns with the control of public expenditure. The terrain was economics, the opposing armies lay in the Treasury and No 10, each provided with their own economic advisers. Seven years later, a different battle was fought – but again on an economic terrain, and again between the Treasury and No 10, and with each side once again armed to the teeth with economic gun power. This time the fight centred squarely on monetary management – the level of interest rates, the importance of the exchange rate, entry to the Exchange Rate Mechanism of the European Monetary System. All this made it entirely reasonable to conclude that as Thatcherites chose economic battles when engaging in civil war, Thatcherism must itself be dominated by economic concerns: people, and political parties in particular, only choose to fight about what matters to them most.

The ostensible evidence in support of the view that Thatcherism is principally concerned with the promotion of free-market economics is, then, impressive. The identification of Thatcherism with free-market economic policy is a view which must be taken seriously. But this is not to say that it is correct. On the contrary, the ostensible evidence is wholly misleading. Thatcherism is not, and cannot possibly be understood as, an economic policy.

Of course Thatcherism has many policies which affect the working of the economy. Thatcherite policies on trade unions and the labour market generally, privatization, local government finance, education and training – all discussed elsewhere in this book – must of necessity have widespread effects on the performance of particular firms and of the economy in general. But these cannot be said to constitute 'an economic policy', any more than a defence policy which causes either a massive increase or a massive decrease in taxation and hence large-scale effects on economic performance can be said to constitute an economic policy. The thesis that Thatcherism is an economic policy – the thesis that appears to be supported by so much evidence – asserts not merely that Thatcherism (like all governments) has many policies which affect economic performance, but rather that Thatcherism offers, or is even mainly constituted by, a general macro-economic policy. This policy, it is said, attempts to achieve certain specific economic effects through the application of certain specific economic principles in relation to critical macro-economic items such as taxation, public expenditure, interest rates, exchange rates, monetary aggregates, control of credit, wages, prices, exchange and the like.

There is no doubt that Thatcherism has economic goals which fit into this category. A room full of Thatcherites could be brought to universal agreement on the proposition that it would be desirable to achieve a permanent combination of stable prices, stable exchange rates, low taxation, high growth and general prosperity. This wish-list is not, however, in any sense a distinguishing characteristic of Thatcherism. A room full of adherents of any other political persuasion would probably also be able to agree unanimously on the desirability of such a state of affairs. Economic policy consists not in listing all the items that would be desirable but rather in making choices between various desirable but, alas, all too frequently mutually incompatible aims. Moreover, an economic policy must contain not merely ends but also means – a set of practical propositions about how generalized economic aims of a particular sort are to be achieved. This is exactly what Thatcherism is not.

It is true also that, for some years, Thatcherism was widely identified with 'monetarism'. This identification has the dubious advantage that, since neither term is well understood, by identifying one with the other the speaker is able to comfort himself that he has grasped both without the need to clarify either. Apart from this dispensable advantage, the identification of Thatcherism with monetarism has no benefits whatsoever. If we take as a working definition of monetarism the proposition that 'the appropriate way to manage the economy is to maintain, so far as possible, stable prices, and the appropriate way to maintain stable prices is to ensure that, so far as possible, the amount of money available to the citizenry reflects the volume of goods and services produced by the citizenry', it is clear, first, that Thatcherites are not the only people who believe this and, secondly, that Thatcherites do not believe it very strongly.

The number of non-Thatcherites who are, on this definition, 'monetarists' is of course legion. To our home-grown Denis Healey, one must add not just a mass of Americans or a mass of Eastern Europeans but also the Bundesbank in Germany (which cannot be regarded as in any way associated with Thatcherism) and succeeding generations of managers of the Japanese economy (many of whom had never heard of Thatcherism). This is not, in point of fact, surprising, since the propositions constituting such 'monetarism' have generally been accepted as true, before the advent of Thatcherism. Who would deny that a degree of price stability is a critical determinant of economic and social well-being (as repeatedly demonstrated by the multitude of economic and social disasters attending high-inflation economies); and there is no doubt whatsoever that the relationship between the amount of money available to the citizenry and the volume of goods and services produced by the citizenry has a marked effect on the degree of price stability obtained and maintained by government. In short, if Thatcherism were identifiable with 'monetarism' in this general sense, it would be both banal and uncontroversial – sins of which Thatcherism has not usually been accused.

If, in an attempt to show that Thatcherism is, in some interesting and controversial sense, identifiable with monetarism, one were to move to a narrower definition of what it is to be a 'monetarist' – insisting, for example, that for a full-blooded monetarist the attention of economic managers must be firmly focused on the monetary aggregates which indicate the amount of money available at any given time to the citizenry, then it becomes immediately apparent that Thatcherites do not believe very strongly in monetarism.

The technical structure of Thatcherite macro-economic policy was devised by Nigel Lawson, Financial Secretary to the Treasury from 1979 to 1981, who though outside the Cabinet exercised great influence on the Treasury and the Prime Minister. He invented a framework of policy known as the Medium Term Financial Strategy (MTFS), designed to reduce inflation by controlling the money supply 'over a period of years'.[3] Trying to control the money supply more rapidly would have required that the base rate of interest be raised even above seventeen per cent, the level it had reached in November of 1979, higher than at any previous time in the century. Raising the interest rate yet higher would have tended to deepen the severe recession that was already under way, besides which it would have tended to raise the pound's already high exchange rate and thus further limit the demand for British exports.

Instead, the government undertook – as the Treasury explained to a Commons committee – to 'frame its policies for taxation and public expenditure to secure a deceleration of money supply without excessive reliance on interest rates'.[4] What this meant in practical terms was that the government undertook in the 1980 Budget to cut public spending by 1 billion, so as to reduce public borrowing, thus decelerating the growth of the money supply and with it the rate of inflation.

But aside from stemming inflation, the reduction of government spending was intended to serve another vital Thatcherite aim. During her years as Leader of the Opposition, Mrs Thatcher had repeatedly attacked the 'pocket-money' regime that had resulted from the confiscatory taxation needed to fund extremely high public spending. Now as Prime Minister she intended to cut back the public sector so as to make more room for private decisions about how much to spend, save, and invest. As the Chancellor of the Exchequer, Sir Geoffrey Howe, explained, this was the ultimate aim of the 1980 Budget: 'At the heart of the medium-term strategy is the need to return to a sensible level of public spending . . . In the last 20 years the ratio of public expenditure to GDP has risen by a quarter. It would be all too easy for this ratio to go on rising indefinitely . . . Expenditure in 1983–84 is planned to be about 4 per cent lower in real terms than in 1979–80. The effect will be a marked shift . . . in the balance between the public and private sectors.' Eventually, albeit not just yet, the decline in public spending would make it possible to lighten the tax burden 'and so to provide scope and encouragement for enterprise and initiative'.[5]

Embodied in the Medium Term Financial Strategy was yet another Thatcherite motif, mistrust of economic 'fine tuning'. Inherent in the practice if not the theory of Keynesian policy – which Thatcherism had rejected – was the idea that as soon as the government observed that any fundamental economic variable (be it output, employment, the price level, or the exchange rate) was veering away from its ideal state, the government ought to take corrective action at once. In an ideal world this would clearly be the right course – if one knew what had been going wrong and if one knew how to fix it. The Thatcherite view was that in the real world these conditions cannot be met because Ministers and officials get their information about economic trends from statistics, and these statistics are notoriously unreliable. What happened in any given month is first approximated a month later – or in the case of GDP, for instance – a quarter later, and then in the form of a 'provisional' figure. Provisional figures keep being revised for months afterwards, sometimes radically, and sometimes months and years later. Equivalent lags are encountered in judging whether the medicine applied by the Government has taken the desired effect because nobody can predict with certainty whether raising the interest rate by, say, one per cent will reduce the money supply too little, too much, or just enough. So months elapse between knowing the extent of the economic disorder and knowing whether the patient is responding to the remedy, or whether, as often happens, the intended cure has exacerbated the original disorder or, alternatively, produced side-effects more troublesome than the original disorder.

Nigel Lawson emphasized that because official statistics arrived slowly and could seriously misrepresent the facts they would mislead practitioners of fine-tuning. He objected to fine-tuning moreover because it stemmed from 'pragmatism', which many have lauded before and since as a special talent of British politicians and officials that enables them to respond to events realistically and flexibly. Lawson, on the contrary, regarded 'pragmatism' as a weak-kneed unwillingness to stick to one's guns,[6] and in this his attitude concurred with Mrs Thatcher's famous refusal to make U-turns in response to fleeting events or momentary fluctuations in public opinion.

The upshot of all this was that the Medium Term Financial Strategy, which Lawson described as an 'essentially . . . monetary – or, if you like, monetarist – strategy', was based on a set of rules. The pivotal rule was that a target should be set annually for the growth of money supply, as measured by M_3 – the broad measure of money supply that includes cash and balances in current bank accounts. The target for 1979–80 was set at growth between seven and eleven per cent, and the government was to arrange its macro-economic policies so as to meet the target and thus to bring inflation under control. Fiscal policy, like monetary policy, should aim at the money-supply target, which meant in particular that government borrowing should be reduced to the extent necessary. The pound should be left free to float against other currencies; this would relieve the government of responsibility for intervening in the foreign-exchange markets, intervention that would often conflict with its prime task of controlling the money supply. And the government should follow an 'active' funding policy: it should sell gilt-edged securities as a means of reducing the supply of money when that was growing too fast, or buy back such securities if and when the supply of money was growing too slowly.[7] Those were the operating rules, the means devised to do away with inflation and allow for reduction of taxes, all in order to set individuals and private markets free to pursue their own objectives.

Despite certain detailed alterations, the so-called monetarist system continued in place until 1985. And it proved successful in bringing inflation down to six per cent, controlling government borrowing, and stimulating a robust and stable rate of economic growth at about three per cent annually.

But during 1985, Nigel Lawson, who had been appointed Chancellor of the Exchequer in 1983, increasingly shifted his attention away from the money supply as the dominant target of economic policy and toward the sterling exchange rate as at least a vital auxiliary target. Indeed in October, after M_3 had been rising about twice as fast as targeted, he explicitly abandoned the target. At the same time he committed Britain to participate in efforts by the leading industrial countries (the so-called Group of Five) to stabilize their exchange rates.[8] For Lawson had abandoned his earlier commitment to a free-floating pound for the belief that the government's policy of monetary discipline would be better solidified and exhibited if Britain joined the Exchange Rate Mechanism (ERM) of the European Monetary System. In this aspiration, he enjoyed the support of Sir Geoffrey Howe, the Foreign Secretary, the Bank of England, and various business organizations who longed for the certainty of fixed exchange rates. But as is well known, he encountered decisive opposition from Mrs Thatcher (for whom entry into the ERM represented an intolerable surrender of British sovereignty as well as a return to the old inflexible controls which destroyed gradual economic adjustments) and from her economic adviser, Alan Walters, who argued that ERM was a 'half-baked' scheme, midway between a unified European currency and free-floating national currencies, offering the advantages of neither and suffering special defects of its own.

For a time all seemed well. Inflation never much exceeded four per cent from 1987 through to the spring of 1988. For this reason, and also to restore confidence following the stock market crash of October 1987, the interest rate was brought down from 11 per cent at the beginning of 1987 to 7.5 per cent in the spring of 1980, its lowest level in a decade. And then in his Budget message of 1988, Lawson capped the good news by cutting the basic rate of income tax from 27 per cent to 25 per cent while the top rate came down sharply from 60 per cent to 40 per cent. The Medium Term Financial Strategy, or what was left of it since Lawson abandoned its rules – an explicit target for growth of broad-money supply, floating exchange rate, and an active open-market policy concerning gilts – seemed to have delivered the goods, or if it had not, Lawson somehow had. Inflation was nearing extinction, tax burdens were shrinking, and the private sector was booming.

But at this moment of triumph, everything began rapidly to turn sour. Inflation doubled within the twelve months after March 1988. In an effort to stem the surge, Lawson doubled the interest rate to 15 per cent. Despite that, after a brief lull, inflation mounted again to reach a peak of 11 per cent in the autumn of 1990. And twelve months of interest at 15 per cent, though it did begin to quell inflation, had the foreseeable effect of decisively throttling economic growth and bringing on the recession of 1990–2.

The causes of this debacle are complex and debatable. There were many different explanations: that Lawson and his advisors erred in overlooking the extravagant expansion of M_3 during 1986, from which monetarist economists inferred that inflation would turn upward in 1988 – but which Lawson, the Treasury and the Bank explained away or disregarded; that Lawson was misled by egregious errors in Treasury forecasts, such as that GDP would grow at the usual healthy rate in 1987 – when in the event it grew fifty per cent faster[9]; that after inflation shot up in early 1988, Lawson should have pushed up interest rates more suddenly than he did. But whatever the whole truth, the episode proved that fixing sterling relative to the Deutschmark failed to forestall (or as some economists claimed, produced) the inflationary outbreak of 1988. Lawson's conviction, that because Germany had 'a very strong anti-inflationary track record ... therefore keeping the pound in line with the Deutschmark is likely to be over the medium term a pretty good anti-inflationary discipline',[10] had been immediately falsified by events.

Nevertheless, that failure did nothing to reduce the enthusiasm that Lawson, Howe and many others felt for British entry into the ERM, which many of them regarded as a step toward European monetary union, to set the stage for European political union. The resignation statements of Lawson, in October 1990, and of Sir Geoffrey Howe a year later, made it clear that they regarded Mrs Thatcher's inflexible opposition to ERM as a tragic error, but for which inflation in Britain could have been suppressed as effectively as it had been in West Germany and other ERM members. Just before Sir Geoffrey resigned, John Major, then Chancellor, and Douglas Hurd, then Foreign Secretary, prevailed on Mrs Thatcher to condone British entry into the ERM and to make the effort to keep the exchange value of sterling within the bounds that ERM permits the sole official target of British monetary policy.

It is true that, during the course of these gyrations in economic policy, with the attendant contraction, expansion, and renewed contraction of the British economy, many Thatcherites came to feel uneasy. But there is no evidence that this unease arose from a clear and settled conviction on the part of Thatcher herself or of Thatcherites in general that there was one true path from which divergences had occurred. Rather, the unease clearly stemmed from the fact that changing circumstances forced them to adopt successively different macro-economic policies. The effort to identify Thatcherism with any particular macro-economic policy is thus bound to fail.

Should one, then, conclude that the impressive array of ostensible evidence linking Thatcherism with economics is no more than sham – that Thatcherism is in reality a purely political doctrine with no special relationship to macro-economic policies? Would this not leave unexplained the fact that so many commentators, both favourable and unfavourable to Thatcherism, have so often associated Thatcherism with economics, and also to leave unexplained the extent to which economic advisers and economic ministers have dominated Thatcher administrations?

A good explanation of anything has not only to justify itself but also to explain why other bad explanations should have been found acceptable. How then can the view of Thatcherism being put forward here account for the widespread conviction that Thatcherism is all about economics, even though Thatcherism is not constituted by a specific macro-economic policy? The answer is that this conviction has been inspired by a fact which has been wrongly interpreted; that fact is a distinctive Thatcherite *attitude* towards economic affairs. Just as an Oxford theologian once said of existentialism, that it is not so much a philosophy as a way of doing philosophy, one can say of Thatcherism that it is not so much an economic policy as a way of doing economic policy – or, more precisely, a way of *not* doing economic policy.

The one common thread running through the many shifts in economic stance witnessed during the Thatcher administrations is the consistent desire that government should set a framework rather than attempt to achieve results directly. This point was made clear by Thatcherites from the beginning. In his famous speech at Preston in September 1974, Keith Joseph stated that: 'the monetarist thesis has been caricatured as implying that if we get the flow of money spending right everything will be right. This is not – repeat not – my belief. What I believe is that if we get the money supply wrong – too high or too low – nothing will come right. Monetary control is a pre-essential for everything else we need and want to do; an opportunity to tackle the real problems – labour shortage in one place, unemployment in another; exaggerated expectations; inefficiencies, frictions and distortions; hard-core unemployment; the hundreds of thousands who need training or retraining or persuading to move if they are to have steady, satisfactory jobs; unstable world prices. There is no magic cure for these problems, we have to cope with them as best we can.'[11] Two years later, Keith Joseph made the point even clearer: 'I will try to restate this view in even broader terms: monetary stability provides a framework within which the individual can best serve his own – and therefore, if the laws and taxes are appropriately designed, the nation's – interests.'[12]

Reading those words again, and in the right light, one can see that the emphasis lies not on 'monetary stability', but on the phrase 'provides a framework'. What was attractive to Thatcherites about monetarism was not its technical concern with quantities of money or monetary aggregates but rather its theory that *direct* management by government to control prices, wages, dividends, exchange and so forth was unnecessary or even counter-productive. In other words, monetarism appealed to Thatcherites not because it was economically true but because it implied a paradigm shift in the relationship between government and the economy, with government acting to provide no more than a framework within which individuals could pursue their own ends. This implication was, for a Thatcherite, the crux of the matter rather than merely a consequence of an economic theory.

The economic theory was welcomed precisely and especially because it had this implication. And the evidence for this proposition lies in the fact that, throughout the many variations of macroeconomic policy visible during the years of the Thatcher administrations, the one consistent theme was the unwillingness at all times to take steps leading to direct management (as opposed to intervening in order to maintain a framework for transactions of the marketplace). Whether monetary aggregates or interest rates or exchange rates were the correct focus for macro-economic policy was, for Thatcherites, a matter to be decided *ad hoc*. But there was consistent resistance to wage and price controls, to direct control of bank lending, to exchange control and, in short, wherever possible, to all forms of direct control by government of the actions of individuals in the economic sphere.

To put this another way, one can say that Thatcherites: (1) accepted the banal and uncontroversial thesis that a high degree of price stability was good for the economy; (2) were willing to adopt a large number of different macro-economic policies to achieve this goal; but (3) have been consistently unwilling to adopt any macro-economic policy which would achieve this end by means of direct management; and (4) have therefore consistently chosen economic policies which depended upon setting a price-signal, through interest rates or exchange rates or the like, rather than through establishing laws and regulations calculated to remove decision-making from the marketplace.

The dichotomies here are clear and classically Thatcherite – between maintaining a framework and managing, price setting and rationing, the marketplace and planning, the labour market and wage control, the commercial market and price control. For the Thatcherite, the first item in each of these pairs represents freedom for the individual under a framework imposed by government, whereas the second involves the government making the decisions in place of individuals. To a politician willing (or even wishing) to intervene continuously in the activities of the citizenry, the choice between the first and second items in each pair is at most indifferent: to the Thatcherite with a political consciousness dominated by the desire to achieve the paradigm shift – to avoid government's becoming an instrument for 'doing something' about every problem – the preference for the first item in each pair is absolute.

There is, moreover, another sense in which Thatcherism can be said to have an attitude towards macro-economic policy. This comes out in the Thatcherite view of inflation. The belief that inflation should on the whole be avoided to the extent possible is, as we have already remarked, entirely banal and uncontroversial. But for a Thatcherite, this is not merely a matter of mild preference as it has been for almost all governments, nor does it stem merely from a fear of the instability which can arise as a result of hyper-inflation (the motive which dominated in the establishment of the Bundesbank). Rather, it is a central belief because it stems from and is intimately associated with the desire to promote independence in individuals and continuity in families. Inflation – even of a relatively mild variety – whittles away savings at an alarming rate. Even with inflation as low as five per cent per annum, the value of savings invested in an ordinary interest-bearing account halves every fifteen years. The result is to make savings and hence the independence (and, for many, the independent-mindedness) that go with such savings unattractive. Particularly at the lower end of the social and economic scale, inflation produces a nation whose citizens perforce depend upon the state rather than seeing themselves as independent actors, because if savings are made unattractive by the erosion of value, people find themselves turning in every necessity and throughout the course of their old age to the state for support. The Thatcherite therefore sees the presence even of mild inflation as a major threat to the success of any programme aimed at promoting the independence of the individual and the ability of the individual to hand down wealth from one generation to the next through a family which thereby strengthens its sense of itself. This is not, of course, strictly speaking an economic attitude, much less an economic policy. But it is a political attitude which is distinctively Thatcherite and which induces the Thatcherite to pay particular attention to those aspects of macro-economic policy which are designed to limit (or even, preferably, to eliminate) inflation.

We have, here, the two great explanations of what is popularly regarded as Thatcherite economics. On the one hand, out of a desire to see savings, and the individual and familial attitudes which go with savings, promoted, the Thatcherite is determined to avoid inflation; and, as a result of his belief in the paradigm shift, the

Thatcherite wishes to eschew all forms of macro-economic management which involve direct interference with individual actions by the government. It is these twin preoccupations which give rise to the Thatcherite's commitment to a preference for controls such as maintaining monetary targets or exchange rates, indeed for any kind of control that can avoid *direct* management of the economy. So, far from constituting a threat to the view that Thatcherism is a moral and social vision, the Thatcherite *attitude* to economics is, therefore, when properly understood, strong evidence for it.

6

Goodbye To Social Contracts

If Thatcherism were renowned for nothing else, it would be remembered as the David that vanquished the Goliath of trade unionism. But the reason why it undertook to do so is profoundly different from that generally supposed.

According to the popular picture, just as the Labour Party is the worker's champion, so Thatcherism, and indeed the Conservative Party as a whole, is the determined defender of capitalists, businessmen, and the wealthy. Whereas the Labour Party tried to tip the balance between trade unions and employers in favour of the weaker party – supposedly the trade unions – Thatcherism aimed to do the opposite. But the true explanation of Thatcherite policies towards trade unions is that Thatcherism takes – what undoubtedly was and to some extent still is – an unusual view of the role that government should perform.

Trade Unionists in Downing Street

The unions had always wanted their leaders to participate in running the country, in the course of beer-and-sandwich parties at Downing Street, as they did most blatantly under Labour governments and more subtly under Conservative governments. The 'social contract' that they made with the Wilson and Callaghan Governments suited them very well indeed, even if in the end they did not quite keep their side of the bargain. But this was just the kind of 'governing' that Thatcherism repudiated.

A government out to 'do the right thing' could not set policies that suited one or another powerful interest group at the expense of the public at large. Thatcherites considered it outrageous that the country should be ruled by an extra-legal 'partnership' between the government and people to whom the laws had given no authority.

In taking this line, Thatcherism set itself not only against the Labour Party but also against an important strand of opinion in the Conservative Party, of which Ian Gilmour was in the early 1980s the leading spokesman. Gilmour argued that British constitutional theory had to be accommodated to new circumstances. The old conception of government had been suitable for a time when 'unions were not powerful and most firms were not large and the Government did not intervene in the economy'. But now, when there were strong 'corporate forces' on both sides of industry, the only way for a representative government to prevent national disintegration was to give up trying to be the 'unique national policymaker' and to seek 'partnerships' or 'contracts' with the other powerful 'corporations', namely industry and the trade unions. Corporatism in this sense was contrasted by Gilmour to 'authoritarianism' of either the Left or the Right, to which 'interest groups are anathema'. 'Authoritarians', by which he meant Thatcherites among others, believe that 'they themselves embody the public interest, and therefore interest groups can only distort that interest and thwart the wishes of the ruler'.[1]

Although Gilmour's corporatism could claim no such ancient and venerable ancestry as he attributed to it – for both Burke and Maitland explicitly opposed the views that he imputed to them – it had acquired a following more recently. In 1930, Winston Churchill had suggested that an 'Economic Sub-Parliament' be established to deal with the intricacies of modern economic life. Harold Macmillan believed that the Economic Council he recommended in 1938 might have been 'the keystone of the structure of a planned economy'. In 1947, L. S. Amery advocated a new Reform Act to create a 'separate House of Industry' or 'Sub-Parliament' to establish the new principle of 'functional representation'.[2] Iain Macleod told the Conservative Party Conference in 1958 that 'Only in a partnership independent of politics, between the great partners – the Government, the trade unions, and the employers – is there any real hope of good, sound industrial relations.'[2]

Gilmour and other corporatists of the eighties wanted a 'partnership' between Government, trade unions and employers to be not *outside* politics but the core of politics. Only then, they believed, would powerful interests be willing to co-operate with each other and the government, and so cease to be destructive of social peace. The Thatcherites, he maintained, destroyed the possibility of such peaceful tri-partite accommodation by their dogmatic aversion to the trade unions, which inspired their hostile legislation.

Gilmour and other corporatists totally failed to see that the objective of Thatcherite legislation was to end 'interest-group politics' – the effort of powerful organized groups to enlist the government as an instrument for pandering to their special interests, an effort whose success culminated in a corporatist 'partnership'. For the Thatcherites this outcome represented an unacceptable triumph of power over authority, which transferred the constitutional functions of government, partly at least, to private persons lacking any constitutional authority to govern. In short, Thatcherite reforms of labour laws, though they certainly reduced the power of the unions, were intended fundamentally to restore and clarify the government's authority to rule.

How Trade Unions Grew

The first step in the Thatcherite battle against corporatism was to attack the immunities from law that had been so lavishly bestowed on trade unions.

These immunities had been acquired partly through historical accident. Whereas company law subjects business corporations to a regime of positive rights and duties, unions had largely been defined by negatives, that is to say, by immunities from the normal provisions of the common law. Their legal status lies somewhere between that of corporations and of unincorporated associations. Like corporations, they can make collective agreements with others, such as employers, but unlike corporations, their agreements are assumed *not* to be enforceable as legal contracts.

The definition of trade unions by immunities from the common law is due to the fact that trade unions began life at a time when Englishmen had become accustomed to managing their own lives by voluntary contracts, free from various restrictions which had for centuries made it difficult for individuals to choose their own conditions or places of work. Eagerness to protect this liberty of the individual employee, fortified by fear of the new repressions being forged by the French Revolution and imported into England, led to the Combination of Workmen Acts of 1799 and 1800 which made it illegal for workmen to associate in trade unions. This prohibition was removed by the Combination Laws Repeal Act of 1824, which Beatrice and Sidney Webb called 'the most impressive event in the early history of the Trade Union Movement'.

From then on, a concern to strengthen the hand of working men against their employers overcame regard for the freedom of individual employees and spurred on the development of the trade union movement. By the middle of the nineteenth century, local unions of skilled workers amalgamated into national unions, each covering a particular craft, and further legislation enlarged their immunities. A Royal Commission set up by Disraeli in 1867 laid the groundwork for the Trade Union Act of 1871, passed under Gladstone's Government, which gave trade unions legal security for their funds and for their Friendly Society activities. The latter were co-operative efforts to provide for the welfare of members by, for instance, setting up schools or arranging for medical care; these were thought of at the time as the leading functions of trade unions. Further legislation in 1875 legalized peaceful picketing and immunized unions against prosecution for criminal conspiracy. For this the TUC, which had arrived on the scene in 1868, warmly thanked Disraeli's Home Secretary.

But though unions had become important enough to appear in an unfavourable light in the novels of Trollope, Dickens and Mrs Gaskell, it was only in the last quarter of the nineteenth century that the unions became industry-wide organizations devoted to raising wages and wielding political influence. Trade unionism became a 'movement', and fighting the 'capitalists' took precedence over helping the members.

The larger and the more powerful trade unions grew, the more they were accepted. Some enthusiasts hoped and expected that they would ultimately bring down capitalism and usher in the utopia of socialism by means of a general strike. Syndicalists hoped that the same means would produce a different variety of utopia. But whatever the particular aspirations of their supporters, unions came to be widely accepted as voluntary organizations no less legitimate in a free society than any other. By the 1950s, they had a wider membership than any other form of association, and as they claimed to represent the interests of millions of voters, it seemed suicidal for any political party to attack their power.

Nor was any party inclined to curtail their power by law. On the contrary, the Conservative Party took great pride in Disraeli's Act of 1875, because it had conferred on the unions such vital privileges. In its Industrial Charter of 1947 it proclaimed that 'the official policy of the Conservative Party is in favour of trade unions'. When the Conservatives subsequently legislated against restrictive practices in retail distribution, none of them suggested that any steps should be taken against the restrictive practices of unions. And the Industrial Relations Act of 1971, which the Heath Government initially regarded as a triumph, proved to be too feeble and contradictory to matter.

The Labour Party, which depended heavily on unions for funds and on union members for votes, and whose policies were so strongly influenced by union delegates at the Party's annual conferences, took even more care not to offend. It was only under extreme provocation that the Wilson Government in 1969 produced the White Paper, *In Place of Strife*, which proposed that unions, like employers who disobeyed ministerial orders, should be fined. That proposal was defeated by the joint efforts of trade union leaders, MPs sponsored by trade unions, and Cabinet members led by James Callaghan. The implications of this episode were described by Richard Crossman in 1972: 'I think we have got to face it, that as a result of our failure to carry our Industrial Relations Act in our time, the price of TUC support for an alternative Labour Party policy is that they will write their own Industrial Relations Act for the next Labour government. I think we have simply got to do what they wish because that is the only basis on which we can hope to work out a common attitude to other problems.'[3] Crossman was proved right.

As soon as Labour was returned to government in 1974, it repealed the Heath Government's Industrial Relations Act of 1971, feeble and inconsequential though it was. The Labour Government legalized closed shops and removed all legal safeguards protecting individual workers who wished to join no union or preferred to belong to a different one than the majority of their fellows. The Government also legalized strikes concerning matters outside Britain (such as apartheid in South Africa) and secondary boycotts of enterprises by whom the strikers were not employed. Unions were given immunity to civil action for injunctions or damages that might arise from strikes or boycotts against firms other than, indeed even far removed from, the firm involved in the original dispute. Employers, however small their business, were compelled to recognize trade unions, to disclose the business's future plans to them, and were exposed to legal action for unfair dismissal on grounds so wide that they were left helpless against troublesome or useless employees. Trade unions were given the right to make pay claims solely on the basis of 'comparability' with pay in other firms or industries, regardless of the conditions peculiar to their own enterprises.

Not much later the Labour Government enlisted the unions in aid of its effort to restrain prices and wages. They promulgated a 'social contract', in accordance with which the unions undertook to practice a degree of self-restraint in pay negotiations and the Government undertook to compensate them in various ways. T. E. Utley articulated the Thatcherite response to the 'social contract' when he described it as 'that almost unbelievably blatant violation of the Constitution . . . the arrangement under which the Government largely abandons the role of governing in return for a partial abandonment by the trades union leaders of the function of wage negotiation.' The 'social contract' was the perfect expression of the view that a trade union leader is not 'the authorised representative of a section of the labour force, employed to protect and advance its legitimate interests' but is 'an actual part of the machinery of government, entitled to a share in the formulation of general economic policy and probably also in the formulation of all other aspects of policy as well'.[4] Thanks to the acceptance of this view of trade unions by the Labour Government, the power of trade unions reached its zenith between 1975 and 1978, when TUC leaders and agents seemed to be permanently installed in Downing Street.

Trade Unions Versus the Vigorous Virtues

What the trade unions had become by 1979 was obviously incompatible with the Thatcherite desire for a Britain peopled by independent-minded, vigorous, self-sufficient individuals. The unions claimed – and were given – support as expressions of the right of free association. But that claim had been under attack for some years.

Enoch Powell had argued that free association 'means nothing unless there is an equal right of non-association. It is contrary to the rule of law that any private association of citizens should be permitted to exercise coercion over those who do not choose to belong to it.' The various privileges bestowed upon the trade unions have given them the power to coerce individuals into becoming members and have enabled them 'to behave in ways that for any other associations would be unlawful and would result in damages for those who suffered injury at their hands'.[5]

The same point was made by the philosopher, Michael Oakeshott, who said that although trade unions appeared to spring from and be justified by the right of voluntary association, they were in reality a self-contradiction. 'A compulsory voluntary association [a union, in other words] is a conspiracy to abolish the right of association.'[6]

T. E. Utley condemned unions for claiming 'not only the right to withhold their labour, which might be thought to be inherent in the free man, but the right to force others to join them on pain of unemployment, the right to commit any minority, however large, to whatever course of public policy is approved by a union majority, however slight, and the right to trick any member who has not troubled to learn the rules into automatically subscribing to a political party of which he may disapprove. What would you say if the British Medical Association allotted a proportion of every doctor's subscription to [Conservative Party] funds unless the doctor took the trouble to specify that he was not a Conservative?"[7]

According to the Thatcherite view of the vigorous virtues, the trade unions could no longer claim to enhance the working man's human dignity. On the contrary, by wielding their closed-shop power which prevented him from taking certain jobs or moving from one job to another under the control of a different union, by prohibiting him from declining to join any union, or deciding to resign from his union – they undermined the worker's self-respect, reducing him to the status of a latter-day serf.

The myth that workers flocked voluntarily to join unions, in order to enhance their sense of independence and self-esteem, was critically examined by the Thatcherite lawyer and economist, Arthur Shenfield. In a pamphlet published by the IEA, he demonstrated that only small numbers of workers had joined before unions acquired legal immunities and backing from the government and before they were able to recruit members by violent intimidation. Only fourteen per cent of the labour force had joined unions before 1906, when the Trades Disputes Act afforded unions protection for their activities in organizing strikes.[8] There were many reasons why some workers joined unions, and why many did not. It was far-fetched to suppose that those who chose to join did it mainly as a means of asserting their dignity as self-determining individuals.

What really distinguishes the free employee from a slave, prisoner, or conscript, Shenfield argued, is the former's freedom to choose his job and to change it at will. The labourer's dignity does not at all depend on a right to strike because the essence of striking is not that employees collectively withdraw their labour, but rather that while doing so they insist that the jobs which they temporarily vacate remain theirs by right. The striker, in short, asserts a proprietary interest in his job. Accordingly, when in the course of a strike the employer hands the job over to a 'scab' or 'blackleg', he perpetrates a sort of theft, which may rightfully be resisted by force.

By the time that Mrs Thatcher became Prime Minister, it had come to be widely recognized that strikes were a form of duress exercised against innocent people by those who had the power to impose their will on others. It had also become evident that not only those outside the unions were victims of these uncontrolled powers, but also that union members themselves were victimized. They could not refuse to join a strike and they were not often consulted about whether there should be one. The closed shop, which meant that union membership was compulsory and that no one but a union member could be employed there, was recognized to be an affront to the dignity and independence of union members. If members acquiesced unwillingly in 'collective' decisions – frequently in fact autocratic decisions taken by self-perpetuating union leaders – they sacrificed their independence to superior power; if they refused to give in, they were likely to land on the dole. In the kind of Britain that Thatcherism envisioned, the closed shop was a monstrous anomaly.

Trade Unions Versus Prosperity

Thatcherism's intention to cure the 'British disease', to restore Britain's vigour, and to raise its standard of living, was another basic reason for changing the legal status and duties of trade unions. Contrary to the unquestioning belief, held by 'middle way' Tories as well as the liberal consensus, that trade unions had raised the earnings and improved the working conditions of their members, Thatcherites concluded that the opposite was true.

That view was founded partly on the work of a South African economist, W. H. Hutt. His analysis of labour markets, *The Theory of Collective Bargaining*, little noticed when it was first published in 1939, became increasingly influential during the 1960s and 1970s. Hutt maintained that in free individual wage-bargaining, the employee suffered no natural or inherent disadvantage. Though in some specific circumstances the employer enjoyed a temporarily stronger bargaining position, in other circumstances the employee had the edge, and in general over the long-run the bargaining positions of the two sides were evenly matched. This was demonstrated, said Hutt, by the fact that in free economies where pay rates were set by individual rather than collective bargaining, wages rose over the long run. As Shenfield put it: 'in every known case of a labour market which has been allowed to be free, the earnings and working conditions of labour have improved, not deteriorated.'[9] This fact disproved the Marxist theory that under capitalism, exploitation results in continued 'immiseration' of the proletariat. Indeed that theory had been abandoned even by German Marxists when they observed at the end of the 19th century how much the wages and conditions of German workers had improved, an advance that could not possibly be attributed to intervention by powerful trade unions.

Overwhelming confirmation of Hutt's thesis was afforded by the case of Hong Kong. Its labour market has been as free as any in the world, and its unions are few and insignificant. Moreover, Hong Kong's population has increased rapidly – ninefold from 1945 to 1985 – which, according to the theory of the employee's inherent disadvantage, should have allowed employers to grind wages down to the subsistence level or below. In fact, the contrary has happened. Earnings of workers in Hong Kong have risen at rates that no union in the West, not even the printers' union in Britain, has ever dared to contemplate.

If a union uses its monopoly to raise wages by force, Hutt concluded, the rise will in the long run be illusory, because it will be passed on in different proportions to employers, consumers, workers in other industries, and ultimately to the union members themselves both as consumers and as workers whose jobs are lost. The only way in which a union can genuinely raise wages is by using its knowledge of the market. In various circumstances individual workers lack timely information about what jobs are available elsewhere and at what rates of pay. A union is better equipped to assemble comprehensive information about labour-market conditions, and it could genuinely improve the bargaining position of its members by passing such information to them. A union which saw this as its chief function might sometimes advise its members to strike, not however in order to achieve artificially high wages by resort to force, but rather to test the market in order to establish higher wages that were economically sustainable and non-injurious.

Others independently reached conclusions similar to Hutt's. For instance, in the sixties, Enoch Powell shocked the *bien pensants* by denying that trade unions had produced any real benefits for their members. Anyone who believed that the rise in workers' standards of living was due to the action of unions would, Powell said, believe anything. 'It is the kind of absurdity which people only entertain when they are desperately determined to do so, for fear of the consequences of disbelief.' The standard of living of the working class had risen because labour had become more productive thanks to causes such as advances in scientific and technical knowledge, the greater availability of capital, and more efficient modes of organization. None of this had anything to do with restraint of trade or restriction of competition. At most, some trade unions might have affected 'the remuneration of labour in certain particular employments relatively either to the remuneration of other factors or to the remuneration of labour in other employments'. But even this possible effect, Powell maintained, conflicted with more experience. Workers in wholly non-unionized occupations, such as domestic service and secretarial employment, have secured advances as great as or greater than those which trade union leaders and shop-stewards were supposed to have obtained by force of combination. Moreover, wages in the highly unionized industries have risen more slowly than in industries where trade unions were very weak. Whether we like it or not, wages are determined by supply and demand. Therefore, any advantage secured by union coercion is bound to be short-lived, and even while it lasts it 'is always at the expense not only of the community at large but of other workers . . . because the higher cost of labour in that employment reduces demand for it and results in workers either being unemployed or being employed less remuneratively than they otherwise would be.'[10]

Nor was it true, Powell said, that unless wages were set by 'collective bargaining' the worker was at a disadvantage in relation to his employer. For labour is not 'the only perishable commodity which is lost if it is not sold'. The individual buyer of labour can no more influence the price by 'holding off' than can the individual seller of labour. Employers own equipment which would decay if not operated; they have bills to pay, overdrafts to service, orders to fill if they are not to lose customers to competitors, as well as a workforce to conserve despite the efforts of other employers to lure them away. For all these reasons, an employer in a competitive industry could not hope to overcome his employees in wage negotiations by locking them out. The effort would be suicidal, as the employer's customers would place their orders with his competitors. It follows that in a free market, employers have no unlimited power to exploit employees.

There is no more reason, Powell continued, to suppose that the price of labour has to be determined by collective bargaining than the price of carrots or cars. Indeed the 'crowning paradox' is that where collective bargaining is supposed to be indispensable, and operative, 'the real bargain' is in fact often determined by unofficial and varying bargains struck at the local level or by a pure market mechanism whereby the individual employer raises pay high enough to obtain or retain as many employees as he needs. The very people who think collective bargaining is indispensable do not and cannot use it in practice.

Michael Oakeshott pointed out a broader failing of unions, which identified them as among the greatest obstacles to the economic improvement of Britain. Strong unions are effective monopolies, which benefit their members at the expense of consumers. Their power to impose such exactions is enhanced if they can enter into collusion with monopolistic employers. So from the unions' standpoint the ideal setting is a nationalized industry, especially one where the demand for its product is inelastic. In that setting the supposed conflict between capital and labour could evaporate, to be replaced by a hidden attack of producers – employers and employees – on consumers, as management and unions colluded to raise both earnings and wages, these rises being funded by hiking up the prices of the industry's products.

The victims of this collusion, Oakeshott concluded, are consumers, among them union members. But they include also would-be workers whose potential jobs have been destroyed by the unduly high wages extracted by the union. The union is thus a contrivance of an organized minority to pursue its self-interest at the expense of the rest of the community, which pays the bill both in monopoly prices and disorder.[11]

Similar views were expressed repeatedly by F. A. Hayek, throughout the post-war years. And when the Thatcher Government came into office, he maintained that unless it instantly suppressed the monopoly power of unions it would be unable to control either inflation or unemployment, and would risk falling.

Others emphasized that unions injured economic efficiency by reducing differentially high payments to workers who were more skilled or efficient than others. In their view the growth of the trade unions accounted for the 'de-skilling' of Britain. Highly skilled craftsmen, formerly the uncrowned princes of the shop floor, lost their special standing as they were swallowed up in huge unions dominated by unskilled or semi-skilled workers. Typical of the destructive consequences was the long dispute between the toolmakers and the Amalgamated Union of Engineering Workers that ran between 1976 and 1979. The toolmakers called a number of strikes over shrinking pay differentials. Their leader was showered with abusive letters from union members. The employer, Leyland, would have wanted to pay its skilled men more but dared not bargain with them separately. As a result unskilled labourers received the same pay as skilled craftsmen, and numbers of Leyland craftsmen went off to become taxi drivers or insurance salesmen. In the three years up to January 1978, the Leyland works at Cowley could recruit only 117 toolmakers to fill the gap left by the 234 who had quit. According to the toolmakers' leader, Ray Fraser, the real reason for Britain's shortage of skilled labour, was not lack of training but the abolition of differential rewards imposed by unions dominated by the unskilled.

Not only did unions distort the patterns of pay. They were able also to extract pay rises quite unjustified by increases, if any, in productivity. In this way they throttled one company after another and whole industries. In the meantime they called for ever greater subsidies to keep the dying industries alive.

The Case of the Newspaper Industry

Nowhere was the power exercised by unions more effective than in Britain's newspaper industry, though the story could not be revealed until after the great battle at Wapping was won by the employer, Rupert Murdoch.

What had been going on in the newspaper industry was explained briefly and with shocking clarity in *The Times* on 3 February 1986, by Bernard Levin, under the headline: 'Fleet Street: now the truth can be told.' He began his account with an apparently irrelevant tale of the beginnings of mass advertising at the end of the nineteenth century. Once the same advertisement began to be placed in half a dozen newspapers, it seemed sensible to prepare one plate that could be used by all the newspapers instead of setting it separately for each paper. But the compositors who no longer did the typesetting for the advertisement that appeared in their paper refused to give up the pay for the work they no longer did. They insisted on being paid as if nothing had changed. And unbelievable though it may seem, the management agreed to pay them for this non-work and continued to do so until the Wapping revolution.

Bernard Levin's little tale was anything but irrelevant to his story about Fleet Street. It encapsulated the practice that became known on Fleet Street as 'fat', the practice of paying printers who did no work, a practice long continued. 'For many years now', Levin wrote, 'newspapers have been produced in conditions which combined a protection racket with a lunatic asylum; the details would have made interesting reading for those who bought the newspapers but any attempt to let the outside world know what was happening nightly would have led immediately to a strike.'

Given some of the happenings, Levin's description is an understatement. A printing press, which elsewhere was operated by four or five men, was run in London by eighteen men. It was in fact impossible for all of them to get near the machines at the same time, but that was of no account as most of the men never appeared. Because eight hours in a press room was uncomfortable, every eight-hour shift was split into two four-hour shifts. But though everyone worked only four hours each day, they were all paid as if they had worked eight hours. Moreover, a machine-room operator worked alternate half-shifts only on alternate days; but he was paid for a full week's work on full shifts. On Saturday nights extra hands were needed to print the Sunday papers. An additional half-shift was accordingly worked by an operator one Saturday in three weeks; but he was paid 'as though he had worked eight hours every Saturday of the month'. If in a certain department five of the fifteen employees left for one reason or another, the remaining ten would not allow the five to be replaced. They would insist instead that the weekly pay of the five non-workers should be divided among the remaining ten. Moreover, those ten now claimed that as they were doing the work of fifteen, they were owed additional payment for overtime (though they were not working longer hours). All this was demanded though the disappearance of the five demonstrated that they had not been needed in the first place.

Then Levin recounted the story of the imaginary button. Once upon a time, there had been a button that stopped or slowed down the presses when there was a snag further down the production line. For years there had been disputes about who had the right to press the button. With the move to Wapping, the button was replaced by an automatic emergency procedure. Nevertheless, union negotiators insisted that three men – one from each of the three unions – should be paid, full-time, to supervise an imaginary button.

Of course the management had no power to hire print workers; that power was reserved to the unions. Neither was the management permitted to reject a useless employee or to impose a retirement age. Since the *Sun*, however, by some anomaly, did have a partial retirement age of sixty-five, some print workers would retire at sixty-four, taking a slight reduction in their pension, and then enrol at *The Times* where they could 'continue until they could no longer climb the stairs to the wages office'.

A linotype operator paid by piece-work could get as much as £800 a week, which was nominally pay for thirty-five hours, though twenty-five hours was the maximum usually worked. To end this somewhat expensive arrangement, the management offered to 'buy out' the job by compensating the linotypers. But as negotiations got under way, similar compensation was demanded by other employees, who were not on piece-work, on the ground that they too might one day be working with new technology. When this was granted, a third group insisted on similar compensation even though the union demarcations would have prohibited them from ever doing such jobs. And finally, the assistants to this group also demanded 'buy-out' compensation, on the ground that their differential had been, or might be, eroded.

The story was the same with the lorries that distributed the newspapers. The unions insisted that if a lorry travelled beyond a certain distance, it must be staffed by three men. In fact, only one man ever appeared, but three were always paid. In addition, if the journey was over seventy-five miles, an hour's overtime had to be paid for every twenty miles of the distance, and paid not only to the driver but also to the two men who never appeared.

There was more to Levin's account and he assured his readers that he had by no means told it all. But, as he pointed out, the unions were not alone to blame. Without 'the ineptitude, cowardice, and folly of newspaper managements' they could never have maintained their empire.

That Murdoch should have become a synonym for Satan among the lovers of powerful trade unions is hardly surprising. For it was he who broke the stranglehold of the print workers by withstanding the year-long strike. But even he could not have done so except for the changes that the Thatcher Government had made in the labour laws and its willingness to enforce them.

New Rules

The Thatcher Government's efforts to legislate new rules for trade unions were not the first of their kind. Labour's dead-born 'In

Place of Strife' and the Heath Government's legislation had tried 'to do something' about trade unions. What distinguished the Thatcher programme was neither its breadth nor even the effectiveness with which it was executed, though there was plenty of both, but its repudiation of what had been the objectives of the earlier efforts. Both the Labour and the Heath governments were out to reform the union movement into a body that could act as a 'responsible social partner' along with industry and government in managing the economy. Their objective was to put in place a more effective corporatism. By contrast the Thatcher measures were designed to restore the contractual freedom of individual employees, to insist on the *voluntary* character of union membership as well as on democratic procedures for reaching union's decisions, and to revive among union members the pride that comes from doing one's job well.

Four pieces of legislation aimed at those results: the Employment Act 1980, the Employment Act 1982, the Trade Union Act 1984, and the Employment Act 1988.

The Thatcher legislation made three main changes. The closed shop was all but abolished. Union officials were made subject to democratic election and dismissal by members and to various safeguards against corrupt practices. Unions were obliged, in order to retain immunity from damages caused during industrial action, to follow prescribed procedures for securing the consent of the members to a strike, and were prohibited from extending their disputes to parties other than their members' employers. Taken together, these changes tended to transform unions by loosening their monolithic structures, autocratically controlled by a permanent corps of leaders, and to reshape them as once again voluntary associations of independent-minded individuals.

i. THE CLOSED SHOP

The 'unions' most potent weapon for enforcing obedience on their members and other employees was the closed shop. Nobody could be employed in a closed shop except members of the union, which had full power both to prevent someone from being employed and to enforce the dismissal of anyone who disobeyed union orders. In short, the closed shop gave the unions unlimited power over employees, and removed the employer's freedom to choose his employees.

Only gradually was the power of the closed shop whittled away. The 1980 Act provided compensation for people unreasonably excluded or expelled from a union in a closed shop; required that a new closed shop had to be approved in a secret ballot by four-fifths of the workers affected; made public funds available for holding secret ballots; and made it unfair to dismiss a person who had a conscientious objection to joining the union, or who had worked for the employer before the closed shop came into effect. The 1980 Act was acknowledged not to have gone very far, because none of this seriously inhibited the unions from pursuing their old practices.

More effective action, indeed a new spirit in industrial relations, was introduced by Norman Tebbit's legislation in 1982. It empowered the Government to compensate those dismissed, under Labour's legislation of 1974 to 1979 because they failed to join a union where there was a closed shop. The 1982 Act made it 'unfair' at law to dismiss an employee for not being a union member unless the closed-shop agreement had been approved during the previous five years in a secret ballot of employees. It outlawed 'union labour only' contracts, which prohibited employers from dealing with firms that were not 'closed shops'. But it was not until the Employment Act of 1988 that all the qualifications in the earlier legislation which allowed some measure of legal protection to the 'closed shop' were finally abolished. That Act made it quite simply 'unfair' to dismiss anyone for failing to join a union, thus leaving individuals free to decide for themselves whether or not to join.

No one denied that the effects of the legislation were noticeable. Whereas in 1978 some 5.2 million people had been employed in closed shops, by 1989 the number had declined to about 3.5 million.

ii. NEW INTERNAL PROCEDURES

The Trade Union Act of 1984 concentrated on reforming the internal procedures of unions. The rules of unions were surprisingly devoid of elementary precautions to protect members against abuses by officials. No accurate registers were kept of the members' names and addresses. No adequate checks disclosed how union funds were acquired, used, or stored. All this was rectified by the 1984 Act. In addition, it required that all voting members of the union executive should be elected by secret ballot at least once in every five years. Members acquired a right to complain of violations of any of these procedures to the courts or to the Arbitration Officer. In addition, there was the not very onerous requirement that a union's political fund, supplied by members' contributions and spent on causes chosen by the executive (such as contributions to the Labour Party), had to be endorsed every ten years by secret ballot. Employers who deducted union subscriptions from employees' pay were obliged to discontinue deducting political contributions from the pay of any employee who so desired.

Furthermore the 1984 Act required a practice which might have been expected to be well established but was in fact a great novelty when introduced. Members were given the right to inspect a union's financial accounts as well as a right of access to the accountant. In addition, elections and compulsory ballots on political funds had to be conducted entirely by postal ballots supervised by independent agencies.

iii. STRIKES

Quite apart from maintaining a closed shop, unions had been able to coerce members by calling strikes without their approval. Power to call strikes was exercised by national officials and by shop stewards as well. Anyone who refused to come out on strike could be expelled from the union and thereby from his job; if he tried to escape that punishment by seeking work in another enterprise he would find himself 'blacklisted' by all unions and so rendered unemployable. Physical intimidation of members reluctant to strike or picket was not unknown, and the power of union chieftains like Arthur Scargill of the National Union of Mineworkers seemed to be unassailable.

One of the most important changes introduced by the Trade Union Act of 1984 was the requirement that a union had to hold a ballot *before* it endorsed or authorized any 'industrial action'. If it held a ballot afterwards, it would be liable for any damages resulting from action taking place before the ballot. If a union failed to comply with these provisions, it could be sued by employers who suffered a loss of custom as a result of the union's action.

All these reforms were made yet more effective by the Employment Act of 1988. Individual members gained the right to seek an injunction against their union if it unlawfully authorized or induced industrial action. Members unjustifiably disciplined for failing to take part in industrial action could now seek legal redress. Under certain circumstances, unions were required to conduct separate ballots in each of its members' workplaces.

By October of 1990 the *Sunday Times* reported that 'Like some increasingly insubstantial ghost, the indefatigable Mr Arthur Scargill is making yet another bid to persuade his dwindling band of followers ... to forgo a large part of their earnings by stopping overtime.' The reporter had discovered moreover that 'although the workforce and the number of pits had been cut by around two thirds since 1985, in 1989, the actual amount of coal produced remained almost exactly the same, at just over 100 million tons.' Production per employee had almost trebled since the strike, from 550 tons to 1544 tons. Workers' earnings had almost doubled, and British Coal had converted losses in the vicinity of 1 billion per year into modest profits. 'The really astonishing irony of the story is that by turning his union into a complete irrelevance and himself into a haunting and absurd figure, Arthur Scargill has actually done more for British miners and for the industry than anyone has for decades.'[12]

The Unions Hit Back

Unions made three dramatic efforts to reassert their power. These were the miners' strike in 1984–5, the strike at Wapping against Murdoch's News International in 1986, and the Dock Strike in 1989. That any of these should have ended in total defeat for the union would have been held to be unthinkable when Mrs Thatcher came to office. Indeed even some of her ministerial colleagues continued to rub their eyes and insist that the emperor was wearing clothes until the very last moment when the awful truth was acknowledged by the unions, even if not by all Conservatives.

The most dramatic of these events was the miners' strike of 1984–5. Arthur Scargill, the leader of the National Union of Mineworkers, did not even pretend that he was merely out to raise wages. He made it perfectly clear that his purpose was to bring down the Thatcher Government. Nor did he bother to abide by his own union's rules which required that 'a strike shall be entered upon as the result of a ballot vote of the members.' The miners in Nottinghamshire, Derbyshire, and Lancashire, who wished to remain at work, were not allowed to vote. Of the seventy thousand miners who were balloted, over fifty thousand voted to continue working. Scargill was undeterred by such opinions. As a result, after the strike was over, some thirty thousand miners broke away to form the Union of Democratic Mineworkers.

Scargill rested his case on opposition to the Coal Board's closing of uneconomic pits, as well as to other changes that might make the coal industry more efficient. As the Minister in charge, Peter Walker, put it, 'He has made one demand throughout – that every pit, no matter what the price of coal produced from it, must be kept going until every ton of coal in it has been exhausted. That is a claim that no leader of the NUM has ever made before. It is one that no Labour Government has ever conceded or even thought about. It is a claim that no management and no one with any sane view about the industry could ever think about.'[13]

The strike kept the television screens filled with scenes of violence which, despite television producers' efforts to give as much prominence as possible to police truncheons, made it difficult to think of trade unionists as starving, weak, oppressed pacifists. Over ten thousand criminal charges were brought during the strike, and Mr Scargill indicated his approval of the miscreants in a statement to a Hungarian newspaper: 'The strike ... offered a challenge against the heart of the capitalist system ... what I am thinking about ... is the influence exercised by the strike on British society.'[14]

One of the more amusing aspects of the affair was its effect on journalists. The pundits of the media argued vehemently, on the one hand (if only by insinuation), that the Thatcher Government – which they insisted on using as a synonym for the Coal Board, whose head, Ian MacGregor, was notoriously formidable and immune to any 'handbagging' by the Prime Minister – had no pity for the poor miners, and was determined to keep them working and living in conditions that no human being should be made to endure. But on the other hand, when faced with the Coal Board's arguments that pits could be closed without any compulsory redundancies, leaving the industry more prosperous and able to raise the pay of its employees as well as to sell more coal, the pundits on television and in the newspapers, and of course Labour politicians, suddenly became besotted by the joys of being a miner. They discovered that mining coal was the most delightful of all possible occupations, that every miner wanted nothing so much as to have his sons follow him down the shaft, that there was no community more idyllic than an old mining village, that never before in the world's history had mines been shut down or miners asked to move away from the villages in which they had been born and lived to villages near productive seams. Unfortunately, the nation was deprived of much harmless amusement because no journalist had the wit to reprint some of the earlier reflections on the joys of being a miner, the moral of which was, to say the least, somewhat different.

Whereas in earlier miners' strikes, the government had been caught napping and responded ineffectively, this time the tables were turned. In 1981, the Thatcher Government had given in when Scargill began blowing his war trumpet; it did not yet feel ready to do battle with the NUM. But by 1984, the Government had amassed great stocks of coal above ground and had made other arrangements to carry the country through without resorting to a three-day work-week. It followed a strategy that had been prepared in 1978 by Nicholas Ridley. Scargill, for his part, had timed his campaign poorly, attacking in the spring when the demand for coal was decreasing.

The last act of the coal strike turned into farce, when Scargill and his cohorts were accused of serious irregularities in the handling of union funds. After many accusations, threats, and counter-accusations, Scargill was neither exonerated nor convicted. But the lion's teeth had been drawn. Scargill lost his reputation for invincibility.

Next to the Coal Strike, the most notorious piece of union militancy was the strike against News International, publishers of *The Times*, the *Sunday Times* and the *Sun*, after it had been formed by Murdoch, who moved the publishing and printing from Gray's Inn Road to what became known as 'Fortress Wapping'. On 23 January 1986, News International announced that the journalists would transfer to Wapping the next day, but not the six thousand print workers. Although the unions had been told that Wapping was to be used to print only the new evening paper, the *London Post*, the company had in fact arranged to move production of all News International titles to Wapping. And it had recruited members of the electricians' union, EEPTU, to run the new plant in place of the print workers, who were less skilled in handling the new electronic technology installed at Wapping. The distribution of the papers, which had previously also been controlled by the print unions, was turned over to Thorns National Transport, a privately owned sub-contractor.

By leaving the print union members behind when it moved to Wapping, News International inaugurated a revolution in the newspaper world. Previously moribund and weighed down by debt, newspapers began to flourish. New ventures in quality newspapers, as well as tabloids, sprang into existence once the new technology, which had been available for some years, could be put to use. Whereas before journalists had been moaning that they would soon all be unemployed, after Wapping not especially talented young graduates, who could learn to work a word processor, readily found jobs in journalism at very generous salaries. None of this could have happened without the long hard fight by News International, and the legislation which had made it possible to destroy the power of the unions to prevent any change in the production of newspapers.

The unions involved, SOGAT and the NGA, decided to resist the management with all their resources. They demanded full reinstatement of the six thousand sacked employees, and mounted a gigantic picketing operation at the Wapping plant to delay or prevent the production and distribution of newspapers by making it difficult for any person or vehicle to enter or leave the premises. Journalists got in only by whipping past the pickets in taxis, while turning a deaf ear to the insults hurled at them.

Every Wednesday and Saturday the drama was heightened by evening marches from Tower Hill to the 'Fortress Wapping', which was protected by barbed wire and spotlights. Marchers were numbered in the thousands; on 6 April, fifteen thousand joined a march from Trafalgar Square to Wapping organized by the TUC. But after the May Day march, of some ten thousand, numbers trailed off sharply.

Throughout the period of massive demonstrations, continuous picketing, frequent arrests and prosecutions for violence, and the sequestration of 400,000 of SOGAT's funds following its refusal to obey a court order terminating its boycott of News International papers, negotiations between management and unions continued. Towards the beginning of May, Murdoch offered the unions 15 million and *The Times'* former premises in Gray's Inn Road so that they could start a newspaper of their own. Later in May he offered 50 million in redundancy payments along with the building in Gray's Inn Road. The *Sun* journalists withdrew their threat to stop working after they were offered a pay increase and sports facilities. In September, Murdoch upped his offer of redundancy payments to 60 million, which the unions rejected. He then offered individual redundancy deals. Finally, on 2 February 1987, SOGAT voted to end the dispute and on 7 February, the NGA followed suit. Peace descended on Wapping, and national newspapers entered a new era of reasonable industrial relations.

The third notable union drama under Thatcherism took place at the docks. Ever since the Second World War, when fear of a dock strike led the government to make any concessions needed to keep the docks open, the employers had been held to ransom by the unions under the Dock Labour Scheme. It guaranteed jobs for life to 9,400 dockers and fostered practices like 'ghosting' – watching idly while another man trained to do your job – and 'bobbing' – clocking in and 'bobbing' off home. In the 1960s, unofficial strike action by dockers was a normal part of British life.

By imposing colossal overmanning, the Dock Labour Scheme had succeeded in bringing major British ports nearly to a standstill. Ports not bound by the Scheme, such as Dover and Felixstowe, attracted traffic from all corners of Britain, often travelling on highly unsatisfactory roads. Ports outside the Scheme flourished while the others languished. Efforts to amend the Dock Scheme by negotiation were all rejected by the unions under the direction of Ron Todd the General Secretary of the Transport and General Workers' Union. When now and then the management did try to make a stand, the government, ever fearful of provoking a strike, invariably removed or neutralized 'tough' managerial representatives from the negotiations. The iniquities and idiocies of the Dock Labour Scheme were thoroughly exposed in a pamphlet, *Clear the Docks: Abolish the Dock Labour Scheme*, by David Davis MP, published by the Centre for Policy Studies in 1988. By then, port employers were beginning to be less fearful and sluggish, and readier to think of developing the twenty thousand acres of industrial land awaiting development in Scheme ports. Finally, in 1989, the Government acted to abolish the Scheme.

The dockers attempted to stage a strike, but the walk-outs were patchy. Since secondary action and mass picketing had been outlawed, the strike had little chance of success and indeed did not succeed in halting the abolition of the Dock Labour Scheme. Within ten days of starting, some two thousand dockers were back at work and by the time the strike was called off, a majority of dockers had returned. Once it was over, the labour force shrank and local bargaining replaced the national agreement.

Peace Restored

By 1989, union ascendancy belonged to the past. At that year's Trades Union Congress in Blackpool, a succession of speakers sponsored a resolution, carried unanimously, which demanded that all the Thatcher 'anti-union' laws be repealed and replaced by legislation enshrining the right to strike. Labour's front-bench employment spokesman, Tony Blair, denounced the last of the Government's Bills, which ended the closed shop, curbed unofficial strikes and restricted sympathy stoppages, as 'extreme and bigoted'. But at the same time, Mr Blair announced that in principle Labour no longer supported the closed shop, and he carefully evaded any firm commitment to counteract the Government's other proposals. That was the last gasp of the old unionism. The only bargain that the TUC was able to make with the Thatcher Government was an agreement to police their political funds more strictly.

To Norman Tebbit, the unions seemed to have fallen into pathetic wishful thinking. At their Conference of 1989, he said, 'the old men of the TUC' sat up late in the bars, 'misty eyed with sentiment and becoming quite emotional as they recalled long-past triumphs of mass secondary picketing, car park mass meetings and legal immunities. They remembered how they once had the power to force businesses or even whole industries into bankruptcy and to punish miscreants for such horrible crimes as refusing to strike, or belonging to the wrong union.' In recent years, 'such retelling of the Luddite sagas of Grunwick, Saltley Coke Works and the busting of British Leyland had been sad occasions, rather like the meetings of Citizens for the Restoration of the Bourbon Monarchy or old cavalrymen reminiscing about Balaclava and the other great charges before the days of the Panzers.' But in 1989 the delegates were full of hope, thanks to Labour's lead in the polls, the Government's economic problems, and the success of strikes against British Rail and the town halls. Tebbit warned them, however, against false confidence. Of course, by 1989 the proportion of people believing that the unions were too powerful had halved since 1979: 'As the architect of the Government's trade union legislation, I would have been appalled had that not been so.' And Tebbit reminded them that if the pollsters had asked instead whether the law should be changed to restore the unions' old immunities, 'the answer to that question would have wiped off a smile or two from the faces of the union leaders assembled in Blackpool.'[15]

There was no longer any ground for a lament like that of T. E. Utley who, shortly before Mrs Thatcher became Prime Minister, had declared that he far preferred 'perpetual strife between government and trade unions, continual disruption of industry, even public and humiliating defeats for political authority at the hands of the unions' to 'the silent surrender of sovereignty which is now going on and which will increasingly reduce Parliament to the function of rubber-stamping agreements reached behind closed doors between the Cabinet and the TUC'.[16]

By 1 May 1991, the government's arbitration service, ACAS, reported that in the past year official strikes had fallen to their lowest in fifty-five years. And days lost due to industrial action were the fewest since 1963. The chairman, Mr Douglas Smith, attributed the change to more realism in the unions and to the legal requirement for pre-strike ballots. He also reported that union membership had declined by one quarter in recent years, especially in industries such as coal, steel, shipbuilding and engineering, and that unions were unable to recruit effectively in growing areas of employment such as finance and part-time work.[17]

So much had the power of unions diminished as Mrs Thatcher began her twelfth year in office, and so much had previous antagonism to them faded, that the *Sunday Telegraph* – whose leader writers never had understood Thatcherism's commitment to 'doing the right thing' – thought that they should once again be heard in the councils of state. It would no longer be dangerous for the government to talk with the TUC, said a leader. 'A chastened TUC could now play a constructive role in the coming months . . . Of course some Tories said, "Don't touch them with a bargepole", but in our view . . . talking this time could be valuable.'[18]

But the issue had been definitively settled in favour of the rule of law. Earlier in the 1980s, fierce disputes had raged in better-educated Conservative circles about whether Lord Denning's bending of the law to protect the rights of individuals against the iniquitous immunities of trade unions should be applauded or condemned. Jonathan Sumption pointed out that there had been a curious reversal in public opinion: whereas in the past 'those who have urged judges to bend the law to some higher social purpose of their own have more often been on the Left than on the Right', now the Right welcomed Denning's flouting of the law because they had become so obsessed with the power of trade unions. Sumption warned against this corrupting tendency. The rule of law, he said, 'depends in large measure on the propensity of the losing party to accept the result. He may not accept with very good grace, but he can always console himself with the thought that he has been defeated by an impersonal body of principles and that the law is an ass.'[19]

Many Thatcherites were inclined to dismiss Sumption's argument as priggish. Not so the Prime Minister, though she never publicly pronounced on the question. She was one of those Britons who knew in their bones, whether they could or did put it in so many words, that if Parliament was to remain sovereign, judges as well as trade unionists had to observe the law; judges had to interpret the law rather than change it.

Temptations to forget that had been removed by the Thatcherite labour legislation. It legitimately changed the law so as to provide the kind of protection that Lord Denning had tried illegitimately to introduce by judicial dictate. Once that legislation was in place, however much the trade unions flourished, no one had reason to doubt that the 'silent surrender of sovereignty' to powerful interest groups, which had distinguished British government since the Second World War, had ceased. No such surrender could be tolerated in the Britain envisaged by Thatcherism.

In taking such 'tough' measures on trade unions, the Thatcher Government was answering a widespread and deeply felt public demand to be liberated from a tyranny which, apart from its effects on employees, had made it impossible for Britons to know from one day to the next what stoppage would produce chaos in their daily life. Indeed nothing served the Government better than to be accused by Labour of 'union bashing', a taunt that damaged Labour as much as it benefited the Tories. The action that the Thatcher

Government took to end the abuse of trade union power was a prime example of the paradigm shift. It identified the problem as one caused by government action and then changed that action. The legislation was designed to remove obstacles to the thriving of Britain and to the freedom needed by individuals to be independent, efficient and honest workmen which had been installed by the immunities that previous governments had bestowed upon trade unions.

7

The Illusion of Local Government

Next to the trade unions, Thatcherism's greatest bugbear has been 'local government'. The picture of the Thatcherite relationship to local councils is usually painted in vivid colours: Mrs Thatcher is portrayed as a 'centralist' dictator mounting an all-out attack on ancient bastions of local autonomy and liberty; the poll tax is represented as the most powerful weapon in her centralist armoury, and one which backfired horribly, contributing significantly to her untimely demise.

This picture raises extremely serious difficulties for understanding Thatcherism as a promoter of the vigorous virtues and a 'paradigm shift'. How can this view of Thatcherism be reconciled with a centralist and dictatorial attempt to stifle local autonomy? Moreover, the usual picture of Thatcherism appears also to have presented insurmountable difficulties for previous commentators – for the subject of Thatcherite policies regarding local government, though admitted by all to be of the utmost importance, has in practice been all but ignored in the various comprehensive attempts to explain what Mrs Thatcher was out to do.

The reason why the usual picture of the relation between the Thatcher Government and local government poses such problems is that it is a radically false picture. Local government was *not* an ancient bastion of local autonomy and liberty; and the Thatcher Government's attack on it was the very opposite of an attempt to centralize. Indeed, once the history of British local authorities themselves and of the Thatcherite war on them is properly understood, it becomes apparent that – whether sensibly or utterly misguidedly – the motives for the policies were precisely those that one would expect if one identified Thatcherism with the promotion of the vigorous virtues and the paradigm shift.

The Myth of Local Autonomy

Both the Conservative and Labour parties have repeatedly declared their devotion to local autonomy. In its 1970 White Paper, *Reform of Local Government in England*, the then Labour Government pledged its determination to reverse 'the present trends towards centralization' and to restore the place of 'local democracy' in 'our democratic system'. In the following year a Conservative government declared in its White Paper on *Local Government in England*, that 'a vigorous local democracy means that authorities must be given real functions – with powers of decision and the ability to take action without being subjected to excessive regulation by central government through financial or other controls'.

These protestations were, however, a matter of ritual rather than reality. In fact, since 1945, there has been a consistent pattern in the relationship between local authorities and the central government: the government declares its devotion to local democracy and self-government; local authorities ask the central government for more money and less control; when economic conditions begin to deteriorate, the central government increases control; local authorities protest that the tyranny of central government has passed all decent limits and must cease.

It ought not to surprise anyone with a sense of British history that the rhetoric of local autonomy fails to be carried through into practice. For local government in Britain has never been autonomous. What we now call local government has a continuous history which can be documented from medieval times. But what we find when we look for its ancestry are two unlikely institutions. One is a court of law, created by Henry II, presided over by travelling justices who came in time to exercise other administrative functions and to act as protectors of local interests. The other is the borough, which was a settlement with a market within walls, which appeared before the Norman Conquest, and possessed, *by charter from the King* and by custom, certain privileges. Historians disagree about which of these two is the ultimate ancestor, but they generally accept that the arrangements developed by the boroughs became the nucleus of municipal government.

The privileges granted by the King to the boroughs did *not* include the right to tax themselves except for the most obvious practical needs, and their annual revenue was accordingly negligible. The boroughs' only court was presided over by Crown officials who also collected payments due to the King. And the Alderman administered the borough community only under the supervision of the King's reeve and with support from the King's sheriff.

Nor were the medieval antecedents of local government anything like democratically elected bodies. Although everyone, apart from the extremely poor, was subject to municipal rates as well as royal taxes, the *communitas burgensium* rarely, if ever, included all the householders. Only traders and master craftsmen were admitted to a gild. Officials and professional men were excluded by their work, and small tradesmen and craftsmen by the entrance fees and property qualifications. The right to elect MPs was more often than not confined to members of the governing bodies, which were mainly concerned with keeping the peace. In the rural parts of the country, the Justices of the Peace in the parishes performed the same duties.

In short, England was never the 'association or federation of self-governing communities' so admired by the German historians who wrote the first general history of English local government.[1] Nor was there ever anything like the 'free and autonomous village community' invented by Beatrice and Sidney Webb in their history of local government.[2]

The only resemblance to the local government of popular imagination appeared in the practice of freeholders in parishes, in the eighteenth and early nineteenth century, to assemble under the sheriff in the counties or the mayor in towns or in the open vestries of the parishes, to debate matters of local or national interest and occasionally to send petitions to Parliament. But before the end of the age of Queen Victoria, such meetings became extinct. The provision of 1872 that a meeting of ratepayers had to give its approval before the borough council could promote a Bill in Parliament, became a vestige long before it was abolished in 1972. Town meetings and parish meetings, except on rare occasions, were attended by very few.

New powers were acquired and new local bodies came into existence not through autonomous local decisions but through Acts of Parliament. Thus bodies were set up to provide drainage, roads, sewers, water, highways. The parishes acquired responsibility for looking after the poor, under the supervision of the Justices of the Peace, through the Elizabethan Poor Law Acts. And through such Acts of Parliament, there grew up between the fourteenth and nineteenth centuries a disorderly patchwork of local bodies engaged in a variety of activities, whose functions and boundaries often overlapped and whose administration was not always distinguished by either probity or efficiency.

The first major effort to give local government a more systematic character, the Municipal Corporations Act of 1835, made explicit the legal limits of local powers. They were defined by the principle of *ultra vires* which, by explicitly prohibiting local authorities from doing anything not delegated to them by law, made it clear that they existed only for the purposes established by an Act of Parliament. The 1835 Act formally recognized what had from medieval times been accepted in practice, that the powers of local authorities were not derived from any constitutional principles (as in the United States) but depended wholly on grants from Parliament which it could give or withhold at pleasure. In other words, the local authorities were not governments but agents of Parliament. Indeed the term 'local government' did not come into use until the latter part of the nineteenth century.[3]

The Growth of Local Government Powers

It was as agents of the central government, engaging in welfare activities, that the local authorities acquired many new duties in the course of the nineteenth century. But the extension of the powers of local authorities went hand in hand with greater control by Westminster. District auditors, who checked the accounts of municipal corporations, were just one of the many kinds of officers appointed to inspect the services provided by local authorities. Indeed, it was because the central government saw itself as the ruler of local authorities that it was willing – through Parliament – to delegate to them increasing powers over welfare. As the Royal Sanitary Commission of 1871 put it, 'local administration under central superintendence [was] the distinguishing feature of our local government'.[4]

The same was true even of London. Because Peel was reluctant to entrust the police to any existing local bodies, a new authority – the Metropolitan Police – was created in 1829. The City of London had its own police force and was a kingdom to itself. Otherwise, there were assorted parish assemblies, local paving trusts, commissions of sewers, and water companies. These were consolidated in 1855 into the Metropolitan Board of Works, which took charge of building a drainage system for London, constructing the embankment of the Thames and streets such as Charing Cross Road and Shaftesbury Avenue, organizing fire and building regulations, gas supplies and the management of parks. As the Metropolitan Board became notorious for incompetence and corruption, Parliament replaced it in 1888 by a directly elected London County Council.

By 1900, local authorities were not only building houses, running schoolboards and employment bureaus, but also dealing with sanitary services, police, highways, water, gas, electricity, trams, buses, libraries, cemeteries, docks, entertainment, racecourses, telephone services, stolen property, blackmail, gambling houses, cruelty to animals, the sale of poisons; they regulated coffee and tea houses, brothels, dairies, and pawnbrokers; and established reading rooms as well as restaurants in parks.[5]

Despite these increasing powers, it was taken for granted until the end of the nineteenth century that local authorities were nothing but convenient administrative units for performing a limited set of activities. By the middle of the twentieth century, however, both the Labour and the Conservative parties were willing to contribute to the creation of far larger and more powerful local authorities which have since waged war on the central government, whatever the ruling party. The London County Council was replaced by the Greater London Council, which, in addition to the old LCC areas, took control of most of Middlesex, and some portions of Surrey, Kent, and Hertfordshire. Although the Redcliffe-Maud Royal Commission on Local Government (1966) admitted that it had found no 'relationship between size and functional effectiveness', it accepted 'the general atmosphere' which surrounded its work and concluded that 250,000 was the minimum population for effectively run educational and social services.[6] The proposal for consolidating small diverse local authorities into large uniform ones was described as 'rationalization' and was praised effusively by the Labour Prime Minister who, however, lost power before he could implement it. The Conservative Government led by Heath accepted many of the Redcliffe-Maud proposals, and in order to achieve what they described as 'a genuine devolution of power from the Central Government'[7], established two tiers of local government – large boroughs and districts and, over these, even larger and more powerful county councils.

But even before this great consolidation, the power of local authorities had been expanding dramatically since 1945. The pattern of growth is well illustrated in the housing policies. By 1975, almost a quarter of local authority capital and revenue spending was absorbed by housing. The GLC alone spent at its height £500 million each year, while boroughs like Camden or Lambeth were spending about £70 million annually (at 1982 prices). Between 1945 and 1965, 670,000 dwellings were destroyed by local authorities and replaced with nearly three million. By 1978, local authorities controlled a third of the housing stock in England and over half in Scotland.

Not unreasonably, given the great extent of their powers as arbiters of planning, education, housing and allocation of priorities for finance and space, local authorities were by the late seventies thinking of themselves as being in charge of the overall economic, cultural, and physical well-being of the country. They remained free to use their rate support grants as they saw fit within the limits set by their statutory functions. They were not seriously hampered by the loan sanction procedure, or the possibility that the central government could withold their grants. Such sanctions existed chiefly in theory and were rarely used. In practice, relations between departments of government and local authorities were a combination of advice, exhortation, promotion and inspection and if a local authority made a determined stand against the advice or guidance offered, the government had neither the authority nor the power to compel submission. When, in 1967, the Committee on the Management of Local Government did a survey of attitudes among local councillors, they found that some were not even aware that the *ultra vires* rule could restrain them.

The Growth of Local Government Spending

One effect of the central government's increasing extension of the power of local authorities was that, unsurprisingly, expenditure rose like a well-made soufflé. In the period between 1900 and 1970, when (allowing for the change in the value of money) national income doubled, spending by local authorities increased elevenfold. A local council officer is reported as saying, 'Members of the public usually leave a good few noughts off the bill when they think of what we spend.'[8] The growth in spending was made possible by a striking growth in the funds supplied by the central government. Regular grants from the central government did not begin until 1879, when they constituted less than a tenth of the total income of local authorities, the rest being supplied by rates, and the rate bills were small – in 1870, they were a sixth of what they were in 1987. After the end of the Second World War, grants from the government constituted about half of the local authorities' income, and, by the 1970s, only a third of local spending was supported from the rates. As Richard Crossman explained to Parliament in 1965, 'the more you are forced to shift the burden from the shoulders of the ratepayers to those of the taxpayers, the more you strengthen Whitehall against the town hall.' He himself assisted this shift by introducing domestic rate relief. In 1976, the Committee of Inquiry on Local Government Finance reported to the Labour Government that 'power has progressively moved towards the government . . . The Rate Support Grant determination has in the last two years become an occasion for the Government to give increasingly detailed guidance to local authorities about their pattern of expenditure.'[9]

The numbers of people employed by local authorities rose even more dramatically than did their expenditure. According to a study which made a considerable stir in the late seventies, there had been almost a seventy per cent increase in the number of local government employees between 1961 and 1975.[10] No one was very surprised when the Audit Commission declared that the same services 'could be delivered in many cases at much lower cost and that the first step for most local authorities must be to reduce manpower'.[11]

By the mid-seventies, the fact that something was amiss in the conduct of many local authorities was widely recognized in the Labour Party as well as elsewhere. The Labour Government of 1974 set good precedents for the efforts of the Thatcher Government to curb the spending of the local councils. In 1975, the Secretary of State for the Environment, Anthony Crosland, declared that 'the party was over'. The following year, local authorities received a circular saying that 'It is now essential that the projections of local authorities be revised so that the overall total of local authority current expenditure be brought into line with the general figure for public expenditure even though rates would have to be increased by fifteen per cent and twenty to thirty thousand jobs eliminated.'[12] The exercise was repeated in 1977 by Crosland's successor, Peter Shore. There were also substantial cuts in grants so that by 1978–9 the rate of grant from the Exchequer was reduced by sixty-one per cent. Even when Labour went into opposition and began attacking the Tory government for not spending enough, their Environment spokesman nevertheless promised that when Labour returned there would be 'no pork barrel for local government . . . no blank cheques, no easy money'.[13]

It had become obvious by the mid-seventies that while the local authorities were spending furiously, the services they provided were in many cases derisory. Even those sympathetic to the Labour Councils concluded that they had 'conspicuously failed to address the problem, let alone resolve, the tension between the interests of producers and the interests of consumers: or to develop clear priorities between policies to improve service provision for the local community and measures to better terms and conditions of staff. This was in part because the rhetoric of the Left constantly confused the two. The struggle that councils were engaged in was "to defend jobs and services" which were seen as inseparable. The uncomfortable reality that services could be protected while jobs were lost, or vice versa, was not confronted. At the most simplistic level, sections of the hard Left identified their interests entirely with those of the town hall unions because they saw them as the key local representatives of the working class.'[14]

Local Government as a Base for Socialism

The significance of the increasing shift of powers by central government to local government, and of the increasing ability of local government to spend money unchecked by Parliament, was not lost on socialists. Even by the end of the nineteenth century, the Webbs and other socialists saw local government as a vehicle for socialism. Before the Labour Party itself was established, socialist and trade union candidates began to stand in local elections. At the Trades Union Congress in 1899, it was reported that at least seventy Labour representatives had been elected to town councils. From 1899, some sort of organization in the Labour Party kept the local authorities in touch with the party's headquarters. Labour groups on town councils were supported with advice and information by the Fabian Society, and by the end of the First World War, Labour had achieved strongholds or complete control in many provincial as well as metropolitan boroughs and county councils.

Nor was it only the Fabians and the Labour Party that used local government as a means of achieving socialist or quasi-socialist aims. Liberals and 'middle way' Tories were as much involved. Again, the history of housing makes the point. The power of local authorities to build houses was established by legislation in 1868 and 1890, on the grounds that housing was an aspect of public health, and that local authorities would in extreme circumstances provide suitable quarters for families living in unhealthy conditions. But this modest aim disappeared by the end of the First World War when Lloyd George called for 'homes for heroes' and subsidized the demolition of nearly three hundred thousand houses and the building of almost a million and a half. After the Second World War, grand strategies for local authority housing continued to be provided by both parties. In 1951, the Conservative Minister of Housing, Harold Macmillan, set himself to build three hundred thousand houses a year, and received a standing ovation at the Party conference of 1952 for showing that the Tories were the party who got things done. When Richard Crossman became Minister of Housing under Labour in 1964 he concluded that four hundred thousand houses had to be built in the next twelve months, and Wilson decided 'that all other social services must be cut back in order to have a magnificent housing drive'. They were certain that it could be done quickly and economically by using 'industrialized methods' or what was called 'system building', and wanted none of that nonsense about rehabilitating old houses or clearing 'one little bit' at a time. Much better, Crossman thought, 'to pull the whole bloody thing down' and 'have a real demonstration that our system building can work'. No nonsense either about local self-government. The Permanent Secretary at the Ministry of Housing loved the New Towns 'because they have been created autocratically from above'.[15]

Nevertheless, local authorities happily obliged the Minister. One of the most enthusiastic was the Greater London Council which destroyed terrace after terrace of solid and handsome houses, leaving whole areas derelict and communities irrevocably dispersed, as the inspectors did not bother to examine the houses carefully or to calculate the comparative cost of redevelopment and renovation. Redevelopment took so long that the shortage of housing was considerably exacerbated. As commercial properties were destroyed, jobs were lost. Cities became disfigured by brutal concrete blocks which spread like a cancer among the houses that were allowed to remain. When Crossman went to visit Wigan where the council, having 'undertaken an enormous building programme', had produced 'thousands of council houses', he found that they were 'of an appalling dimness and dullness, and I am afraid that they have built a Wigan that in 2000 will look just as bad as the old 1880 Wigan looks in the eyes of the 1960s'.[16]

Those whose homes were demolished were not consulted and preservation societies who demonstrated that more housing could be had at a lower cost by rehabilitation were scorned. The official excuse for the destruction was obsolescence, but in many cases, such as in Camden, Wandsworth, Hackney, Islington and Lambeth, it was inspired by antipathy to middle-class owner-occupiers. By the seventies the damage that had been done began to be recognized. It was a Labour Environment Secretary, Anthony Crosland, who in January 1975 expressed concern and refused to confirm more compulsory purchase orders, pointing out that the 'housing gain proposed by the Council can only be gained, if at all, at the cost of immense disturbance and disruption', that 'the redevelopment . . . will result in a numerical housing loss; the substantial majority of existing houses are in good condition . . . A high proportion . . . are in occupation by owners who wish to retain them.' When in 1978, the Department of Environment required local authorities to take into account the effects of demolition on the people whose houses had been destroyed, along with the comparative costs of renovation, it was too late.[17]

One of the unintended consequences of the housing spree was to change the character of many Labour councils. The inner cities lost their skilled workers and were left with those, like the old and immigrants, who could not so easily move. But in place of those who had gone, there came younger professional people to fill the many jobs and to staff the various organizations of the local authorities. These people, who had earlier been connected with a variety of radical organizations, became the 'activists' who founded the 'new urban Left'. Their takeover was assisted by Labour's heavy losses in the 1968 election, which removed many of the old Labour hands from the scene.

The new lot joined the Labour Party with the object of shaking it out of its 'lethargy' and fighting the 'paternalism' of the Labour councils. Adept at forming alliances, when the Campaign for

Labour Party Democracy began demanding mandatory reselection of Members of Parliament, they came into the open. Each ward became a battleground between Left and Right in the Labour Party. Wherever the New Left took over – the number of their strongholds had increased markedly by 1971 – they set out to spend and to redistribute wealth. Rates rose and kept rising. Waiting lists for municipal housing were scrapped and tenants boldly relocated thus providing blocks of safe voters. Organizations to liberate women, gays, blacks proliferated. Public transportation was made free of charge, but services like the collection of rubbish or the removal of litter languished. Socialist republics in practice, and sometimes with names, statues and flags to match, flourished in South Yorkshire, Manchester, Lothian, Liverpool, Merseyside, Lambeth, Hackney, Islington and Camden. All of them gave priority to jobs and higher pay for council employees on the ground that more jobs meant better services.

The New Left councillors described their objective as achieving socialist change. What it meant in practice was campaigning against a vast variety of evils such as apartheid in South Africa, exploitation in the Third World, police brutality in Britain, the threat of nuclear warfare, discrimination against gays, women, the handicapped; organizing festivals for the women encamped on Greenham Common, renaming halls and streets to celebrate heroes of socialism, investing (and losing) money in the *News on Sunday* to promote a left-wing press. That the new sorts of officers appointed did not always please those whom they were designed to serve was irrelevant. It did not matter that the local black community objected when a Militant supporter was appointed as race adviser in Liverpool.[18] As late as 1987, Hackney Council installed plaques of Lenin and Stalin.[19] During 1984–5, some £20 million was spent on propaganda – 1500 cartoon guides on police powers were distributed to children by the Manchester City Council urging them to 'resist threats from officers'.[20] The flagship of the flotilla sailing towards utopia was what became known as the Socialist Republic of South Yorkshire. When it was elected in 1974, the Council provided every new member of staff with a copy of the Labour Manifesto, tried to set up a fully integrated public transport system, standardized fares, and finally free transportation. The provision of transportation would thus be completely monopolized and centralized by the city councils; users would be subsidized by tax-paying non-users regardless of need; and once fares were abolished, transportation would be rationed by queues or provided with such wasteful abandon that no one ever need wait. The model, of course, was the holy land, the USSR, whose remarkable efficiency in transportation matters, as in so much else, as well as in dispensation of justice was an indisputable fact for the rulers of the Socialist Republic of South Yorkshire.

Other sections of the Labour Party were inclined to concentrate more on improving and increasing publicly provided services. A GLC pamphlet in 1984 went so far as to say that as council services had become 'literally indefensible', it was all too easy for the Tories to justify privatization, penalties, and rate-capping. But when Ken Livingstone took over the Greater London Council, he was bent on confrontation. And he had a talent for notoriety. Whether he played Cassandra – 'I fear that within ten years there will be a coup and that all gays, trade union activists and left-wing politicians will be led off to the gas chambers', or defended the IRA after an attack that killed an innocent passerby – 'they have a motive force which they think is good', he was rarely absent from the headlines or television. He declared that his aim was 'to use the council machinery as part of a political campaign both against the government and in defence of socialist policies'.[21]

A Power-Base for the Unions

Special relationships between unions and councillors enabled the unions to dictate the terms of employment, to cover up scandals such as the ill-treatment of residents in an old people's home, to prevent the realization of plans for improving the refuse service, or to close schools and libraries whenever the staff fancied a grievance. Campaigns for equal opportunities and against the government took priority. And councils who were recalcitrant soon found themselves paralysed by 'industrial action' and ordered by the local Labour

Party to give in to their employees' demands. Occupation of council housing by squatters and properties vandalized by the workforce became regular occurrences. And no matter what happened, a cry went up for more money and more 'local self-government'.

The 'direct labour organizations' of the local authorities provided just what public sector unions needed. Between 1948 and 1974, the percentage of unionized employees rose from sixty-two per cent to eighty-six per cent. And the two public sector unions, NUPE and NALGO, soon became distinguished for their militancy. Whenever proposals were made to improve the efficiency of a service, the union could bring out the workforce on strike. This was especially easy where Labour was in control. Union organizers were often also active in the party and were ready to use 'industrial action' to influence the decisions of the council about matters in which they were directly interested. Unions were thus able to set staffing levels, hours, and standards as well as wages. As the councils never punished the unions for striking, and striking workers usually did not even lose pay, to stop work became 'cost free'. Even if giving up a restrictive practice did not involve redundancies, the unions refused to allow it.

Refuse collection, for instance, was always handled by the direct labour organization and was one of the leading reasons for complaints about local services. The bonus schemes in refuse collection had been devised after the end of the Second World War and were based on productivity levels and work schedules of that time which bore no resemblance to what was being done in the seventies. Thanks to new methods, the workman now finished work at one or two in the afternoon, three hours earlier than he would have done previously and yet he was paid for full time. The bonus schemes accounted for a quarter of the cost of labour in refuse collection, and the 1984 report of the Audit Commission concluded that there was no relationship between bonus schemes and performance, and that £20 million could be saved annually without any loss to the existing standard of service.[22] Yet such practices could not be altered without producing a strike.

The resulting state of affairs was summed up by Dave Sullivan, Labour leader of Lewisham Council between 1985 and 1987, in a paper addressed to the local Labour parties. He condemned the Labour assumption 'that somehow the need to manage can be replaced by concepts of workers' control or industrial democracy'. The councils' policies had become, he said, a 'quagmire of bureaucracy' and their operations were distinguished by 'absenteeism, high sickness levels, high staff turnover, low productivity, flexitime abuse, excessive overtime, poor quality work, low self-esteem, and low public esteem'. If the council did not 'urgently begin the process of transforming this authority into one that truly serves the interests of working people by using efficiently and effectively the large sums of money we take from their pockets', it would be 'nothing less than a rip-off'.[23]

A Base for Revolution?

Municipal socialism was not a matter merely of the takeover of local councils or the promotion of union power; in its most extreme forms, it came to mean using the authority and spending power delegated to local government as a basis for quasi-revolutionary activity. The first instance of this phenomenon came as early as 1918, with the notorious case of Poplar, a parish in the poorest part of the London dock area. When the reforms of 1892 and 1894 lowered the property qualifications for voting, the Labour Guardians on the Poor Law Board (which was then the public agency for assisting the unemployed) began to dominate the Board. Under the leadership of the socialist, George Lansbury, they abandoned the rule that the able-bodied should not get relief outside the workhouse and substantially increased the amount of outdoor relief. The number of paupers and the money being spent rose dramatically and ratepayers revolted, but until 1918 the Labour Guardians were inhibited by the disfranchisement of paupers because the more people they provided with Poor Relief, the fewer the votes that they could rely on. When pauper disfranchisement was abolished, the Labour Party won decisive control of both the Board of Poor Law Guardians and the borough council. By 1921, the rate had doubled over what it had been three years before.

The council embarked on grand projects such as building new baths, widening streets, adding playing fields, until Poplar went bankrupt and the councillors were imprisoned for defaulting on their debts. But the government found their imprisonment embarrassing and they soon marched out of Brixton gaol to the tune of 'The Red Flag'. A new Bill allowed Guardians to borrow money and required the richer boroughs to contribute to poorer ones. But that was not enough to keep Poplar solvent, as by 1923, almost two out of every ten people were on Poor Relief. An employer in Poplar wrote to the Minister saying: 'Our employees who live in Poplar have pointed out to us that they can get more money by being unemployed than by working for us, and as we have no wish to prevent them from getting as much as possible, we propose to dismiss them so that they can take advantage of your relief.'[24]

The level of poor relief in Poplar was finally declared illegal; the borough councillors and Guardians were repeatedly surcharged; the Labour Party was incensed; the surcharges were remitted. Nevertheless, by September 1925, the Guardians could no longer pay either the poor or their officers and finally agreed to the conditions set by the Minister so that they were permitted to borrow the money they needed. But they continued to give relief with a generous hand and officers were accused of fraud and misconduct. Only when the Local Government Act of 1929 handed over the duties of the Guardians to the counties and the county boroughs did 'Poplarism' end. The object of the operation was explained by George Lansbury: 'We are all clear class-conscious Socialists working together using the whole machinery of local government and Parliament for the transformation of Capitalist Society into Socialism.'[25]

By the time that Mrs Thatcher came to power in 1979, the Poplar phenomenon was re-emerging. The Government was confronted by a large number of local authorities whose leaders were avowedly determined to defeat her and to establish socialism in Britain. Their design was not hidden. Apocalyptic calls for revolution appeared in a variety of publications. One of the earliest of these, published in October 1980, was by Frank Hansen, later a Brent councillor, which was a clear call to arms: 'Only political action backed by concerted industrial muscle, plus the mobilization of entire working-class communities can confront and turn back Thatcher's onslaught.' He asked for a commitment from all Labour groups that they would not 'under any circumstances' implement the Government's policies and would recognize that 'if we want to win we must be prepared for the possibility of a general strike if necessary and the removal of the Thatcher government.'[26] In the following year, also in *Briefing*, Ken Livingstone called for 'industrial action by the Trade Union movement and disruption of Parliament by the Parliamentary Labour Party' to defeat the 'massive attack' launched by the Tory government.

In practice, the two great set pieces were played out in Liverpool and London. Of the two, the revolutionary intent was more seriously evident in Liverpool. But Derek Hatton's Liverpudlian Militant Tendency never succeeded in capturing the popular imagination to anything like the extent of Ken Livingstone's GLC, even if many ordinary Liverpudlians revelled in their new-found status as the thorn in Thatcher's side and lauded their bolshie leaders.

The GLC's chief responsibility, when Livingstone arrived, was for London Transport, which Livingstone tried to operate so as to provide the maximum number of jobs and reduce fares to nothing. As many more would benefit from the perk of free fares than those who lost by paying higher taxes, and as the Labour Party would be the benevolent provider, a Labour victory in the national election would be assured, or so Livingstone supposed. But when he brought in Keith Bright as chairman, he was faced by someone trying seriously to administer London Transport as efficiently as possible. When Bright's efforts were repeatedly blocked by Livingstone and his henchmen, Bright began negotiations with the Minister of Transport which ended, in 1984, in the removal of London Transport from the GLC and the setting up, as a separate nationalized industry, of London Regional Transport.

After that, as there were very few administrative responsibilities exercised by the GLC, Livingstone's policies consisted principally of spending money. He had good precedents for doing so. In 1973, the GLC committed itself to such a grandiose programme for housebuilding and increasing services that the councillors became too embarrassed by the projected rate and fare rises in London to proceed. Even so, GLC rates rose by eighty per cent in 1975, but still, within three weeks the council found itself obliged to make housing cuts in order to avoid further raising the rates.[27]

During his reign between 1981 and 1986, Ken Livingstone increased GLC expenditure by 170 per cent (when the rate of inflation had been 29 per cent). In 1984–5, he handed out £47 million. There were the usual good causes such as blacks, gays, one-parent families and peace campaigners, as well as a Police Committee which used its budget of 2.9 million in 1985–6 to fund forty-nine anti-police organizations (which supplied schools and council estates with officers to explain the iniquities of the police and to encourage antagonism to them). And there were also more exotic causes – the United Filipino Association, the Armenian Democratic Front, the Marx Memorial Library, and Babies Against the Bomb. The Women's Committee, which cost thirteen million pounds a year, had duties like vetting the song 'There Is Nothing Like A Dame', in the pre-Christmas panto, for sexism. And the GLC promoted its causes blatantly: 'The GLC has got more billboards than any other advertiser in London and it has the best sites,' Ken Livingstone boasted.[28]

Although the GLC was responsible for only eleven per cent of local services in London, it had over twenty thousand employees, ninety-two councillors and a budget (in 1985–6) of just under £1 billion (without counting spending on education). Only about twelve thousand employees were really needed, according to Illtyd Harrington, the senior Labour councillor and chairman of the Special Committee on Matters Relating to the Council's Future Existence. But the crowd of assorted eccentrics who congregated amidst the marble columns in the halls of the GLC were not of the same mind. They were determined to bring about fundamental changes in the nature of British society, and they regarded the GLC as an ideal base from which to do so. They saw local government as 'the only arena in which alternatives to the "values" of Thatcherism [could] be developed and where these ideas [could] be translated into action': in order 'to demonstrate a very different set of values based on democratic accountability' they were 'determined to redistribute local resources, to experiment with new approaches to collective provision and local planning and to act as a platform for socialist alternatives'.[29]

Thatcherism and Local Government: the Inevitability of Confrontation

No one acquainted with this history and with the nature of Thatcherism could reasonably have doubted that local government and Mrs Thatcher would soon collide. Here, after all, were manifestations of everything distasteful to a Thatcherite – local authorities, established by and delegated great powers by Parliament, engaged in huge public sector projects to 'cure' every local problem, spending vast amounts of individuals' money for them, acting as allies of the unions, and providing platforms for socialism (sometimes in an extreme form).

The Thatcherite response was absolutely predictable: the government set out to achieve a 'paradigm shift' through the introduction of privatization of local services; to increase the scope for individual choice (and hence encourage the vigorous virtues) by reducing local government's tax-based expenditure; and to make 'local government' accountable to the local populace in the hope that this would restrain councillors from engaging in the promotion of their fancies at the expense of their ratepayers.

The Privatization of Local Services

The textbook case of the Thatcherite effort to privatize local services is the Borough of Wandsworth in London. When, in the 1978 local elections, the Conservatives took over what had been a Labour stronghold, they pledged themselves to bring down rates by improving efficiency. The first service to be 'contracted out' was street cleaning. By March 1982 the councillors had moved on to the refuse service, and the inevitable collision with the unions ensued. The white collar and manual worker unions in Wandsworth staged a strike; and brought the administration of the council to a halt. Neighbouring councils and the GLC sent in workers whose obstruction compelled contractors to use refuse sites as distant as Kent. The strike was in full force when the 1982 local elections came up, and collapsed only when the Conservatives were again returned to office.[30]

There were always some problems in the course of a privatization, but by 1985, Wandsworth had privatized thirteen services – 'We cut our teeth on street cleaning and never looked back' – and had saved some four million pounds through privatization.[31] The cost of some services was reduced by forty-five per cent. And the staff of the Borough was reduced by a third between 1980 and 1985.[32] Whereas in 1978, Wandsworth's local taxes were as high as those of other inner city boroughs, they fell quickly to being one of the lowest in London.

Nor was Wandsworth by any means the only example of the Thatcherite drive for privatization. By 1986, sixteen per cent of councils were putting services out to competitive tender, and substantial savings were reported by Labour-controlled as well as Conservative authorities. In 1986, further legislation compelled local authorities to put refuse collection, street cleaning as well as four other services out to tender.

The monopoly over bus services was first attacked by the Transport Act 1980 which made it easier for private sector operators to be licensed for bus services and established three trial areas where private operators could operate a bus service without first getting a license. In 1985, the system of licensing was abolished for the whole of Britain and replaced by a simplified registration system. Councils operating bus services had to form them into companies, which were to operate on market principles and pay their way. The National Bus Company was privatized and divided into smaller, commercial units. And all local authorities and other transport authorities were prohibited from interfering with competition and required to promote private enterprise. The only subsidies that local authorities were still permitted to give were to unprofitable but socially desirable routes, after they had been opened to competitive tenders. Something like eighty per cent of the old route system has since come into private hands, the level of public subsidy to transportation has decreased by some thirty per cent, and more than two hundred mini-bus services have come into existence.

The most spectacular dispersal of power occurred in connection with housing. It was heralded by a radical change in language. In the Conservative manifesto of 1979 and ministerial statements afterwards, the language of the housing lobby was discarded: there was no mention of planning, or projections of need, or a housing shortage or crisis. Instead, the talk was about 'what the country can afford', about under-used resources, especially empty houses, about the capacity of the private sector to provide what people wanted as well as needed.[33]

The Local Government Planning and Land Act 1980 gave the Secretary of State power to oblige local authorities to release unused or under-used land owned by them. As a result, between 1979 and 1986, enough land was sold to private builders for about fifty-two thousand houses. Schemes whereby private builders worked in partnership with local authorities produced some sixteen thousand five hundred houses for sale. Local authorities on their own built some seven thousand low-cost homes. But it was the Housing Act and the Tenants' Rights Act of 1980 that made something near to a revolution.

The sale of council houses, by giving tenants a 'Right to Buy', built on policies that, much earlier, had been adopted by local Conservative councils such as Birmingham in the 1960s. Even before 1945, local authorities had had the power to sell housing with ministerial consent. As the Heath Government encouraged such sales, by 1972 some 46,000 council houses had been sold. The Right to Buy legislation of 1980 gave tenants of three or more years standing the right to buy at two thirds of the market value, with a further one per cent discount for each year of tenancy, but if the house was sold again within five years, the discount would have to be repaid. If tenants could not buy outright, they could, by paying £100, acquire a two-year option to buy at the original price.

Local authorities, Conservative as well as Labour, resisted this policy both openly and clandestinely. The councils delayed responses to applications; they insisted on explaining the disadvantages of ownership; and they used various threats such as that 'a "problem family" would be moved in next to households purchasing their homes'; they refused to carry out repairs to the homes of tenants who were trying to buy; they imposed difficult conditions on sales; they circulated incorrect information about the level of service charges. The unions assisted and sometimes led the campaign against buying. Some two dozen Labour authorities manned the front lines. The Labour Party committed itself to repealing the Right to Buy legislation. Some acknowledged that it was not altogether clear whether this campaign 'was a struggle for the working class or the preservation of local, paternalistic, bureaucratic empires'.[34] But in the end, most local authorities reluctantly complied; only a few had to be given final warnings and the Government went to court only with Norwich, which lost its challenge. On the other hand, some authorities, especially Conservative ones, pursued the policy energetically, selling besides vacant properties, sometimes whole estates, which had been in their possession but unused.

As a result of the Right to Buy, the owner-occupied sector grew from a little over a quarter of the total housing stock to almost half between 1978 and 1985. More houses passed into private ownership between 1979 and 1982 than in all the years since 1945. By 1983, half a million houses had been sold.

Local privatization on a Grand Scale – the UDCs

Privatization on an even grander scale was brought to the inner cities, through the creation of Urban Development Authorities. In place of the grants for redevelopment, which had been given to local councils for many years by both Labour and Conservative governments, the new scheme initiated by Michael Heseltine in 1979 emphasized the involvement of private investment and the need to create economically self-sufficient projects.

The proposal was supported by the Prime Minister against opposition from those who feared the creation of new quangos and new openings for public spending, and from local authorities who were hostile to private investment and to the intrusion, as they saw it, of foreign powers into their territory. The Urban Development Corporations were given powers to own and acquire land, build factories, and invest in both the infrastructure and the environment in a fashion that would attract industry as well as commercial and residential development. The funding was to be provided as far as possible from private sources, but public investment to initiate the projects, along with governmental intervention to assemble land and provide regulations and transportation, was expected to create conditions that would attract investment from the private sector. Local authorities were encouraged to co-operate with private investors to construct projects which would compete for approval and funding from the Department of the Environment. As a result, Heseltine believed, civil servants would be forced 'to enter into a dialogue with the business world', and local Chambers of Commerce, rather than local councils, would become the engine of enterprise.[35]

The earliest and most successful project was the London Docklands development, where the investment by government turned out to be, as it was hoped, not so much a subsidy as an encouragement to private enterprise. But even here, during the recession, some of the gargantuan projects remained partly empty, producing calls for aid from the Treasury, and much public agitation about the collapse of the investing companies. Elsewhere, in areas such as Merseyside, private enterprise never took over and the effect was mainly to make a hopeless place pleasanter to live in for those who could not leave it. Old warehouses which had been standing empty on a swamp because the barriers to the river had not been tended and the river swept up to the doors, were converted into offices, restaurants, pubs, shops. And in some instances, the government investment remained wholly a subsidy. Derelict property was turned into parks and other amenities which yielded no economic return. Nevertheless, the aspiration was quite different from that of the housing projects of the sixties. The Thatcherite aim was clearly to stimulate independence, not to create new projects for management by the public authorities.

The Control of Local Expenditure

Privatization of local government services, through contracting out and the UDCs, was valued by Thatcherites not only for its contribution to the 'paradigm shift' (its effect in reducing government's role as a solver of every problem), but also for its effect on local government expenditure. Mrs Thatcher herself, and successive Secretaries of State for the Environment, argued forcefully that 'contracting out' would reduce costs, and hence leave more money in the pockets of individuals – a contribution to the promotion of individual choice and the vigorous virtues. But neither Mrs Thatcher herself nor her ministers ever believed that privatization alone would suffice to control local government's tax-borne expenditure. Direct controls were also put firmly onto the agenda.

The attempts to limit local spending came in a succession of stages, in each of which, as the local authorities found a way of evading the constraints placed upon them by new legislation, the government responded by imposing a new restriction. The programme proceeded incrementally.

The first change came in 1980, in the system for allocating central government support. Under the old system, what the local authorities already spent became the basis for calculating the grant, on the assumption that expenditure indicated need. As this way of calculating the grant gave the councils an incentive to spend more, the new Block Grant was calculated according to assessments of local need made by the central government on the basis of an established formula. It was accompanied by a provision for financial penalties on authorities which spent more than ten per cent above the assessment for need. That obliged them to fund the extra spending out of the rates or by borrowing. From 1981 – 2 the government also had the right to control the power of local authorities to borrow money in order to fund capital expenditure.

The next attempt to control the expenditure of local authorities was a system of targets for spending whereby councils were penalized for exceeding the target by cuts in the Block Grant. By 1983 – 4, the Inner London Education Authority and the Greater London Council succeeded in spending their way past the entitlement to any grant. Money for extra spending was obtained by raising the rates and the rises were often spectacular. But the local authorities blamed the central government for the rises and, according to a public opinion survey in 1982, so did nearly sixty per cent of the ratepayers.

Restrictions directly on spending were followed by attempts to control the level of rates. First, councils were prohibited from setting supplementary rates, that is to say, levying an addition to the rates in mid-year to avoid being subject to a cut in the grant. And finally the government instituted ratecapping, putting a limit on the rates allowed. Labour local authorities, who were more likely to over-spend, tried to organize a campaign to refuse to set rates. But as the Labour Party did not support them and many councillors were reluctant to engage in illegal action, the campaign failed. But by 1987–8, twenty councils were 'ratecapped' (one controlled by the Alliance, the rest by Labour) in addition to the twenty made subject to 'automatic precept control' in the previous year.

All along there were dire predictions of cuts in local services and manpower; after ratecapping was introduced they grew even more ominous. Lewisham Council claimed that ratecapping would force them to eliminate fifteen hundred jobs;[36] Ted Knight, Leader of Lambeth Council, warned that they would have to sack three thousand workers [37]; the Deputy Leader of the GLC predicted that the GLC would have to sack a thousand fire-fighters and a thousand GLC staff, withdraw grants from two to three thousand voluntary organizations, increase rents for GLC tenants and cut many services.[38] Margaret Hodge, Leader of Islington Council, lamented that 'services across the board [would be] simply stopped'.[39] None of these things happened, and there were protests against the exaggerations: journalists in Islington's publicity department were 'totally disillusioned and resentful of the scaremongering tactics adopted by threatening cuts which never materialized, and asked that they should not again be forced to lie to the consumer'.[40]

Local authorities had found a new way of evading the constraints on them, the way of 'creative accounting'. A variety of devices constitute creative accounting. Mortgage debts, land and other assets were sold to produce an income that could be used for capital spending. Debts were re-scheduled so that they need not be paid until some time in the future. Items such as repairs and modernization, which had in the past been listed as current expenditure, were recorded as capital expenditure. Deferred purchase schemes arranged for a finance company to buy an asset for the council, which agreed to repay the company at some time in the future. The most cunning arrangements were the 'lease and lease-back' schemes such as that of Manchester City Council. It raised £200 million through a deal with the Manchester Mortgage Corporation, which it owned, by giving the Corporation a long lease on some thirty civic buildings (including swimming pools, art galleries, an abattoir) in return for which the Council was given the money. The Corporation borrowed the £200 million in the City by using the buildings as security. And the council invested this money to produce an interest of £15 million in the first year. Some five billion pounds may have been borrowed in this fashion by Labour authorities.[41]

The creative accounting was wonderfully effective. According to a Labour Party document, 'the collective debts of Labour councils nationally amounted to about £2 billion' in 1986. An official in Sheffield estimated that repayments on the council's loans of £110 million would cost up to £25 million a year for around seven years. Camden, Hammersmith and Fulham in London also had debts of 100 million or more.[42]

The government responded to 'creative accounting' with legislation which restricted the sale of mortgage debt and later blocked 'lease and lease-back' schemes. But although these further controls did somewhat limit capital spending (on housing, schools, and roads), all the efforts at restraint did not substantially reduce the great bulk of current spending by councils.

The Accountability Experiment

Driven in part by the failure of external controls on council spending, in part by the increasing anger of Conservative as well as

Labour councillors about the controls, and in part by subscription to the myth of 'local autonomy', Thatcherites determined to try a bold experiment. Instead of using local privatization and central spending controls to eradicate municipal socialism and the dependency culture which they believed it engendered, they decided to combine local privatization with true local accountability. The mechanism of accountability was to be a community charge. The intention was that this tax, together with a radically revised grant system, and the introduction of a uniform national business rate, would remove the need for any central controls on spending by making each member of the local populace bear (and hence, presumably demand justification for) each additional pound spent by the local authority.

The Conservatives had been promising reform of the rates ever since the general election of 1974. Opposition to the rates had been a feature of local government for over a century. They were recognized to discourage the maintenance and improvement of property because every bathroom added subjected the owner to higher rates. They were considered unfair because there was little correlation with ability to pay. In 1965 the Allen Committee showed that the lower the level of income, the higher the proportion claimed by the local authority. The inequity of the old lady on a small pension living alone and paying the same rate as all ten high earners living next door to her was common knowledge. Although rate rebates assisted households with the lowest incomes, the rates continued to bear most heavily on that section of the population with incomes just above the rebate level. From 1895 on, there were repeated attempts to devise an alternative. But no government could summon the courage to tackle a change that was bound to offend vested interests.

The Government's arguments for the community charge emphasized that rates were no longer suitable because rates were a tax on property. They had been suitable in the past, because the services provided by local authorities had then been chiefly services to property. But as the services grew into the Welfare State, they became services to people. It was therefore more appropriate to have a tax on persons rather than property. This argument was supported by the fact that of thirty-five million electors in England, only eighteen million were subject to rates; and even of those, a third received a full or partial rebate, so that only twelve million, a third of the electorate, were full ratepayers. When only ratepayers were eligible to vote, this disparity did not matter. But once universal suffrage came in, those who did not pay the tax had the power to determine its use. Businesses, which provided a major part of the funds, had no vote. And the other ratepayers could easily be outvoted by the majority who paid nothing. Moreover, there had been no revaluation of property since 1973, which meant that the rates paid in some parts of the country bore little relation to the value of the property, so that a corner shop in Edinburgh paid four times as much as a corner shop in central London and rates for a business in Newcastle could be three times as much as for an identical business in Kensington. The high rates in the North drove businesses out to locate in the South, which made the economy as a whole much less efficient. Yet a revaluation of property was certain to create an uproar.

An income tax had been considered and rejected. In a letter in 1990 to Mr Ashdown, leader of the Liberal Democrats, answering his proposals for a local income tax, Mrs Thatcher said that a person with a national average male earnings of £12,800 taxable income in his Yeovil constituency would have to pay a bill of £955 under local income tax compared with £363 poll tax. And the most unfair feature of a local income tax would be, she said, that it would allow millions of people who benefit from local services and who could vote in local elections to avoid paying a penny directly towards the cost of those services.[43] In choosing the community charge, the Government claimed to have chosen 'local democratic accountability', rather than greater central control. As they did not want 'to go on legislating until we have a framework of law within which the abuses can be contained with more central control', the Government had chosen to 'make local authorities fully accountable to their electors and ensure that those who vote for local extravagance and depravity pay for it'.[44] The new system would make it possible not only 'to relax controls from the centre' but also to 'abolish the present complicated and creaking rate support grant system . . . There will be no "targets", "recycling", "penalties", "holdback", "slopes" or "thresholds".'⁴⁵

When the community charge was first introduced, it seemed to meet with universal approval among Conservatives. The Green Paper was presented to Parliament jointly by Kenneth Baker, Malcolm Rifkind and Michael Edwards in 1986. It had been produced by a group headed by William Waldegrave. As Nicholas Ridley succeeded Baker at the Department of the Environment, he steered the Bill through Parliament.

The Tory Conference of 1986 welcomed the Green Paper with enthusiasm, only nine hands being raised against it. Rifkind commended the new tax for introducing 'greater accountability' and being fairer to 'little old ladies living on their own'; Michael Forsyth, the MP for Stirling, was sure that its earlier introduction in Scotland would 'demonstrate its advantages'. Later that year, the minister for local government, Rhodes Boyson, declared that 'The new system will be fairer, easier to understand and, most important of all, it will restore local accountability and thereby enhance local democracy.' When the Party Conference of 1987 was told by Nicholas Ridley: 'People know rates are unfair. We promised them a fairer system, and we shall not disappoint them,' his audience applauded not only him but also Gerry Malone who asked to have the tax 'introduced in one go' so as 'to maximize the political benefit', since at the time the tax was planned to be brought in over four years.⁴⁶

At the second reading of the Bill in December 1987, backbenchers enthusiastically commended it for 'bringing about a better system of accountability' and reestablishing the principle of 'no taxation without representation'. Peter Walker, Secretary of State for Wales, approved of the proposals 'because they are positive for Wales'.⁴⁷ Michael Howard expected the community charge to become the 'real scourge' of the hard left and to secure a return to 'good, honest, old-fashioned local government'. The *Telegraph*, *The Times* and the *Sun* supported the new tax as the only sensible way to pay for services since it would increase accountability and put an end to the local government gravy train.

Opposition parties saw nothing good in the community charge

and argued that all taxes should be progressive and that property owners should be made to pay more. They did not concern themselves with defending the anomalies of the rates or remember Neil Kinnock's condemnation of the rates, as recently as 1980, for being 'the most unjust of all taxes . . . which take most from those who can afford least'.[48] The most notorious Labour Councils took the lead in girding themselves for a campaign against the community charge.

Expectations for the level of the charge turned out to be well below the reality. In 1988, a government spokesman had argued that a majority of households would gain from the proposals. By 1990, it was clear that the tax Tories had voted for was not the tax they got. At the start, the Government had guessed that the level of the charge would be between £160 and £170 per person. In 1987, they predicted that it would be £183 for Reigate and Bansted – the charge there was set at £445. Simon Burns (Chelmsford) declared: 'I will face my electorate with pride. While the average rates bill in Chelmsford is £540, if the community charge had been introduced this year . . . the charge would be £181.' In fact it was £397. David Shaw (Dover) said: 'I met an elderly lady who was forced to leave Camden and become a refugee in Dover, where her rates bill is only £300 a year. She is looking forward to the community charge which will be £150 a year'. It was £298. Mrs Teresa Gorman (Billericay) was confident that 'pensioners who are able to pay a full contribution will be pleased to do so,' but she did not expect that the poll tax would be £478. The Environment Minister, Christopher Chope, had predicted that the 'community charge in many holiday areas would be £160 or £200'. It was £345 in East Devon and £390 in Suffolk Coastal.[49]

Conservatives now joined the Opposition in arguing that requiring the same payment from everyone regardless of income was unfair. The Government answered that the elaborate system of rebates allowed for cases of hardship and that going further in that direction would turn the charge into an income tax. In any case, they said, local government was, as it long had been, still chiefly supported by progressive taxation because most of their revenue came from the central government, and therefore from the progressive income tax. Only a quarter of local expenditure was supported by the community charge. Thus in an area with a poll tax of £363, the total contribution to local revenue varied considerably from one person to another in accordance with their ability to pay, because of rebates and the different levels of income taxation: a student paid £72; a person earning £12,000 paid £650; a £20,000 a year primary school head, £1,390; an airline captain on £50,000 a year paid £3,300; and a barrister earning £100,000 paid £7,242.[50]

The business lobby opposed the business rate because some had been benefiting hugely from rates on property which had not been revalued since 1973. They were really objecting to the revaluation of their property that came with the business rate. Of course, some businesses, in areas where the local authorities subsidized the rest of the community from the rates paid by business, benefited greatly from the new business rate. They, however, were not heard from. Businesses providing local services were not penalized because their competitors were in the same position and would also have to put up their prices. But businesses not dependent on serving local people were more likely to be themselves worse off. It did not comfort them that the new business rate would increase the country's economic efficiency by giving them an incentive to move instead of remaining in an area that was overcrowded, short of labour and land.

When Wandsworth set the second lowest charge in the country, a cry went up that Wandsworth had achieved this by being given an unusually high grant from the government. Its leader, Sir Paul Beresford, wrote in to *The Times* saying (as he had said elsewhere) that 'Wandsworth achieved the lowest community charge in mainland Britain despite the lowest level of government grant in inner London. Although Wandsworth benefits from the safety-net redistribution between authorities, we benefit less than several other London boroughs, and the sum involved is so small that without it we would still enjoy one of the lowest charges in England.'[51] Similar complaints were made against other councils that set low charges. Those councils who had set high community charges busied themselves with organizing protest meetings and marches.

In boroughs like Camden the residents were flooded with leaflets proclaiming the iniquities of the community charge and urging them not to pay and to take part in protests.

Criticism of the community charge came also from some who generally supported Thatcherite policies – Ferdinand Mount denounced it as quite simply unfair. All other flat rate charges, such as the BBC license fee, he argued, could be avoided by not buying a television. This was 'not simply an unpopular tax. It is a rotten piece of legislation, vilely expensive to administer and likely to clutter up the courts with non-payers in arrears for years to come . . . '[52]

A report on the poll tax published by the Institute for Fiscal Studies calculated that households with net incomes of less than £400 per week would be worse off, and that the hardest hit of all would be households on 'middle incomes', ie £150 – £300 per week, losing out by roughly £190 a year on average.[53] What had been altogether forgotten in the rush to install the community charge at once was the likely response of local councils. They saw and grasped the opportunity to increase their revenue while blaming the increase on the government's reform.

The Conservative backbencher, Michael Mates, gained considerable support for his amendment which proposed 'banding', meaning that non-taxpayers pay half the community charge, standard taxpayers pay the full charge, and higher rate taxpayers, one and a half times. Rhodes Boyson, the minister who had earlier strongly supported the reform, appeared on television as a critic. He, like others, objected especially to the 'safety net' provision which meant that people in low-spending local authority areas were subsidizing poll-tax payers in high-spending and often Labour-controlled areas. Backbenchers from constituencies in the south of England, where the new business rate reflected the sharp rise in the value of property, were beside themselves with rage, rage directed chiefly at Nicholas Ridley, then Secretary of State for the Environment. No one remembered the enthusiastic welcome given to the community charge in 1986 and 1987.

The most radical suggestion came from Peter Kellner, in the *Independent*, who proposed that each council be permitted to levy what tax it chose: 'If Bromley wants a poll tax, Westminster a sales tax, Sheffield a property tax, Richmond a local income tax, and Eastbourne a system of site value rating, so be it. A quintet of taxes may lack the poetic imagery of a thousand flowers, but the point would be the same: encourage variety and let people decide for themselves. Central government would still fund a large slice of local spending through grants; the uniform business rate might be kept. But for the rest, let variety flourish. To make this change would not only 'remove an albatross' from the necks of MPs and augment the accountability of local government, but it would allow us to 'admit our doubts and turn them into practical advantage'.[54]

Defenders of the community charge explained that councils had gone on a once-in-a-lifetime spending spree and nothing else should have been expected as the councils could blame every extra penny that they screwed out of the local populace on the nasty new charge and the rotten government that had introduced it. They pointed out that the number of 'gainers', who would pay less than they had for rates, slightly exceeded the losers. The gainers included not only the rich but also pensioners living in large houses, single parents who had to pay rates for a whole flat or house, couples who had moved into larger houses to accommodate growing families, people whose houses were revalued as a result of adding central heating or a bathroom. While Surrey residents were up in arms and there were protest marches in Maidenhead, a household in Islington which had been paying £2800 in rates was now paying £1000 in community charge.

A persistent criticism of the community charge was that it would be difficult to collect. Certainly, the rate of collection was low. Defenders of the charge argued that technical ineptitude explained the low rate of collection. A survey in the *Local Government Chronicle* revealed that the reason why the community charge was not being collected in some areas was that computers had failed and bills had not been sent out. Places like South Tyneside, Eastleigh, Elmbridge and Hereford, Woodrow Wyatt pointed out, where the software was working, had collection rates of eighty per cent or above, as compared with Plymouth, which had a fifty per cent collection rate because it had sent out only eighteen per cent of its bills by the week ending 9 June. He concluded that 'the trend seems to be that collection and refusal to pay are no worse than under the old rates system, often better' and that MPs, ministers, and journalists reported that complaints about the charge 'have almost vanished from our mail'.[55]

Within the year after the charge was introduced, the government announced that it was studying plans for revisions to soften the anomalies that had become evident. The poll tax safety net would be reconsidered. In the meantime, twenty Labour councils were 'charge-capped', and others, including a Conservative-led Council, were capped later. There were protests that the need to 'cap' meant that the charge would not, as had been claimed by the government, increase accountability and there were the usual predictions that capping would produce cuts in spending on vital services like education. As usual, too, came the answers pointing out that no such cuts were needed: in reply to the head of the policy review on the Oxfordshire County Council, who complained of the dreadful cuts they faced as a result of capping, the leader of the Conservatives pointed out that the joint Labour and Liberal Democrat Budget, as well as the Conservative Budget which had been defeated, had budgeted for an increase in spending of 3.4 million and 2.8 million respectively, from which he concluded 'that the Secretary of State could cap Oxfordshire's expenditure without any risk of cuts to the education service' as it had been maintained before the capping.[56]

Whatever else one may think of it, there is no doubt that the introduction of the community charge persuaded local authorities that the party really was over. They had been severely shaken by the Tory victory in 1987, for they had relied on the return of a Labour government to bail them out of their difficulties. With no such hope in sight, they had to set about paying for their creative accounting. Once the community charge was in place, it became impossible for them to raise money from business and the wealthier sections of the community to provide for the causes dear to the hearts of Labour activists. Even opponents of the community charge lamented that it had become all too clear that councils pursuing a 'high taxation, high service' policy would be hitting 'the pockets of the poorest residents'.[57] Labour councillors were warning that while the new tax-payers would not mind paying for street lighting, refuse collection, or the maintenance of parks, they might be expected to resent spending their money on maintaining huge workforces who appeared only sporadically to do the required jobs, let alone the various 'causes' patronized by local authorities. At the same time, competitive tendering was making it all too obvious that some jobs could be done much better at a much lower cost once the management ceased to be dictated to by the unions.[58]

Some academic observers, whose sympathies lay entirely with 'local government', indeed with Labour control of it and not at all with Thatcherism, acknowledged that some of the councils had refused to adapt to 'the changing pattern of modern wants in their communities'. They pointed out that the failure to turn increased spending into a visible improvement in services had cost the Left's councils the support of local people. They had 'remained wedded to old orthodoxies: the importance of "class struggle" and the paternalistic model of local government with power restricted to a few leading councillors and party activists'. They had continued to fund counselling services and propaganda in schools and elsewhere to promote acceptance of lesbians and gays, arguing that they were not seeking to encourage homosexuality but merely countering discrimination. The die-hards were still bent on 'confrontation' and spent the time and energy that should have been devoted to improving services on wrangles about how to defeat Thatcherism. Even the soft Left refused to face hard choices and seemed to be more concerned to keep up the level of spending than the quality of services: 'By failing to demonstrate that collective provision could be innovative, efficient, and successful, Left councils failed to win the public support that was needed to hold back the Thatcherite revolution.' When the government accused such councils of being inefficient and profligate, their arguments made sense to the users of their services. Had they been more innovative, they might have developed 'new initiatives or better services' and withdrawn from some activities in order to do so.[59]

The strongest evidence for the effects of the community charge on the behaviour of local authorities came from the authorities themselves. A new spirit began to haunt the town halls. The vehement Labour leader of Islington Council, Margaret Hodge, renounced defiance of the government: 'The days of hoisting up red flags on the road are over,' she said. Labour councils would have to cut jobs in order to save services: 'We . . . have to accept that the "agenda" will be dominated by the Government . . . and work within a tight and worsening legal framework with necessarily limited resources.'[60] The leader of the Association of London Authorities produced a new strategy to make the services offered by the councils popular. It consisted of a resolve to resist the unions and to make changes in working practices 'which would allow two people to do the job three had done previously'. Even if they cut expenditure, he was sure that the councils could offer better services than before. The only dissent came from the leader of Lambeth, Linda Bellos, who nevertheless managed within eight months to cut some 40 million from the Lambeth budget.[61]

The old talk about the natural superiority of public services was gone. Instead, the authors of *Councils in Conflict* – Stewart Lansley, Sue Goss and Christian Wolmar – concluded their book with proposals for new strategies. They suggested that local authorities should develop 'joint initiatives with the private sector' and act as 'a local entrepreneur by identifying gaps in provision and attempting to pool resources across sectors'. Publicly provided services had to be supported by 'large-scale public surveys to assess services through the eyes of consumers' and 'to tailor objectives to the quality or to the extent of provision rather than to the convenience of bureaucracies'. Gone was the fear of a commercial outlook, of pampering consumers rather than producers. Councils were told by their leaders to adopt a 'client-centred approach', unions were told to recognize that better terms and conditions for staff without improving efficiency 'are bought at the expense of consumers'. Everyone was warned that a whole new way of thinking was required: 'A new balance of power must be based on the primacy of service delivery.'[62]

How much was being wasted became obvious once the party was over, and left-wing leaders began to talk about 'savings' and 'freezes' instead of 'campaigning' and 'confrontation'. In Haringey, whose hard Left leader was replaced, his successor managed to remove fifteen million from the budget despite opposition from Labour councillors. Other councils took similar measures by using rent increases and freezing job vacancies. Lambeth froze three quarters of the job vacancies; Southwark cut white collar workers by eighteen per cent, and manual workers by ten per cent. Sheffield, which cut the 1988–90 budget by 27 million and jobs by two thousand, nevertheless avoided compulsory redundancies while housing and libraries were left intact, and social services were cut by only about five per cent of a £50 million budget. The councils began to conduct consumer surveys and consultation for 'identifying objectives and retraining needs'.[63] When Brent made its cuts too late and very ineptly, Ken Livingstone, Brent East's MP, compared it to the Pol Pot regime in Cambodia. But if Brent and Hackney sacrificed their nuclear-free zone officers, they succeeded in preserving the race and women's units, although hardly anyone believed that their achievements were worth anything like the money spent on them, or indeed that they achieved anything at all.

Co-operation with the police was no longer forbidden. The Association of London Authorities, representing the thirteen Labour Councils in London, declared that a general policy of co-operation with the police had been agreed. Mr Peter Chalk, Left-wing councillor of Haringey and prominent in the Troops Out of Ireland Movement, went to Tottenham police station to promise support in countering drug abuse on the Broadwater Farm estate. 'There is a new realism in Haringey Labour politics', he said. 'I think we are adopting a more practical approach. In the past, Labour councillors have been reluctant to talk to the police, but I think talking to the police should be natural.'[64] 'We have to be honest', the formerly revolutionary Margaret Hodge said – 'one of the clear messages we received is of the failure of local authorities to inspire support. One of the reasons Thatcher was able to exploit their unpopularity was because they were seen as bureaucratic, inefficient, unresponsive and paternalistic by many of those people who are dependent on what we provide.'[65]

Socialism was re-interpreted to suit the times. Labour authorities began to talk cheerfully about their 'customers' and to boast of the public contracts they had developed. They guaranteed to clean streets, empty bins, and maintain street lighting to given schedules, with hotlines for complaints and promises to publish the performance of their workforces. Newcastle, Norwich and Southampton proclaimed a new 'municipal socialism' which was clean, efficient, enterprising, customer-oriented, ready to work with the private sector and even with the government's once-hated development corporations.[66]

When Ealing passed into Conservative control after the 1990 elections, the Union Jack replaced the Red Flag and the African National Congress emblem that used to fly from the town hall. The new officers set about scrapping self-defence lessons for lesbians, research into the oppression of Irish women in west London, the 'change agents' appointed to schools to enforce the right views on racism and sexism, the animal rights officer who campaigned to close pet shops and a 'bunny park' in a children's playground, the £80,000 a year to the Southall Black Sisters advice service, the forty jobs in the economic development unit which was supposed to encourage industrial growth and succeeded only in buying one set of workshops.[67] They thus made redundant some two hundred workers each with salaries of up to £30,000. Removing the forty jobs in race equality and women's units saved over a million pounds from the budget.[68] Even militant activists were beginning to acknowledge that however desirable it might be to promote good relations among different races and to end discrimination against homosexuals, the money being spent for such purposes by the local authorities did nothing more than 'provide jobs for the boys' who neither did nor could do anything to earn their keep.

But if some of the changes were dramatic, the old practices did not altogether disappear. Costly 'twinning' arrangements with foreign cities and the associated junkets abroad for the boys continued, if mainly in Labour-controlled councils, but also in Tory Bournemouth. Camden put its refuse collection and litter services out to tender but it was always won by the in-house group, who continued to be as inefficient as before. Rent arrears in Camden amounted to £14 million in March 1990, apart from another £14 million of uncollected debts, while a million a year continued to be spent on the Lesbian and Gay committee and the Woman's Committee. Rotherham announced that a thousand redundancies were due to the government's restrictions on spending, yet on the same day the council gave a seven-course dinner for two hundred guests. Tories on Derbyshire County Council complained that although the council was threatening to close libraries, its publicity department spent over a million pounds each year and the Equal Opportunities and Race Relations department had a budget of £630,000. The council of Southwark continued to spend £100,000 a year on a trade union support unit, apart from what it spent on supporting homosexual groups, a carnival to raise apartheid awareness, race relations and race equality officers.[69]

But on the other hand, the Camden Council cut seven million from the overtime budget, imposed a recruiting freeze, began a 'budget scrutiny', and embarked on a great publicity campaign to persuade its charge payers that it was turning over a new leaf, with new managers. It went so far as to acquire the larger refuse bins which residents had been requesting for years, to repair some of the broken pavements, and was finally compelled to privatize the refuse collectors and street cleaning services, with revolutionary effects. Sir Paul Beresford of Wandsworth was inundated with requests from Labour councils, among others, for advice on how to put their houses in order. The newspapers only occasionally carried dire warnings about the astronomical heights to be reached by the community charge in the coming year. Anti-poll tax meetings attracted fewer and fewer and ceased to be called. The millennium had not yet arrived, but it was not quite business as before.

While more and more people were coming to believe that everyone ought to contribute something to the upkeep of services which they use, discontent with the poll tax continued to rumble on especially among Conservative backbenchers. Certainly in some marginal, and even in some safe, Conservative constituencies, people who lived in modest terraced houses and had paid low rates were outraged by a community charge more than double what they had been paying. That the tax was full of unexpected anomalies no one denied. Many Conservative backbenchers, including many Thatcherites, had become strongly opposed to it, and their dissatisfaction was effectively exploited by opponents of Mrs Thatcher. After the downfall of Mrs Thatcher herself, the poll tax was abandoned with little ado.

The irony is that the poll tax saga, often represented as the evidence for the picture of Mrs Thatcher as a centralizing opponent of local autonomy, in fact directly demonstrates the invalidity of that picture. Unlike the legislation on contracting out, the establishment of the UDCs and the efforts at central control of local government spending, the poll tax was an experiment in autonomy: an attempt to undermine municipal socialism *without* centralization. With understandable logic, the failure of the experiment has led many Thatcherites in the post-Thatcher era to begin talking of the need to reduce local government to being in practice the agent of central government that it has always been in constitutional theory. This illustrates nicely that, for Thatcherites, the fundamental issue is neither the autonomy of local government nor centralization, but rather the desire to eradicate so far as possible from all government (local as much as central) the apparatus and practice of socialism – the desire to ensure that in place of dependence on the public sector, private activity and enterprise are encouraged to flourish in the hope of promoting the vigorous virtues and a prosperous Britain.

8

Invalids or Consumers?

If Thatcherism is committed to promoting the vigorous virtues in individuals and enabling them to take responsibility for managing their lives, what are we to conclude about the Thatcher Government's repeated insistence that the National Health Service – Britain's largest public enterprise absorbing almost thirty billion pounds a year and employing nearly a million people – was 'safe in our hands'?

Accusations Against the Government

The Opposition, and even some Conservatives, simply dismissed the claim as bogus and argued that in reality the Thatcher Government starved the NHS of funds. And they produced statistics that, according to them, prove it. In 1986, the Social Services Committee of the House of Commons concluded that the NHS was 'underfunded' by some 1.3 billion; and in 1988, the 'accumulated deficit' had risen, according to their calculations, to almost 1.9 billion. Compared to the 1970s, expenditure during the period from 1980–1 to 1987–8 was much reduced. Current spending on hospital and community health services rose at a much lower rate than previously, by only ten per cent in real terms, even including the funds internally generated by the government's cost improvement drive.[1]

The government replied to these accusations with another set of figures, showing that the total spending on the NHS had risen from 7.7 billion, for 1978–9, the year when Labour left office, to 29 billion in 1989–90. And the proportion of Gross Domestic Product spent on the Health Service had increased from 4.9 per cent under Labour to 5.2 per cent. The number of patients treated in hospital per available bed in England had increased by 61 per cent; the number of day-cases had nearly doubled; hip replacements and cataract operations were 50 per cent more in 1986 than in 1978. More than a thousand heart transplants had been done since 1979, and more patients had had successful kidney transplants than in any other European country. Britain had ten thousand more doctors and dentists in 1987 than in 1979, and sixty-three thousand more nurses and midwives, all being paid significantly more for a shorter working week. More hospital facilities were being built than ever before; some three hundred and fifty major projects, each worth over 1 million, had been completed, with five hundred more, costing over 4 billion pounds, in progress. Not only had more been spent on health care but also, as the Secretary of State for Social Services said in 1987, 'better value for money, combined with the hard work of dedicated staff, have resulted in substantial improvements in the level of care provided'.[2]

To tell who was right is not easy as the critics argued in terms of 'inputs' and the government in terms of 'outputs'. It was not unreasonable for the government to emphasize output, because whether resources are adequate depends on how they are used. But whether the NHS used its resources 'adequately' there was no way of knowing because there was no established way of measuring the quality of service. On the other hand, the shocking total of 'underfunding' did not necessarily indicate what everyone supposed. For whether there is 'underfunding' in one year can only be known by comparison with the funding for another year. The Social Services Committee took 1980 as the base year, but there was no reason why that should have been chosen. If they had selected another year as the base, they might have found that the 'underfunding' of the NHS was non-existent or twice as bad. Moreover, not even the Government tried to include spending on *private* health care as part of the picture. If they had, even on the Social Services Committee's reckoning, there would have been no underfunding. And yet, although the proportion of the population covered by private health insurance had risen from five per cent in 1979 to ten per cent in 1987, Britain still spent considerably less on private health insurance than any other European country.

What no one denied was that complaints about the NHS, although endemic from the outset, had grown peculiarly fierce in the 1980s. It was evident too, that grounds for complaint abounded. At the end of 1986, almost 700,000 people were waiting for treatment in NHS hospitals, half of whom would wait more than two months for treatment and one in fifty more than a year. Administration of the NHS was criticized for other reasons as well. Junior doctors, for instance, worked hours which would not be imposed on prisoners sentenced to hard labour; besides being exhausted by overwork, they were also compelled to change jobs every few months to suit some invisible administrative schedule of vacancies. Confusion in hospitals' administrative structure made it axiomatic that nowadays Florence Nightingale would be walking the corridors with a lamp in search of the person in charge.

The chain of command was hardly simple. It was certainly not what Aneurin Bevan had had in mind when he assured a meeting at the London School of Economics in 1948 that the administrative costs of the NHS would be negligible. At the apex of the pyramid sat the Secretary of State who, as a part-time sideline, also ran the 40 billion social security system. He was assisted by a number of junior ministers, who would be transferred to other departments almost as soon as they had learnt their jobs at the DHSS. The ministers were served by one hundred thousand civil servants, who divided their time between health and social services. The National Health Service Management Board consisted of a ministerial chairman, a deputy chairman, a chief executive, a chief medical officer, a chief nursing officer, six executive directors and three others. In addition there were inter-regional co-ordinating committees, as well as individual health authorities in the Regions, and the Districts. Down at the bottom, underneath all this apparatus, stood the hospitals and the GPs, vainly trying to avoid being crushed by the weight of the massive administrative structure above them. Each of the administrative tiers had what civil servants call 'a degree of autonomy', a euphemism meaning that they spent their time battling against one another – the Management Board against the civil service, the Regions against the centre, the Districts against the Regions, and everybody against the Secretary of State. When something went wrong, the game of pass-the-buck was played with practised brilliance.

Reorganization followed reorganization but without easing the resentment against central control. The DHSS inspired a great stream of complaints about its habit of 'proffering advice on unattainable objectives', and the rigidity imposed by national agreements about numbers of staff and levels of pay. At the same time, governments kept failing to discover ways of making the various tiers of the NHS more accountable.

As things were organized, it would not in any case have been easy to change much. Room for adjustment was squeezed out at every level. Consultants were given long-term contracts with the NHS and limits on total expenditure, in exchange for which they enjoyed job security and 'clinical freedom'. As a result, in order to change the specialists on its staff, a health authority had to wait for death and retirement. Unionized nurses and staff were governed by national agreements on wages, working conditions and job security. General practitioners were well organized and not disposed to yield any of their 'rights'. Managers had every incentive not to 'rock the boat' by trying to shorten their waiting lists. For if management and consultants in a District referred patients to other Districts with excess capacity and thereby reduced their waiting lists, they risked ruining their campaign for more buildings, equipment, and staff.

Any suggestion for change, other than additional funds, was bound to provoke 'sick baby turned away from hospital' headlines. Nor did anyone within the NHS want anything altered. The officials whom the Health Minister encountered, the medical and nursing officers, the luminaries of the Royal Colleges, the British Medical Association, the Chairmen of Regional and District Health Authorities – all of them regarded any proposal for reform of the NHS as a threat to themselves. For a Conservative government to suggest change was peculiarly outrageous. It was bound to be seen as a plan for destroying the NHS because everyone knew that the NHS was 'safe only in the hands of Labour'.

The Myth of the NHS

That conviction rested on a myth, which had become entrenched in all parties, that the National Health Service had been brought in by the Labour Party in the teeth of strong opposition from everyone else. The historical truth was rather different. The idea had been germinating in all parties since the 1920s, and before then, socialists were by no means universally in favour of a health service – a number preferred alternatives like a national insurance scheme. In 1948, the National Health Service Bill was supported by all parties, as the spokesman for the Labour Government acknowledged during the Lords Debate. The Bill, he said, was 'not the product of any single party or any single Government. It is in fact the outcome of a concerted effort, extending over a long period of years, and involving doctors, laymen and Government, to improve the efficiency of our medical services, and to make them more easily accessible to the public ... Responsible people were advocating a much wider and more comprehensive service long before this ... '[3] Nor was the health service introduced because the existing health care was considered to be so poor. On the contrary, a White Paper on a proposed National Health Service, produced by the Coalition Government in 1944, affirmed that 'Reform in this field is not a matter of making good what is bad, but of making better what is good already,'[4] a conclusion supported by the fact that in the six years before the introduction of the NHS, infant mortality fell more quickly than in the six years afterwards. Moreover, recent research has revealed that a century before the NHS was established, voluntary schemes for ensuring medical care (such as The Great Western Railway Medical Fund Society of Swindon or the Llanelli and District Medical Service) were flourishing.[5]

By 1909, most working men were covered by voluntary insurance. These schemes were killed by the 1948 reform, when all political parties agreed that Britain could not do without a comprehensive health scheme funded by taxes and run by Whitehall.

In the end, although they supported the scheme for a National

Health Service, the Conservatives voted against the National
Health Service Bill on the second Reading because they objected
to the nationalization of hospitals, which had been included in the
Bill at the last moment. The Conservatives' objection was shared
by many in the Labour Party. Not only had the Labour Cabinet,
the local authorities and the great majority of the medical profession
opposed the nationalization of the hospitals – opposition to it had
been the announced Labour Party policy. Just five weeks before
Bevan's Bill was published, the House was told by Herbert Morrison that the Government felt that 'it would not be right to take the
hospitals over into a national concern'. Otherwise, the principles on
which the Bill was based had all along been supported by the
Conservatives. Their spokesman for health assured the House
that his party were wholly agreed on the principle of 'a national,
comprehensive, 100 per cent health service . . . We accept the
principle and we accept the consequences that flow from it . . . an
enormous expansion and development of the health services as a
whole . . . a far greater degree of co-ordination, or planning, as it
is usually called, than we have ever known before.'[6] Indeed so firm
was the Conservative enthusiasm for the NHS, that they came to
regard their having voted against the Bill as a disastrous error.

Nevertheless, there was also good reason for the conviction that
only the Labour Party truly loved the NHS. If many different
strands of opinion had collaborated to support the NHS, the shape
it was given by Aneurin Bevan's Bill rested on an assumption that
few were aware of but that had nevertheless determined its character. This was the assumption that buying health care is nothing
like buying a car or a house because the consumer of health care
cannot know what is good for him. Or to put it another way, the
NHS was designed to satisfy 'needs' rather than 'wants'. 'Needs'
are given by nature, and only experts, doctors and social scientists
can know how to satisfy them. Therefore the patient is to be seen
not as a consumer, deciding what he wants, but as a passive
recipient of whatever the all-knowing powers on high decide that
he ought to have. Therefore consumer sovereignty would defeat
the purpose of a national health service.

Because the NHS was shaped by this assumption, it was

designed to treat patients as packages of needs whose personal preferences or wants are irrelevant. That was why socialists like Beatrice Webb and Aneurin Bevan passionately refused to consider a national insurance system, which would confer on the patient the status of a consumer. Such socialists were determined to have a 'free' health service for everyone, and not just for those who needed financial assistance; they subscribed to the view, succinctly articulated by Sidney Webb, that 'The perfect and fitting development of each individual is not necessarily the utmost and highest cultivation of his own personality but the filling, in the best possible way, of his humble function in the great social machine.'[7] Machine parts cannot be expected to know what will keep them in good working order.

The ethos that shaped the NHS in 1948 accounts for the aggressive, self-righteous austerity of waiting rooms and wards, practices such as requiring patients to wait about for hours because several people are always booked for the same appointment, the insistence that patients spend a day or two in hospital for a test that private laboratories perform in half an hour on outpatients, the obstacles to changing doctors, and the hostility to any questions that a patient might ask about his treatment. For the patient was regarded not as a customer who should be satisfied but as a damaged machine to be repaired as and when the experts found it convenient to do so. A report by Dr Joe Collings in 1950 told of 'minute consulting rooms, with no chairs for the patients, queues for the doctor 200 yards long and a practice of five doctors seeing 500 patients in a day and proud of it.'[8] When the NHS promised equality of access, it was taken to mean that no one should be denied access to medical services through inability to pay. As interpreted by the administrators, 'equality of access' came to mean that no one should ever get more than anyone else, that amenities such as telephones, private rooms or choice of doctor should be available to everyone or to no one. It was an attitude entirely appropriate for an organization that aimed to treat passive bundles of 'needs', rather than independent consumers with a will to choose what they wanted and a right to complain about how their wants were being satisfied.

For those who share this ethos, the spirit in which the NHS

looks after the nation's health is more important than its efficiency. What matters most to them is that the NHS is a nationalized service with a monolithic structure, empowered to impose on the public its conception of what the public needs. That the NHS is unresponsive to 'consumer demand', far from being a defect, is proof of its virtue. And any intrusion of private medicine, regardless of its effects on health, is a corruption of the proper character of the NHS. In other words, the NHS stands *in loco parentis* for the whole population, and any proposal to modify its structure must therefore be an act of impiety. Understood in this fashion, the NHS is a model of how things should be done in the utopia dreamt of by socialists like Beatrice and Sidney Webb (which led them to discover in Soviet Communism the perfect civilization of the future). Though not even all socialists shared the Webbs' dream, in the general enthusiasm for the great reform, everyone who supported the NHS accepted unwittingly the ethos that had shaped it. Thus the health service acquired the aura of a model of perfection. That is why 'the health issue' has become 'the holy cow' of Britain and arouses such violent passions.

The original Bevanite ethos of the NHS also explains why criticism has for so long concentrated on 'underfunding'. If the aim of the NHS is to satisfy 'needs', then it is reasonable to suppose, as almost everyone did at the outset, that the longer the NHS existed, the less it would have to do. For needs, unlike wants, are fixed, and can accordingly be fully satisfied. It was therefore expected that the demand for NHS services would steadily dwindle or, at worst, stabilize. When it turned out instead that the more patients the NHS treated, the longer grew the queues, the only possible explanation, given acceptance of the Bevanite ethos, was 'underfunding' – the government had not provided enough to satisfy unfulfilled needs.

The NHS Fallacy

The founding ethos of the NHS is, of course, wholly alien to Thatcherism. And this might justify or at least explain the chronic suspicion that the health service was not safe in the hands of the Thatcher Government. What that suspicion overlooked is that the Thatcherite's antipathy to the ethos of the NHS does not oblige him to reject all other arrangements for ensuring that no one goes without medical care. Such arrangements, however, would necessarily have a different character than the NHS. They would be seen as a way of satisfying, not fixed 'needs' – except for a certain minimum on which everyone agrees – but wants, for which there is no given order of priority and no limit because they are decided by each individual in accordance with his personal circumstances and tastes. Some wants may come to be regarded as more urgent as a result of changing standards and medical knowledge. But just what medical care a person requires, even if it is a matter of saving his life, remains a 'want' as long as the patient is assumed to retain ultimate responsibility for deciding what is to be done. That way of thinking about providing for health care follows from the Thatcherite understanding of Britain as a nation of individuals who can and should run their own lives, and whose self-respect would be violated by bureaucrats or doctors who ordered them about like children being forced to do what is good for them.

Because the Thatcherite sees the NHS as an arrangement that, whatever its founders may have intended, satisfies wants, he is not surprised that the gap between public expectations and the capacity of the NHS has continued to widen and seems set to go on doing so. For wants unlike needs are not fixed in either kind or number. The healthier people are, and the more that medicine can achieve, the greater will be the demand for health care. In other words, the more effective the NHS, the more it will be asked to do – which is exactly what has happened.

Once the Health Service is understood in this fashion, deliberating about how to make it better assumes a different character. A serious concern to provide decent medical care for everyone becomes perfectly compatible with contemplating changes in or replacement of the NHS. What to do about the NHS turns into a practical question, to which people of equal goodwill may give different answers. If Thatcherites decide that the NHS is 'safe in their hands', it is not because they stand in awe of it or regard it as a holy relic but because they consider it the most suitable arrangement for the current circumstances. They are not, it is true, thereby committed to retaining the NHS in its current form for eternity. But neither need their present support for it be anything other than genuine.

For the same reasons, Thatcherites think of patients as consumers. That is not because they translate every human relationship into a commercial transaction but because they feel obliged to treat all people, even when ill, as persons whose preferences ought to be respected.

Because providing medical care in Britain has become inextricably and unwittingly bound up with the Bevanite ethos of the NHS, any attempt to introduce consumer sovereignty into the NHS exposed its advocates to grave political dangers. The health service accordingly became the most vulnerable flank of the Thatcher Government. It was the issue that Conservatives feared most in the 1987 election, and on 'wobbly Thursday', 9 June 1987, it looked as if 'the health issue' might lose them the election. The story of a boy whose heart operation had been delayed, coupled with Mrs Thatcher's announced use of private health insurance for herself, far outweighed the statistics – 'a 31 per cent increase in government spending on health after allowing for inflation, 10,000 more doctors and dentists, 63,000 more nurses, millions more patients being treated' – cited *ad nauseam* by Conservatives, as testimony to the Government's generosity to the NHS. Yet no such statistics could dent the widespread belief that the NHS was crumbling, that nurses were leaving in droves, and that people were dying as they waited in queues – all because the Thatcher Government was short-changing it.

Yet there was nothing new in the dissatisfaction with the Health Service after 1979. If there were 700,000 on the waiting lists in 1986, there had been 750,000 in 1979 when Labour left office. Many years before, it had become evident that 'the NHS began to outstrip the absurdly optimistic spending projections of its founders' almost as soon as it was established.[9] As the Thatcher Government continued to spend vast sums of money on the NHS without stemming the discontent it began to be suspected that the

National Health Service suffered from a fallacy that should have been obvious from its inception – that the demand for 'free' medical care will always quickly outrun any possible provision for it. Newspapers published dire predictions, 'Today the situation is out of hand, though it is in nobody's interest to admit it,' warned Brian Walden, formerly a Labour MP, converted to Thatcherism: 'The proof that we cannot go on in the old way is that we never spent so much on the NHS and people have never been more dissatisfied with it. We shall spend ever larger sums on health care and the clamour against what is on offer will rise to a shriek ... The inescapable truth about the National Health Service is that, because its services are offered free from the constraint of price, the demands upon it are literally unlimited ... We are chasing our tail, for if the NHS is as grossly deficient in providing the care required as most people say it is, imagine what they will say as their expectations rise and additional expensive treatments are devised. The way we ought to take is to provide health care free for those who cannot afford to pay for it and insist that those who can afford to pay do so. They should be encouraged by the tax system to take out insurance against the cost of medical treatment.'[10]

Circumstances had exacerbated the consequences of the NHS fallacy. A nation that had formerly endured serious ailments with utter resignation had learnt that doctors could help them. At the same time, medicine became increasingly ingenious and able to cure, with extremely expensive technology, illnesses that had previously been fatal. As people lived longer, diseases of the aged flourished and still more demands were made on the Health Service. At the same time, the austerity of the early post-war years when the National Health Service was founded had given way to affluence. When everyone had had to queue for rations of sugar and meat, queuing for the doctor was hardly remarkable. But things had greatly changed by the eighties. It no longer seemed natural to be pushed from pillar to post in casualty departments, one's injuries growing more painful as one was being registered and docketed like a parcel in a railway station and then left to moulder quietly on some hard bench. People who owned their own homes and regarded a television set as a necessity were not so ready to put up with being shoved into bleak wards with no privacy, poor food, and little access to telephones, television or visitors. Moreover, the growth in private health insurance made it easy to see that one's neighbour, who had such insurance, was being treated quite differently.

The complaints of the patients received fulsome support from within the NHS. For those working in the Health Service had what Enoch Powell described as 'a vested interest in its denigration'. The more they shouted about the shortcomings in the NHS, the better they could justify their claims to additional resources: from the chairman of the hospital board to the nursing auxiliary, anyone 'who professed himself satisfied with what was being spent could not unreasonably be represented as a traitor to his colleagues, his profession, and his patients – on the basis, namely, that more money means improvement and that complaint and dissatisfaction are essential to extracting more money'.[11] There was no effective way to dispute a demand for more money because 'nationalized' medical care is virtually insulated, by its universality and its free provision to the consumer, from comparison with similar services. As Britain grew more prosperous, it is hardly surprising that a 'crisis' erupted in the NHS every three years, accompanied by predictions of imminent collapse.

Breaking up the Monolith

When the Conservative Party took office in 1979, they came in, as had all their predecessors, having pledged to reform the Health Service. Their manifesto proclaimed that they would 'simplify and decentralize the service and cut back bureaucracy', and suggested that they would reject the administrative 'rationalization' previously dear to both parties, which had given ever more power to the bureaucrats of the NHS. And there was a promise to halt 'Labour's vendetta against the private health sector' as well as intimations that the government would consider changing the method of funding the NHS.

In keeping with these pledges, the new Secretary of State, Patrick

Jenkin, abandoned the policy of phasing out pay beds, scrapped the Health Services Board, restored tax relief on medical insurance schemes run by employers, and negotiated a new contract with consultants which permitted them to engage in some private practice without loss of earnings. Legislation in 1982 simplified the NHS structure by eliminating the central tier, which had been introduced by the Conservative reforms in the 1970s. It was replaced by some two hundred District Health Authorities, to be established 'for the smallest possible geographical areas within which it is possible to carry out the integrated planning, provision and development of health services'. Thus the government repudiated the dream of the 1960s of a giant District General Hospital, and stressed the value of small, local hospitals.

No longer did government spokesmen invoke the norms and financial targets which had been all the rage when 'central planning' was the vogue. The heavy representation of local authorities on the District Health Authorities was reduced to a quarter of the total membership and worker representation was abandoned. For it was recognized that here, as elsewhere, giving 'local authorities' less control meant giving bureaucrats (hiding under the euphemism of 'local') less power, and making the District Health Authority more responsive to those who used and operated the service. Family Practitioner Committees became free-floating bodies. And Patrick Jenkin declared that, 'First and foremost, I believe that we must see the NHS, not as a single national organization, but as it is perceived by those who use it and those who work in it at the local level – as a series of local services run by local management, responsive to local needs and with a strong involvement from the local community.' But he also recognized that this would be difficult to do 'in a service where virtually the entire finance comes from the centre – from the Exchequer'. A search for new methods of financing health services was put on the agenda but produced nothing more than the oft-tried gambit of raising charges for prescriptions and encouraging the District Health Authorities to promote local fund-raising activities, which was promptly denounced by the Labour Opposition as a return to the days when voluntary hospitals had to hold bazaars in order to survive.

These measures did not much alter the NHS, but they signified that the government had turned its back on a centrally planned monolithic structure, so exposing itself to the outrage of those who regarded any such change in the NHS as a betrayal of it.

The first serious inquiry into the management of the NHS, published in October 1983, was conducted by [Sir] Roy Griffiths, managing director of the grocers, Sainsbury's. The Griffiths Report was a radical departure from other inquiries because the committee consisted of only four people, who completed the Report in a mere six months; they worked quickly without formally taking evidence from the many people consulted, and unlike Royal Commissions, did not try to represent and reconcile all parties. The Report stated in blunt language what others had been whispering for some time – that the NHS was suffering from 'institutionalized stagnation', that health authorities were being 'swamped with directives without being given direction', that it was 'extremely difficult to achieve change', that consensus decision-making led to 'long delays in the management process'. And it concluded with the aforementioned remark, endlessly repeated thereafter: 'If Florence Nightingale were carrying her torch through the corridors of the NHS today, she would almost certainly be searching for the people in charge.'

The Griffiths Committee advised that the management structure of the NHS must be changed radically, a conclusion that the Thatcher Government adopted to the letter. The suggestion that the final word would rest with a Supervisory Board distinct from a Management Board was tried but failed, and the Minister of State eventually took charge of both. Everywhere else, new managers were brought in from industry, commerce and the armed services to work along with nurses and doctors. The nursing and medical staff lost their power to veto the management. Managers were given an incentive to mobilize support for change, rather than to thwart it, by linking their salaries and contracts to their performance. As a result, porters, nurses and consultants were no longer beyond reprimand in their own sphere, but were subject to correction from the manager in charge. Questions of all sorts that had never before been raised, such as why there was a queue at a hospital, began to be asked as a matter of routine. Perhaps the greatest effect of managerial scrutiny was that it inspired the medical profession to examine its own practices.

New Constraints

By assuming that a good manager is obliged to deliver a good product to the consumer, the Griffiths Report for the first time directly challenged the ethos of the NHS. It declared that whereas businessmen 'have a keen sense of how well they are looking after their customers', no one could tell whether the NHS was meeting the needs of the patient and the community. The growth of claims for medical negligence and the increase in the size of the awards made by the courts also contributed to changing the status of the patient in the NHS to a consumer. The Report's insistence on 'quality assurance' repudiated the leading shibboleth of the NHS, that its immunity from the corruption of seeking profit guaranteed a high quality of service.

The same heresy appeared in another context when in September 1983, health authorities were asked to put out cleaning, catering and laundry services to competitive tendering. These ancillary services had usually been provided by the 'in-house' workforce, the direct employees of the health service. Stories of dirty wards, badly washed laundry and poor food were legion. The complaints by the ancillary staff of being overworked were disposed of by the strike of 1982, when newspapers were filled with pictures of doctors doing the laundry along with their medical duties, and spending considerably fewer hours on the task to much better effect. At first the Health Minister suggested that these services should be privatized, but he was forced to retreat to 'competitive tendering' so that, as in the case of the local authorities, the in-house employees could compete on equal terms with private contractors.

The results suffered from the same defects as in the local authorities. Comparing the private and the in-house bids was not easy because of the different circumstances. It was all too easy for the in-house workforce to adjust conditions to its advantage and so it won the contract more often than not, although its service left much to be desired. Nevertheless, the need to compete for the contract and the possibility that it might not be renewed did something toward improving the quality of work. Despite vigorous campaigns waged by unions and attempts to interfere with the tendering, the virtual monopoly of the in-house providers was broken. The savings were not dramatic – 86 million pounds by 1986, and only eighteen per cent of the contracts went to private firms. But the exercise forced NHS managers, for the first time, to specify standards of service and to devise ways of assessing the quality of provision.

A more powerful interest group was taken on when the government addressed itself to reforming the arrangements under which general practitioners (GPs) worked. There had never been any check on what GPs prescribed or why they referred patients to consultants and hospitals, and the rates of prescription and referral varied enormously and mysteriously. As the cost of prescriptions accounted for almost half of the total spent on primary health care and was expanding at a rate in real terms of more than five per cent a year, the government braced itself to do what some had long advocated – to restrict the right of general practitioners to prescribe particular products without regard to their prices or the availability of less expensive substitutes. There was no medical reason for prescribing a drug sold under a brand name, which cost two or three times as much as the identical formula sold under its chemical designation. Yet GPs regularly prescribed the former. Of course, patients could continue to obtain the drug they preferred if they paid for it. Needless to say, the pharmaceutical industry were outraged. In an unholy alliance with the medical profession and the Labour Party, the industry campaigned energetically to persuade the public that they would be deprived of medicines they needed, that the proposal would create a two-tier system (one of the regular bogeys wheeled out by stalwarts of the NHS), and would restrict research by the drug companies because of the drop in their profits. In the end, the government extended the list of 'permitted' drugs.

Nevertheless, a new principle had been introduced, that the Health Service was subject to the same constraints as other public bodies, and that, like any other enterprise, the Health Service could be managed well or badly. Doctors and hospital administrators deserved no more immunity than any other interest group from scrutiny of their expenditure and practices. In short, it was established that even the NHS could not claim automatic or unlimited freedom to use public resources as it saw fit; taxpayers who had supplied its funds had a right to demand that their money not be wasted. Though politicians refrained from saying it, the government's new policies implied that the NHS was but a means to an end, and not necessarily the best means to that end.

Yet not even the Prime Minister dared to spell this out. When in 1987, she gave what was acclaimed by *The Times* as the best speech 'she has made to a Conservative Conference ... no mean feat', she carefully refrained from any bold statements about reforming the health service. The NHS continued to be an explosive issue. Soon after the 1987 election the storm broke. The furore began with the death of a baby who had been kept waiting for some six weeks for an open-heart operation and died soon after it was performed. Television produced dramatic tales about the closing of hospital wards because of cash shortages; consultants complained that they had to leave patients to die because they lacked the resources for the necessary operations; nurses went on strike to protest about closures and shortages. Labour MPs talked of 'murder', and the *Daily Mirror* described Mrs Thatcher as 'coldhearted'. Prime Minister's Question Time was nearly monopolized by the health issue. Everyone clamoured for more money for the NHS. Not only the leaders of the medical profession, the Presidents of the Royal Colleges, condemned the Government in strong language. Ronald Butt of *The Times*, though formerly a supporter of Thatcherism, repeatedly attacked the Government for its indifference to a pressing need. Opinion polls and the BBC assured everyone that the nation was thinking of nothing other than 'the health issue'.

The government tried to calm the storm with a series of emollient measures. It gave the NHS top-up grants to finance new pay awards. It symbolized its concern for medical care by carving a separate Department of Health out of the DHSS under a Secretary of State for Health who was no longer charged with and diverted by responsibility for social security. In November 1988, Kenneth Clarke, the Secretary of State, announced that during the coming financial year the NHS would be provided with an additional 1.8 billion pounds, enough to close the 'underfunding' gap as calculated earlier in the year by the Commons Committee on Social Services.

An Internal market

In the meantime the government had begun to rethink the NHS, looking toward basic and permanent reforms rather than short-term expedients. Immediately after the election of June 1987, discussions were set in motion among representatives of the DHSS, the Policy Unit at Downing Street, the Cabinet Office and the Treasury. Though no formal hearings were mounted, ministers and officials met with representatives of the medical professions and other interested bodies, and solicited comments and suggestions. By January 1988 the Prime Minister announced that the NHS was undergoing a major review. By November 1988 the review resulted in a White Paper.

During the course of the review, the government – that is, principally the Prime Minister and her Policy Unit – considered and rejected various proposals. One was a suggestion by the Treasury that additional charges should be levied for the use of NHS services; it was rejected on the ground that it would brand the reform as a penny-pinching exercise, without even producing much additional revenue. John Moore, the then Secretary of State, favoured a 'health tax', from which people who bought private health insurance could be exempted; but this too was rejected on the ground that it would be attacked as establishing a 'two-tier' system.

The idea that finally won out was to liberalize the NHS by establishing an 'internal market' within it. Its merit was taken to be that, without privatization, it would replace a bureaucratic allocation of resources with one which mimics the actions of the market.

As originally designed, the NHS had been assigned two functions. It would pay for medical services, so that they would be provided to every patient free of charge. In addition the NHS would actually provide all medical services by establishing, as it were, a 'direct labour organization'. These two functions are intrinsically separable. The first is an insurance function, the second a supply function. It would have been quite possible, in other words, to establish a national health insurance – financed, in exactly the same way as the NHS, by specific insurance contributions *plus* funding from general tax revenues – while leaving the supply function in the hands of private doctors and private hospitals. In fact that is just how provision for health care is organized in various other countries. But the Thatcher government recognized that to reform the NHS by privatizing doctors and hospitals would be politically unacceptable.

What the 'internal market' undertook to do was something else. Without fundamentally altering the dual function of the NHS, it introduced the idea that the NHS general practitioner could 'buy' for his patient the best NHS hospital service available. Instead of being compelled, as was previously the case, to send the patient to a hospital within his own District, he could send him to any NHS hospital that could provide the required facilities. Waiting times would thus be reduced for many patients – because at the same time that certain services in some hospitals were subject to month-long queues, other hospitals had idle capacity. Moreover, the 'internal market' would tend to increase efficiency in hospitals – since the most efficient would tend to be preferred by practitioners, and the least efficient would be marked out as such by the relatively low demand for their services.

Three basic ideas underlay the practical working of the reform. The first was that funds should follow the patient: whichever hospital provided the services would earn the corresponding fee. The second was that each hospital would determine for itself the prices of the various services it offered. In order that hospitals should be able to do so, they would be liberated from direct control by the health authorities and each would be empowered to negotiate its own pay settlements with its staff. The third was that the NHS would be authorized to buy services from and sell services to the private sector. This would enable the NHS to relieve pressure on its own facilities when those were overloaded, to earn revenues from the private sector at other times, and thus to widen the scope of the NHS internal market.

Some elements of the reforms changed administrative practices in ways which pointedly repudiated the old ethos of the NHS and gave patients the status of consumers whose wants should be satisfied. Such changes are encapsulated in the contrast between the old NHS health card and the new conditions. The old card listed seven 'Rules of Conduct' – the patient must produce his Medical Card, obey the practitioner's instructions, do nothing to retard his recovery, make no unreasonable demands upon the professional services, attend the surgery at the hours appointed by the practitioner, not summon a doctor to visit him between 8pm and 10am, give notice before 10am of wanting a home visit that day. Under the new regime, instead of being handed rules of conduct, patients were invited to consult lists of available GPs and information about their services. The patient was enabled besides to change GPs at will, without having to ask the abandoned GP to sign a form releasing him. Hospitals were required to make individual appointments that could be relied on, so eliminating the previously frequent waits of two to three hours in out-patient clinics; patients were to be rapidly notified of the results of diagnostic tests; patients were permitted to pay for additional amenities such as single rooms, personal telephones, or a wider choice in meals.

Other changes were designed to promote the 'internal market', the essence of which is that services will be 'bought' and 'sold' within the Health Service. Those providing services would compete for business, and those who do not provide services for which there is a demand would have to look to their performance. It is an attempt to secure some of the benefits of privatization within a nationalized health service. The object was to restore vitality to an enterprise grown increasingly parasitical on the taxpayer and to produce better results in health care. By allowing more decisions to be made by the GPs and hospitals, and emphasizing that they were there to serve rather than command, the patient would come to think of himself differently and take a more active part in deciding what care he should receive. Doctors and administrators, it was hoped, would be similarly inspired. They would have to take responsibility for providing what their clients wanted at a reasonable cost. That was the only way, proponents of the reforms argued, to make it impossible to evade the questions that needed to be asked about the NHS: 'Why is it that some GPs refer twenty times more than others? Why is it that some hospitals find it so difficult to make efficient use of operating theatres? Why is it that one-third of all people waiting for over one year are concentrated in one-sixth of districts? Why is it that death rates vary so much between doctors?'[12]

Health authorities would no longer be responsible for providing health services but for buying the best services either from the NHS or private hospitals. District Health Authorities and GPs would be allowed to use whatever hospital in their judgement provided the best service; they were no longer restricted to local hospitals. Hospitals had been averse to accepting additional patients because – as their budgets were determined beforehand – additional patients simply meant additional costs. But once patients carried the money on their backs, hospitals had an incentive to try to attract more patients. Districts would pay directly for the services provided to their patients by other Districts, leaving each District free to buy the best service it could, whether from self-governing hospitals, private hospitals, or NHS hospitals in other Districts. A District thus ceased to be a monopolistic domain of its local hospitals, and hospitals that had spare capacity could take on patients who would otherwise be waiting in a queue at the local hospital of some other District.

Controlling the Experts

Another aspect of the reform, a new contract for GPs, provoked the most troublesome opposition. The BMA spent millions on an advertising and leafleting campaign. The Labour Party had a field day. Kenneth Clarke, the Secretary of State for Health, was accused of trying to reduce the number of GPs and to force doctors to work longer lists and give patients less time.

What especially outraged GPs was the increase in the proportion of their income to be derived from 'capitation fees' – payments per patient on their list. Other conditions considered too onerous to be endured were that GPs should be available to patients for at least twenty-six hours a week, spread over at least five days a week, at times convenient to the patient; that they should provide illness-prevention services; that they should visit everyone over seventy-five in their homes once a year, examine all newly registered patients, and give 'life-style' checks to their patients every three years. For patients over seventy-five and for services like vaccinating or screening they were to get additional payments. But they had to meet certain 'targets' for the number of patients screened or vaccinated. Nor were GPs pleased by the provision that when a deputized doctor visited a patient at night, he should get only a third of what that patient's own doctor would be paid. They resented the introduction of medical and financial auditing of their activities: their prescriptions and referrals to hospitals were now to be checked by the Family Practitioner Committees, which were required regularly to appraise the quality and quantity of services provided, to set disease prevention targets and to carry out consumer surveys. Giving bonuses of up to ten thousand pounds to doctors working in inner cities, in order to induce more doctors to take up such onerous practices, was denounced because the same bonus was not given for other needy areas.

In introducing these measures, the review recognized a question – To whom should experts be accountable? – which had been ignored in the discussions that had led up to the NHS. In the heyday of socialist reform it had been assumed that expertise was its own monitor. As the Webbs and Fabian pamphlets explained tirelessly, only the greed for profit distorted the truth known to experts. Remove profit, and selfishness would vanish. By the 1980s, many people knew better. It was widely if not universally recognized that whoever defines 'need' makes a political decision and exercises power over those who are dependent on his definition. The review accordingly introduced an elaborate apparatus for monitoring medical experts.

The GPs' anger was exacerbated by the fact that the new contracts were being introduced at the same time as the pay of doctors was being negotiated, a tactical error for which Conservatives blamed Kenneth Clarke, then Secretary of State for Health. The ill will inspired by the nature of the new contracts undoubtedly flowed over on to the pay negotiation. Eleven million leaflets, explaining the horrors of the new conditions for GPs, flooded the surgeries. In the Commons, the Opposition spokesman on health, Robin Cook, explained that 'One needs a word other than contract to describe such a document ... something that captures more honestly than centralizing, the authoritarian nature of the Government that imposes it. Perhaps edict or decree more accurately captures the flavour ... '[13]

In reply, Kenneth Clarke pointed out that, as almost one in four family doctors had been found to work fewer than thirty hours a week on their general practice, their remuneration ought to reflect that fact. The wide variations in the number of referrals to hospitals suggested that something was wrong, and according to the Office of Health Economics, hospital consultants felt that more than forty per cent of the referrals were 'possibly' or 'definitely' inappropriate. Clarke added that there was no sound reason to suppose that getting a larger part of their pay from capitation fees would induce GPs to take on more patients than they could serve adequately; after all, paying consultants a fixed sum per year did not induce them to treat only 'easy' cases.

Another ironic consequence of the review was that the British Medical Association, having previously argued so vehemently that the NHS was collapsing, now took to celebrating its perfection. They assured the government review that only 'a relatively small percentage increase in funding' would solve all problems and that it would be 'a serious mistake to embark on any major restructuring of the funding and delivery of health care in order to resolve the present difficulties'. And they launched into a eulogy of the NHS as 'the most efficient way of providing a truly comprehensive health service, while at the same time ensuring the best value for money in terms of the quality of health care: because the NHS, better than any other system, could control the cost of health care'.[14]

By the end of 1990, the fuss had subsided. The dire consequences had not followed. Instead of the predicted decline in the number of GPs, the Medical Practices Committee had a rush of applications from GPs wanting extra partners. GPs began to carry out more minor surgery and most were reported to be doing between one and four extra clinics a week for selected groups of patients, thus cutting down referrals to hospitals. Doctors were reporting that they were spending up to four hours more each week with patients, and some reported ten or more extra hours. More than a quarter of GPs were doing more home visits and of these the majority were doing an extra five visits a week, while ten per cent said they were doing ten or more extra home visits. Other changes also suggested that GPs were enlarging their activities. In the six months from October 1989 to April 1990 the number of practice nurses employed by GPs increased by a third and there was an even bigger jump in the number of receptionists and secretaries. The number of doctors involved in postgraduate education had multiplied several-fold. Half the GPs had computers and within a year three quarters were expected to do so. Most striking was a statement in the September 1990 issue of the *General Practitioner*, never renowned for its support of Thatcherite policies: 'Suddenly targets [for the number of patients treated] don't seem so bad after all . . . like it or not, the net result of the introduction of targets has been that the necessary proportion of immunizations needed to prevent the spread of wild viruses is close to being achieved; it has meant that the cervical cytology screening programme really is becoming something worthy of the name; and at the same time it has resulted in an increase in GPs' gross pay. A satisfactory state of affairs if there ever was one.'[15]

All this was pointed out by Kenneth Clarke in an interview in the *Independent*. He declared himself to be well pleased with the results of the reforms in the NHS – 'It was a battle worth fighting.'[16]

The Government claimed that these measures had made the NHS more 'consumer oriented', giving patients more choice and more control over the service they received. But even observers who approved of the reforms pointed out that the methods used were those of the planners – setting targets and monitoring progress towards their achievement were the same old 'rational administration long admired by planners'. According to one of the more knowledgeable students of the NHS, Rudolf Klein, 'It is centralization speaking a different language, with the accent on outputs ... priorities expressed in terms of ... targets of activity.'[17] But on the other hand, in two measures, one affecting GPs and the other, hospitals, Klein saw a genuinely new departure. The Thatcher Government presented these changes as the way forward, because they would stimulate the 'internal market' which was the next best thing to a real market, while avoiding any fundamental alteration in the NHS. As free health care would be combined with consumer choice and accountability, the best of all possible worlds would be achieved.

For GPs it was proposed that those who wished to do so, and had over eleven thousand patients either individually or in combination with other doctors, could become budget holders. The budgets would be set by the number and characteristics of the patients on the panel. GPs would then be able to provide the money to pay for whatever services they wanted from whatever hospital, and hospitals could no longer turn away patients referred to them from other districts on the ground that they lacked the funds to care for them. As budget holders, doctors would be able to move resources to where they were wanted. Whatever funds were left over could be used to improve their practice.

This arrangement, it was hoped, would be an incentive for GPs to choose treatments more discerningly and for hospitals to compete for more patients by providing better services. It would also make it easier to send patients to hospitals where they could be attended to immediately instead of being compelled to rely on a local hospital with a long waiting list. But the GPs' budget could be used only for conditions which were not threatening to life. Cases involving life and death, as well as treatment costing more than five thousand pounds, would be paid for by the health authorities in the usual way.

The proposal to allow hospitals to become self-managing trusts enabled them to regain some of the independence that the early supporters of the NHS never wanted to destroy, and that had been wholly removed only later; it has been forgotten that teaching hospitals were not nationalized until the Conservative reforms of 1974 put the health authorities in charge of them. By becoming self-governing, hospitals would be free to employ the staff they wanted on whatever terms they chose. The management would also be able to acquire and dispose of assets, plan their own capital projects, and finance their projects by borrowing. Self-governing hospitals would get their revenue from selling their services either to the NHS, through contracts with health authorities or GPs, or to the private sector.

Criticisms of the Reforms

These more radical reforms did not provoke the outcry caused earlier by the GPs' new contracts. But still Clarke was criticized widely for being too abrasive and too much in a hurry. It was felt that there were too many unanswered questions. People wanted to know what financial penalties would be imposed if GPs overstepped their drugs budget, what would really happen if GPs ran out of money, what would happen if a self-governing hospital went bankrupt, who would pay for a patient to travel to a distant hospital? Instead of giving every hospital in the country the right to opt out and every GP with a list of eleven thousand the right to become a budget-holder, why had the government not launched cautious pilot studies?

Other criticisms were more fundamental. It was pointed out that the reforms had not released the government from the obligation to make the difficult political decision about how much money to spend on the NHS. Nor had the reforms provided a way out of the dilemma of choosing between political and financial costs, between satisfying the demand for free medical care and containing expenditure. By making central control stricter and management more efficient the government hoped to make better use of the available resources. It had also provided encouragements for demand to move into the private sector. But in the end it tried to buy off the opposition by providing more funds: 'The last act of the play – when expectations had been aroused that a combination of rising political embarrassment and financial demands would bring about a fundamental re-appraisal of the NHS – saw impending melodrama turn into familiar farce: the corpse got up and took its bow.' Nevertheless, there had also been an important change of direction: 'behind the stately facade, the workmen are beginning to gut the old building . . . ' The review had confirmed and encouraged a trend towards 'a mixed economy of health care', 'a more loosely articulated system', 'less bureaucracy, less centralization and less deference to professional expertise, more self-help, more consumer participation and more tolerance of diversity'.[18]

Other critics were less charitable. They saw the NHS reforms as a 'great missed opportunity' because the reforms did not tackle the fundamental difficulty, the way the NHS was funded. Only reforms in funding could relieve 'under-funding' and the 'poor record of responsiveness to consumers'. The most telling criticism came from David Green, Head of the IEA Health and Welfare unit, who charged the government with having 'gone native': 'If the Government had been true to its own declared philosophy, it should have attempted to restore choice and personal responsibility to consumers, and it should have attempted to end the paternalism of providing services in kind, paid for by taxes on the people.' Late in the day, some references to consumers and choice were added to the proposals but these were largely window dressing. Consumer choice was never really on the agenda and the idea of talking about consumers only came later when the Government was thinking about how to present its plans.[19]

Green predicted that the reforms would neither allay fresh demands for funds nor win votes. After all, only a few years earlier the British Medical Association had assured us that 1 billion more pounds would put everything right; now the BMA was demanding 5 billion. The government spent 64 million pounds in two years up to 1989 on its waiting list initiative, 230,000 additional patients had been treated, but the total waiting lists remained as they were. As a political gimmick, too, the reforms had failed; they had alienated many without winning new friends other than the new general managers. The government had forgotten its commitment to 'reducing the scope and power of government and its agencies, and increasing the power of individuals and families'. Instead ministers had 'fallen into the same trap as earlier Tory governments, namely believing themselves to be the best managers of public services. Witness Mrs Thatcher's boast to the Tory 1922 Committee in the summer of 1989 that she would make the NHS so good that no one would want to use private hospitals.'[20]

Instead of pursuing a 'clear conception of the proper scope and limits of government', the government's aim seemed to be to seek votes wherever it could find them. Although Mrs Thatcher had said that 'the reforms on hospitals were designed to give more powers and responsibility to the people,' that was not what they had done. The reforms might make the health pound go further but 'they do not restore power to individuals and could not do so without radically reforming the funding of the health service.' Allowing money to follow the patient, Green pointed out, did not give patients the power to decide where the money went or how much was spent. Not their personal preferences, but contractual arrangements between health authorities and doctors determined where they were treated.[21]

What is supposed to be the great virtue of the NHS, that it provides health service free of charge to the patient, is really, according to Green, its central defect. The chief losers are the poor and the more vulnerable because they lack the skills which enable the better-off and more energetic to extract better service. If the poor and frail were given purchasing power instead of services in kind, they too could insist on 'a more responsive service from producers'. There is only one way that the consumer can really choose, and that is by paying for what he wants. When he hands his buying power over to the government in the form of taxes, he surrenders his ability to choose: 'The White Paper provides no answer. The best solution is a fully-fledged competitive market in which consumer choice would be based, not on a Government promise, but on that personal power to inflict economic pain on unsatisfactory producers which consumer payment alone can bring.' Nothing short of radically changing the way of funding health care would achieve the desired results.[22]

The Thatcherite answer to this criticism was that Rome wasn't built in a day. To have attempted so radical a change as that suggested by David Green would have been political suicide, which was why Mrs Thatcher had put strict limits on the review. What had been put in place could, however, evolve in the direction of increased consumer sovereignty. Much had been moved in that direction. The paternalist ethos of the NHS had been replaced. A new spirit now reigned in hospitals and among doctors. As people became increasingly impatient with their lack of control over the treatment they received, they would press for further changes.

Whether this is a reasonable expectation remains to be seen. For the moment, the movement seems to be in the opposite direction. For early in February 1991 William Waldegrave, then Secretary of State for Health in Mr Major's Government, announced that opted-out hospitals would not be allowed to borrow money and would have to pay junior doctors according to the national agreement reached for the rest of the Health Service. By the end of February 1991, in the midst of the Gulf War, complaints about the NHS were again in the headlines.

The rhetoric, the declared intentions, as well as many effects of the Thatcher Government's policies for health can be explained by the Thatcherite determination to change political expectations and practices in Britain. What was actually done, however, fell far short of what might have been expected. To what degree the disparity was due to a prudent recognition of what the nation would tolerate, disingenuousness, or a lack of courage is a subject ripe for speculation.

9

Education: Thatcher versus Bismarck?

The tensions within Thatcherism become obvious in its educational policies. Some of the more radical steps towards clearly Thatcherite objectives were taken in this area. But it is also here that the Thatcher Government adopted policies most blatantly at odds with its fundamental commitments.

Unlike other advocates of a market economy, Thatcherism does not share the view of Dr Bernard Mandeville, who caused such a scandal in the eighteenth century by arguing that public benefits rest on private vices. On the contrary, Thatcherism emphasizes the dependence of public benefits on characters distinguished by the vigorous virtues. In the Thatcherite view the agency for bringing up individuals armed with such virtues is the family. But in Britain as elsewhere some of the family's duties have long been delegated to schools. While Thatcherism accepts that practice, it emphasizes that the school is a surrogate for the family. This view rejects the widespread understanding and practice of schooling that developed in Britain and manifested itself clearly since the Second World War.

Not Schools But 'A System of Education'

As arts and sciences have grown more abundant and elaborate, transmitting them has increasingly become the province of specialized teachers. As a result, schools have come to seem to be wholly distinct in purpose from the family, rather than an extension of it. At the same time, the connection between school and family has been weakened by a growing disposition to think of schools as part of the state, because most schools have become parts of a publicly

228

administered and funded 'system of education'.

Such a 'system' took root in Britain in 1870, when elected school boards were established by law. Further legislation in 1902 transformed school boards into local educational authorities (LEAs), and the finishing touches were added by the Butler Education Act of 1944, which was supported by both the Labour and Conservative parties in the wartime Coalition Government which sponsored the Act. It required children to be schooled from the age of five to fifteen, and established three sorts of secondary schools – secondary modern, technical, and grammar. Whether a child would attend one or another was to be determined by an examination taken at or soon after the age of eleven, 'eleven-plus' examinations as they came to be called. As a great number of the existing schools were schools run by the Church which were in a state of great disrepair both financially and otherwise, the Act made two kinds of provisions. A Church school could choose to be funded completely by the state, with the Church retaining a minor voice in governing it, thus becoming a 'voluntary controlled' school. Alternatively it could choose to be 'voluntary aided', which the majority did. In that case the Church had to provide a certain proportion of the capital expenditure; in return it retained control of the governing body.

By 1979, some ninety-three per cent of all schoolchildren were attending schools maintained by the state, which made it seem reasonable to regard schools as part of the state. For Thatcherites, however, the objective of ensuring that all children have access to an adequate education does not necessarily imply that all, or almost all, should be educated in state schools. This heterodoxy was fortified by the belief that, far from serving as an effective surrogate for the family, British schools were performing very poorly. Of the three kinds of schools set up by the Butler Act, only grammar schools functioned well; many became as renowned for academic excellence as the best independent schools. By contrast, secondary modern schools were widely criticized. Yet it was the grammar schools that the Labour Government began to attack from the 1960s onwards, as part of a drive to reduce all schools to uniformity. When, in January 1965, Anthony Crosland became Secretary of

State for Education and Science, he declared that he was determined to destroy every grammar school in the land. They and all other schools would be turned into comprehensives. The process of turning schools into comprehensives annihilated not only most grammar schools as well as the secondary modern schools but also more than four hundred technical schools.

The great virtue claimed for the comprehensives was that they eliminated selection, that is to say, they made no distinctions between different kinds of ability, either in admitting children to a school or in the curriculum to be followed by pupils. Comprehensives, it was said in their praise, taught the same subjects in the same way to all children, whatever their interests or talents. The drive reached its apotheosis in 1976 when the Labour Secretary of State for Education, Mrs Shirley Williams, made it compulsory for local education authorities to turn all schools into comprehensives. By 1977, three quarters of all pupils in secondary schools had been emancipated from the bad old distinctions.

What Went Wrong

Emancipation was accompanied by the spread of a new theory of education. Change in the structure of schools had coincided with the growing influence of 'progressive' education, whose patron saint was the American philosopher, John Dewey, and which came to dominate schools in the United States by the end of the Second World War. In Britain, 'progressive' education gained admirers because it accorded so well with the egalitarianism and antipathy to all things traditional that inspired the reforms of the Labour governments. It had been tried in the school run between the Wars by Bertrand Russell, as well as a few others, none of them notorious for success.

Wherever the 'progressive' outlook took over, the established attributes of English schools – rules, uniforms, assemblies, rituals, set subjects, timetables, games – were repudiated. In the new open-plan schools, classes were not held in separate rooms and children were not required to remain seated, keep quiet, learn tables or memorize dates. The aim was to replace old-fashioned 'passive reception' by 'active participation' in doing things 'relevant' to contemporary life. Old subjects were crowded out by peace studies; discussions of racism, feminism, community problems, and homosexuality as well as other unconventional sexual practices. Children were encouraged by 'progressive' teachers to think of themselves as victims of 'social forces' and 'the class structure' and to blame shortcomings in their own lives or in Britain as a whole on the failure of the state to provide for the needy. Problems such as pollution were attributed to the iniquities of capitalism and said to be curable only by socialism.[1] Far from learning to put duty before pleasure, pupils were encouraged to pursue instant gratification of desires and to resent any discipline that interfered with 'spontaneity' or 'self-expression'.

A leading objective of the new vogue was to reshape schooling so as to make it impossible for any child to appear any more or less competent than others; this objective was described as ending 'social divisiveness'. Thus the Development Programme for Race Equality, which was lauded as 'a well-planned initiative to deal with the low achievement' of blacks, far from providing special or additional instruction for children who made poor progress, aimed to relieve blacks even more than whites from the pains of learning. To enforce the programme, local educational authorities assigned to every secondary school a monitor whose duty it was to 'coordinate race equality initiatives and make them an integral part of the whole work of the school'. Instead of being required to 'conform' to 'bourgeois' standards of grammar and spelling, children were 'stimulated' to 'express themselves' in the language that they 'naturally' spoke, however remote it might be from standard English. This was what the monitors for the 'race equality initiatives' were required to ensure. Instead of being given literary classics to read, children were encouraged to appreciate unknown writers who did not use idiomatic English or meet ordinary literary criteria. Teaching 'the ascenders and descenders' of an organized handwriting was abandoned, along with the traditional lined paper, in favour of self-expression on blank sheets. 'Equality of outcome' was the theme song of the new education.

One particular school became notorious for its zeal in abandoning the old repression. Teachers at the William Tyndale School in Islington, London declared their loyalty to a 'democratic, egalitarian and non-sexist philosophy', and their opposition to 'arbitrary standards of attainment and behaviour'. The teachers pledged themselves to let children 'make their own decisions about what they should learn, where, when and how', so as 'to diminish role-difference' between teacher and pupil 'to a point where each could be seen to have something of value to offer the other on an equal level'. The result was described by observers as 'complete turmoil'.[2]

Some comprehensives and some teachers did manage to insinuate traditional teaching into their classes. But head teachers with such sympathies and the ability to put them into practice were not welcome. Those, like Lawrence Norcross, Headmaster of Highbury Grove School in Islington, who maintained a staunch resistance, suffered constant attack by the education authorities and their minions. Rebellious teachers were bullied by colleagues into conforming to the new 'freedom'.

Although the 'complete turmoil' of the William Tyndale School was not matched everywhere else, there was a sufficiently close approach in enough other schools to produce large numbers of nearly illiterate and innumerate young people, who had little idea of disciplined behaviour and 'were incapable of enduring any form of steady labour'.[3] The reason was not far to seek. A survey conducted by the Schools Council, whose sympathies lay wholly with the new fashion in education, showed that teachers put 'making children happy and cheerful' at the top of a list of seventy objectives, and ranked arithmetic twentieth, 'writing clear and meaningful English' forty-fourth, and mastering 'basic grammar' fifty-first.[4] The effects on the behaviour of children were dramatic. In the year 1971–2, more than two thousand violent incidents and nearly a thousand threats of violence were reported. In 1974, nearly a tenth of the pupils in middle and secondary schools were found to be truant on the day surveyed. In the Inner London Education Authority's schools, spot checks in 1977 revealed an average of eighteen per cent truancy and an extreme of twenty-eight per cent. When the Baroness Cox and Dr John Marks assembled striking evidence showing that academic performance in the comprehensives was well below that of the grammar and the secondary modern schools, the DES dismissed their evidence. Only after an investigation by Sir Keith Joseph did the officials admit that they had been mistaken.

The consequences of these practices were hidden from public view by changes in the examinations. From 1960 onwards, with strong approval and support from the Schools Council and the National Union of Teachers, O-level and A-level examinations were graded not according to a fixed standard but by allotting a certain percentage of candidates to each grade – a practice called 'norm-referencing'. The grades accordingly merely compared each pupil with others taking the same examination at the same time. As the grades revealed nothing about how well a child measured up to some fixed standard, children who received the highest grades in English might be unable to spell or read, with no one the wiser.

As parents could not choose schools, and schools could therefore not compete for pupils, the only check on the performance of schools was surveillance by Her Majesty's Inspectorate. When Sir Keith Joseph became Secretary of State for Education, he had high hopes for improving the schools by making the Inspectorate more influential. But what inspired the inspectors' reports was not necessarily a concern for education in Sir Keith's sense. A good illustration of the Inspectorate's prejudices was encountered by Professor Sig Prais, Senior Research Fellow in the National Institute of Economic and Social Research. During 1984 and 1985, he was approached by headmasters from about twenty-five independent schools who complained about interference from inspectors. As there was no national curriculum at the time, they felt that the inspectors had no right to dictate the curriculum. But the inspectors persisted. In particular they issued a report on a school in Hackney run by the Hasidic community, declaring that if the school did not wholly change its curriculum, the Secretary of State for Education would cancel its registration. Although the inspectors announced bluntly that they were making a 'test case' of the school, the Secretary of State, Sir Keith Joseph, was told by his officials that he could not justifiably refuse to sign the order for shutting it.

The school's legal advisor said that the report on which the closing order was based was invalid. On visiting the school, Professor Prais found that the children were working in an unusually orderly fashion. In the standard test on mathematics, their grades stood a shade above the national average. In English their grades fell a touch short of the national average, as they were taught mainly in Yiddish which they also spoke at home. There were, however, classes in English, as well as in mathematics, geography, history and other traditional subjects of an English school. A-level results were remarkably good despite the restricted curriculum, and a high proportion of the pupils went on to university. But the inspectors had administered no tests and had made no serious investigation. As none of them understood Yiddish, they had no idea of what was going on in many of the classes. They condemned one of the headmasters, a rabbi, for being unqualified, although he was an Oxford graduate, with a degree in English.

The case was finally heard by the Independent Schools' Tribunal, consisting of a retired president of the Law Society, sitting with two assessors who were headmasters. The DES presented their case at length, and their witnesses were cross-examined by counsel for the school, who sought to establish that the inspectors had acted on personal prejudice. On the tenth day, the DES withdrew, before the school's side was heard, and the case was dismissed.

The attack had been in keeping with what a very senior official in the Department of Education had told Professor Prais earlier: 'we shall do our best to close down all these independent schools that are teaching a restricted curriculum. They should think themselves lucky that we are allowing them to exist at all as independent schools.'[5]

As Her Majesty's Inspectorate were no less infected than most teachers by the doctrine of 'progressive' education, they assumed that their job was to rid the schools of traditional methods. When the inspectors' reports were required to be made public in order to alert the parents to the inadequacy of the schools that their children were attending, there was no such effect as Keith Joseph had hoped for. Indeed even after the national curriculum with all its appurtenances was installed, inspectors continued in their accustomed ways. The 1989 report on the King Edward VI Grammar School in Stratford-upon-Avon still applied all the old progressive standards. It criticized the school for its 'high proportion of teacher exposition', excessive formal written work, and 'classroom discussion dominated by teachers'. The fact that the school produced high academic standards, excellent examination results, and good behaviour did not impress the inspectors. They urged the school to adopt 'new procedures, new methods and new courses' more appropriate to the 'late twentieth century'.

Towards the end of 1990, the inspectors outdid themselves. They harshly criticized Hyland House School in Waltham Forest, north-east London for stressing the three Rs, Christianity, and good behaviour. The inspectors were appalled to find that the school had no 'curriculum guidelines on technology', and insufficient 'multi-cultural resources' in social studies despite the fact that the pupils were all Afro-Caribbean. The Seventh-day Adventist Church, which owned the school, was shocked by the inspectors' criticism of 'an over-emphasis on English', 'over-use of comprehension exercises', and 'over-emphasis on the use of textbooks and arithmetical work copied from the blackboard', despite the inspectors' finding that reading standards were satisfactory, that due attention was given to spelling and grammar, and that 'most of the children have a fairly secure grasp of number and basic arithmetical processes'. Nor did the inspectors consider it important that children were put down for Hyland House at birth, that some of the children travelled from Brixton, at the other end of London, and that although the school charged fees of £340 a term, it had a waiting list of 150.[6] In short, given the nature of the Inspectorate, what was supposed to be the cure for the maladies of schools became an important cause of the disease.

If the education that most children in Britain were getting in state schools could hardly have been better designed to destroy the vigorous virtues, Conservatives were not the only ones to complain. By 1979, all parties had recognized that something was badly wrong in the schools. But whereas the Opposition concentrated on calling for more spending on education, the Thatcher Government, although it in fact substantially increased expenditure, addressed itself to altering the way in which schools were run.

What impressed Thatcherites was that the manner in which the schools were administered effectively eliminated the attributes of a school seen as a surrogate parent. The performance of state schools was so much poorer than that of independent schools, they came to believe, not because state schools had less money but because they had no freedom to manage themselves. That view was not then widely held.

Instead, it was generally supposed that the schools were free from interference by government because the administration of schools was 'local' and 'decentralized'. The reality was that the schools were run by bureaucrats in the local education authorities. That these bureaucrats were 'local' did not deprive them of the power or the inclination to destroy the independence of schools by not only deciding the number and size of schools, but also appointing the headmaster and the governors, and exercising overall financial control through their power to allocate the funds received from the central government. Moreover, as the local education authorities were permitted to 'hold back' part of the money for purposes such as central purchase of school supplies, and as no limit was set on how much could be held back, local authorities could and did deprive schools of a large fraction of the money that the government had allocated for their use. As late as 1990, it was found that the education authority of Cumbria held back 28.8 per cent, Lincolnshire, 18.6 per cent; Newcastle, 28 per cent; Sunderland, 20 per cent; Barking, 28 per cent; Havering, 18 per cent.[7] In addition, in the mid-eighties, the 525,000 teachers in state schools were complemented by no less than 362,000 full-time non-teaching staff, the need for whose services was far from obvious.

In local authorities dominated by the Labour Party, it was often trade unions who ultimately determined the choice and policies of head teachers and governors. No local authority needed to fear that pupils would be withdrawn by their parents, because children were distributed among schools entirely in terms of 'catchment areas'. In order to transfer a child to a nearby school that seemed preferable though outside his catchment area, parents had to move house. The use of 'catchment areas' and the limits on the number of pupils that each school could take were supposed to ensure that children would be distributed equally among all the available schools. In practice, it meant that good schools were not allowed to take on more pupils even when they had spare room, while many bad schools were filled to the brim.

That the local educational authorities should keep the schools on a short rein seemed entirely appropriate to those who regarded schools not as surrogate parents but as instruments of social policy. To Thatcherites this way of administering schools seemed to destroy the essence of a school. If a school is a surrogate for the family, it ought to have the same independence and the same freedom to conduct its affairs as it thinks best. The head of a school ought to decide the curriculum, the rules of conduct, the appointment of teachers and the selection of pupils. As a result each school, like each family, would have a distinctive personality and respect for its own traditions. Whether the surrogate role of a school was fulfilled was for the parents to decide by choosing which school their children would attend.

The Search for Ways of Letting Parents Choose

This understanding of a school inspired Thatcherites to advocate early on that state schools should be funded by a wholly different method. An 'education voucher' should be issued for every child, which could be used in any accredited school selected by the parents. Funding by vouchers, Thatcherites argued, had the great virtue that it would disengage schools from the control of both the central government, which provided the funds, and the local authorities, which administered the funds. Vouchers would restore a more intimate and effective connection between the school and the family.

Parents as consumers could then choose the schools for their children in much the same way as office workers, given luncheon vouchers, choose where to eat. The school voucher, equal in value to about the national average amount spent per pupil, could be 'redeemed' at any school with a spare place. Parents could top up vouchers if they wished to choose a school that charged fees higher than the voucher's value; in this way vouchers would make independent schools more accessible to all. State schools would be as free as independent schools to decide how much to pay teachers and to charge pupils. As inadequate schools would lose custom and cash, they would be forced to improve in order to avoid closure through bankruptcy. With control over budget and management restored to the schools themselves, local education authorities and the Department of Education could 'fade away'. There were disagreements about the details of a voucher scheme, as for instance whether it should apply to independent schools. But the fundamental argument for vouchers was that they would enable parents to choose schools and would free schools to run themselves.

The opponents of vouchers argued that such schemes were founded on the false supposition that all parents are competent to judge how their children should be educated. Vouchers, said their opponents, would widen the gap between good and bad schools and significantly increase inequality and social divisions. Children of parents who were poor, ignorant, or unmotivated would soon find themselves concentrated in 'sinking' schools, from which middle-class parents, vouchers in hand, had fled. What parents really wanted, said the opponents, were decent neighbourhood schools, an objective more likely to be achieved by reform rather than by a voucher revolution.

An active campaign for vouchers began in 1974 when Marjorie Seldon, with the support of both the National Council of Women and Catholic Mothers, set up The Friends of the Education Voucher Experiment to campaign for a trial run. When Sir Keith Joseph became Secretary of State for Education in 1981, he declared that he was 'intellectually attracted' to the idea and set his special advisers, Stuart Sexton and Oliver Letwin, to devising practical proposals. But to every suggestion that they put forward, DES officials, led by Walter Ulrich and Nicholas Stewart, enthusiastically found objections. Although the advisers believed that they had answered all the objections, in the end Keith Joseph dropped vouchers. Not only had his officials persuaded him that it would be too difficult, if not impossible, to put the scheme into effect, there was also strong opposition, within the Cabinet and the Party, to establishing a new nationwide set-up before testing it with pilot schemes. But it was impossible to arrange pilot schemes because no local authority was willing to take the risk of being the first reformer, especially as the next election might return a Labour government committed to abolishing any such arrangement. The campaign both for and against vouchers was so fierce that it became politically damaging even to speak of vouchers, or so some of its advocates believed. To achieve the same ends something different, certainly in name and probably in substance, had to be found.

Keith Joseph turned to heightening the public's awareness of the sad state of British schools. He courted unpopularity by going about the country saying that children arrived in school at the age of five, 'keen and eager to learn' and left at the earliest opportunity 'bored and disenchanted'. He attacked teachers' training colleges as the chief source of the pollution; but though the review he set up proposed some salutary changes, it suggested no such radical shake-up of the colleges as he considered essential. In opposition to the colleges, he advocated that children should be selected and streamed according to their different talents, but found little support among middle-class parents who feared that their children would not qualify for the academic stream.

Not until the end of 1990 was an experiment in vouchers undertaken. Then the Wandsworth Borough Council in south-west London proposed to issue vouchers for full-time nursery places to all children aged three or four. Wandsworth planned to increase the number of its nursery places by more than a third to meet the additional demand, and to pay for this expansion by cutting subsidies to child-minding services. Private day-care centres would be allowed to compete with state nursery schools, but parents could redeem the vouchers only at non-profit schools or playgroups. Vouchers, said the Council, would ensure that everybody 'is being dealt with fairly', because they could accommodate 'different people with different needs'.

Whatever the disagreement about vouchers, it was never in doubt that Thatcherism sought to extend parental choice. But the Government felt its way slowly about how that should be accomplished. When Margaret Thatcher became leader, the Conservative Party had pledged itself to cease compelling grammar schools to become comprehensives, and to restore Direct Grant Schools, funded directly by government and totally independent of local educational authorities. The first legislative act of the Thatcher Government was to repeal in 1979 the law making comprehensives compulsory. The Education Acts of 1980, 1981 and 1986 enlarged parental choice by a variety of measures. They required school boards to include representatives of parents, obliged schools to publish inspectors' reports (which had previously been confidential), and gave parents the right to choose schools outside the catchment area in which they lived. With the 1986 Act, elected parent governors were given equal representation with the Local Education Authority's nominees, the governors were empowered to oversee discipline and to modify the LEA's policy on the curriculum, to spend a small proportion of the school's budget, and to have a say in the appointment and dismissal of staff.

A more radical extension of parental choice was provided by the Assisted Places Scheme introduced in the 1980 Act, which provided for over five thousand places in independent secondary schools able to prepare pupils for university. To qualify for a place, a pupil had to pass the entrance examination for the chosen school. Parents had to pay a small proportion of the fees, or perhaps none, depending on their income, the rest being paid by the government.

Some Thatcherites, like Sir Rhodes Boyson, then a junior minister of education, considered the assisted places scheme to be superior to the direct grant schools because, whereas the latter subsidized everyone regardless of need, the former directed subsidies to those who could not otherwise afford to pay. The scheme began life modestly in 1975, as an Opposition amendment to the Labour Government's education bill of 1976. It was drawn up by the adviser to Norman St John Stevas, Stuart Sexton; Tory MPs were whipped into supporting it, and a commitment to inaugurate an assisted places scheme appeared in the Conservatives' election manifesto of 1978. When Sexton was invited to defend the scheme at the Headmasters' Conference in 1979, where it was opposed by John Rae, Headmaster of Westminster School, because it diverted funds from the public to the private sector, the fact that all but fourteen out of more than two hundred headmasters voted for the scheme attracted considerable attention in the newspapers and helped to assure its inclusion in the 1980 Act.

In the first year of the scheme's operation, almost a third of the places (about seven thousand in all) were given completely free of charge, and this proportion increased in later years. The largest group of places went to children of one-parent families, followed by children of unemployed parents. Others had parents who were bus drivers, coal miners, railwaymen, or shop assistants. The average parental contribution was £285 per pupil per year, while the state's contribution was £1090 per pupil per year, which was less than the average cost of secondary education in maintained schools.

The most significant innovation introduced by the assisted places scheme was the principle of *per capita* funding – money following the pupil. This became an increasingly important theme in Thatcherite policies.

Schools Take Control

A broader effort to give choice to parents and independence to schools was introduced by Kenneth Baker when he became Secretary of State for Education in 1986. He proposed three new ways of organizing schools, which were sanctioned by the Education Reform Act of 1988. The three proposals were, first, to give every school powers to manage its own budget and to accept as many pupils as it could accommodate (open enrolment); secondly, to authorize schools to 'opt out' of control by local education authorities and to be funded directly by the government; thirdly, to set up City Technical Colleges.

Changes of this sort had been considered too risky politically when Keith Joseph became Secretary of Education in 1981. But by 1986, the idea that schools should be given greater autonomy, far from shocking anyone, was being widely advocated. The idea was not new. As early as 1969, Stuart Sexton, inspired by schemes tried in Australia and Canada, had drawn up a proposal for self-managing schools. In 1985, while serving as special adviser to Sir Keith Joseph, Sexton replied to a request from the Policy Unit in Downing Street for new ideas by putting forward a plan that embodied his earlier proposal. It would turn existing state schools into self-managing trusts or charities funded per pupil. Others were thinking along the same lines. Just before the Parliamentary recess in 1986, the No Turning Back group of Tory MPs published a document on the future of schools which found favour with Mrs Thatcher. They proposed that schools' governors should be elected by a postal ballot of parents, that all schools should receive a direct grant from the government allocated *per capita*, and that schools should be run like small public companies, leaving the decision to hire and fire teachers to head teachers. They also advocated a new breed of 'specialist' schools, both academic and vocational.

By the election of 1987, public opinion both within and outside the Tory party had moved a long way from 1979. The *Daily Telegraph* was voicing a popular view both when it demanded repeatedly that the government produce something more than good intentions, and when it announced just before the election that 'the next Secretary of State for Education (who may well be Mr Baker again) will be taking office on the basis of something approaching a new public consensus . . . Labour and the Alliance are still busily promoting their plans to abolish the Assisted Places scheme, remove charitable status and inflict all sorts of other unpleasantness on the independent schools. This is more than the usual humbug, since most people now agree that the right way to run a school is much like the way the independent schools are run. The supremacy of local education authorities has grossly distorted not only the cause of education, which in the big cities has suffered a near-fatal dose of party politics . . . The requirement from the next Secretary of State is therefore as simple as it is urgent: a new Education Bill which sets out in full the future powers of and relationships between the Government, the local authorities, the school governing bodies, and the head teachers.'[8]

The Education Reform Act of 1988 was what the Thatcher

Government provided after it was returned. The proposal to allow schools to manage themselves did not by then produce hysteria among Conservative backbenchers, or even among the Opposition. The success of pilot schemes for self-managed schools in Cambridgeshire and Solihull provided models. Local authorities still spent some of the government's grant on centralized functions such as administrative and advisory services and school transport. But school governors were made responsible for selecting and dismissing staff, funds were provided for training governors and headmasters for their new responsibilities, and computerized management systems were made available to schools. As each school had a strong incentive to administer such housekeeping matters as catering, maintenance, and transport as efficiently as possible, by employing no more people than it needed and making use of voluntary help, more money became available for books, equipment, and teachers' salaries. The introduction of open enrolment, which accompanied the right to self-management, left schools free to determine their own admission policies, and to be rewarded by the patronage of satisfied parents.

Although headmasters complained at first when they were asked really to manage their schools, to decide how to spend money and to make hard choices about staff, maintenance, and books, they gradually began to relish the opportunity to run their schools as they thought right and to enjoy serving parents rather than the Town Hall. But the new powers given to parents and governors were not always exercised effectively. Parent governors were outflanked because they lacked expertise about committee procedures. Indeed after visiting schools struggling with the birth pangs of self-management, Stuart Sexton concluded that it would have been a mistake to introduce vouchers before schools had learnt to run themselves. In addition, local authorities often tried to obstruct the schools. In Shropshire, the local council simply imposed its own choice of head teacher on governors who had chosen a different candidate. In another place a row broke out because a pupil's parents wanted her to attend a school where English rather than Punjabi was spoken. The Secretary of State, Mr MacGregor, approved the transfer, as he was obliged to do by the Acts of 1980 and 1988. But the LEA remained 'reluctant' to implement Mr MacGregor's decision; Doug McAvoy, of the National Union of Teachers, warned that the decision could bring about complete segregation of the schools; Mrs Ann Taylor, a Labour MP, called the decision 'a racist charter'.[9] It was denounced in the newspapers as the 'Birth of the Ghetto School'; and the Opposition condemned the decision as implying that 'parental choice is more important than race relations'. Other critics argued that the new arrangements would weaken 'the control of the local education authority over its schools'. Though they conceded that increased independence of schools meant increased opportunity for choice by parents, they argued that independence would diminish the rights of future parents: some existing schools might shut down due to low patronage, and parents of the future would not be able to restore an opted-out school to its previous position under the local authority.

Once schools had been given the power to manage themselves it was natural to move on to giving them the right to 'opt out' from control by the local authorities and become grant-maintained, that is, funded directly by the government.[10] The concepts of money following the pupil and open enrolment would, the Government argued, provide an incentive for the LEAs to be more responsive to parents' wishes and would make available a greater variety of schools. Education would no longer be led by producers, academic theorists, administrators, or teachers' unions. It would be controlled by the consumers – parents acting on behalf of their children.

Some said that the procedure for opting out was too elaborate. The ballot had to be open to all parents, and either the governors had to agree at two separate meetings to hold a ballot, or twenty per cent of the parents had to petition for one. The complexity was defended on the ground that it protected schools from opting out on a whim or a conspiracy by a minority of parents, when there was no wide support for the move and perhaps no capacity in the school to deal with the new status. It was left to the Secretary of State to judge whether there was a sufficiently competent governing body and enough commitment among the parents to ensure the success of 'opting out'.

Schools that opted out could expect fifteen per cent more than the sum they had previously received because they were now given their share of what the council had kept back for spending on central resources. Opponents of opting out sneered at this as a 'golden hello'. But the money received by opted out schools had all along been allocated to *all* schools by the government, only it had been withheld from them by some of the councils. Under the new arrangements, which made it obvious that such councils were depriving schools of funds that were due to them, local authorities were moved to revise their accounting procedures so as to allow schools that stayed with them to control a greater share of the available funds.

The effects of 'opting out' were sometimes spectacular, for reasons made clear by the headmaster of Haverstock School in Birmingham: 'We are not leaving Birmingham,' he said, 'We are leaving a particular local authority which has given education a very low priority. The Labour-run Birmingham council had come 84th out of 96 in spending per pupil on books and equipment. Schools in cities such as Coventry or Leicester are like palaces. Their classrooms are well decorated, their floors have carpets, and there is a reasonable provision of science laboratories, textbooks, and equipment. We have faced niggardly resourcing.'

When Haverstock became a grant-maintained school, its income was increased by a fifth because it received its share of Birmingham's funds withheld for 'central administration'. The school was refurbished, acquired a permanent caretaker and full-time nurse, and ten new teachers to do specialist teaching: 'Under Birmingham, we could never get specialist teachers,' the headmaster explained. 'We always had to take fill-ins. We've had woodwork teachers taking science and home economics people doing French. Opting out has allowed us to advertise nationally and pick up graduates in every subject.' The number of parents making the school first choice for their children rose from 26 to 240. All 1050 girls and boys wore uniforms, and its rulebook had only one entry: Treat all people in our school as you would like them to treat you.[11]

Despite opposition from organized groups, individual teachers responded enthusiastically to opted out schools. One of the first schools to opt out, Audenshaw High School, in Tameside, Greater

Manchester, advertised ten posts after fifteen staff decided to seek redeployment; within ten days the school received a hundred firm inquiries about the vacancies from teachers of remarkably high quality. In another school, twenty applications were received as soon as it became known that the school was to become grant-maintained, although no vacancies had been advertised. By September 1990, almost all opted out schools reported sharp rises in the number of applications, averaging over forty per cent. Headmasters reported that even in areas with high-rise flats and a high dependence on social services, the morale and the quality of schools appeared to have improved. Schools seeking to opt out were spread throughout the country. An advisory network was established with the help of the Grant Maintained Schools Trust. By the end of 1990, fifty schools had chosen to be grant-maintained. By May 1992, two hundred and fifty schools had become grant-maintained and seventy had applied to opt out.

Before the 1992 General Election, a number of schools had reported that they were inhibited by the fear that opting-out would be reversed by a Labour government. And they were being actively discouraged by local authorities, Conservative as well as Labour. A 'Local Schools Information Service' was organized and funded by the local authorities to fight proposals for opting out. Bedfordshire County Council removed two thousand books from Queensbury School, Dunstable, when it opted out; in Birmingham, the council requested the return of three thousand five hundred books from Small Heath School.[12] Nevertheless, by the end of 1990, national Labour leaders declared themselves ready to embrace the principles that power to manage themselves should be devolved on schools and that funding should 'follow the pupil'.[13]

Only weeks after Margaret Thatcher's resignation, a wider move toward opting-out began. Until then barely a hundred schools had balloted parents on changing to direct funding by Whitehall; now in one month, thirty-five schools were preparing to hold ballots. The director of the Grant Maintained Schools Trust described it as an extraordinary turnaround which he attributed to the disappearance of political uncertainty. The increase was also encouraged by the government's announcement in October 1990 that, for the first time, small primary schools would be eligible to opt out. Six prepared to do so at once, and a number of others were planning for it. The word had got around that schools managing themselves did considerably better.

A further move to increase the financial autonomy of even those schools that did not opt out was made by Kenneth Clarke, soon after he took over as Secretary of State when John Major became Prime Minister. He proposed to limit to about fifteen per cent the amount that local education authorities could hold back to pay for administration, training, advisory teachers, and school inspectors. According to the government's estimates, the 109 local education authorities in England and Wales held back more than 2 billion a year. If half of that sum were released, each school on the average would have an extra £50,000 to spend. A move in this direction was supported by David Hart, General Secretary of the National Association of Head Teachers, who said that if schools were responsible for arranging their own training programmes and supply of teachers rather than having to rely on those provided by local authorities which did not always suit their needs, the resources of schools would increase by some £515 million pounds.[14]

A small step towards the 'fading away' of superfluous local bureaucracies was taken on 1 April 1990, when the Inner London Education Authority (ILEA) was abolished. It had long been known that although the children in ILEA schools ranked above the national average in intelligence tests, the O-level results in ILEA schools were well below the national average. Besides, ILEA spent considerably more: while it educated only four per cent of the nation's pupils, it spent eight per cent of the national total; it spent in total thirty per cent more than Manchester and sixty per cent more than Birmingham. Sweeping away what was deemed to be the unnecessary superstructure of ILEA, the Government argued, would enable the Inner London boroughs to run more effective local services. Borough councillors would be directly responsible to local parents and would perform their educational duties at considerably less cost than the ILEA.

'Unashamedly Different' City Technology Colleges

The third proposal made by Kenneth Baker was to establish a number of City Technology Colleges. These were to be 'unashamedly different' from other secondary schools, and to serve as 'beacons of excellence'. Being outside the normal system, they would be more flexible. Class hours would be longer per day and year, pupils would be required to do homework, and parents would be engaged in their children's education. Their funds would be supplied partly by the DES and partly by industry, at the same level as other schools. By enrolling pupils of a wide range of abilities, they would not 'cream off' the most able but rather demonstrate that efficiently organized schools could produce better education for children of all abilities. It was hoped that the City Technology Colleges would operate as a spur to opting out, since they were in effect independent schools funded on a *per capita* basis by the central government.

But there was ambivalence about the character of the CTCs. Considerable emphasis was placed on technical training designed to meet the requirements of British industry, and on the 'relevance of the curriculum to modern needs'. It was by no means clear whether the Colleges were designed above all to be centres of superior education or of better vocational training.

Some of the opposition to the CTCs was simply an objection to the introduction of more variety into state education. Labour Party spokesmen, notably Jack Straw,[15] argued that the CTCs were a mere gimmick, providing education for only twenty thousand children, a mere 'drop in the ocean'. Yet Labour politicians also argued that the CTCs would 'wreck' the education plans of the local authorities because they would drain children from other schools. Such critics were described by the defenders of the CTCs as 'rent-seekers within the all-powerful educational bureaucracies', resentful of anything that would infringe on their power and disturb the uniformity of the state 'system'.

Opposition came also, however, from those who generally welcomed the introduction of variety, but were disturbed by the CTC emphasis on technology. One of the most lucid of these critics,

Anthony O'Hear, Professor of Philosophy at Bradford University, argued that 'there cannot be a technological education in the strict sense'. Technology, he said, 'is about getting things done, about building bridges or spaceships, producing more energy or setting up information networks ... But a person trained in technology alone will lack that richer conception of the world and of human life which comes from a study of the humanities and the natural sciences and on the basis of which he might be able to discriminate between better and worse in the choice of ends. He will lack that knowledge of human things, and that training in disinterested reflection about them which true education strives to instil. He will not, in short, be an educated person ... even if, in terms of time, due attention in CTCs is given to Latin, to history, to literature, to physics and to biology, there is such a thing as the spirit of a place. If the whole emphasis of the school is on the relevance of school work to industry and commerce, I fear for the chances of that generosity of spirit and culture which a liberal education provides.'[16]

In the event, the CTCs, like most projects, turned out rather differently than anyone had expected. For one thing, their costs exceeded the forecasts, because local authorities refused to let them take over unused buildings, and the Government felt that compulsory purchase would take too long. Sir Cyril Taylor, who was put in charge of the programme to found City Technology Colleges, managed by various stratagems to discover the whereabouts of disused buildings belonging to local authorities and eventually to acquire them. But the obstructive tactics of local authorities meant that some Colleges could not be located in inner city areas, and others had to be housed in expensive new buildings. Nor were parents always delighted to have the local school turned into a CTC. But on the other hand, the Churches, though originally very sceptical, discovered a source of income to be had by selling unused school buildings to the CTCs. Six CTCs were set up before the end of 1990, another six were expected to open in 1991, and the total expected to reach fourteen or fifteen by the end of 1992.

Towards An 'Enterprise Culture'

The uncertainty about the leading purpose of CTCs was part of a much larger ambivalence among Thatcherites about the proper nature and purpose of schools and universities. This ambivalence emerged in connection with provisions for vocational training and new examinations. What to do about the 'lower thirty per cent' had preoccupied Sir Keith Joseph when he became Secretary of State for Education, and he addressed himself to heightening public awareness of the needs of non-academic children. But allied to this concern was another, not adequately distinguished concern about the failure to train the kind of people needed by British industry.

This concern was encouraged by the thesis, put forward by the Cambridge historian, Correlli Barnett, among others. He argued that Britain's industrial decline was due to British education having been dominated for a hundred years or more by the 'academic liberal arts'. Barnett blamed this sad state of affairs on 'the triumph in the Victorian educational debate of such as Newman and Mill over the protagonists of a more practical preparation for life.' He maintained that the public schools and Oxbridge, by insisting on 'liberal education', had 'emasculated the sons of manufacturers into "gentlemen" ', and created 'a governing class and an intelligentsia ignorant of, and disdainful of "trade" and technology. The pecking order of British values was established whereby tax-eaters [consumers of wealth] came to be admired above wealth creators; and "gentlemen" went into the public service or the professions, leaving industry and commerce to the socially and educationally second-class.'[17]

The same lesson was taught by an American professor, Martin Wiener, of the Massachusetts Institute of Technology, whose *English Culture and the Decline of the Industrial Spirit 1850–1980* was much admired in Britain. The Prime Minister, Sir Keith Joseph, and Lord Young all strongly approved of this doctrine, as indeed did almost everyone else. Hardly anyone remembered that the traditional idea of the gentleman was not the decadent one popularized in recent years, but the very opposite ideal of self-sufficiency, moral courage, industriousness, and a detestation of snobbery. In short, the Barnett-Wiener thesis provided historical justification for emphasizing Britain's need for more 'wealth creators', and an 'enterprise culture', which Sir Keith Joseph had made into a Thatcherite theme song. That Oxbridge showed little enthusiasm for Thatcherism, to the point of refusing to grant Margaret Thatcher the honorary doctorate that Oxford had awarded almost as a matter of course to other prime ministers, seemed to prove that they were right.

Nevertheless, there were also impressive dissenting voices, some of them ardent Thatcherites. Professor Sir Geoffrey Elton provoked a heated correspondence in the columns of *The Times*[18] when he wrote in praise of a leader page diatribe against the Correlli Barnett thesis, which pointed out that Montesquieu had noted – to his dismay – that the English aristocracy and gentry engaged in commerce and had regularly married into, or been recruited from, the world of commerce and industry.[19] Professor Elton dismissed the Correlli Barnett thesis as 'ignorant parrot talk'. Similar criticism came from the Professor of Economic History in Cambridge, Donald Coleman, who said that one might as well argue that the decline of British industry was caused by the class war or toilet training, depending on whether one puts one's faith in Marx or Freud. In 1990 the controversy, fed by a new book from Correlli Barnett, was still raging, and provoked Lord Annan to ask: 'If science and technology were so scandalously neglected between the two wars by the effete humanists who controlled our education,' how did Britain produce radar, penicillin, the Spitfire, and the wartime artificial harbours? 'How between 1945–88 did British scientists win 40 Nobel Prizes, far more than any country except America?' He pointed out that 'We would have lost a great deal . . . if in most sixth forms there was never any chance of pupils' discussing the matters raised in Aristotle's *Ethics* . . . If the pursuit of knowledge for its own sake were to disappear from universities they would cease to be universities. Nor do I accept that intellectuals think civilized values incompatible with the creation of material wealth. Neither of my mentors (E. M. Forster and Keynes) thought so.'[20] T. E. Utley voiced the opinion of many other Thatcherites when he repeatedly protested that 'enterprise culture' is a 'monstrous phrase'.

Strangest of all in the Thatcherites' enthusiasm for the Barnett-Wiener thesis were the bedfellows that they thereby acquired: egalitarians, corporatists, collectivists, and the educationalist establishment. The corporatist view could hardly have been better expressed than by Correlli Barnett's assertion 'that education must take as its primary task the development of individual and national capability to create wealth'.[21] It is the proper conclusion of the corporatist argument: Britain is a productive enterprise; Britain's people are this enterprise's workforce; this workforce should be taught whatever is needed to improve the efficiency of production. Barnett accordingly lamented that Britain 'has now slipped to 14th in the non-communist world as a whole in terms of annual gross national product per head, and trails all the advanced countries of Europe'. He attributed the 'slippage since the Second World War' to 'Britain's chronic shortage of skilled manpower at all levels from boardroom to shop-floor; shortages stemming from the persistent national neglect of training over the last Century and which the vaunted Butler Education Act of 1944 failed to remedy. If we do not match, and more than match, the national training efforts of our most dangerous rivals in world markets, nothing can save us from descending into Third World status when the North Sea oil take gradually dries up.'

That 'education' should or could be distinguished from 'training' was denied by Barnett. It was a distinction 'first foisted on British opinion by the high-minded Victorian academic "liberal arts" lobby'. Something very different was wanted now: rather than perpetuate our Victorian intellectual snobbery, 'we should surely think of a continuous process of "formation", whereby "education" is the shaft and "training" the spearhead of our competitive capability to survive and prosper in a fiercely competitive world.'[22]

For those who believe that education, like all other matters, ought to be controlled by the state, the Thatcher Government's drive to promote training for 'wealth creation' could hardly be more congenial. Egalitarians were delighted by the denigration of the academic 'elite' and the levelling down of everyone to 'wealth creators'. Such levelling had long been the object of the education-alist establishment, who considered that the route to equality lay through eliminating any distinction between a liberal education and vocational training. That was after all the point of turning all schools into comprehensives. Thatcherites who were pleased with the reforms remained either unaware of the strange bedfellows they had acquired or were unwilling to consider what such support signified. They concentrated on schemes for providing more vocational training.

Apart from the City Technology Colleges a number of pro-grammes were designed to increase and improve vocational train-ing. The Department of Employment had been active in the field through the Manpower Services Commission (MSC) set up in 1974, which was said to have 'terrorised education'.[23] When the Thatcher Government came in, the MSC acquired a substantial proportion of the education budget in order to provide vocational training not just for school leavers but also for pupils in secondary schools. In 1981, the MSC announced the Youth Training Scheme, which guaranteed one year's training for all sixteen-year old school-leavers without jobs; in 1986 such training was extended to two years. Trainees were to receive an allowance from their employers according to scales laid down by the MSC. Where necessary, they could be enrolled also in classes to improve their literacy and numeracy. Experience in work went along with training, both being provided by the employer or arranged by co-operation between employers and educational institutions.

The scheme was generally regarded as a success, though trade unions represented it as a capitalist trick to reduce wages. Sixty per cent of the 389,000 boys and girls aged 16 and 17 who joined the YTS in 1984–5 gained permanent employment in the firms where they had been trained. Another six per cent were sent on for further training. And a rapidly increasing number of companies began recruiting from YTS instead of from schools or colleges.

To improve the technical and vocational education of pupils between the ages of fourteen and eighteen and to link schools to experience of employment, the Youth Training Programme was supplemented in 1982 by the Technical and Vocational Educational

Initiative, which was extended to the whole country in 1987. The subjects taught ranged 'from agriculture and catering to computer studies, office technology and design technology', and the programmes were established by schools in co-operation with colleges of further education and employers.

In 1988, the Prime Minister launched Training and Enterprise Councils, modelled on the American pattern of 'private industry councils'. It was hoped that by having businessmen run the councils, private industry would take the lead in providing training. The chairman and managing director of a council had to be 'substantial local decision makers', such as the chief executive of a major company or local authority, so as to encourage especially small and medium sized firms to invest more in training the local labour force. In just over a year, eighty-one Training and Enterprise Councils were operating across England and Wales.

A more radical step was taken when, on 27 March 1990, Michael Howard, Secretary of State for Employment, announced that the Youth Training Scheme would be replaced by vouchers or 'credits' to all sixteen year-old school leavers with which they could buy training of their own choice. The new scheme enabled school leavers who did not go on to some form of further education to receive a training voucher, which could be used to pay for day-release courses, at local authority schools or accredited private colleges, for qualifications in skills like engineering or hotel and catering management. The costs of the voucher scheme were to be met largely by asking employers to pay for the training of their employees; money that had previously been paid to employers for training was redirected to vouchers and to providing more places in colleges. The vouchers, it was estimated, would be worth around £1500 each. The new approach was introduced through ten pilot schemes covering some ten per cent of all those leaving full-time education, and the training credits or vouchers were issued by the Training and Enterprise Councils. 'Training credits represent an entitlement to young people to train to approved standards', Mr Howard said. 'They will be issued to young people, who will be able to present their credit either to an employer who makes training available or to a specialist provider of training if the young person is unable to find employment.'[24]

Opposition to what some saw as the new 'barbarism', exacerbated by the suggestion – never adopted – to merge the Department of Education with the Department of Employment so as to ensure a closer match between what industry wanted and what schools produced, continued to rumble on, most of all among Conservatives. Such critics were dismayed by the new practice in schools of showing fourteen year-old pupils charts of 'Occupational Training Families', where learning chemistry was linked with a window-cleaning job, geography with bus-driving, English with being a traffic warden. Nor were the critics cheered by school corridors lined with advertisements from banks, oil companies, and commercial organizations. All this encouraged the young, they argued, to define themselves not as individuals but as workers, not as citizens but as industrial fodder. Moreover, the reduction of education to vocational training would fail to achieve its purpose because, given the rapid changes in technology, much training becomes almost immediately obsolete, whereas an educated employee is flexible, informed, adaptable, and therefore better prepared to learn new ways.

But it was in the rest of the educational programme, in the introduction of a new examination for the General Certificate of Secondary Education (GCSE), the National Curriculum, and in the policies with regard to universities, that the contradictions in the Thatcherite commitments became still more troublesome.

New Examinations

The new examination for the GCSE was introduced by Sir Keith Joseph in 1986 and used for the first time in the summer of 1988. The GCSE was supposed to test practical skills as well as knowledge and to be suitable for children of all levels of ability. It was ironic that a government and a minister committed to undoing the damage caused by the destruction of the grammar schools should have introduced the GCSE. For it finally destroyed the distinction between grammar and secondary modern pupils, which had survived in the distinction between O-levels and CSE examinations, thus completing the ascendancy of the comprehensives.

These consequences were not what Sir Keith Joseph had intended. He meant instead to bring higher standards to bear on the education of pupils with few academic talents. In a speech to the council of Local Education Authorities[25] he talked about the need to raise the 'standard achieved by 80–90 per cent of pupils to the level now expected of the average pupil in a number of subjects and over a broad range of knowledge and skills'. In order to achieve this, he said, what was needed was 'first, a clear and broadly agreed statement of the objectives of the school curriculum; second a system of examinations which secures not only courses based on agreed curricular objectives but also assessment methods which show more precisely what pupils understand, know and can do in relation to the agreed objectives; and third, improvements in teaching quality.' Teachers would thereby be given the motivation and the understanding needed to avoid 'ill-directed endeavour'.

He accordingly proposed to secure agreement 'on the broad content and organization of the 5–16 curriculum' and to establish 'attainment targets at age 11 and age 16', and he expected that these ideas would not be 'a blueprint offered by the holder of my office', but would be translated into practice through 'the work of many hands' (the Inspectors, the School Curriculum Development Committee, teachers working on curriculum development, LEAs). He refused to engage in 'fruitless controversy' about whether acquiring 'skills' was the hallmark of practical and vocational learning, as distinct from acquiring 'knowledge', the special purpose of academic learning. The new examination would be graded not according to the old system of 'norm-referencing' which 'tells us a great deal about relative standards between different candidates' but 'much less about absolute standards'. Instead, criterion-referencing would provide 'clear definitions of the level of knowledge and performance expected from candidates for the award of particular grades.'

What emerged from the new examinations, however, was far from what Sir Keith had envisaged. Indeed later on, during the second reading of the Education Reform Bill in the House of

Lords, he expressed dismay at the way the GCSE had turned out. The examinations were written by the same old educational establishment who continued to make the new scheme serve the old orthodoxy, indeed to entrench it. Within the host of apparently innocent words (whose meaning was a mystery) setting forth the virtues of the brave new requirements – empathy, oracy, school-based assessment, skills, breadth, balance, differentiation, relevance – lay hidden the same old orthodoxy of progressive education. Learning dates in history, grammar and spelling in English, tables in mathematics – all those were definitely excluded. 'Criterion-referencing' turned out in practice to set standards no more fixed than 'norm-referencing'. Children brought up on the new history could leave school with no idea, for instance, of the century in which the First World War took place. The engineering faculty of Cambridge University announced that it needed an extra under-graduate year to make up for the mathematics that was no longer being taught in the schools. The head of history at Priory School in Lewes, Sussex lost his post because, having demonstrated that primary schoolchildren without any historical knowledge could achieve good marks in a GCSE history examination intended for sixteen year-olds, he decided to coach his pupils for the Scottish Ordinary Grade, which he considered to be a more suitable examination.[26] A series of vigorous pamphlets from the Thatcherite think-tank, the Centre for Policy Studies, was devoted to exposing the folly of the new examinations. The Social Affairs Unit of the IEA published a pamphlet arguing that the GCSE, having been hijacked by left-wingers, was far less rigorous and far more politicized than the O-levels that it replaced: one art paper asked pupils to draw a mural for a village involved in the miners' strike and another paper asked candidates to compare NATO spending with spending needed to improve health in poorer nations.

The educational establishment, having triumphed over O-levels, moved on to attack A-levels, which had served to qualify students for universities. In this the establishment was supported by John Rae, Headmaster of Westminster School, who argued that Britain should emulate Japan by eliminating A-levels and having everyone take the same examination at eighteen. In the meantime the road to eliminating A-levels was being paved with ploys for lowering their standard. Letters to the newspapers asked: 'Who in Mr Mac-Gregor's department is instructing the examining boards to lower the standards in this way? Who in his department has given the Schools Examination and Assessment Council the right to try to force into A-level syllabuses matters which have nothing whatever to do with the subjects, but represent the obsessions of the feminist and racist lobbies? . . . Mrs Thatcher is presiding over an edu-cational catastrophe: the very people who should have been removed from the system at the time of the Education Reform Bill have been given *carte blanche* to wreck it.'[27]

Led by the headmaster of Eton, the Headmasters' Conference, which represents more than two hundred leading public schools, criticized the proposals by the School Examinations and Assess-ment Council to alter A-levels. Changes must not be a 'vehicle for imposing lower standards by stealth', the heads said. Against the Council's principle that A-level syllabuses should avoid 'religious, cultural, political, gender, ethnic, age and other forms of bias,' they argued that 'a true culture and the education tradition which flows from it is bound to be deeply coloured by the values which inform it. A Christian school is biased in favour of Christian values. The SEAC proposals amount to a prejudice in favour of secularism.'[28]

Given what was going on, it might almost have seemed that the Headmaster of The Perse School, Cambridge, was in earnest when he wrote to *The Times*: 'My proposal is to replace all existing GCE A-level, GCSE and BTEC examinations with one single, compulsory examination to be taken by all pupils at 18. This would sweep aside all the outmoded traditional subject disciplines, and replace them with a single examination in interpersonal skills, widely acknowledged as the only skill that will see Britain through 1992, the greenhouse effect and the Apocalypse . . . Expensive laboratory and scientific equipment would no longer be required, pupils would no longer be required to explain the chemical reaction that took place when an egg was boiled, but instead be required to explain what it felt like to be an egg . . . I feel this proposal is the logical extension of all our recent advances in educational and examination theory, and have no hesitation in asking for your readers' support.'[29]

Revolution by National Curriculum

The most widely praised of the educational reforms, the imposition of a national curriculum, became the most difficult for Thatcherites to justify in their own terms. Although Sir Keith Joseph had said emphatically that he did not intend the curricular objectives set forth in the GCSE syllabus to lead to a national syllabus, it did become its precursor. A national curriculum seemed to fit with the other reforms because, like them, it was designed to 'raise standards'.

Some who, like the Prime Minister, at first supported the national curriculum, expected it to be something quite different from what it became in fact. Mrs Thatcher had seen it as a commonsensical proposal for a core curriculum in maths, English and science, with compulsory testing. 'When we first started this, I do not think I ever thought they would do the syllabus in such detail as they are doing now.'[30] The policy of the national curriculum started from the conviction that teachers and educational authorities had failed to ensure that all children left school with a solid grounding. The national curriculum was meant to put that right, by 'cutting through the fog of methodology and sociology which filled the teacher-training colleges, and installing a few simple and necessary goals at the heart of the educational system'. But those charged with working out the details of the curriculum – officials at the DES, members of HM Inspectorate, and professional educationalists – instead of dispelling the fog 'transformed it into something solid, elaborate, and enduring'.[31]

A national curriculum was in any case a dangerous remedy because, as Mrs Thatcher remarked, 'once you put out an approved curriculum, if they have got it wrong, the situation is worse afterwards than it was before.'[32] Those who had hoped that the national curriculum would provide an antidote to the progressive orthodoxy were sorely disappointed. All the sins of the GCSE were writ large in the National Curriculum.

The Saunders-Watson report on history for the national curriculum argued that it would be 'a value judgement' on the part of teachers to require some facts rather than others to be mastered; besides, any so-called 'facts' learned by a student would sooner or later be superseded. So learning history properly, said the report, has nothing to do with facts and everything to do with pursuing objectives such as 'source evaluation', 'skills', 'empathy', 'conceptual attainment'. The report's critics condemned it for recommending nothing more or less than indoctrination in a wholly hostile attitude to Britain and its inherited civilization.[33]

Other proposals for the national curriculum equally incorporated the orthodoxy of educationalists. It was suggested that English literature should disappear as a separate subject; instead pupils should be introduced to 'the richness of contemporary writing', unrestricted by antiquated notions of classics of good writing or great literature. Even the proposals for design and technology were found to be 'depressing'. Professor Anthony O'Hear was outraged by the equation of 'aesthetics' with something to be used to sell products and influence consumers: 'Anyone sensitive to what Ruskin and Morris used to say about the human or spiritually uplifting aspects of the aesthetics of good design will be appalled . . . '[24] Not even geography escaped the rot. The Geographical Association insisted that teachers ought to ignore the names of cities, hills, plains, and rivers in order to focus attention on more noble subjects such as poverty and pollution.[35] The Conservative-dominated Kent County Council published a Curriculum Statement which declared that 'experience in Kent has yet to come across a topic or activity that is not eligible for a multicultural perspective and enhanced by it.' It also commended 'child-centred learning' and 'subject integration'. In short, the national curriculum, like the GCSE, fell into the hands of those whose power it was meant to destroy.

Yet the National Curriculum was one of the most popular measures of the Thatcher Government. Those who, given their political allegiance, might have been expected to be its natural critics were full of praise. The director of education for the borough of Croydon rejoiced that at last schools and teachers would be united 'into a truly national education system'. The requirement that everyone must pursue the same curriculum was welcomed as a new instrument for achieving the same old objective of ironing out all distinctions. On the ground that education must be 'broadened', it was argued that pupils with a special aptitude for science should be compelled to pursue a wide range of other subjects. When Mrs Thatcher expressed her doubts about the National Curriculum in an interview, the president of the Secondary Heads Association, Mr John Horn, declared that she was taking a greater interest 'than she should' in such matters: 'Are we to have a national curriculum or a government curriculum?'[36] John Rae was certain that as soon as the commotion died down everyone would see the undoubted advantages of a curriculum prescribed from the centre.

If praise came from the wrong people, some of the fiercest criticisms came from the Government's supporters. Peregrine Worsthorne, doyen of the conservative *Sunday Telegraph*, reprimanded Mrs Thatcher for being even more ambitious than the socialists in trying to impose 'an educational system geared to the creation of entrepreneurs'. 'The dangers of central planning or state control do not disappear', Worsthorne warned, 'just because the central planners and State in question are Right minded.'[37]

Thatcherites who found the whole idea of a National Curriculum repulsive regarded it as a 'nationalization of education'. Sir Rhodes Boyson described the National Curriculum as 'the ultimate triumph of the comprehensive socialist philosophy, part of the command economy'.[38] Lord Joseph led an unsuccessful attempt in the Lords to cut the curriculum down to a few core subjects. Stuart Sexton explained that, 'What the government has done, or, more precisely the officials at the Department of Education and Science, is to say – having devolved management to the schools . . . having decentralized we are now going to impose our view of what that national curriculum should be, even down to the detail of which periods of history should be learnt . . . The same old lot of so-called educationalists are having a field day imposing their rather idiosyncratic view of what children should learn.' He suggested that the government should 'suspend forthwith any more directives on subject content, on assessment, on examination syllabuses . . . disband the umpteen councils and committees on the curriculum, assessment and examinations . . . [and] concentrate on the one issue that will really bring the higher standards we all desire: effective management and responsibility in the schools themselves. Better still, make all schools grant-maintained.'[39]

As criticism mounted, the Government began to think again. By October of 1990, Mr Baker's successor as Secretary of State for Education, John MacGregor, announced slimmed-down testing in mathematics, English and science: 'We are concentrating on fundamentals and that I believe is what parents want,' MacGregor said. 'The tests will be rigorous and will promote higher standards, identifying strengths that can be built on and weaknesses which can be tackled. It is if you like the three Rs plus science. We are making the national curriculum come through exactly as it was intended . . . We are cutting the external testing to what really matters.' For children aged fourteen to sixteen, the national curriculum was reduced to a compulsory core of English, maths, science and technology and a modern foreign language – which together would occupy no more than about half the timetable. But the contents and the inflexibility of the modified national curriculum still aroused opposition.

Newspapers began to offer more support for the opposition to the new 'unification' of education. They carried many reminders that 'Our competitors generally continue to separate academic and vocational courses . . . European experience suggests that the academic and vocational courses should remain largely separate.'[40] Those who called for the abolition of A-levels in favour of a single qualification were told that the A-level science syllabuses 'constitute the broadest, indeed the only secure and practical foundation for absorbing and initiating technological change . . . The fact that this work has been done up to now in the sixth form rather than at university is the reason why this country has produced engineering and science graduates at 21 who can hold their own academically with the products of foreign systems who are two or three years older.'[41]

The Government responded by trying to loosen further the

national strait-jacket. Selectivity and streaming were brought in
from the cold. Schools were encouraged by the Government to
develop vocational streams offering courses in basic engineering,
construction, agriculture, business studies, accountancy, information technology, design, care management, and hotel and catering skills. 'We must give schools more room to manoeuvre within
the basic framework of the national curriculum,' the Education
Minister, Tim Eggar, said. 'Instead of trying to broaden A-levels
to include everybody, we should be concentrating on raising the
status of vocational qualifications. To achieve that, we must have
two parallel streams – the vocational and the academic – from half
way through secondary school so that children can concentrate on
what interests them. One of the options we are considering is
allowing schools to offer a BTEC (Business and Technician Education Council) qualification as an alternative to GCSE. Also, now
that schools have local management and power to opt out of council
control we expect a considerable degree of differentiation to
develop.'

The Government had begun to recognize the embarrassing truth
about a national curriculum. Although it had long been a favourite
project of the DES, the Department's civil servants had not been
able to persuade any of the socialist governments to adopt it. Nor
would the first two Secretaries of State for Education under Mrs
Thatcher, Mark Carlisle and Sir Keith Joseph, touch it. Kenneth
Baker saw it as a way to produce noticeable results quickly and
impressively, whereas all the other measures could do their work
only slowly, hardly in time for the next election. He was accordingly
described by the *Spectator*'s political columnist as 'a busy man and
a man in a hurry. With a whole repertoire of major reforms to
cram into his great Education Reform Bill, he was prepared to
compromise on every one of them in order to ease them past
the professionals and the officials ... Mrs Thatcher looked on,
meanwhile, with surprise and increasing impotence'.[42] Earlier, however, Mr Baker had not been alone in his enthusiasm for a national
curriculum. It had been supported by the Prime Minister and
others as the way to promote the vigorous virtues and to make
Britain a flourishing nation.

Taming the Universities

The strain in Thatcherism that led a Government committed to encouraging variety and choice to establish a national curriculum also determined the Government's policies towards universities. It was here, rather than in the pursuit of privatization or monetarism, that economic objectives dominated and, by doing so, put Thatcherism seriously at odds with itself.

By the late seventies, the beautiful baby to which the Robbins Report had given birth in 1963 had acquired gargantuan proportions. Within little more than a decade the number of universities had doubled, thirty-two new polytechnics appeared, colleges were upgraded, two new research councils were created, the University Grants Committee quadrupled in size, the Open University was founded, business schools were started, and government funding of postgraduate study increased. There were jobs galore for would-be academics. Universities provided lavish services for health, sport and careers, and student unions became increasingly ambitious and powerful as their income grew. The trade unions joined the act to make universities pay more for non-academic staff as well as for technicians at the laboratories. At the same time, the projections of student numbers and forecasts of expenditure turned out to be statistical fairy tales. Some 135,000 places in science and technology were not taken up. It was all ruinously expensive.

Any government, and certainly one committed to restraining public spending, was bound to call a halt. Even before Mrs Thatcher took office, university salaries had been falling in real terms; dons' incomes lagged further and further behind those of civil servants with which they used to be on a par; instead of earning as much as professionals, academics were paid as little as semi-skilled workers. Vice-chancellors told the government that they could make no more economies and could not balance their budgets.

Sir Keith Joseph, as the Secretary of State for Education, made several efforts to reduce expenditure by limiting student grants. He suggested a graduated scale of contributions by parents who could afford them. Middle-class parents and students were outraged, even though he pointed out that their university education was being subsidized by people much poorer than themselves. He went three times to the Cabinet with proposals to replace student grants by student loans, and three times the Cabinet turned him down. Passionate opposition came from the Lord Chancellor, Lord Hailsham, whose grandfather had invented polytechnics.

A new regime for higher education was established by the 1988 Education Reform Act. Its provisions were shaped by two assumptions: that the universities were monopolies of producers who had for too long been pampered by handouts; that the universities had failed to achieve what was now regarded as their leading duty, to contribute to Britain's economic growth.

Even before Robert Jackson became the Under-Secretary of State for Higher Education in 1987, he had attacked the 'university culture' for the 'power which it gave to producer interests' and had argued that in order to prevent these 'cartels of producer interests' from obstructing 'the strategic design of Britain's economic revival', it was essential that 'the apparatus and ethos of the self-regarding academic producer-monopoly be dismantled'.[43] Later he explained that the government had showered money on the 'producers' in the universities while leaving them free to decide how many students they would take in. The result was that 'unit costs' were far too high. It was time that 'new thinking in academe' addressed itself to producing 'graduates of acceptable quality at lower unit costs'.

Robert Jackson's dicta were entirely in keeping with the recommendations of the Croham Committee,[44] which concluded that the Government had 'a responsibility to form a view about the size of funding and the objectives for the tertiary sector of education',[45] and that 'the mechanisms of conditionality and earmarking available to the UGC [University Grants Committee] will be required in order to manage public resources effectively.'[46]. It proposed that the UGC be replaced by a body which would 'initiate and promote such plans for the development of university teaching and research as may from time to time be required to meet national needs'.[47] It defined the 'principal responsibility' of the new body as constructing 'a national strategy for the investment of public funds', and reconciling the universities' separate strategies 'with perceived national needs'.[48] The new body should have an 'unambiguous' power to attach conditions to grants 'including the positive or negative earmarking of elements of the grants',[49] so that it could 'allocate student places and concentrate and rationalize provision in individual subjects' with the help of 'indicators of output'.[50] To ensure 'that it becomes strong, effective and capable of meeting the formidable challenges facing the universities and of acting as an agent of change, its Director General should have the required 'professional and leadership skills'.[51]

These recommendations were put into effect when the Education Reform Act established a Universities Funding Council to replace the University Grants Committee. More of the same appeared the following April in the White Paper, *Higher Education Meeting the Challenge*, which declared that 'Higher education has a crucial role in helping the nation to meet the economic challenges of the final decade of this century and beyond,'[52] and promised that, in aid of precise 'manpower planning', the government would monitor the demand for university places, and the 'prospective needs for new graduates by industry, commerce and the public services'.[53] The Government would 'in particular be concerned to see that the UFC's arrangements for making funds available to universities properly reward success in developing co-operation with and meeting the needs of industry and commerce.'[54] In the same spirit, the Secretary of State for Education, Kenneth Baker, speaking in the House of Commons, promised that the Universities Funding Council would address itself to the 'precise targeting of funds'.[55]

To ensure that the Universities Funding Council would not be distracted by frivolous or effete pursuits, more than half of its fifteen members were to be businessmen. Lord Chilver, who was appointed chairman, was not disposed by his professional interests to favour learning as an end in itself. He was an engineer, a Fellow of the Royal Society, and had been chairman of the Advisory Council for Applied Research and Development. He explained that 'Every university in its charter is required to disseminate knowledge and . . . that knowledge must be universally applicable.

That's the meaning of the word university.' Of course he considered arts and the humanities 'terribly important', but if they were not to turn into one of those 'decaying parts of the university system . . . which lose their contact with the real world' and become reduced to nothing more than 'armchair things', they had to be 'relevant'. If historians did not discuss what 'people are interested in', such as 'the history of urban development' or the 'history of political systems', they would be 'turning out the same sort of things all the time' and in effect be 'dead'.[56] Under the new regime funds would be allocated on the basis of plans submitted by each university, which would be 'detailed, separately costed for research and teaching' and supported by 'open publicly judgeable indicators of quality'; Lord Chilver therefore felt confident that the decisions of the Funding Council would be perfectly objective and indisputable. The UFC would scrutinize, he promised, 'each history course on offer in the competition for the grant. If they all look the same, "We'll say we've got enough of those", in other words, the funding will encourage diversity. The wise university will pick up differentiation and you don't differentiate by doing "a history course", do you . . . '[57]

Relations between the University Funding Council and the universities were mediated by the Committee of Vice-Chancellors and Principals (CVCP). Founded after the First World War, the Committee was designed to enable the universities to 'discuss their common problems'. But with the proliferation and expansion of universities during the 1960s, the Committee's activities became 'operational as well as deliberative'. By 1986, the CVCP had become what the Croham Report described admiringly as 'a strong effective national body, representative of the universities and able to undertake collective action on their behalf'. It monitored academic quality, 'staff performance and development', and promoted 'selectivity in research function, rationalisation, better management'.

The Croham Report's admiration of the Committee of Vice-Chancellors and Principals was not universally shared. Nor did the CVCP accord with Robert Jackson's view of the universities as 'cartels of producers'. Far from trying to defend the 'privileges' of the universities, the CVCP acted as pliant handmaidens of the

Department of Education. They were accordingly described by dons as 'yet another layer of outside control' designed 'to stifle the autonomy of supposedly autonomous corporations'. The growing power of the Vice-Chancellors to negotiate with the Association of University Teachers and with the Secretary of State was denounced in the House of Lords. The CVCP had 'become committed', Lord Adrian said, 'to acting collectively and to imposing changes on their universities by agreement with Ministers in which they may have had individually only a minimal part. They become middle managers and ultimately just employers – employers of an increasingly casualised academic labour-force. More and more, as vice-chancellors accept that role and as the UGC has increased its grip on individual universities, as the paradigm of university education becomes industrial rather than collegiate, so the behaviour patterns of the industrial world spread in the universities.'[58]

The managerial activities of the CVCP included monitoring university admissions 'so as to ensure that students from ethnic minorities are not being discriminated against'. It was doing that, the CVCP explained, in order 'to establish facts which will assist the appropriate public bodies in the development of a multi-cultural society'.[59] And in keeping with this resolution the DES ordered that from the autumn of 1990 application forms for both university and polytechnic courses had to include a question on ethnic origin. In addition, the CVCP assumed the power of inspecting universities in order to identify publicly 'departments guilty of consistently poor teaching'. And the head of the policing unit, the Principal of King's College, London, warned that the time would come 'when names will be named'. This 'monitoring' was represented not as an interference with the autonomy of universities but rather as the reverse. The CVCP boasted that the unit doing the monitoring 'will demonstrate to ministers' that dons are 'capable of policing their own teaching'.[60]

But this was only a small part of the machinery to ensure 'accountability'. Not only did the National Audit Office check the universities' accounts, but the Universities Funding Council was to do its own internal auditing and conduct 'value-for-money' studies. The Council in turn was to be monitored by the Department of Education and Science. In addition a new Higher Education Internal Unit was established within the DES with the right to examine the universities' books.

Complexity was compounded when the Universities Funding Council embarked on Laputian schemes of appraisal. Dons had to spend many days each year filling out forms displaying their achievements such as success in obtaining Research Council grants and studentships, contract research income from industry and government departments, and other equally telling signs of recognition. They had also to engage in a yearly ceremony of mutually appraising one another. Each university was required to produce 'research plans'. And the great stock of information thus amassed emboldened the Universities Funding Council to propose closing or merging more than thirty small 'unviable' departments of physics, chemistry and engineering, which happened to include some of the most distinguished in the world, on the ground that departments with fewer than twenty full-time staff could not offer a sufficiently wide range of courses or maintain up-to-date equipment. This proposal was dropped, but other evaluation schemes were prosecuted energetically. 'Research selectivity exercises' provided data for grading each university according to its research performance. The results of this examination were published with great fanfare but treated with scant respect. The progress to ever more scientific modes of assessment culminated in 'bibliometric profiling', whereby dons could be assessed without reading their works by merely counting the number of times that their publications had been cited by other writers.

That the Committee of Vice-Chancellors and Principals was dedicated to assisting, rather than impeding, the government's control of universities became especially noticeable in connection with the Government's proposal to abolish tenure – the right of dons to continue in their positions until they reached the age of retirement. The Government argued that giving academics tenure made it difficult, as Robert Jackson explained, 'for the management of universities to manage their institutions rationally'.[61] Others denounced tenure as an 'outmoded privilege'. The Vice-Chancellors nodded in hearty agreement.

The Backlash

The abolition of tenure was represented by the Government as just another step in its fight against cartels of producers bent on preserving inefficient practices. Some academics, both Thatcherite and non-Thatcherite, approved. Lord Annan, who had been Provost of King's College, Cambridge and of University College, London and raised to the peerage by a Labour Government, had long opposed tenure as a practice that loaded down universities with drones and made it impossible to bring in new blood where and when it was wanted.

On the other hand, these moves to reform the universities elicited criticism from people of all political colours. Enoch Powell accused the government of being 'engaged in establishing – so far as it lies in the power of any government to establish – that economic utility is to be the criterion of all organized human behaviour ... The old Prussia claimed to decide how its citizens should be educated to make them efficient instruments of its imperialism. The new Prussia, now being daily built here, demands, after having substituted economic competition for military aggression, that its citizens be so educated as to maximise their return on the capital invested. Compliance with that demand means an end to the university. Let those who know and love it repel the attack.'[62]

The editor of *Marxism Today*, Martin Jacques, also denounced the 'staggering' transformation of the relationship between higher education and the government produced by the Education Reform Act: 'Historically the universities have enjoyed a strong degree of independence from the government. The bill will remove this at a stroke.' It was all in keeping with the Thatcherite dictum: 'If you can't privatize, then control or even abolish ... Anything that does not lend itself to the market principle is treated with suspicion and regarded as a suitable case for "state" treatment.' Because of this, Jacques continued, the Thatcher Government regards universities 'with as much contempt as it does the trade unions'. It is 'a know-nothing government whose philistinism is dangerous to the economic and cultural health of the nation'.[63]

Education: Thatcher versus Bismarck? 271

The former Leader of the Liberal Party, Jo Grimond, blamed the universities for embracing 'what passes as "Thatcherism". I say "pass as" because I do not believe Mrs Thatcher is solely responsible for that mixture of greed, belief in public relations, materialism and bureaucracy which has gripped the upper classes, and now is invading the universities . . . they seem anxious to lick the boots of government and big business and to show how they appreciate "the contracts" they are offered . . . Yet "contracts", as the main method of finance, and an academic league grading professors etc are the antithesis of what a university should stand for. They might as well offer themselves to the Department of Trade and Industry and become technical colleges.' Grimond lamented decisions like that of Aberdeen University to abolish the teaching of philosophy while it 'glories in a new filing system'.[64]

Indeed criticism came from all quarters. On the one hand, Professor John Ashworth (currently Director of the London School of Economics), who had become known for establishing links between Salford University and the business community, denounced the new arrangements for importing into the universities 'those features of the management of the nationalized industries which have made the commercial performance of those industries so lamentable'.[65] On the other hand, the Bishop of Rochester reminded the House of Lords that: 'Universities must not be thought of as though they were departments of state subject to central control, not as the different regiments of an army under the leadership of a commander-in-chief. Universities are distinct and independent institutions, no two of which are alike. They have come into being at different times. They each have their own history, traditions and statutes. What some of us look for above all else is that the individuality and the particular ethos of a university shall not be put at risk any more than the academic freedom of the teaching staff.'[66]

The most passionate and telling criticism came from a staunch admirer of what the Thatcher Government had achieved elsewhere. In a pamphlet which the Centre for Policy Studies had commissioned but refused to publish because it was so trenchantly critical of the Government's policies, Professor Elie Kedourie, of the London School of Economics, denied that university teachers were 'so many oil sheiks grown fat on the exactions and extortions of an academic OPEC', and attributed the false belief that they had done so to an 'inverted world'. In the real world, he said, the universities are almost wholly dependent on what funds the government chose to give them. The charge that 'unit-costs' are 'unnecessarily high' in British universities is 'make-believe economics' because there is no real market and hence no way in which the costs of a university education can be compared with a market price. Nor does it make sense to 'compare' the costs of one university with another, let alone the whole British system with that of another country, because to decide 'what to leave in, what to leave out, whether to include current costs, and over what period, whether capital costs should count, whether teaching only, or also research costs should be included' requires the 'dazzling arts of the prestidigitator'.[67]

Kedourie attacked the Government's assumptions that since universities were financed from state funds, they must serve the public interest, and that because ministers were the elected representatives of the taxpayers, they ought to lay down what the public interest requires universities to do. 'This sweeping doctrine', Kedourie argued, leads 'to the centralization which is the distinguishing feature of enlightened absolutism. Accountability (which implies scrutiny after the event) has given way to management (which is the setting of goals and methods before the event) . . . is it the case that government is always able unerringly to define the public interest? Is it not the case rather that, in the circumstances, management more often than not must be bad management?'[68]

Above all, the general attitude to universities displayed in the new arrangements was subjected to withering criticism by Professor Kedourie. The attempt to promote the 'efficiency' of universities by putting businessmen on the UFC failed to understand the meaning of efficiency, for 'efficiency is not a general and abstract attribute. It is always relative to the object in view . . . a university is not a business. What then is the ground of the presumption that someone who can speed up a production line for fashion hosiery

or can set up a profitable factoring business is *ipso facto* able to say
how best a university should be run? The intellectual qualities
required, for instance, to marshal the evidence relating to the
Elizabethan House of Commons, or to the theory of quantum
physics, and to set them out coherently and convincingly cannot be inferior to those required in running a multinational
company.'

Making everything taught in a university 'relevant', as Lord
Chilver wanted, meant that unless the 'wares' of universities 'have
that special, seductive zing, so much prized by, say, lingerie manufacturers, the merchandise will not be shifted'. As Britain is a free
country 'there is no reason why Lord Chilver should not indulge
his taste for the study of urban development or 'political
systems' ... But how can he establish that they are less dead or
more relevant – relevant to whom, anyway? – than the Jacobite
rebellions or the government of Florence under the Medici? For
what in history is living and not dead is that which pulsates with
the life of the enquiring and critical mind, not that which the latest
evanescent fashion decrees to be "with-it" and "relevant".' The
new system of appraising dons 'conjures up a vision of Cairo and
Calcutta office-wallahs, which one had assumed to be worlds away
from the sceptical sobriety of civil servants in London'.[69]

What had reduced universities to their present sorry state,
according to Kedourie, was the growing discrepancy between the
student grants and the real cost of educating a student. When, in
1960, it was established that all students admitted to full-time first-
degree courses should receive awards from public funds, the grant
given to a student 'was the actual sum charged by the university'.
But as the grant 'did not keep up with the rising costs of university
education,' the universities became increasingly dependent on the
block grant from the University Grants Committee. The only way
of ending this client status and of achieving genuine accountability
in the financing of universities, Kedourie concluded, is to make
universities wholly dependent on fees by raising the student grants
enough to cover the real cost of both their tuition and maintenance.

Kedourie was not the only one to suggest some such way of
financing universities. Indeed by the end of September 1989 even

the Vice-Chancellors had proposed that students be charged the full cost of their tuition, even though the fee would in most instances be wholly paid for by the government. From many different directions came agreement that higher education had to be liberated from the stranglehold of uniformity, so that different institutions could levy the charges and pay the salaries that best fitted in with their particular circumstances. It would then be possible for universities to pay enough to retain academics who could command two or three times as much elsewhere, without, as previously, having to raise salaries all around. The Government had already acknowledged as much by its introduction of merit awards, which enabled universities to pay some of their staff more than the salary on the established scale. Universities had also been learning that they could find funds from private sources and that charging foreign students higher fees increased their revenue. By funding universities in the simplest fashion, by letting the money follow the student, it was argued, the government could and should free universities to manage their own affairs.

But the great Education Reform Act, as Mr Robert Jackson frankly avowed in the House of Commons, had aimed to do the opposite, to effect 'the nationalization of higher education funding'. That he felt some discomfort over this is suggested by his adding that the Act would also 'strike in the direction of decentralization'. This 'decentralization through extreme centralization', Kedourie said, sounded like 'one of those antinomian heresies which hold that salvation can only come through sinning and the greater the turpitude the more certain the salvation.'[70]

The greatest mystery in all this was why the Thatcher Government should have embarked on a university policy wholly at odds with its ideals and objectives, and indeed with the policy for schools introduced in the very same Education Reform Act. It was a university policy, moreover, which far from bringing political advantage embroiled the Government in difficulties and unpopularity that it might easily have escaped by following its natural bent. Although the policy was clearly inspired by the Thatcherite commitment to making Britain flourish, that aim was implemented in a fashion that violated all other Thatcherite commitments. In part this was due to the efforts of the Department of Education and Science which, through all the changes in governments and ministers, retained a strong *dirigiste* ethos and ruthlessly used its power to design the practical details of the government's policies so as to defeat Thatcherite intentions. But it is also true that the officials in the Department of Education did not meet effective resistance from the ministers. That was because Thatcherites had not seriously reflected on the role of education, and especially of universities, in the kind of Britain they hoped to shape. No one had done for education what the Institute of Economic Affairs had done for economic policy.

The fundamental commitment of Thatcherism to promoting the vigorous virtues and a flourishing Britain does not imply that universities should be treated as a training ground for industry. But Thatcherite politicians had never addressed questions such as: what distinguishes a university from other educational institutions? What have the ancient universities and the practices they developed contributed to the character of British civilization? Because of their practical orientation, they were disposed to dismiss serious academic writing on such topics as irrelevant for their purposes. Since they were more familiar with the principles of economics, they were easily seduced by arguments such as those of Correlli Barnett which treated education as a means to economic success.

Moreover, the spirit of the age was hardly likely to encourage clear thinking about the reasons for cherishing professors of Greek. Nor was a career in politics in the late twentieth century a natural home for those who were steeped in humanistic learning. It is not surprising that the politician who most vigorously criticized the government's policies for universities – Enoch Powell – should have been a classicist. Ordinary Thatcherite politicians could more easily see the reasons for restoring the independence of schools, making them more accountable to parents, improving standards, and promoting vocational training because such policies were the obvious means to promoting the vigorous virtues, a flourishing Britain, and a paradigm shift. But with respect to higher education, the Thatcher Governments defeated themselves by pursuing objectives that conflicted with their basic commitment. They failed to

understand how profoundly different is the role of universities in
a Britain made flourishing by individuals possessed of the vigorous
virtues from the function assigned to universities in a Britain made
to flourish by Bismarckian directives.

10

We British

No account of Thatcherism could be complete without an explanation of the attitudes and policies taken up by Mrs Thatcher herself and Thatcherites generally towards Europe. It was in the responses to the developing European scene that Thatcherism came to see itself and came fully to be seen for what it was.

Nothing But a Free Market

The saga began with the 'Common Market' debates of the 1970s. Scanning the columns of *Hansard* that cover the critical Parliamentary occasions, one finds no major utterance by Mrs Thatcher herself before 1975, when she intervened in the debate about a referendum that the Wilson Government proposed to call on whether Britain should withdraw from the EEC. In the course of arguing against the referendum she dismissed the suggestion that Britain had acquired a written constitution by virtue of her affiliation with the Common Market, and emphasized the sovereignty of Parliament and the collective responsibility of the government for such decisions. And she denied the propriety of using a referendum 'to override a treaty obligation which had been through all its parliamentary stages and had been in operation for two years'. Such a step, she said, 'would have a damaging effect on Britain's standing in the world'.[1] She is recorded as having voted in favour of the Common Market on all the relevant occasions. She was, of course, at that time a particularly domestic politician – one who later, on the eve of her premiership, admitted to having rarely left the United Kingdom on business. But so studious and conscientious an MP can scarcely have failed to have read the published papers or to have taken note of the repeated assurances given by her own party's leaders and experts about the nature of the exercise.

Although the opponents of Britain's entry into the Common Market, most notably Enoch Powell, argued that, by joining, Britain would be surrendering her sovereignty, the advocates of entry strenuously denied any such possibility. The Prime Minister, Mr Heath, assured the House of Commons on 25 February 1970 that 'There will not be a blueprint for a federal Europe ... What is more those members of the Community who want a federal system but who know the views of Her Majesty's Government and the Opposition Parties here are prepared to forgo their federal desires so that Britain should be a member ... I believe this to be of great importance.'[2] The *White Paper*, recommending Britain's entry into the EEC, issued in July 1971,[3] declared that 'The Community is no federation' and 'there is no question of eroding any national sovereignty.'

Similarly unequivocal repudiations of federalism came from other members of the Government who were in a position to know the true state of affairs. The Foreign Secretary, Sir Alec Douglas-Home (now Lord Home of Hirsel), told the House of Commons that Britain could not be forced into federalism because 'great countries with the history of the European nations cannot be dragooned or coerced into a pattern of political association which one or other of them does not like.'[4] The chief British negotiator, Mr (now Lord) Rippon was just as certain that there was no danger of Britain being moved into a federal Europe. When the European Communities Bill was debated during 1972, the most impressive affirmation that joining the EEC would not in the least affect British sovereignty came from the Solicitor-General, Sir Geoffrey Howe. He asked: 'What is the position concerning the ultimate supremacy of Parliament?' and he answered: 'the position is that the ultimate supremacy of Parliament will not be affected.'[5] On 1 January 1973, Britain joined the European Economic Community, along with Denmark and Ireland.

There is no reason to doubt that, like everyone else, the earnest Secretary of State for Education, Margaret Thatcher, took these assurances at face value. And if she did so, she will have thought

of the European Economic Community as what it was regularly
described as being by its advocates in the UK – a Common Market,
meaning an area of free trade with no customs or other barriers
to the free movement of goods, services and people. In a speech
in London, on 24 November 1976, attacking the Labour Government's lack of enthusiasm for the European Economic Community,
Mrs Thatcher was obviously talking about an association of sovereign states dealing with one another as independent equals: 'This
Government has run down our bargaining strength in Europe to a
dangerously low level. It will be one of the first tasks of the new
Conservative Government to restore it.' The same view of the EEC
was stressed in an interview in January 1977: 'I believe we should
continue to have a partnership of national states each retaining the
right to protect its vital interests, but developing more effectively
than at present the habit of working together.' The next generation
might grow 'impatient with the bargains and compromises' but that
is 'the price we pay for a Community of partner states'. What had
to be firmly resisted, Mrs Thatcher emphasized, was 'drawing up
blueprints for the next generation'.[6]

None of this meant that Mrs Thatcher and the Conservative
Party were anything but whole-heartedly committed to the
Common Market as an established feature of the political scene.
The Right Approach, by the Conservative Central Office, first published in 1976, declared that just as 'NATO provides the framework within which we plan and implement our defence policies,
so the European Community provides the framework not only
for many of our domestic policies but also increasingly for the
development of our foreign policies. For the last fifteen years, the
Conservative Party has consistently believed that the best hope for
Britain lay in membership of a free, strong, and democratic European Community.'[7] The Conservative Party *Campaign Guide* of
1977 praised the Common Market membership for presenting
'valuable opportunities for industry and agriculture as well as providing real help in grants and loans from the various EEC funds,'
and pointed out that the Conservatives had opposed Labour's
efforts to withdraw: 'In government and opposition Conservatives
have fought successfully both to bring Britain within the European

fold and to keep her there.'[8] The Conservative Election Manifesto of 1979 assured British electors that 'The next Conservative Government will restore Britain's influence by convincing our partners of our commitment to the Community's success ... We shall work for a commonsense Community which resists excessive bureaucracy and unnecessary harmonisation proposals, holding to the principles of free enterprise which inspired its original founders.'[9]

In the early years of the Thatcher administration the one source of serious irritation in relation to Europe was the argument over the net contribution of the UK to the European Economic Community as a whole and in particular to the Common Agricultural Policy. The 1979 manifesto contained a promise to reform the CAP so as to 'reduce the burden which the Community budget places upon the British taxpayer' and to ensure that 'national payments into the budget should be more closely related to ability to pay.'[10] It is noteworthy that this dispute was not, in any sense, an argument with or against the Community itself, but rather against other member states. It was a sheer battle of national interests, in which Mrs Thatcher was determined to 'repatriate' large sums which Britain had contributed to the other nation states and which had not been fully offset by contributions from those states to Britain. It was, in other words, a dispute of a form all too familiar – both to the Commission and to the representatives of the other member states – it was an argument about money.

Britain's contribution to the Community budget was second only to Germany's although (in terms of GDP per capita) Britain was only the seventh richest member state. At the same time, as Britain had a relatively small agricultural sector, it received the least benefit per head – some ten per cent – from the Budget. Besides, because Britain had worldwide trading links, she paid a disproportionate amount in customs levies and agricultural duties on goods imported from outside the Community. By 1979, Britain's net contribution was close to 1 billion, far more than that of any other member state, apart from West Germany. Within a few months of becoming prime minister, Mrs Thatcher gave notice that she intended to do something about that: 'Britain cannot accept the present situation.

It is demonstrably unjust. It is politically indefensible . . . the imbalance is not compatible with the spirit of the Community.'[11]

After seven months of negotiations, an agreement was reached in May 1980 whereby, for 1980 and 1981, Britain received refunds amounting to £1.4 billion. No progress was made toward reforming the system as a whole by May 1982, but the Community agreed to refund 589 million net for 1982. At last, however, at the Stuttgart Summit in June 1983, it was agreed not only to refund the £440 million to the UK for 1983, but also to introduce fundamental reform. Mrs Thatcher insisted that the reform must impose effective controls on the rate of increase in agricultural and other expenditure, and distribute the financial burden more equitably.

An impressive victory was scored by Mrs Thatcher at the Fontainebleau Summit of 25–6 June 1984, when the Community established for the first time permanent arrangements which dramatically reduced the contribution of Britain to half of what it had been. Under the new system UK budgetary imbalances would be corrected by an automatic refund known as 'the abatement'. Instead of contributing at a net rate of up to twenty-one per cent to Community spending, Britain would now contribute no more than seven per cent. On her return, Mrs Thatcher's 'tough stand' was widely praised. 'Europe United, Maggie Wins a New Deal for Britain', 'Maggie Home with a Bargain', the headlines proclaimed.[12] It was reported in the Tory press that, 'Flushed with triumph', Mrs Thatcher last night hailed the outcome of her Common Market budget battle at the Fontainebleau Summit as 'a good deal for Britain . . . We've got a settlement we've been trying to get for five years.' And she praised both President Mitterrand and Chancellor Helmut Kohl for their 'marvellous co-operation'.[13] Doubts were expressed about whether the Community would really deliver and about whether the other members had truly come to recognize the absurdity of the Common Agricultural Policy. Some were dismayed that it was an agreement only for 'a limited period' and that Mrs Thatcher had not got all of what she wanted. But it was generally agreed that relations with the other members of the Community were now much improved: 'By exposing the unfairness and absurdities of the Community's present finances, Mrs That-

cher has advanced the cause of true European unity.'[14] 'It is an
agreement which permits the Community', *The Times* said, 'after a
year of existential crisis to turn its collective mind and energies to
other things besides the accounts.'[15]

It is true that, in the course of extracting cash from the other
member states, Mrs Thatcher was willing to use constitutional
devices, such as the delay of the Budget, to achieve her ends. But
there was no suggestion in the first few years of her administration
that the British Government was challenging the constitutional
structure of the EC as a matter in its own right. On the contrary,
it was the Labour Party who, in their 1983 manifesto, argued that
Britain required tariff protection and called for withdrawal from
the EEC: 'The next Labour government, committed to radical,
socialist policies for reviving the British economy is bound to find
continued membership a most serious obstacle to the fulfilment of
these policies . . . British withdrawal from the Community is the
right policy for Britain – to be completed well within the lifetime
of the parliament. That is our commitment.'[16]

The Conservative Manifesto of 1983, by contrast, carried a
ringing endorsement of Britain's membership of the EC: 'The
European Community is the world's largest trading group. It is by
far our most important export market. Withdrawal would be a
catastrophe for this country . . . It would be a fateful step towards
isolation, at which only the Soviet Union and her allies would
rejoice.'[17] In the House of Commons the point was hammered
home by backbenchers and the Prime Minister. And Mrs Thatcher
said that it would be a 'disaster' for 'this country to withdraw from
Europe'.[18]

The Train Moves On

It was thus with a sense of victory on the financial front, and with
a continued belief that the EC was, in essence, a 'Common Market'
that the second Thatcher administration entered discussions on
the Single European Act. It was an amendment to the Treaty of
Rome, to which Britain agreed in December 1985, and which it

presented to Parliament in March 1986. Within the government, and within the Conservative party at large, the Single European Act was regarded, first, as a matter of foreign affairs and, second, as a move towards free trade. Thatcherites, who were in any event more concerned with pressing domestic issues such as recession and the miners' strike, were easily persuaded that the Single European Act fitted firmly into their preference for a wider and more comprehensive free trade area.

Yet the preamble to the Act made commitments that had little to do with promoting free trade. It said that the member states were 'determined to work together to promote' the European Social Charter and equality, that 'the results achieved in the fields of economic integration and political co-operation' had led 'the democratic peoples of Europe' to believe that a 'European Parliament, elected by universal suffrage is an indispensable expression', that Europe would 'aim at speaking ever increasingly with one voice', and would seek to 'improve the economic and social situation by extending common policies and pursuing new objectives'. But all this was regarded as little more than window dressing, and scant or no thought was given to the extension of the power of the Commission which the Act in fact made mandatory.

Once again, Sir Geoffrey Howe assured Parliament that 'We are not talking about the declaration or proclamation of a United States of Europe or about vague political or legal goals. We are talking about practical steps towards the unity (not union) that is essential if Europe is to maintain and enhance its economic political position in a harshly competitive world.'[19] The same point was made by another Foreign Office Minister, Mrs Lynda Chalker: 'what the Single European Act will not do – and I think it is worth emphasizing this – is that it will not lead to a federal union.'[20] The Conservative Campaign Guide for 1987 included an assurance that 'The Single European Act does *not* represent a fundamental change in the structure of the European Community or in our relationship with it. The Act simply brings the Community Treaties . . . more into line with the practical needs of the 1980s and 1990s.'[21]

It was acknowledged that mechanisms such as majority voting created what might perhaps be unfortunate precedents, but in the light of the importance which Thatcherites attached to the promotion of the single market these technical defects seemed hardly worth the candle. To the extent that either Mrs Thatcher herself or Thatcherites generally had any worries about the real purpose of the Single European Act, these were largely allayed by the fact that the Act had replaced the Draft Treaty of Union – a document which had been put forward by the European Parliament as an effective blueprint for a federal Europe, which on 14 February 1984 was adopted by the European Parliament by 231 votes to 31 with 43 abstentions. The Draft Treaty proposed among other things that 'the law of the Union' should 'take precedence over national law',[22] that citizens of Member States should become 'citizens of the Union', that the national veto be completely abolished within ten years,[23] that the Union should have the power to tax and raise loans, conduct foreign policy and be represented by the Commission and its embassies *vis-à-vis* non-EC states,[24] that the Treaty should become effective once ratified by two-thirds of the member states of the EC, regardless of opposition from the remaining third of member states.[25] Following its adoption by the European Parliament, the Draft Treaty was approved by the Belgian, German and Italian legislatures but not by the others; the British Government strongly objected. Thus almost before it was heard of in Britain, the Draft Treaty was replaced by the Single European Act which was designed as a compromise.

For the majority of Thatcherites, and even to a great extent for Mrs Thatcher herself, the years between 1984 and 1987 saw little change on the European front. There was considerable enthusiasm for the introduction and completion of the single market by 1992. This enthusiasm remained dominant before and through the 1987 election, and the Conservative manifesto in that election fully reflected what was at that time the official Thatcherite view when it said that: 'Britain has led the way in establishing a genuine common market, with more trade and services moving freely across national boundaries ... We will continue to play a responsible leading role in the development of the Community while safeguarding our essential national interests.' Immediately after the 1987 election on 4 June, the effervescent Lord Young of Graffham moved to the Department of Trade and Industry and began an active campaign advertising the merits of 1992 and the need for British businessmen to prepare themselves for the new world of open competition in Europe. So far, so good.

Troubles with Delors

In early 1988, this picture of harmonious and orderly development of the European Community and of Britain's relationship to the Community was indeed all that publicly presented itself. But, looking back on the same events, it becomes possible to see that during the period from 1982 to 1988, the wind was filling with straws of a different kind. The Falklands War, as well as initially increasing the stature of Mrs Thatcher herself, had brought the Thatcher administration substantively and emotionally close to the Reagan administration and had demonstrated that it was upon the Anglo-Saxon and Atlantic connection rather than upon our allies and trading partners across the Channel that Britain could depend most firmly at a time of national crisis. The Westland saga, which was a searing experience for Mrs Thatcher herself and those who worked closely with her, had illustrated the gulf between the market solution of an American partner for the Westland company and Heseltine's interventionist pro-European stance.

There had been besides a number of irritating encounters with the European Parliament in relation to Northern Ireland – an issue regarded by the Thatcher administration as firmly domestic. In 1984 the European Parliament's Political Affairs Committee, under the direction of the Danish MP, Neil Haagerup, conducted an investigation into Northern Ireland, for the purpose of advising Britain on how to settle the conflict. The Report called for power sharing and an integrated economic plan for Ireland. Mrs Thatcher refused to co-operate and ignored the Report. In addition, there had been disagreements about the extent to which frontiers would be free from passport checks, which perhaps seemed at first sight not a significant matter. But its connotations for the control of terrorism and Northern Ireland were reinforced by the IRA bombing of the Conservative Conference at Brighton in 1986, by which time the disagreements were by no means without emotional significance. There had been, too, an increasing awareness in Whitehall and around the Cabinet table of the extent of jurisdiction that had been conceded to the European Court of Justice. Incidents, trivial in themselves, such as a ruling which imposed the need to provide hundreds of millions of pounds in grants for students from other European countries, had brought home the extent to which the European Court was becoming in practice what it had been for many years in theory – the supreme court of the UK. (This realization was confirmed explicitly when in 1989 and again in 1990, the European Court of Justice ruled that national courts can be obliged to freeze legislation until its compatibility with community law had been decided in Luxembourg.)[26] Everything from construction standards, textile production, and tests and standards for professions, to the control of financial services, company law, and taxation of corporations and securities had become a subject for the flood of Regulations or Directives pouring out from Brussels in pursuit of the completion of the single market.

Monsieur Jacques Delors became an important factor in the relations of Britain, and especially of Mrs Thatcher, with the Community by the middle of 1987. He had been President of the European Commission since 1985, but became more aggressive in 1987. In December 1987 *The Times* headline 'Thatcher-Delors Clash Looming' summed up the story of how Monsieur Delors had disdainfully dismissed Mrs Thatcher's demands for strict curbs on farm spending and declared that Britain could afford to contribute more to the EC budget. His speech on 6 July 1988, to the European Parliament in Strasbourg, stunned even some of the MEPs. They heard that thanks to the Single European Act, which had abolished the national veto and introduced majority voting, more decisions had been taken in the past six months than in the previous ten years. Within ten years, Delors promised, eighty per cent of economic legislation 'and possibly fiscal and social legislation as well' would be of European rather than national origin.[27]

The Challenge from Bruges

Mrs Thatcher herself and at least some Thatcherites were beginning to realize that the spirit of the Draft Treaty of Union was not in fact dead and that there was a serious possibility of the European Community becoming an interventionist federal state rather than a free trade area encompassing and dependent on nation states. From the moment when this realization was expressed, and federalism openly rejected by Mrs Thatcher at Bruges in September 1988, it was as if the film had moved into the fast forward mode. Event followed event with astonishing rapidity. In two years and two months, Mrs Thatcher found herself in deep and bitter dispute not merely with Delors but also with Mitterrand and Kohl, with Heath and Heseltine, and finally with her own Chancellor and her own Foreign Secretary.

The movement from the Bruges speech to the resignation did not, however, proceed in a simple straight line. It seemed at times that conflict would be avoided, either by Mrs Thatcher's winning, or giving in, or by the arrangement of a compromise. At any one moment, one could find support for and predictions of all the possible outcomes, and the opposing views often cited the same texts as evidence for their conclusions.

All through 1989 and 1990 the debates over Europe became more frequent and rancorous. Hot anti-federalist tempers were not cooled when Delors came to meet with the TUC and told them: 'You have totally failed to defeat the Prime Minister in this country, but you have an opportunity through Brussels and Strasbourg to bring in social legislation which would be helpful to your cause.'[28] Nor did Mrs Thatcher add a pacifying note when she said that Labour was 'seeking socialism by the back door' and more jocularly, 'by the back Delors'.[29]

In the *Daily Telegraph* and *Sunday Telegraph*, though broadly pro-Thatcher, strong dissenting voices also appeared. Ferdinand Mount took an optimistic view of European union. While he did not welcome the Social Charter and preferred that entry into the ERM be delayed, he thought it was a pity that Mrs Thatcher tended to see the Community as a 'threat rather than an opportunity'. EC membership had brought many good things and opinion in Britain was accordingly 'swinging round to the view that the Community is something that we can *use*', and away from 'fear of a European super-state'. What Mount picked out of the Bruges speech was Mrs Thatcher's declaration that 'our destiny is in Europe, as part of the Community,' and he deplored her instinct to 'kick hard against each and every manifestation of that destiny'. Her vision of 'a looser Europe in which the sovereignty of national government would remain pristine and virginal' was fantasy and 'it would be a sad irony' if chasing after that fantasy were to unhorse 'the greatest realist in modern politics'.[30]

But W. F. Deedes warned that 'Our future in Europe is in danger of being determined on the absurd basis of whether Mrs Thatcher is supportable or insupportable.' German liberals, he pointed out, were reminding Britain of the dangers of an overweening central power, which Britons had struggled against all through their history.[31] And in the *Sunday Telegraph*, Peregrine Worsthorne regularly denied that the British people wanted or ought to want a federal Europe: 'Whenever the British economy gets into trouble, the cry goes up: merge more with Europe as if that were a panacea. Joining the EEC failed as a panacea in the 1970s. Recovery waited upon Thatcherism, not Europeanism and to revert now to the God that failed at the expense of the God that at any rate nearly succeeded' would be high folly. Mrs Thatcher may have been 'appallingly undiplomatic in her language' but her policy towards Europe was 'sound, statesmanlike, and in keeping with public sentiment'.[32]

David Owen, former Labour minister and founding father of the Social Democrats, emerged as a firm supporter of Mrs Thatcher's views in the debate over the Delors plan for economic and monetary union. M. Jacques Delors must be told, Dr Owen said, 'that much of what he was proposing was arrant nonsense'. To force the European Community down the federalist route would not only damage the EC but possibly destroy it. 'An unnatural beast, it had never before been given such a massive federalist twist as by the Delors report.' If Britain gave up 'its right to fix its own level of direct taxation and its own borrowing requirement', it would be 'emasculated'. 'We have seen in the war cemeteries of Europe a massive demonstration of the folly of nationalism. But we also see in the stresses and strains, and potentially, even the break-up of the USSR, the danger of forcing independent nations into an artificial grouping.' It was right for the British Prime Minister to be in a minority of one. Moreover, West Germany had similar reservations but was happy to let Britain take the flak.[33]

Support for the Bruges stand also came in a variety of other contexts. Mrs Lynda Chalker, Minister for Overseas Development with a pro-European reputation, attacked the other members of the Community for pretending to be 'good Europeans' while they broke all the rules. While her partners went on paying enormous subsidies, Britain enthusiastically supported greater competition in air fares, road transport and telecommunications. 'It's time', Mrs Chalker said, that 'the foot-draggers in the Community followed suit and helped us build a consumer's Europe, not a producer's Europe.'[34] The same lesson was taught by the economist, Norman Macrae. Although the push to join the ERM had replaced the enthusiasm for CAP, he said, the French, Italians, and Spanish broke EC rules by maintaining exchange controls, imposing illicit protectionism such as their quota restrictions against imports of Japanese cars, and when Margaret Thatcher dared to tell them the truth about themselves they 'are liable to arraign her for . . . actions Latin politicians do every day'.[35]

In the House of Lords, Lord Harris of High Cross, chairman of the Bruges Group which was formed to support the thesis of the Bruges speech, carried on a steady but lonely campaign against federalist dreams. Would M. Delors, he asked, prefer to have his pension rights fixed 'in a newly invented EMU or . . . like the rest of us, prefer Deutschmarks?'[36] The Governor of the Bank of England, Robin Leigh-Pemberton, urged the Government to resist pressure to join the European exchange rate mechanism before the economy was in better balance. Premature entry would be bad not only for Britain but also for the Community as a whole. Against suggestions that European countries should follow collective monetary targets, the Governor argued that individual countries should be responsible for achieving internal price stability, using the monetary tools best suited to each one separately.[37]

But on the whole, it was the opposition to Mrs Thatcher's stand that was more frequently heard in the press and on television. Sir Leon Brittan, who had been exiled to Brussels to become one of Britain's European Commissioners, urged that Britain should join the ERM at once without waiting for inflation to fall, and implied that full economic union in some form was inevitable. Sir Leon's brother, the economist, Samuel Brittan, once part of the Thatcher entourage, accused Mrs Thatcher of opposing European Monetary Union only because she hated letting anything escape her control. What was really at issue was 'an elective dictatorship in which the views and prejudices of one person who holds the strings of political patronage and also approves the chief civil service appointments are dominant'. Like others of his persuasion, Brittan argued that sovereignty is a matter of degree and that there was nothing 'special about money which makes the possession of a national currency the hallmark of an independent nation'.[38]

Opponents of Mrs Thatcher frequently charged her with fighting to prevent an already accomplished fact. They took the line of the EC competition commissioner, Peter Sutherland, who described the Community as a federal structure in embryo and concluded that the only question was about when the baby would be born.[39] Others maintained that no one would notice the difference if Britain became part of a federal European state. One of the pillars of the left-of-centre establishment, David Marquand, explained, on the one hand, that federalism was a meaningless expression and, on the other hand, that it meant political union which was the only antidote to 'xenophobic and destructive nationalism' and to the reduction of Britain to the status of Nevada.[40] He accordingly warmly praised Jacques Delors and his dream of a united Europe.

The Liberal Democrats supported a federal Europe on another ground – that it would replace Britain's adversarial system of justice with the inquisitorial system, installed on the Continent by Napoleon. It was far preferable, they argued, to have an inquisitor appointed by a central authority, who would be concerned only to find the truth, and would accordingly prosecute, hand down the verdict and determine the sentence, than the ridiculous ritual of two counsels arguing for opposite sides of the case. Mistakes, such as the case of the Guildford Four, the Liberal Democrats were certain, could not occur in the inquisitorial system.

An Interval of Peace

But at the two meetings of the heads of state in the European Community, in Madrid in October 1989 and in Strasbourg in December, harmony reigned. At Madrid, Mrs Thatcher said that Britain would join the European Monetary System on certain conditions – that other countries should first abolish exchange controls, establish freedom of financial services, allow free movement of capital, and reduce subsidies to their industries. 'When you join any system,' she explained, 'you must all play by the same rules.' At present the rules were too 'higgledy-piggledy': 'I really can't have Britain worsted by other people having a different set of rules from the ones we have.'[41]

Not everyone, however, had the same idea of what had been agreed to in Madrid. Some said that Mrs Thatcher had accepted the 'progressive realisation of European Monetary Union', others, that the conditions she had laid down could not be realized until some distant time in the future, when ideas about monetary union might have changed out of recognition. Sir Geoffrey Howe put the emphasis where he preferred it in a speech that he sent directly to the newspapers instead of letting it be circulated by the Conservative Central Office. He praised Lawson as 'a chancellor of great courage' and stressed the importance of keeping the commitments that he, Mrs Thatcher, and Lawson had agreed to at the Madrid summit.[42]

At the Strasbourg meeting of the European Council the dominant note was again that of concord. Whether rightly or wrongly, it was taken to be a 'sign of the times' that at the Cabinet meeting before the Summit, the discussion was led by the Foreign Secretary, Douglas Hurd, who presented a paper. And Mrs Thatcher proposed that the Cabinet agree that the position to be taken in Strasbourg be in accordance with the Foreign Secretary's presentation.[43] At the meeting itself, Mrs Thatcher emphasized that she shared the long-term aims of the other heads of state and praised Britain's record in implementing the Single European Act. President Mitterrand went out of his way to allow her to register her disagreements in a low key. The Political Editor of *The Times*, Robin Oakley, believed that the Prime Minister had taken account of a stronger pro-European sentiment at home, and that her new Foreign Secretary, Douglas Hurd, irritated her much less than had his predecessor, Sir Geoffrey Howe: 'What Strasbourg appeared to signify was that it has become an argument not so much about direction as about pace.'[44] Others, too, concluded that 'the unhappy chapter' begun with Mrs Thatcher's Bruges speech was now closed.[45]

Mrs Thatcher also held out an olive branch to the Euro-MPs, whom she had been accused of ignoring, by inviting them to meet with her early in 1990. They, for their part, tried to play down their differences with Mrs Thatcher over monetary and political union, in order to persuade Mrs Thatcher to repudiate Norman Tebbit's charge that they were disposed to go native and desert Conservatism. But although few would confess to being federalists, a number wanted to establish a unitary central authority in Europe.

Nevertheless, by the end of 1989, not only the pro-European and anti-Thatcher *Independent* but also *The Times* were insisting on the dangers of Britain's 'isolation' in Europe, the desirability of playing down the rhetoric about loss of sovereignty, and the need for a 'positive' attitude. Even the *Daily Telegraph* was saying that the Government could not afford to be seen as either split or 'marginalised', and the two might go together. The two-speed Europe, with Britain in the slow lane, which Mrs Thatcher would undoubtedly prefer, would be difficult to present as anything but 'humiliating', and would undermine 'her claim to have led Britain back to the centre of events'. In short, the European issue had taken its place alongside the Corn Laws, Ireland and India as a threat to the unity of the Conservative Party.

But from a distance the chief impression was of immense confusion. The left-of-centre establishment who took up the crusade for European federalism never managed to state their views in plain

English. Michael Heseltine who seemed to be working very hard to promote European federalism denied that he was a federalist. The British people told opinion pollsters that they disapproved of Mrs Thatcher's attitude towards Europe, but when they were told the nature of Mrs Thatcher's doubts, sixty-eight per cent agreed with her. In many circles, certainly, the sudden enthusiasm for European federalism was a way of abusing Mrs Thatcher and declaring that she was 'out of touch with reality'. Sometimes, in odd corners, support for her emerged: Ian Aitken, the staunchly socialist commentator on the *Guardian*, kept saying that on this issue the Prime Minister was probably right.[46]

The Third German War

Only one thing was clear, that the peace which had reigned briefly at Madrid and Strasbourg would not last through 1990. The reunification of Germany provided an effective irritant. When it was first proposed, the headlines were occupied with what Ferdinand Mount described as 'the third German war'. The prospect of a united Germany was taken up by the pro-federalists as a decisive argument in their favour because a Germany with eighty million people was sure to be a menace unless constrained by being made part of a European state. The anti-federalists were equally certain that a European state including the new Germany would necessarily be dominated by Germany and reduce all the rest to vassals.

It was reported that Mrs Thatcher had taken to 'denouncing the West German Chancellor' to all her visitors, regardless of whether they had come to talk to her about South Africa or power dressing for women. 'The tabloids were fully armed with epithets to hurl at the Boche. Dr Conor Cruise O'Brien was firing massive anti-German shells across the top of *The Times* oped page, striking terror into timorous souls sheltering in the correspondence columns.'[47] And the City Editor of the *Daily Mail* wondered how many more wars were needed before people realized that Germany would remain a menace, whatever its form of government.

The excitement about a united Germany persuaded some that

Britain ought to be proposing a more definite constitutional structure for the Community. Mrs Thatcher was said to have been impressed by the suggestions of Dr Frank Vibert, in a series of IEA papers, that national parliaments should be explicitly recognized as the ultimate authority in new European treaties, that the Commission should be restricted to an executive role, and the European Court – which Mrs Thatcher repeatedly dismissed as 'not a proper court at all' – should act as an impartial referee rather than as an active promoter of European union.

The German war ended quickly once Dr Kohl confirmed explicitly that he had no intention of questioning the Oder-Neisse border with Poland. Skirmishes continued, however, and open hostilities were again provoked by an interview with Nicholas Ridley, in the *Spectator* on 14 July 1990. Ridley made plain not only his opposition to European federalism but also his distrust of Germany. He ended with remarks which were taken to be immoderately hostile, even by some members of the Bruges Group. In fact, the impression was created not so much by Mr Ridley's words – which were widely misquoted – as by the conjunction of his reference to Hitler with the cover cartoon by Garland showing Herr Kohl wearing a Hitlerian moustache. The heavens opened up; everyone was outraged; Mr Ridley resigned, leaving Mrs Thatcher without any powerful senior supporter in the Cabinet.

One of the less noticeable but nevertheless very important issues in the debate on Europe was how Britain's membership in the Community or a federal state would affect the 'special relationship' with the US. In April (1990) Mr Gorbachev gave Mrs Thatcher an opportunity to show that the Anglo-American partnership was still flourishing. She was in Bermuda, conferring with Mr Bush, and about to leave when news came that Gorbachev was threatening break-away Lithuania with economic sanctions. Mrs Thatcher had been presenting Bush with her vision of a European Community as a free-trading, non-protectionist alliance of outward-looking European countries, and declaring her conviction that what mattered even more was what she called the Atlantic Community. When Bush and Thatcher decided to respond at once to Mr Gorbachev's move, and stood side by side before the already wait-

ing media, the whole world was informed that the special relationship was alive and well.[48]

U-Turn?

But the leading issue, especially after Chancellor Lawson's resignation, was about whether Britain should join the European
Exchange Rate Mechanism and ultimately the European Monetary
Union. The latter issue was temporarily defused when the new
Chancellor, John Major, proposed the 'hard écu'. It was presented
as a compromise between monetary union and complete rejection
of it. The 'hard écu' was to be a parallel Euro-currency which
would be controlled by a new European Monetary Fund, to ensure
that the écu would not be inflationary. If the écu became common
currency, Mr Major argued, then there might be gradual advance
to a unitary currency. The suggestion was generally regarded as
'an exercise in Europolitics and none the worse for that'. Mr
Major's speech, *The Times* said, 'was thus a classic case of jaw-jaw
being better than war-war. He hopes to keep Brussels talking at
least through the next British election and through the next
German one as well . . . Mr Major is to be congratulated on a very
modest coup.'[49] The pundits declared that Mrs Thatcher had done
a U-turn on Europe when she seemed to accept John Major's
proposal for the 'hard écu' in June of 1990.

The Chancellor's gloss on his proposal was not quite the same
as the Prime Minister's. Major said, 'In the very long term, if
peoples and governments so choose it, [the Ecu] could develop
into a single currency.' On the following day, Mrs Thatcher said
that the scheme would allow nations who wished to replace their
own currencies with the écu could do so, but she doubted that any
would. It was subsequently 'revealed', however, that Sir Charles
Powell, Mrs Thatcher's trusted private secretary, had persuaded
her to accept an institution to be called the European Monetary
Fund and that some of the words in John Major's speech had
been dictated by the Prime Minister herself over a telephone from
Cornwall. At the European summit in Dublin, on 25 June 1990

she confirmed her support, saying that although conditions were not now ripe for a single currency, in fifteen or twenty years, who could know what might happen. Peter Jenkins concluded: 'It will not be the first time that Mrs Thatcher has clambered down from the last ditch at the last moment. That has been the consistent style of her European diplomacy: throwing nationalist scenes, digging in her Gaullist heels, interposing her body – but always succumbing in the end, giving in, and claiming victory.'[50]

By July it became evident that Mrs Thatcher had also agreed to accept British entry into the Exchange Rate Mechanism. It was well known that Lawson and Howe had both favoured it long before and been resisted by Mrs Thatcher. Now, when both Hurd and Major urged joining the ERM, it was said, she had to surrender because she could not afford to sack or lose either of them.

When, after joining the Exchange Rate Mechanism, Britain continued to suffer rising inflation, as opponents had predicted, Lawson and his supporters argued that it would not have happened if Mrs Thatcher had allowed Britain to join earlier. And Sir Geoffrey Howe continued his campaign for full monetary union. He wrote to *The Times* denying Tim Congdon's charge that Howe and Heseltine did not really know what European Monetary Union meant: 'Successive governments of the UK, Labour and Conservative alike,' Sir Geoffrey said, 'have committed themselves on many occasions since 1973, to a common objective: "progressive realisation of economic and monetary union."' He regretted having to take issue with Congdon whom he admired, but 'When he touches on matters European', his judgement became clouded by 'an instinctive fear of some "Euro-political establishment" '.[51]

As interest rates were raised while inflation stubbornly maintained its hold, the head of the Bank of England became more impatient to use a stronger pound as the treatment instead of the interest-rate prescription under which the patient seemed to be growing ever weaker. He pointed out that two successive Chancellors had argued for a European Monetary System with exchange rates fixed by adjustable parities, and that Britain had reserved its sovereign right to change the pound's parity, when necessary, by agreement with her partners. But now parities had stayed put for three years and re-alignments were deemed beyond the pale – 'the very last resort, something to be avoided beyond everything else'. Christopher Fildes, the economic commentator in the *Daily Telegraph* and the *Spectator*, remarked that the whole ERM drama was a remake of 'Tales from the Bretton Woods, when the fixed but adjustable parities lost the knack of adjustment,' and he advised that one should come prepared with plenty of popcorn and Kleenex, because it promised to be 'a weepie'.[52]

Alan Walters, economic adviser to Mrs Thatcher, architect of the early success against inflation, who became notorious by being blamed as the cause of Lawson's resignation, continued to dismiss the Exchange Rate Mechanism as 'half-baked'. He warned that far from bringing the stability promised, it would do the opposite, while leaving Britain with its hands tied and unable to take appropriate action. Much less publicity was given to the alternative to the hard écu that he favoured. While he doubted that 'there can be any agreement on a Eurofed with a single managed currency for Europe which satisfies the German need for Bundesbank hegemony and the requirement of the other eleven for some effective control of the Eurocurrency, there was a way out – a new currency which, unlike the hard écu, was in no way related to existing currencies. A unit of that currency, an 'ecom' would always buy the same defined basket of commodities, just as under the old gold standard, a pound or dollar was convertible into a quantity of gold. Such a currency would not require a Eurofed or central bank to determine monetary policy; through arbitrage by the private sector, the quantity of 'ecoms' would automatically adjust to satisfy the wishes of people at the constant price of the commodity basket.'

Establishing the 'ecom' would 'entail some surrender of monetary sovereignty, but it would not involve transferring sovereignty to ... the clever operators on a Community committee'. The scheme would resemble a 'resuscitation of the gold standard but without gold's well-known disadvantages'.[53]

The Gulf Effect

In September of 1990 the 'train' to European unification encountered a wholly unforeseen obstacle. Saddam Hussein's invasion of Kuwait had the bizarre side-effect of severely dampening Euro-enthusiasm. Even before Saddam Hussein's invasion of Kuwait, the chaos produced in Germany by political reunification had begun to encourage doubts about further extending monetary union. When the breach with Iraq threatened the loss of business, recession, higher inflation and a distortion of trade, finance ministers began to insist on going more slowly. When they refused to endorse an early start to Stage Two, which M. Delors' timetable required, he scolded them for using the crisis for selfish ends and setting up a 'common front' against Europe, and accused the Spanish finance minister, whose support for John Major's compromise had tipped the scales, of playing to the gallery.[54]

In Britain, the response to the Gulf conflict by her European partners did not make them look like ideal mates in a trench. Whereas the United States, partly perhaps thanks to Mrs Thatcher's influence with President Bush, nonetheless took and maintained a firm stand, the European countries tried to wheedle their way out of making any response, and in the end contributed feebly and in relatively painless ways. The reluctance of Italy and most other Mediterranean countries to back any policy with force contrasted sharply with Mrs Thatcher's affirmation of Britain's close links with Washington and her denunciation of other Community members for pusillanimity: 'Hopes for a new world role for a united Europe have run into the Arabian sands,' concluded *The Times*: 'Bickering has opened up old divisions, a cacophony of discordant policy has prevented concerted action, and the vibrant new Community that so impressed Washington with its purpose has been revealed as a mere fairweather friend.'[55]

Even the federalists acknowledged a set-back. Jacques Delors felt compelled to tell the European Parliament, 'This time the United States did our work for us. We were lucky. But we may not always be so lucky.' The leader of the British Conservative MEPS was applauded when he told them, 'Not for the first time

Europe owes the United States an immense debt.'[56]

Everyone agreed that the confrontation with Saddam had destroyed the image of a forceful and coherent unity in Europe. Of course different camps drew different conclusions. Sir Leon Brittan argued that it showed that the EC must now move rapidly toward full military co-operation. But even Sir Geoffrey Howe admitted that it was too early to expect a greater security role for Brussels.

The Last Act

The last act of the European drama in which Mrs Thatcher played the starring role took place in Rome, towards the end of October 1990. According to the agenda for the summit, some solution to the problems raised by the common agricultural policy (CAP) was to be the chief subject. The US was threatening a trade war if Europeans did not mend their ways. But instead, led by Signor Andreotti, the other members wanted to agree on a deadline for economic union. Mrs Thatcher argued that it was 'putting the cart before the horse' to set a deadline for something whose nature was not yet known. She criticized the French for blocking a crucial agreement on cutting farm support in Europe which was jeopardizing a world trade deal and described the Community as 'living in cloud cuckoo land'. And when she returned to report on what had happened in Rome, she uttered those fatal three Nos.

The response of Tory backbenchers was mixed. Euro-enthusiasts were dismayed by Mrs Thatcher's strong words. The chairman of the European movement, the Tory MP, Hugh Dykes, 'feared Mrs Thatcher was leaving Britain out in the cold'. But Norman Tebbit believed that she had the support not only of many Conservatives but also of many in the Labour Party. Teddy Taylor, the robust Tory MP for Southend East, said, 'This ridiculous EC summit shows that while the European leaders can write the constitution for the year 2000 they were wholly unable to find any solution to the urgent crisis of the common agricultural policy.' These sentiments were supported by Dr David Owen who said that the eleven other EC countries were 'showing every indication' of wanting to force 'the issue of a United States of Europe on Britain'.[57]

From outside Parliament came many voices hostile to the Prime Minister's stand. Only *The Times* said that the summit 'was a disgrace' – 'Nothing might have done more for federalism in Rome than for M Delors and his colleagues to have picked up Mrs Thatcher's farm price gauntlet and thrashed out a deal that very night. They funked it. They opted for a vague easy-going future, rather than the nasty, difficult present.'[58] But elsewhere she was accused of making Britain 'Europe's permanent outsider . . . relegated to the guard's van'; of being 'the old crone in the corner who can see only the past'; of playing a role that had become dated – 'dressing up as Britannia, ready to repel with her trident any continentals who would tamper with our coinage'.[59]

In a matter of days, the resignation and resignation speech of Sir Geoffrey Howe, the leadership challenge from Michael Heseltine and the desertion by the backbenchers led to Mrs Thatcher's departure from Downing Street. With fitting irony, she was pictured on television screens during the closing days not at No 10 but at a meeting with her European counterparts in Paris.

Conservatives and Thatcherism

The story is one of high drama, in personal and national terms. What does it tell us about Thatcherism as a phenomenon? One might argue that the tale, whilst significant as an indication of Mrs Thatcher's character, tells one little about Thatcherism itself since it was the Prime Minister rather than the Cabinet or the Party as a whole that led the charge and became unseated. But that argument ignores the extent to which the true die-hard Thatcherites – the grandees, Joseph, Ridley, Parkinson; the younger generation of prominent ministers, Lilley, Portillo and Redwood; and the backbenchers of the No Turning Back Group – supported and agreed with Mrs Thatcher. It would be easy to underestimate also the mood amongst the Thatcherite activists, the overwhelming applause at the 1990 and 1991 Conservative Party conferences for any speaker who unequivocally rejected a federal Europe and the at best half-hearted acceptance at the 1990 conference of Britain's entry into the ERM. The saga of Europe, in other words, reveals more than Mrs Thatcher's personal views. It tells us something important about the nature of Thatcherism. But what?

The key is the speech at Bruges, one of the two or three great set pieces of Thatcherism. The themes of this speech, like its crisp and concise prose, are clear and distinct. From the start, it enunciates a firm belief in the continuing values of the independent nation state: 'My first guiding principle is this: willing and active co-operation between independent sovereign states . . . Europe will be stronger precisely because it has France as France, Spain as Spain, Britain as Britain, each with its own customs, traditions and identity. It would be folly to try to fit them into some sort of identikit European personality.'

Nor is this preference for the independent nation state merely paraded as an abstract ideal. On the contrary, it is applied directly and repeatedly to the specific case of Britain. The separate political culture of Britain is announced, and announced with pride: 'We in Britain are rightly proud of the way in which, since Magna Carta in 1215, we have pioneered and developed representative institutions to stand as bastions of freedom. And proud too of the way in which Britain is a home for people from the rest of Europe who sought sanctuary from tyranny.'

There is, moreover, a clear – and, as it must have seemed to some of the listeners in the hall at Bruges, a strident – claim that Britain's separate and independent political culture has been the one guarantee of political freedoms across Europe: 'We British have in a special way contributed to Europe. Over the centuries we have fought to prevent Europe from falling under the dominance of a single power. We have fought and we have died for her freedom. It was British support to resistance movements throughout the last War that helped to keep alive the flame of liberty in so many countries until the late day of liberation. It was from our island fortress that the liberation of Europe itself was mounted. And still today we stand together. Nearly 70,000 British servicemen are stationed on the mainland of Europe.'

Beyond this, there is a distinct affirmation at several points in the speech of the close connection between Anglo-Saxon Britain and the United States of America, and an equally distinct suggestion that it is this Anglo-Saxon dimension which constitutes the main bulwark of present freedom: 'Nor should we forget that European values have helped to make the United States of America into the valiant defender of freedom which she has become . . . People went there to get away from the intolerance and constraints of life in Europe. They sought liberty and opportunity; and their strong sense of purpose has, over two centuries, helped create a new unity and pride in being American . . . let us have a Europe which plays its full part in the wider world, which looks outward not inward and which preserves that Atlantic Community – that Europe on both sides of the Atlantic – which is our noblest inheritance and our greatest strength.'

The speech does not, however, rest with the assertion that Britain, with its separate Anglo-Saxon political culture and its Anglo-Saxon former colony constitutes the surest defence of Europe against tyranny in time of war. It also claims for Britain a leading, indeed the leading, role in promoting economic freedom: 'The Treaty of Rome itself was intended as a Charter for Economic Liberty. But that is not how it has always been read, still less applied . . . The lesson of the economic history of Europe in the 1970s and 1980s is that central planning and detailed control don't work, and that personal endeavour and initiative do . . . by getting rid of barriers . . . we can best compete. And that means action to free markets, action to widen choice, action to reduce government intervention . . . Britain has been in the lead in opening its markets to others . . . the City of London . . . our market for telecommunications . . . air transport . . . our coastal shipping trade . . . free movement of capital . . . a genuinely free market in financial services . . . I wish I could say the same of many other Community members.'

Finally there are two vivid attacks directed against European federalists. First there is an explicit objection to federalism as such: 'to try to suppress nationhood and concentrate power at the centre of the European conglomerate would be highly damaging ... let Europe be a family of nations, understanding each other better, appreciating each other more, doing more together but relishing our national identity no less than our common European endeavour.'

And second, there is the now famous attack on an interventionist federal state: 'working more closely together does not require power to be centralized in Brussels or decisions to be taken by the appointed bureaucracy ... Our aim should not be more and more detailed relations with the centre, it should be to deregulate and to remove the constraints on trade ... It would be a betrayal if ... the Community were to erect greater external protection. We must ensure that our approach to world trade is consistent with the liberalisation we preach at home ... We have not successfully rolled back the frontiers of the state in Britain, only to see them reimposed at a European level, with a European super-state exercising a new dominance from Brussels.'

Here, then, is the classic exposition of Thatcherite views on Europe, an exposition in which Britain is portrayed as an independent nation with a separate political culture, as a bulwark for her defence of freedom, linking Europe to that great defender of freedom, the United States, and providing for Europe an example of a liberal economy; an exposition which ends with a forceful attack on federalism and federal interventionism. What does this speech tell us about the nature of Thatcherism?

It tells us first, as it has been argued here throughout, that Thatcherism is to be understood not as an abstract theory but as a practical political doctrine applying to a particular time and place. The contrast with 'political theories' is clear: Thatcherism, as embodied in the Bruges speech, can hardly be said to provide an analysis or an argument let alone one that might be valid for different times and places. It provides instead an assertion about what is right for Britain now. The faint attempt to argue that independent nationhood is 'the best way to build a successful European community' or is 'the source of Europe's vitality throughout the centuries' is scarcely even meant to carry conviction. The force of the speech resides not in the shadow of an argument but in the repeated emphasis on British desires and interests: 'my country', 'we British', 'our nation', 'we in Britain are rightly proud'. In this speech, ostensibly on Europe, the words 'Britain' or 'British' are used no less than seventeen times in nine pages.

If proof were needed that Thatcherism is concerned with the practical politics of Britain, this speech is such proof. Certainly, one might imagine an analogue of Thatcherism in some other country – but to be such an analogue, the ism in question would need to rest on and assert its own sense of nationhood. Except in this analogous sense, it would be absurd to speak of Thatcherism in another country. Unlike Marxism or Libertarianism, or any of the other great isms, Thatcherism is non-exportable.

Nor is this merely a matter of geographical location. For Thatcherism, as represented in the Bruges speech, Britain is not just an island, but one with a distinctive and precious history: 'Visit the great churches and cathedrals of Britain, read our literature and listen to our language . . . From classical medieval thought we have borrowed that concept of the rule of law which marks our civilized society from barbarism. And on that idea of Christendom, with its recognition of the unique and spiritual nature of the individual, we still base our belief in personal liberty and other human rights . . . This is no arid chronicle of obscure facts from the dust-filled libraries of history. It is the record of nearly two thousand years of British involvement in Europe.'

Indeed, to the extent that there is an argument at all, it is the historical argument that 'our destiny is in Europe' because of 'the cultural riches which we have drawn from Europe' and the fact that without the European legacy and political ideas we could not have achieved as much as we did. 'We British are as much heirs to the legacy of European culture as any other nation. Our links to the rest of Europe, the continent of Europe, have been a fundamental influence on our history.' Nor is this simply a matter of the speech itself. The entire record of the Thatcherite response to Europe can be understood only when one recognizes the dominance of the desire to retain the existence of a nation whose history, whilst inextricably linking it with Europe, has at the same time created a separate political tradition and national identity. Whether this desire is right or wrong is besides the point. The mere fact of its existence shows that, whatever its tenets may be, Thatcherism is not an abstract or general economic or social theory but a view about what Britain in the twentieth century has become and ought to be.

The speech itself and the series of events of which it forms the core also demonstrate the extent to which, in Thatcherism, substantive and structural aims are fused together. The welling feeling of resentment, which built up in the years leading to 1988, were so powerfully expressed in the Bruges speech and then became the basis of Mrs Thatcher's downfall, were not simply associated with the fate of Britain as an independent nation but also with the character in a sense of the federal government which Mrs Thatcher believed was being promoted. The fear is as much of Delors, Heath and Heseltine – interventionists to the man – as it is of the federal constitution and of its implications for the independence of Britain. Hence the attacks on regulation from the centre, the powerful references to rolling back the frontiers of the state, the emphasis not merely on Britain's separate political culture but upon the enshrining of civic and economic freedom in Britain and in its Anglo-Saxon partner, the United States.

If, reading the Bruges speech and contemplating the record of events, one were to ask whether the principal objection is structural (a dislike of being reduced to a mere part of a superior whole, a wish to retain Britain as a nation state as a matter of history and national identity) or substantive (an objection to interventionism and centralized regulation, and a sense that Nato rather than the EC constitutes the bulwark of defence), one could not answer sensibly.

In the speech, as in practice, Thatcherism has placed equal emphasis on the structural independence of Britain and on the substantive freedom of Britain from centralized regulation. As a practical political view, rooted in time and place, Thatcherism does not have a conceptual apparatus with which to distinguish between structure and substance. The substance – the threat of an interventionist government in Brussels – draws attention to the perceived deficiencies in the structure of a huge pan-European federal state. And there is simply no knowing what view Thatcherites would have taken about the structure if this substantive threat were absent.

The Bruges speech and the events which surround it show Thatcherism to be, in the deepest possible sense, Conservative as opposed to Liberal. Whether the Conservatism of Thatcherism is seen as something to be praised or blamed, the fact of its being Conservative is undeniably disclosed in its attitude towards Europe. The Thatcherite stance on Europe is a set of practical political preferences, not separating substance from form, rooted in history, British by essence not accident, and based upon the belief that Britain should be a well-defended island power with affiliation to its Anglo-Saxon brethren and secure against any danger that the vitality of its people would be compromised by managerial government. Europe is the mirror in which Thatcherism came most clearly to see itself as a Conservative doctrine – and, by a curious irony, it was that picture in that mirror which did not suit the Conservative party.

III

Anglo-Saxon Attitudes

11

The Response to Thatcherism

The Change in How People Think

More important than the immediate practical effects of Thatcherism (and certainly more telling as evidence of its nature) has been its effect upon how people think. The proof that Thatcherism has indeed been an 'ism' rather than merely a motley collection of political actions lies above all in the fact that it has fundamentally changed political attitudes in Britain. It has changed the conception of what is true, what is possible and what is desirable.

In 1979, socialism, in the sense of the dependency of the individual upon the state in a series of vital areas including industry, education, health and housing, was regarded by Britons as 'here to stay'. The possibility that the 'great advances' of the 1940s and 1950s could actually be reversed was hardly entertained. Nationalized industries; the spread of mass-produced, concrete blocks of public housing estates; the disappearance of terraced houses and private gardens; industrial growth resting on government decisions about where to invest how much public money; the multiplication of state schools and the attrition of independent schools; ever-increasing state subventions to the arts; the public ownership and centralized management of all utilities; the death of many small independent enterprises due to the inevitably superior efficiency of large, centralized, bureaucratized organizations; the opening of family homes to inspection by more and more officials – all this was taken for granted.

Most important is the reason why it was taken for granted. It was seen not as a matter of choice but as a necessity imposed by irresistible 'forces' which well-informed people were bound to recognize and accept. Not only Communists and dogmatic socialists saw the developments in Eastern Europe as the wave of the future. Though more keen on seeking modifications and qualifications and more often pinched by guilt, Conservatives, too, were persuaded that things were bound to go in that direction. When Mrs Thatcher proclaimed the need to drive back the tide of socialism, to let freedom of choice and the vigorous virtues flourish, in short to change the course of British history, few if any of the commentators believed that she could do it. A senior tutor at Jesus College, Cambridge, who lectured on industrial relations, reported that 'When Margaret Thatcher declared she would curb the power of the union bosses, we academics scoffed. Others had promised as much, and the unions had outfought and outlived them. No matter what laws she made, the workers would disobey them, for they would be seen as illegitimate: steps against secondary picketing or the closed shop would be perceived as class-based legislation and would therefore collapse. If Churchill, at the height of his powers and popularity could not curb the miners in 1942 – he was even forced to supply petrol coupons to bring colliery brass bands down to march in support of a Kent pit dispute – how could she?'[1]

The talk for the first year and more was all of 'U-turns' because Mrs Thatcher was expected to follow the way of Heath, to encounter obstacles that would prove to be immovable, to capitulate, and eventually to end by implementing yet more 'middle way' policies. The fact that things did not turn out this way, that even after Mrs Thatcher's own departure the trend towards private activity in place of public has continued almost unabated, has confounded the early sceptics and changed ideas about what is feasible. Notably, former Heathites such as Mr Hurd, when questioned in the last days of Mrs Thatcher's own administration, made it clear that she had persuaded them that it was possible to reverse the tide and to choose which way to go.

Although no one in the Government entertained any such expectations, the most profound effect of the Thatcherite privatizations was on a metaphysical assumption. By demonstrating so concretely that nothing in human arrangements is inevitable, that what seems irreversible today may be reversed tomorrow, the success of privatization destroyed the foundation of the liberal consensus. It suggested that everything which had been taken for granted – and not only by avowed 'liberals' – might be questioned and rejected. Very few Britons ever read Karl Marx, but almost everyone had picked up somehow the central message of Marxism – that history is moving in a given direction and that human beings are moulded by irresistible 'forces' to which they are obliged to accommodate, and that any other response is futile. But when privatizations spread to Malaysia, Jamaica, a dozen African states including Nigeria, as well as New Zealand, Japan, Canada, Spain and France, frequently under the supervision of former Downing Street advisers, when Eastern Europe turned out to be nothing but a badly tattered house of cards and the successful rebels hailed Mrs Thatcher as their patron saint, the world that had been assumed to be forever, by Conservatives as well as Communists and Socialists, crumbled to dust, and with it the view of history that had underpinned it.

In less profound ways, too, Thatcherism changed the attitudes of Britons to how things might be. In industry, a different way of thinking became at the very least more prominent. The effect of nationalization had been that managers and employees in the nationalized industries began to think of themselves as bureaucrats with a natural role in government, while politicians and bureaucrats saw themselves as managers with a natural role in industry. The idea that industrial managers and employees should take a pride in the craftsmanship that leads to top quality goods and services at low prices was replaced by the view that managers and union leaders should spend their time (often together, sometimes apart) persuading, cajoling and bullying the state into policies more favourable to their industries and wage packets. The idea that politicians and bureaucrats should take pride in defending the public interest as a whole against special interest groups was replaced by the notion that they should spend their time 'getting on' with executives and union leaders in the nationalized industries, understanding their 'problems', dealing with their concerns, defending their record and bringing them to a 'consensus'.

Reversing the trend towards nationalization brought about a major shift away from such attitudes. The paralysing awe of trade unions vanished. In 1989, the Master of Fitzwilliam College in

Cambridge found that his students were wholly baffled by his questions about the influence of trade unions on British life. Then he remembered: 'They're all too young to recall those pictures of the TUC trooping in to see Harold Wilson.'[2] Satisfying the consumer was again seen as a field of activity in which providers work to satisfy customers, each as an independent agent, and the state was expected to act as the guarantor of the conditions that made it possible to work harmoniously and efficiently. Instead of being absorbed in trying to stop strikes, managers began to spend more of their time trying to make a profit and succeeding. And the fact that privatization had made shareholding a mass activity and produced substantial employee holdings in almost every privatized industry gave this return to what had once been just common sense a new gloss.

This changed attitude to industry was accompanied by what Ferdinand Mount called 'the decline of acceptable idleness'. On Mrs Thatcher's tenth anniversary, he selected the rejection of idleness as the greatest difference 'to the way we live' made by the decade. It affected all classes. 'I dread to think,' Mount said, 'what modern opinion would have made of the months Stanley Baldwin used to spend in Aix-les-Bains. And what a contrast with a day in the life of the Windsors in Paris? The City lunch that lasted until 4pm had become a thing of the past.' Although holiday entitlements had steadily lengthened for all classes and the official working week had diminished, 'the average number of hours actually worked had increased during the Thatcher years. Men now worked longer in Britain than almost anywhere in the European Community. And this meant, as so many more women are employed here, that a higher proportion of the adult population was at work in Britain than in any other EEC country except Denmark.' Longer hours do not necessarily produce greater efficiency, but they do indicate a change in attitude toward 'acceptable idleness'.

The most remarkable decline was in middle-class idleness: 'Whatever became of all those naval and military officers and city merchants (often in a quite modest way of business) who used to retire in their early forties to the country or the seaside and who feature so vividly in the pages of 19th century novelists . . . Nowadays they would be embarking on second careers as fund-raisers, personnel managers, school bursars, and Hon Secs of every organization known to man. These days the correct answer to "How are you getting on down in Sidmouth or Budleigh Salterton" is "keeping busy"!'

The same transformation was noticeable in the working class: 'you now hear far fewer of those jokes about the plumber's mate and the workman leaning on his shovel that used to infest the pages of *Punch*.' Only the young, Mount thought, still clung to the delights of idleness. And he attributed to this renunciation of idleness the fact that Britain had become so attractive to investment by the Japanese and others who 'can expect to find an eager workforce, unrecognizable from 10 years ago'. In short, British national character – 'that mysterious entity' – seems to have been transformed.[3]

Not everyone might agree that British habits had been quite so thoroughly altered. But no one can reasonably deny that something of the sort has occurred. Otherwise there could not have been the effects which are evident in the statistics about the improvements in Britain's productivity.

A similar if less exciting effect was produced by the novelty of the Thatcherite responses to problems like unemployment. The dark side of the Thatcherite drive for efficiency and the phenomenal rise in productivity was the sharp rise in unemployment. As 'lame duck' companies ceased to be subsidized and competition became the order of the day, managers were moved to tackle the overmanning and restrictive practices that had given rise to the British disease. The outcome was a wholesale shedding of labour. As unemployment figures rose, pundits like the Tory columnist, Peregrine Worsthorne, prophesied that rioting in the streets would bring down Thatcher.

But, despite the riots in 1982, the public remained surprisingly apathetic. Indeed by the end of the Thatcher era newspapers had come to dismiss the idea, which had earlier been a self-evident truth, that a rise in 'unemployment' was a sure cause of failure at the polls. One reason why the predicted crisis never materialized (apart from the provision of unemployment compensation and other

welfare arrangements and the often temporary nature of unemployment for any one person) was the novel response of the Thatcher
Government. While the media were promising disaster, the
Government was emphasizing making it easier for people to move
from areas of high unemployment to those where jobs were waiting
by removing rent controls and selling council houses and flats.
Norman Tebbit's notorious advice to the unemployed to 'get on
your bike' offended the *bien pensants* more than the bike riders.
There was a new emphasis, too, on training schemes, on incentives
for workers to take lower-paid jobs when others were not available,
on part-time work. The Labour Party began attacking the Conservatives not with unemployment figures but with demands for
more investment in training. Many of these ideas had once been
taken for granted in Britain but had been forgotten as the welfare
state had come to dominate public thinking. The Thatcherite
response to unemployment suggested – to many for the first time
– that they were not so dependent on the state and its welfare
agencies as they had supposed. The classic radio soap opera, *The
Archers*, began running episodes in which an unmarried mother is
saved from the social workers' zeal to reduce her to dependency
by neighbours who teach her how to look after her baby and to
earn a living. If the kind of mobility that Norman Tebbit envisioned
did not quite arrive, still getting on your bike became something
one might consider.

At the Conservative Party Conference of 1984, Mrs Thatcher's
message stressed still other aspects of the Government's drive to
restore the vigorous virtues. The remedy for unemployment, she
said, was, on the one hand, the 'spirit of enterprise' for that alone
would provide new jobs, and, on the other hand, cutting taxes,
bringing down inflation, removing the regulations and other
obstacles to the growth of small businesses 'for that is where
many of the new jobs will come from'.[+] What mattered for future
prosperity, she said, was the fact that over the past year (1983–4)
more than a quarter of a million new jobs had been created.

What was novel in Mrs Thatcher's response was not her optimism – democratic politicians are professional optimists – but her
emphasis on recognizing that in the human world nothing is fixed

forever, that there are always new, as yet undreamt-of possibilities, that what seems impossible today might become commonplace tomorrow. The Thatcherite view also taught that your gain is not necessarily my loss – that both parties to a commercial transaction might win. It was the very opposite of what had been the prevailing view, and not just among socialists – that every voluntary transaction is necessarily a 'zero-sum game' in which, if anyone gains, the other must be a loser. All that was repudiated by the Thatcherite outlook. It rested on a very different axiom, that the increase in new businesses benefited everyone – entrepreneurs, workers, employed as well as unemployed, consumers, the country as a whole.

As these Thatcherite responses became increasingly familiar, Britons began to think less in terms of unchangeable security and more in terms of the potentialities of taking a risk; they became readier to recognize the blessings of uncertainty. They may not have acquired the vigorous virtues but they had at least become familiar with a more vigorous attitude to the vicissitudes of a human existence. Of course there were those who painted Britain as a land where the streets were filled with the poor freezing in cardboard boxes. And though such people were to be seen in the streets of London and on television (sometimes alongside their would-be benefactors like Lady Howe) and no one could deny that their condition was lamentable, it had become thinkable that people sleeping in cardboard boxes might be at least in part responsible for their plight, that they had perhaps failed or even refused to look for other possibilities.

Nor has it been merely a question of indicating possibilities. For with the recognition that things done by the state did not *need* to be done by the state, the obvious correctness of the solutions posed by socialism began to fade. The 'paradigm shift', while still by no means universally or even generally accepted, has nevertheless become part of the common currency of British politics and political comment. One does not any longer expect as a matter of course to hear the interviewer ask what government is going to 'do about' a given problem. One does not any longer reel with shock when one hears somebody saying that some problem is not the government's responsibility. In short, just as the conception of what is politically possible has been altered by Thatcherism, so the conception of what it is possible to say has been altered. It has become feasible in polite society to argue for the vigorous virtues and for their political implications. This is not at all to say that such arguments have won the day. But it does mean that Thatcherism has changed the intellectual agenda of political discourse.

The Effect on the Labour Party

The least contestable effect of Thatcherism has been the change in the opinion of its opponents. If one contemplates the Labour Party platforms of the forties, fifties, sixties, seventies and early eighties, and contrasts them with what the Labour Party, by the end of the Thatcher administrations, has come to consider desirable, one can see the true extent of the effect of Thatcherism upon British political thinking.

When Labour issued its policy document, 'Looking to the Future', on 4 May 1990, *The Times* leader said – 'One individual stalks the pages ... Mrs Margaret Thatcher. In the last 11 years, her Government has changed the language and outlook of friend and foe alike, and not least of Mr Neil Kinnock.' The policy review jettisoned the Labour Party's past commitment to renationalization, to government controls over the economy and industry, to taxes to enforce the repatriation of overseas capital and to the repeal of all Conservative trade union reforms. It reduced to 'near-invisibility' the addiction to unilateral nuclear disarmament. It was, *The Times* concluded, a 'retreat not just from some naive socialism' – socialism was reduced to 'dust on the shelf'.[5]

Labour proclaimed its belief in the market, even if alongside praise for a 'partnership between the private and public interest'. It forswore any 'irresponsible dash for growth'. Talk of renationalizing was replaced by the declaration that 'Government must create a stable economic framework within which industries can flourish,' and that 'We welcome and endorse the efficiency and realism which markets can provide.' It promised that Labour would 'not spend ... more than Britain can afford'. Even in industrial relations, almost all the Conservative reforms were accepted, including the end of the closed shop, ballots on strikes and union elections. Although 'sympathy action' and secondary picketing would be restored, picketing would be severely restricted and mass picketing or flying pickets prohibited.

Whereas the previous document spoke of abolishing the remaining non-comprehensive schools, this one talked only of a commitment to maintaining comprehensive education and raising educational standards. Of the old promise by Bryan Gould to return privatized utilities to public ownership, all that remained was a proposal to renationalize water and British Telecom. Controls on incomes and prices, exchange controls, were no longer on the menu.

Critics had plenty to say about the shortcomings of the policy review as a wholehearted renunciation of socialist sins. Michael Howard, the Conservative cabinet minister, writing in the *Independent*[6], described the policy document as a strikers' charter and a recipe for chaos. Ferdinand Mount pointed out that 'In some cases, Mr Kinnock has managed to gain credit twice or even three times over for abandoning the same outdated socialist shibboleth'. But nevertheless 'Labour is no longer in the embarrassing position of standing somewhere between the Soviet Communist party and the National Salvation Front in Rumania.'[7]

The subsequent policy document, *Opportunity Britain*, issued in April of 1991 dropped any mention of equality – (in the 1988 statement, *Democratic Socialist Aims and Values*, the party was still committed to 'a more equal' society). It firmly ruled out a statutory incomes policy. While promising to raise the top rate of taxation to fifty per cent, it was clear, *The Times* said, that 'This time there is no Labour Denis Healey threatening to squeeze the rich until the pips squeak. The top rate of tax will plainly not return to the eighty-three per cent at which it stood in 1978–9, even if Labour wins.'[8] There were only two specific spending pledges, to raise child benefits and pensions.

Again, of course, Labour's critics pointed out, as the *Daily Telegraph* did, that 'Labour's plans breed dependence on the state.

Its offers tend to be gestures ... It is a sophisticated version of George Brown's National Plan and the Department of Economic Affairs set up by Harold Wilson.'[9] It was certainly a programme for restoring the corporatism, the 'beer and sandwiches' at Downing Street, that Thatcherism had fought off. Nevertheless, the spirit of Margaret Thatcher still obviously haunted the appearance, if not the reality, of Labour policies, as it continued to do in the 1992 election manifesto.

The Passion of Thatcher's Critics

In sum, Thatcherism – for all its concessions and inconsistencies, and for all its failures – has not only manifested a clear intention but also achieved in its own terms both considerable practical effects and a significant shift in British political thinking. It remains to consider why a political venture, by a democratically elected government, in many respects so successful, should have become the object of such remarkable dislike. Even if everyone might not accept Mrs Thatcher's own conclusion, 'I believe that our policies have brought out the very best in the British character, a sense of freedom and responsibility, and it is that I am proud of, because it is that which made Britain great,'[10] why should she have aroused such a violent hostility? That Thatcherite policies were criticized, however sharply, for a variety of sins, whether for being 'uncaring' or ineffective, is not in the least surprising – it is part of the usual give and take in British politics. But the passionate hatred among people who pride themselves on their rationality is certainly unusual. The antagonism of the liberal clergy, for instance, is understandable, given their political views, but the harshness of their language in this secular age is, to say the least, remarkable. In his Easter 1988 speech, the Rt Revd David Jenkins condemned Mrs Thatcher's administration as 'wicked'. Another Church of England Bishop and a leading Methodist minister dubbed the Government's social security reforms 'iniquitous'.[11]

In its milder forms, the antagonism to her was like that expressed by the Tory columnist, Peregrine Worsthorne during the earlier part of Mrs Thatcher's premiership. To him, it was Mrs Thatcher's 'preachy manner, with that self-righteous, censorious "this hurts me more than it hurts you" – schoolmistressy voice' that was so annoying. He saw Thatcherism as a kind of puritanism, out 'to turn Britain into a land fit only for Roundheads to live in, and not just temporarily for the duration of the emergency, but for ever and ever, amen'. As by 1985, he believed that the recession was over, Worsthorne thought it was time to escape from the Thatcherite lessons in 'thrift, sobriety, hard work' and turn to indulging the 'rumbustious, Falstaffian, devil-may-care strain' in English Toryism.[12]

The Times columnist, Ronald Butt, who had earlier on been an enthusiastic supporter, suggested that Thatcherism had become associated with witchcraft: 'What is most remarkable about the political phenomenon of Mrs Thatcher is not that her adherents regard her as something like a miracle worker, but that those who detest her also invoke her as such, though they attribute the wonders she works to diabolical power.'[13] Ronald Butt's impression was confirmed by the strongly anti-Thatcher barrister and playwright, John Mortimer, who saw Mrs Thatcher as a terrifying figure, someone who inspired people with fear.

But these were comparatively mild criticisms. When the *Sunday Telegraph* published a series of interviews with leading figures in the intellectual and cultural establishment, the vitriolic attacks recorded by the interviewer, Graham Turner, became something of a scandal. 'They have about them', Kingsley Amis said, 'the same venom and unreason as anti-semitism.' To Jonathan Miller, doctor and impresario, the reason he and his like were so deeply hostile to Mrs Thatcher was 'self-evident' – 'It's the same as why the bulk of the human race is hostile to typhoid.' He himself found her 'loathsome, repulsive in almost every way'. He could not endure 'her odious sub-saccharine patriotism, catering to the worst elements of commuter idiocy'. The Baroness Warnock, philosopher and Mistress of Girton College, Cambridge, was positive that even if Mrs Thatcher's policies towards universities became more acceptable, there were deep personal reasons for detesting her. Mrs Thatcher's 'patronising elocution voice', the 'neat well-groomed clothes and hair, packaged together in a way that's not exactly vulgar, just *low*' filled Lady Warnock with 'a kind of rage'.[14]

Similar responses were reported also earlier, in 1983 in the *New Statesman*. The publisher, Carmen Callil, who had started the Virago Press which republished forgotten women writers and pursued a feminist line, declared that Mrs Thatcher 'terrifies me, she repels me, and I think she's ruining everything that is best about this country'. Melvyn Bragg, novelist and television producer, was revolted by the 'gloating incantations from a woman dangerously in love with her own publicity'. And the novelist, Angela Carter, felt that the voice summed up 'the ambiguity of the entire construct. She coos like a dove, hisses like a serpent, bays like a hound', a form of ' "toff-speak" now reminiscent not of real toffs but of Wodehouse aunts'.[15]

When Mrs Thatcher was asked by the intrepid interviewer, Brian Walden, 'What do you think of this constant characterisation of you as an authoritarian virago?' she replied: 'You cannot have my job and have had a vision, a dream, a will to turn Britain round, to live up to the best of herself, without being more than a chairman of a committee . . . a prime minister has a task of leadership. If the trumpet give an uncertain sound, who shall prepare himself to the battle? . . . if one has a sense of purpose, they call that authoritarianism. It is totally false, but there you are.'

When he pressed her further with, 'Why do they hate you so much?', she moved on to: 'Success is not an attractive thing to many people – they do not like it. And, of course, some of them are snobs. They can never forgive me for coming from a very ordinary background. It does not bother me at all. I cannot stand snobbery of any kind.' And the greatest snobs of all are the intellectuals and academics: 'They think they have a talent and ability that none of the rest of the human race has. That is the ultimate snobbery, the worst form of snobbery there is. Only put them in charge and the poor will have everything. So the poor put them in power and discover the rulers have everything and the poor have nothing.' She herself believed in giving people what they wanted, not what the snobs thought they ought to want. Perhaps, too, she suggested, successful, purposeful behaviour was not what men expected from a woman. And when Walden wondered why she did not simulate the kind of 'style' that her colleagues preferred, she was shocked: 'I could not! I could not!' 'Pretence is alien to her, part of the foreign world of the snobs and patronisers,' Walden concluded. 'She wants to persuade, but will use no artifice to do it.'[16]

No doubt the reasons Mrs Thatcher gave for the passionate response to her played some part. Lady Warnock and Jonathan Miller themselves attributed their hostility to snobbery, which they considered perfectly respectable – it was looking down on what was inferior. Colin Haycraft, chairman of the independent publisher Gerald Duckworth, suggested that the trouble was due to Mrs Thatcher's being the first modern politician who denied that the world owed every would-be intellectual a living. Lord Annan, former provost of King's College, Cambridge, and the Vice-Chancellor of London University, believed that intellectuals resented no longer being constantly invited to sit on government bodies. Besides, their dream of an egalitarian society free of competition had turned into a nightmare in the 1970s and Mrs Thatcher had substituted her vision of a highly competitive world, which had been a rude, and much-needed, awakening.[17]

Why They Hated Her

None of these explanations, however, goes to the heart of the matter. They do not explain how the emotional outbursts are connected with the more serious charges brought against Thatcherism. For the personal attacks were linked in the minds of Mrs Thatcher's critics with what they regarded as the damaging effects of her policies. Their accusations on this score fall into two categories. On the one hand, Thatcherism was charged with being 'authoritarian' (a word regularly misused nowadays to mean autocratic); on the other hand, it was found to be philistine in the broadest sense of crude, harsh, and insensitive. What needs to be explained is not just what gave rise to the belief in these shortcomings, but why they made Thatcherism such a peculiarly irritating substance.

i. THATCHERISM SEEN AS 'AUTHORITARIANISM'

At first sight, it might seem obvious why Thatcherism should have seemed to be 'authoritarian'. The obstacles that Thatcherites encountered when they set out to correct what, in their view, was badly wrong with the state of Britain were undeniably tough; so too was the language of Thatcherism; and so also the action taken. In relation to the unions, there was literally bloody conflict; in relation to local government, something not far off; and even in relation to schools, hospitals, and industries, toughness of an unprecedented order. Moreover the transformation was driven by one person, and that a woman, from the top. That together with the toughness of language and action made it plausible to see Mrs Thatcher as a tyrant.

On closer examination, however, the charge becomes more puzzling. Why did a government whose leading commitment was to enlarging freedom and choice and to reducing interference by the government, which even some of its opponents admitted had achieved that objective to a remarkable degree, become reviled for having made the state more 'intrusive'? What makes this charge more mysterious is that it was often complemented by the opposite accusation, that the Thatcher administration did too little because of a doctrinaire commitment to a market economy. And often both charges were made by the same people.

The answer is that Thatcherism rests on a distinction between two different kinds of governmental intervention which was never explained nor probably even understood by most Thatcherites. The distinction was a profound lacuna in Thatcherite thinking. Because of it, Thatcherites, along with everyone else, talked as if the issue were about 'more' and 'less' government. And in doing so they reinforced the popular fallacy – which they should have been combating – the fallacy that a government can do only one of two things, intervene or not intervene. Thus the rhetoric defeated their objectives.

Thatcherites failed to explain what they were unwittingly assuming, that 'government intervention' can take many different forms and that these differences are far more important than the *quantity* of governmental activity. As the history of the Tory Party shows, it was a misinterpretation with a long and venerable lineage going back to a misunderstanding of Adam Smith's 'invisible hand' and the role of *laissez-faire* in nineteenth-century Britain. What Thatcherites failed to make plain, both to themselves and to their opponents, is that a preference for a market economy, far from prohibiting government intervention, requires especially firm and steady intervention. But it is intervention of a particular kind.

The 'paradigm shift' entailed a change not so much in the amount of government control as in its character. It was a shift from direct government action – to set prices, wages, dividends, exchange rates, to build houses or invest in and manage industries – to very different sorts of measures, designed to set a 'framework' which would make it easier for individuals to initiate and pursue their own projects, to buy and sell goods and services at the prices they choose to pay. For such free arrangements among individuals to be possible – as Eastern Europe is painfully beginning to learn – there must be a strong state to enforce appropriate laws and to maintain the value of money, apart from maintaining peace at home and security against external enemies.

In short, the Thatcherite preference for a market economy is not a repudiation of government intervention but a commitment to a certain manner of intervening. That manner relies on devices which make it easier for labour to move to areas where jobs are available rather than on make-work projects; on encouraging new enterprises through lower taxes rather than by government invest-ment; on using local authorities as 'enablers' rather than 'providers' of services. The simplest analogy that illustrates what distinguishes the two manners of governing is the difference between enforcing traffic rules and planning an itinerary or driving the car.

Thatcherites are not – and, being practical politicians, could not be – completely averse to activities analogous to planning the itiner-ary or driving the car. No modern state can wholly avoid such activities. What the 'paradigm shift' implies is that such activities are not the essence of government but rather an inescapable anom-aly which should be restricted as far as possible. Only in this sense do Thatcherites believe in 'less' or 'limited' government. That is why there is nothing in the least incompatible between the Thatcherite devotion to 'the paradigm shift' and their belief in a strong state.

But far from clearly distinguishing the different kinds of government intervention, Thatcherite rhetoric helped to blur and confuse such distinctions. When Thatcherites warned against the dangers of tampering with the market and ignoring 'the laws of economics', when they promised 'to roll back the state', when Mrs Thatcher took up Hayek's remark – out of context – that 'there is no such thing as society', they re-enforced the mistaken belief that the only choice is between a more and less 'intrusive state'. Given that belief and the incessant, far-reaching legislative activity of the Thatcher Government, it became plausible to conclude that Thatcherism had promoted an 'intrusive state' while preaching the opposite.

In other words, Thatcherism suffered from a serious lack of self-understanding. And this defect, as it so often does in human relations, inspired a peculiarly strong antagonism. For it led people to feel that Thatcherites were being devious, which made what were interpreted as the policies of an increasingly 'intrusive state' all the more offensive, especially to those who, for whatever reasons, opposed the Thatcherite kind of intervention.

Another reason why Thatcherism seemed to be 'authoritarian' was that it suffered from a tension between its commitment to efficiency and its devotion to freedom. Thanks partly to the grisly experiment in Eastern Europe, it has become almost universally acknowledged that the most efficient way to organize the economic life of a highly industrialized nation is through a market economy. As the market consists of independent agents choosing to make arrangements with one another in accordance with rules which both are obliged to observe, a market economy is also a paradigm of how human beings can associate and remain free. There is no conflict then between a commitment to improving economic efficiency and a commitment to freedom. It is one of the rare cases where we can eat our cake and keep it. Therefore, as long as Thatcherites concentrated on economic policies they did not face any conflicts between these two of their aims. But when the Thatcher Government turned to other matters, as it did in its later years, the harmony between freedom and efficiency disintegrated and was replaced by a painful tension.

The tension became especially troublesome in the educational policies. It was produced by the Thatcherite acceptance of the diagnosis which blamed the British disease on admiration for the liberally educated gentleman. The marriage of this diagnosis with their eagerness to cure the British disease made Thatcherites hostile to the tradition of liberal education which, for many centuries, had been so eminently developed in independent schools like Eton, maintained schools like Manchester Grammar, and in Oxford and Cambridge. The huge amounts of public money absorbed by the universities during the Robbins expansion, the antics of students in the 1960s, the noisiness of socialist dons, all helped to strengthen this hostility. 'Some academics and intellectuals . . . are putting out what I call poison,' Mrs Thatcher said. 'Some young people who were thrilled to bits to get to university, had every decent value pounded out of them.'[18] The Thatcherite concern to improve the efficiency of British industry accordingly took shape as a conviction that all the established educational institutions, universities like Oxford and Cambridge along with the chaotic comprehensives, had failed in their duty to contribute to the productive capacity of the nation, and that therefore a liberal education was incompatible with the cultivation of the vigorous virtues.

Having identified both the 'progressive' education of the comprehensives and the liberal education of Oxbridge as enemies of the vigorous virtues, Thatcherites tried to find an alternative to both. But they did not look to those views of education which were eminently compatible with Thatcherism, such as they might have found in the writings of Michael Oakeshott and Richard Peters. These authors did not use the practical language that Thatcherites found congenial.

Instead Thatcherites took up the utilitarian or corporatist view of education. Their concern to cure the British disease made Thatcherites peculiarly susceptible to a view that explicitly and emphatically regarded education as a means to improving economic efficiency. And they were not clear-headed enough to see how incompatible that view was with the 'paradigm shift' that they also valued. For it treated individuals not as independent, self-sufficient agents distinguished by the vigorous virtues, but as instruments of production. Hence the Thatcher Government's education policies introduced precisely the kind of intervention that it had renounced in its economic attitude. These policies gave good reason even to its friends to attach the 'authoritarian' tag to Thatcherism. Again, the fact that Thatcherites talked of freedom while acting as corporatists exacerbated the antagonism to its policies.

Thirdly, a hostile view of Thatcherism as 'authoritarian' was encouraged simply by the degree of change that it introduced. It had long been assumed in Britain that respect for tradition was one of the conditions that accounted for the preservation of British liberties. Respect for tradition is compatible with change, since traditions are constantly changing. But they do so without noticeably breaking away from the past. A respect for tradition would then seem to require letting change come about through the slow modification of established practices.

But the Thatcherite project could not have been achieved by such modifications. As Thatcherites saw things, what was needed was a sharp repudiation of many established practices. No slow modifications were going to stop Arthur Scargill from bringing in flying pickets, or turn schools where children rushed about expressing themselves in chaos into educational institutions teaching the three Rs in disciplined fashion. Thatcherites wanted radical change, drastic enough to undo, among other things, the changes that had been introduced by the Labour Party since the Second World War.

Radical change, however, even if introduced – as the Thatcherite changes were – with strict regard for constitutional procedures, are in themselves, however much they are desired or desirable, an affront to freedom because the natural tendency of most human beings is to go on doing what they had done in the past. Despite the new opportunities for choice opened up by the changes, as they compelled people to abandon an accustomed way of doing things, they were bound to be seen in the first instance as a restraint.

What made the Thatcherite changes especially irritating to some was the feeling that they were antagonistic to important British traditions. Certainly the fact that the changes were radical distinguished them sharply from the slow adaptation of traditions. But whether a change attacks a significant tradition or merely an entrenched practice is always difficult to say. It was not therefore implausible to see every radical change introduced by Thatcherism as an attack on British 'traditions' and hence as a destruction of British liberties.

Of this, the efforts to reform local government are the supreme example. There was (and is) widespread ignorance of and indifference to what precisely is entailed in 'local government' and to how local authorities came to be established and financed – even so seasoned a political journalist as Hugo Young complained that the poll tax made local authorities newly dependent on Whitehall for seventy-five per cent of their funding, whereas in fact something close to that had been true since the Second World War. The ignorance, combined with the energetic campaigning by the many powerful vested interests attached to the local authorities, made it all too easy to see any proposed change as an attack on 'traditional British liberties'. Thatcherism was accordingly labelled as 'centralist', implying that it had moved power from local government to the central government when it removed schools from the control of local authority bureaucrats and turned them over to the control of headmasters, governors, and parents so as to give more responsibility to those who would directly suffer the consequences.

And finally, what helped to make Thatcherism appear to be autocratic was its determination to repudiate pressure group politics and to promote the vigorous virtues. To a nation that had forgotten the jeremiads of the great British statesmen against governments that acted as mouthpieces for special interests, at a time when public opinion polls ruled the headlines and when people had long grown accustomed to seeing the heads of unions and industry going in and out of Downing Street, a government that resolutely refused to bargain with such groups, appeared to be breaking with well-established 'democratic' practices. On this account Thatcherism was intrinsically vulnerable to the charge of 'refusing to listen' and of handing down orders from on high without regard to the opinion of the public. Moreover, the way in which Thatcherites responded to such accusations only made matters worse. Instead of explaining their concern 'to do the right thing', they protested that they were just as open-minded and 'ready to listen' as their critics and succeeded in sounding hypocritical as well as high-handed.

Nevertheless, the most adroit rhetorician would not have found the task easy. To explain the policies and intentions of Thatcherism is peculiarly difficult, especially under current conditions. Even if Thatcherites had understood perfectly all the assumptions that they were making and all the reasons for their decisions, they would have found it nearly impossible to put their case to a popular audience so as to avoid misinterpretation, let alone to secure agreement. It is intrinsically easier, given three minutes and a mass audience, to justify an incomes policy than to argue for controlling the money supply. Of course, ministers developed slogans on which they relied – 'our first priority is getting inflation down'. But if such simplifications persuaded some, they easily gave others the impression of an autocratic dogmatism. When added to this was a Prime Minister with unusual energy, quickness, and forcefulness, and a woman at that, who was able to talk down the most intrepid interviewers and whose Cabinet emerged after every Thursday lunch with well-bruised egos, who repeatedly emphasized her determination not to give in to any interest group, the ingredients for arousing a passionate antipathy to Thatcherite 'authoritarianism' were complete.

ii. THATCHERISM SEEN AS ENERGETIC PHILISTINISM

The tone of certainty in Thatcherite pronouncements contributed also to the second charge, that it was a philistine enterprise which was determined to turn every acre of Britain's green and pleasant land into a Tesco supermarket. Auberon Waugh, though not wholly antagonistic to Thatcherite aims, proclaimed that 'The new class struggle is to reassert the ascendancy of the bourgeois culture in all the fields where it is being crushed by the Murdoch-Thatcher juggernaut; in political and administrative leadership, arts, education, entertainment, television, newspapers.' By 'bourgeois culture', Waugh explained, he meant 'the standards of intelligent liberally-educated people such as still hold the strings of power in most of Europe'.[19]

At first sight, it is not obvious why a political enterprise dominated by a desire to change the underlying morality of Britain, to reinstate the vigorous virtues, and to do 'the right thing' should have been seen as a philistine project bereft of humility. But the explanation lies to some extent in Thatcherite rhetoric. Partly because it developed out of an economic analysis of the evils of socialism, partly because economic theory provided a readily available vocabulary for explaining the difficult new outlook, Thatcherism regularly used the language of the market and of economics. Although that language is only a shorthand for the language of choice and responsibility, it came to be taken by Thatcherism's advocates to be a description of its essence. The scientific jargon of economics conveyed an air of dogmatic certainty. And as the term 'free market' came to be associated with Thatcherism, for many people it was the 'market' rather than the 'free' which stuck and identified Thatcherism with crass commercialism.

This image was enhanced by the talk of creating an 'enterprise culture', a phrase that grated on ears attuned to good English and offended people who felt that a good life consisted of something other than getting and spending.

The Thatcherite attack on the great interest groups was accordingly seen as an attack on the cultivated establishment beyond academe. This was taken to be of a piece with Mrs Thatcher's choice of ministers who did not come from the shires or even Oxbridge. In the early days, this disposition was interpreted favourably, as a readiness to recognize new talent and to abandon stuffy Tory prejudices. Everyone 'knew' that Mrs Thatcher could not bear Old Etonians or members of grand families, although Nicholas Ridley, who qualified on both counts, had long been an ally and close friend. But when the charge of philistinism began to dominate the public's attention, this supposed antipathy to Eton and the aristocracy, combined with the very real suspicion of Oxbridge and a liberal education, fortified by the talk of an 'enterprise culture', served to confirm the belief that the beauties of 'this emerald isle' were not safe in the hands of Mrs Thatcher. It became plausible to conclude that Thatcherism was bent on barbarizing Britain, on destroying everything that cultivated people cherished. A suggestion, such as that museums might solve their financial problems by charging entrance fees, was seen not as a possible device for funding museums but as yet another attack on 'culture'.

Hatred of Thatcherism for what was seen as its philistinism became directed at Mrs Thatcher herself because of the tone she adopted. Instead of trying to be as emollient as possible, she was abrasive and aggressive. Instead of wrapping her objections in mellifluous compliments and voicing her opposition in sweet murmurs, she shouted, No, No, No. Far from cultivating agreement, she provoked conflict, stating her views forcefully, without the benefit of comforting qualifications. To an audience who had acquired the decadent belief that gentility consists in malleability, a readiness to compromise and to tolerate evil, an anxiety to avoid conflict, that tone signified – not candour and fearlessness as it might have done a century or more earlier – but a philistine lack of civility.

That impression was re-enforced by the intimation that Thatcherism had no sense for the tension between striving to improve things and reconciling oneself to the dissonances of a human condition. No government, just as no individual, can escape this tension. But in a government that does nothing very radical, it easily goes unnoticed. When people spoke of Mrs Thatcher's certainty, arrogance, and abrasive vulgarity, and complained about her treating her ministers as Elizabeth I dealt with her courtiers, they were complaining about what they took to be a lack of humility or diffidence. Whether or not Mrs Thatcher or Thatcherites genuinely lacked this quality, it is impossible to know. But one can see that the persistent drive 'to do more', combined with a rhetoric that emphasized always the virtue of doing something to change things for the better, displayed no awareness of the dangers lurking in projects for reform.

A greater gift for displaying such an awareness might perhaps have made Thatcherism less offensive. But it could never have rid itself of its peculiar vulnerability to the charge of lacking diffidence.

The reason is that Thatcherites are neither revolutionaries nor ideologues. Not being ideologues, they have no way of even seeming to establish – at least to the converted if not to others – that the changes they are making are indisputably necessary and the best possible ones. Not being revolutionaries, they cannot believe or argue that change for the sake of causing upheaval is in itself always desirable. Deprived of both the ideologue's comforting absolutes and the revolutionary's assurance, yet displaying an offensive energy, Thatcherism easily appeared to be compulsively activist and unyielding. It came to seem increasingly arrogant as public concern about the state of Britain gave way to irritation with the activity involved in trying to cure the patient. And the more Thatcherism achieved its aims, the easier it was to find it objectionable.

For the broad mass of the British electorate, including no doubt a great many of those who supported the Thatcher administrations as well as a great many of those who opposed her governments without hating them, the real complaint arose from the feeling, both deep and characteristic of the British consciousness, that the whole enterprise was simply too energetic. Ultimately, Thatcherism lost its grip on power because it failed to heed sufficiently the words of St Augustine: 'It is an established fact that peace is the desired end of war. For every man is in quest of peace, even in waging war . . . peace is so great a good that even in relation to the affairs of earth and of our mortal state no word ever falls more gratefully upon the ear, nothing is desired with greater longing, in fact nothing better can be found.'[20]

Of course, peace can also mean stagnation, inertness, passivity, death. And that aspect is what preoccupied Thatcherites. But in trying to shake Britain out of what they saw as a deadly torpor, Thatcherites inevitably appeared to be destroyers of peace. Even when things are going badly, a considerable number of people are so fearful of disturbing the peace that they continue to support their oppressors. In Britain under Thatcher, as inflation and stagnation receded, as more people became owners and investors, despite the opposition's taunts about 'running out of steam', there seemed to be less and less reason for disturbing the peace. And when, after all the activity, the Government ran into difficulties, that was blamed not on the absence of Thatcherite initiatives but on a superfluity of them.

After so many years, people in Britain at last came to see the depth of the seriousness of the Thatcherite project. In an incoherent and inarticulate fashion they began to understand that Thatcherism actually aimed to encourage continual vigour and advance. And when Mrs Thatcher kept repeating, 'there's so much more to do', they concluded that with 'that woman' around there never could be any peace. What eventually 'got under the skin' was the feeling that Thatcherism might really be a *permanent* revolution. Thatcherism had not developed an understanding of how vigour once recreated in Britain could be translated into something calm, gentle, pleasant.

12

A British Individualism

Beyond the Aims of Thatcherism

The most obviously lethal failure of Thatcherism appeared in the area where it had previously scored its most notable victory. In the late eighties, what many regarded as the supreme achievement of Thatcherism – the control of inflation and the reduction of unemployment – disintegrated. The economy appeared to be returning to the sorry state in which the first Thatcher Government had found it. In 1989, the rate of inflation reached 7.8 per cent; by October 1990 it had moved up to 10.9 per cent. Interest rates rose from a low of 8 per cent to a high in 1990 of 15 per cent. Unemployment rose steadily in the late eighties to 1,700,000 by October 1990. The house-buying spree began to look like a disaster as, thanks to high interest rates, borrowers found it increasingly difficult to meet the payments on their mortgages. The fact that Britain was the only European country where the public sector absorbed less than half of the national output – in 1988 government spending was under forty per cent; that taxes had been dramatically cut; and that Britain had, as a result, attracted far more investment in industry from Japan and the United States than any other European country went unnoticed. The media were more interested in the complaints of industrialists – aggrieved by the lack of government hand-outs – and of corporatists in all the parties that manufacturing had been sacrificed to the City and that Britain had been reduced to a Third World country.

Even if one takes a less lurid view of it, the economic failure of the third Thatcher Government is undeniable. But it is equally clear that the failure was not intrinsic to Thatcherism. Its opponents showed no signs of expecting disaster until it was unmistakable.

The Chancellor remained a hero at Tory Conferences. It was an arch Thatcherite, the economist Tim Congdon, who raised the alarm as early as 1985. If 'the burst of high money growth' continued, Congdon warned, the country was heading for a severe bout of the boom, inflation, recession syndrome. He urged the Chancellor to act at once to restrict the money supply – there was still time to save the economy from serious damage.'[1] But instead, the Chancellor decided that the broad money measure, M_3, gave a misleading picture of monetary conditions, ceased to use it, and dismissed objections from 'teenage scribblers.'

In January 1986, Congdon wrote in *The Times* that 'Every day more evidence becomes available that the rapid growth of sterling M_3 is not misleading but is having standard and predictable effects on economic behaviour.' He pointed out that 'Surplus cash in the corporate sector' is financing takeovers and driving up share prices; surplus cash in the personal sector is starting to affect house prices.' And he told the Government to take 'a firm, clearcut decision to reinstate a broad money target and to stick to it.'[2] In October 1986, Congdon predicted that 'inflation will accelerate in the next few years, perhaps to as much as 10 per cent.'[3] In July 1988 Congdon congratulated the Government on having at last 'accepted what most economic scribblers, from the teenage to the geriatric, have known for many months', that Britain was in the throes of a full-scale boom such as had not been seen since Barber's 'dash for growth' in the early seventies. It was an impressive tribute to Mr Lawson's presentational skills, Congdon concluded, that he was still regarded by the media and most Conservative MPs as the most successful Chancellor since the war, even though he had, in the last three years, 'effectively destroyed all that he stood for, in terms of the structure of policy, in the previous five'.[4]

By 1987, Mrs Thatcher, urged on by her adviser, Sir Alan Walters, was becoming persuaded that the Government's monetary policies were on the wrong road. It became known that she was not on the best of terms with her Chancellor even though she described him as 'brilliant' at the 1988 Tory Conference. No doubt Mr Lawson and Mrs Thatcher will in time give their own accounts of what happened. But whatever they say, just as monetarism was never of the essence of Thatcherism, neither were the policies that produced the inflation and recession of the late eighties. Although a commitment to ending inflation is at the heart of Thatcherism, the policies required to achieve this do not follow from the nature of Thatcherism. Therefore a failure to adopt the right means might discredit a particular Chancellor or Government, but cannot make Thatcherism either more or less admirable. None of this can by itself exonerate Thatcherism from blame for either its commitment to ending inflation or for the policies that were pursued. It means only that, according to the understanding of Thatcherism presented here, the concern of Thatcherism with bringing down inflation was not inextricably tied to certain policies. One may therefore approve of the Thatcherite emphasis on ending inflation while deploring the policies pursued, or disapprove of both the objective and the means adopted to achieve it. Both views are compatible with the understanding of Thatcherism presented here because what makes Thatcherism distinctive and coherent is not any set of policies but a particular attitude and response to the condition of Britain.

This was not, however, the popular view. Thatcherites as well as their opponents believed that Thatcherism as such had been discredited. And the same shortcoming that had all along promoted confusion about Thatcherism made it impossible to distinguish the economic bungling from the essence of Thatcherism. Moreover, by the late eighties, a clear exposition of the aims of Thatcherism would not have sufficed. Something more was wanted to sustain a Thatcherite government. The irritating character of Thatcherism, exacerbated by its economic failure and highlighted by the press and television, inspired more probing questions. To answer them, Thatcherites had to make it clear not only that Thatcherism is committed to 'doing the right thing', to promoting the vigorous virtues and the paradigm shift, and to preserving Britain's independence, but also why. In short, a complete explanation of Thatcherism was wanted. No politician proved equal to that task.

An Unidentified Morality

Thatcherism can be fully explained only by answering a question that is not usually considered in discussions of contemporary politics: what understanding of the human world shaped the way that Thatcherites interpreted and responded to the conditions of their time? Or, to put it another way, what assumptions or postulates made the aims of Thatcherism seem reasonable to its advocates? Because Thatcherism is a coherent project, it makes sense to suppose that there is an answer to that question. For the coherence of a project rests on a steady understanding of the human world. If we could not find any such understanding, that would cast doubt on the validity of speaking of Thatcherism.

The answer is a surprising one. Despite the revolutionary character of Thatcherism, the understanding that holds the key to it is very old. It was not invented by Margaret Thatcher, her colleagues, mentors, or immediate predecessors. On the contrary it has a long and curious history. It is a distinctive but unidentified British morality.

Although intimations of it have appeared elsewhere, only in Britain has it prevailed since medieval times. It has enabled the British to cultivate over many centuries a combination of qualities which was greatly admired by other Europeans but regarded by them as a miracle. For Britain had managed to combine freedom with order. A broad tolerance even for eccentricity flourished alongside a sturdy tradition of constitutional government and civility. Whilst that morality flourished, no one doubted that the practices and institutions of Britain embodied an outlook peculiar to that country. Foreigners regularly commented admiringly on the oddity of Britain. Readers of English literature discovered in writers from Chaucer to Trollope a moral attitude which they considered to be quintessentially English. And that notorious English oddity, the gentleman, understood as a kind of character rather than as a member of a social class, was universally acknowledged to be a moral phenomenon unknown elsewhere.

But so unselfconsciously was this moral outlook taken for granted in Britain that it began to disappear without ever having been identified. By the end of the nineteenth century, it was being displaced by a quite different morality imported from France and Germany. And as this foreign morality gained more influence, the British grew increasingly well disposed to collectivism, which consequently dominated British politics until the appearance of Thatcherism.

The old morality did not, however, completely lose its hold on the people of Britain. Like a faint melody, more nearly felt than heard, it remained an important strain in the atmosphere of the country and continued to impart a distinctive quality to life in Britain. Many yearned to hear the melody more distinctly. But being unaware of having heard it at all, they could hardly give voice to their yearning.

It was Margaret Thatcher who did that for them. Her ability to appeal to the public over the heads of their representatives, what has been called her 'populism', was due to the affinity between her understanding of the human world and that of a large section of the British public. It gave to her government, and to her fall, an unusual dramatic quality. But though she often talked of her 'philosophy', she was wholly unaware of the understanding that was postulated by her convictions. Indeed, far from supposing herself to be engaged in a crusade to restore the traditional morality of Britain, she believed herself to be doing the opposite. And both colleagues and opponents agreed with her. In reality, however, she had – unwittingly and instinctively – translated the morality that had by the 1970s become a vestige in Britain into a diagnosis of what had gone wrong and a coherent conception of what needed to be done, thus creating Thatcherism.

The traditional British morality which ultimately explains Thatcherism bears the same relationship to it as the Abbot Suger's cosmology to medieval Gothic cathedrals. Those who built the cathedrals had no inkling of the cosmology which had shaped the structure of what they had built. Yet the discovery of Suger's cosmology has given us a much deeper understanding of medieval cathedrals and solved many puzzles about them. In the same way we can more fully understand the practical political enterprise known as Thatcherism once we see its connection with that unidentified British morality.

Reason, Freedom and Order

One thing about that strange British morality is obvious – why it should have persisted for so long without being identified. Its conception of human beings is far more difficult to explicate and utterly unlike that of the classical morality which has dominated Western thought and practice since ancient times.

The latter, which still shapes how most people think nowadays, takes human beings to be divided between two elements – reason and passion, or mind and body. Each person is seen as an unstable compound of two warring parts. Insofar as reason dominates, order prevails. For reason is understood as a power to discover universal truths, laws, and patterns. It imposes order on the human world by reducing multiplicity to unity and variety to uniformity. But order is threatened by the irrational element in human beings, which is a chaos of desires and aversions. Since these operate in no regular fashion, they produce an endless, disorderly diversity in behaviour.

As reason necessarily leads everyone to be and think alike, insofar as reason dominates, people must lack individuality. Only when reason is overcome by the irrational element, the source of diversity, can individuality flourish. Therefore the only way that human beings can cultivate their individuality is to refuse to obey the commands of reason. It follows that, in this picture, the individualist is a restless, selfish, aggressive creature, concerned wholly with getting and winning. This is the understanding of individualism that is familiar nowadays to both its admirers and critics.

But whether or not they are individualists, all those who accept this classical picture of human nature are bound to associate order and reason with uniformity and unity. They are consequently obliged to assume that their only choice is between promoting unification and yielding to disorder. Some may describe this gloomy dichotomy in a more inspiring fashion as a choice between self-sacrifice and egoism, or between fraternity and alienation. Others may hope that through a fortunate accident, relatively mild repression might suffice to procure an adequate uniformity. Nevertheless, they are all certain that human beings are obliged either to submit to losing their individuality so as to secure order, or to rebel against order if they wish to preserve their independence or freedom.

In politics, this picture of the human world leads to the conclusion that, in order to avoid conflict and the oppression of the weak by the strong, all activities have to be organized by a highly centralized, unified system. Any relationship between human beings must consist in either submission or aggression. But these alternatives are judged differently by collectivists and classical individualists.

Both see a market economy, in which buyers and sellers compete for goods and services, as a 'free-for-all' in which the strong necessarily succeed and the weak fail. Both regard a market economy as a zero-sum game in which no one can win without imposing a loss on someone else. But whereas collectivists, in order to establish peace, want to eliminate competition and the market economy it sustains, classical individualists, of whom Herbert Spencer is the most eminent example, approve of a market economy for allowing the 'natural struggle for survival' to flourish and to eliminate the weak and inefficient. Moreover, such individualists are necessarily always at war with 'society' because they regard a legal order, the disciplines of education, the requirements of civility, indeed any conformity to established rules or conventions as repression.

Both collectivists and individualists of this breed regard the British talent for combining freedom with order as either an illusion or a miracle. Their understanding of the human world makes it impossible to see how relationships among human beings can be orderly and peaceful without being directed by a higher power which organizes everything in accordance with some grand, all-encompassing plan.

The world looks very different, however, if it is understood in the manner of the traditional British morality. Then no miracle is needed to reconcile freedom with order. For in the British picture, human beings are not divided between reason and passion. They are completely rational. Everything they do is permeated by their rationality because reason is not a power to discover indisputable arguments and universal patterns. Its essence is the power to choose what to see, feel, think, and do. In other words, reason is a faculty that enables human beings to interpret and respond to experience as they will. In this view, emotions are no less rational than mathematical calculations, because what causes fear or any other emotion and how people respond to it depends on how they interpret what they experience. And every interpretation is a rational activity.

When reason is understood in this fashion, what a human being does voluntarily cannot be caused in the way that a trigger sets a bullet in motion. Human behaviour is never a mechanical process, because human actions are not the products of internal 'drives' or external 'forces'. Of course everyone has to deal with biological processes within his body and events outside it, and human beings can by force be deprived of their faculties or prevented from exercising them. Nevertheless, anyone who retains his rationality cannot but choose how to understand and respond to what happens to him. In this picture then, a human being in possession of his faculties is never merely potter's clay. He is himself both potter and clay because he necessarily decides what to make of whatever happens to him.

Given this view of reason, the variety and uncertainty in the human world cease to be sinister products of irrational forces. On the contrary, the variety and uncertainty are attributed to the fertility of rational activity. For here reason is a creative power, which enables each person to choose differently from others, indeed even from what he himself did yesterday.

Seeing the human world in this fashion has five leading implications. They can explain what makes it reasonable for someone who accepts this outlook to pursue the aims of Thatcherism.

Diversity without Conflict

It follows, first, that beyond the sustenance (in one form or another) required to secure biological survival, no 'needs' are given to human beings by nature or any other non-human source. All desires or wants are created by human beings for themselves. What we call a man's 'needs' are simply those wants that he or someone else believes that he ought to have satisfied. Though we may speak of a 'need' for medical care and assume that it can only be satisfied by doctors, the personal preferences of patients are not irrelevant. Respect for medical expertise does not eliminate room for choosing whether to consult a doctor; when, where, or whether to proceed with treatment; how much time, money or energy to devote to medical care; whether to be despairing or hopeful. Thus the first implication of understanding reason as a creative power is that depriving people of the freedom to decide by treating them as bundles of needs, at the mercy of experts who know what is good for them, deprives them of the respect due to human beings.

This assumption has led Thatcherites to explore new ways of providing public services which give the recipients greater freedom to decide how they will be treated. It explains the Thatcherite rejection of the old ethos of the National Health Service, and their determination to give parents more say in where and how their children are educated. It explains as well why such measures are condemned by opponents of Thatcherism for 'commercializing' everything. Those who see people as bundles of needs are bound to regard any increase in diversity and freedom to choose as an invitation to conflict. As they associate such conflict with economic competition, they consider 'commercialization' an appropriate description for those measures. But from the standpoint of the British morality, it is respect for human dignity that inspires, indeed requires, the expansion of choice and diversity.

A second implication of this view of the human world is that what people think or do is determined not by their circumstances but by how they have learnt to think and behave. This means that human beings are seen not as passive victims of their circumstances but as agents able to choose how to understand and respond to circumstances. What they choose will depend on how they have learnt to behave. And what they have learnt is what they have chosen to learn. Therefore, from how a man earns his living, nothing necessarily follows about what he will think. If he is a waiter he may believe himself to be a lackey or a superior craftsman; someone who regards himself today as a self-confident, skilled artisan might learn tomorrow to think of himself as a formerly deluded member of the oppressed proletariat. Whatever the circumstances, different people can understand and respond to them differently.

That is why it does not make sense to a Thatcherite to blame crime on poverty. In advising the unemployed to 'get on your bike', Norman Tebbit was reminding them of their power to choose how to respond to their circumstances. And when Thatcherites emphasized the role of the family in shaping character and tried to restore the vigorous virtues, they were assuming that a human being is what he learns and teaches himself to be.

Thirdly, it follows from the British morality that there need be no conflict between society and individuals bent on cultivating their individuality. On the contrary, because a human being is what he learns to be, each individual is dependent on his life among others for the materials with which to fashion his individuality. 'Society' is the name for the body of civilized practices to which the members of a community subscribe. Society is therefore the cradle rather than the coffin of individuality.

What enables individuals to make use of the wealth of materials, which constitute civilization and are made available by living in society, are the disciplines of social life. Foremost among these disciplines is education. Here education is not regarded as society's weapon for 'repressing' individuality by 'conditioning' people to conform to society's demands. And individuals are not required to rebel against either discipline or society if they wish to preserve their independence. That is why Thatcherism rejected the view, which dominated the introduction of comprehensive schools, that children should be released from the agonies of learning and any obligation to acknowledge that individuals differ in their ability to learn different things. Instead, Thatcherite policies assumed that education is an initiation into the arts, skills, and sciences that constitute civilization and that the discipline and distinctions needed to effect such an initiation are the essence of education. It is the only view of education compatible with understanding reason as a creative faculty.

A fourth implication of the British morality is that human activities cannot be arranged in a hierarchy. The belief in a hierarchy of occupations rests on the conception of reason as a 'higher, spiritual' faculty as opposed to the 'lower' bodily part of human beings. Then the more intellectual and the less physical an activity is, the higher it must be considered. Ultimately this view rests on a belief in a cosmic hierarchy of being which ascends from matter to spirit. But as, in the British morality, reason has nothing of this character, there is no justification for considering philosophy 'higher' than carpentry or business, or for regarding plumbers as inferior to poets. The human world is seen not as a hierarchy but as a highly intricate web of many different practices which cannot be reduced to one or measured by any single principle. What matters is how well each practitioner performs his work and conducts his life.

When Thatcherites insisted that the skills of the businessmen were as worthy of respect as those of dons, they were not, as they believed, combating the traditional British attitude but defending it. When that attitude was still dominant in Britain, to look down upon certain occupations was the mark of a snob, who was regularly ridiculed and castigated by moralists. Only in the twentieth century, when the new, imported outlook took over, did that cease to be the case. In combating the imported prejudice against dirtying one's hands in business, Thatcherism was returning – albeit unselfconsciously – to the traditional British morality.

Fifth and finally, it follows from that traditional morality that, as reason is an unceasing power to create diversity, the human world cannot be understood in terms of inevitabilities. Under certain conditions, some sorts of behaviour may be more likely. Of people whom we know, we may be able to predict how they will respond. Within a given practice, we can rely on certain regularities. Hence economic theory is a useful tool, though no more, for the management of economic affairs. But no human behaviour follows of necessity from any 'cause'; it is always the product of choice. Therefore nothing is inevitably so. And what is suitable or desirable in one set of circumstances may not be in another.

Because Thatcherites considered no arrangement to be inevitable, they could reject the truisms of their time and feel free to choose whether to continue or to halt the collectivization of Britain. They could question the commonplace that prosperity depends on manufacturing industries rather than on commerce or service industries. They could disagree with one another on how to direct the economy so as to avoid inflation.

The equation of respect for individuality with respect for human rationality and hence with respect for human dignity disposed Thatcherites, on the one hand, to emphasize measures that allowed and encouraged individuals to take responsibility for themselves and, on the other hand, to reject big plans, drives for unification, strategies for mobilizing the nation's resources, which are so beloved by collectivists. For all such projects treat individuals as parts of 'the great social machine', the ideal preached by the British socialist, Sidney Webb. The fundamental postulate of Thatcherism is the opposite – that human beings are and should be treated as self-moving makers of their own destinies.

This explains also the connection, which Mrs Thatcher mystified some followers by emphasizing, between Thatcherism and Christianity. For it is a central tenet of Christian doctrine, at least in some versions, that each person is an immortal soul who has to answer to God for what he makes of himself. In doing so, he has no access to indisputable knowledge of God's will. He can rely only on Revelation, his church's interpretation of it, and other human institutions. This view of Christianity underlies the British morality and renders it both sceptical and individualistic.

An Unfamiliar Conception of Government

Human beings understood in this fashion can become associated in many different ways for an unlimited variety of purposes. Associating with others is compatible with maintaining one's independence as long as the association is voluntary. But human association requires something more because the individuality of human beings gives them also a talent for disagreeing. Even those working on the same project can arrive at irreconcilable interpretations of their shared practices. Conflicts among different projects are, of course, even more likely.

In this picture, disagreement is inescapable not just because human beings may be wicked but because they are rational. Even if everyone were always ready to yield, there has to be a way of deciding when the yielding should stop. If then human beings wish to work and live together in peace, without fear of arbitrary interference, they must find a way of settling or preventing conflicts. They must be compelled to accept some sort of agreement about the conditions for civil peace. And this gives rise to a dilemma: how can the agreement needed for civil peace be made compulsory without destroying independence and diversity? In other words, how can political association, where the judge's decision is enforced by handcuffs and iron bars, be reconciled with the independence of its members?

The traditional answer in Britain has been the rule of law. It is a form of association in which the members are united not by their pursuit of a common objective but by their readiness to observe a set of rules. These rules define offices, duties, and procedures for making and enforcing rules, thus making it possible to know who has the right to decide what. What constitutes a desirable or 'just' rule is decided by those who have been given the right or authority to legislate. The legislators may be selected by universal suffrage, as in a democracy, or by some other device. But if the rule is enacted in conformity with the required procedures, it is an 'authentic' rule whose 'authority' the members of that association are obliged to accept. In acknowledging the 'authority' of a rule or decision, those subject to it recognize that whoever issued it had a 'right' to do so.

The great virtue of the rule of law is that it enables us to distinguish 'authority' from 'power', and thus to recognize that the policeman's baton, though physically like the hoodlum's club, has a wholly different character. The hoodlum's use of the club is an exercise of power. But the policeman is exercising authority because – if he is behaving in conformity with the law – he has been given a 'right' to act as he does by rules whose authority can be acknowledged even by those who are bruised by his baton.

If I recognize the right of someone to command me to do something, I can obey him and at the same time retain my independence because I choose to recognize his right to command me. That is why the freedom to emigrate must complement the rule of law. For only then does my remaining within a community signify that I have chosen to acknowledge the authority of the established law. If, however, I submit to the will of another because I lack the strength to resist it, I retain no independence. Thus to live under the rule of law means submitting to authority, not power, and such submission is compatible with preserving the independence of individuals.

Although subjects of the law are obliged to obey authentic law, questioning both the authority and the justice of laws is entirely compatible with the rule of law. As long as the questioning abides by the procedures laid down in the established rules, neither the legal order nor civil peace is threatened. Thus in Britain, since the seventeenth century, laws have been regularly questioned, and changed, sometimes radically, without drastic constitutional upheavals. No other country can claim as much.

This understanding of the rule of law is the postulate that explains how Thatcherism could introduce radical new laws and at the same time claim to be defending the traditional legal order. What matters is whether the new laws were introduced and promulgated in accordance with the procedures required by the established law. That some people considered the new laws undesirable or unjust, as is bound to happen, does not derogate from the validity of the law. It merely highlights the importance of abiding by the established legal procedures in order to settle differences peacefully.

Because it is the only way in which individuals can be compelled to associate without losing their independence, the rule of law is a central postulate of Thatcherism. It explains why Thatcherites believe that governments should aim 'to do the right thing' instead of yielding to interest groups or making bargains with barons of industry or labour who have not been given the authority to make public policy.

Socialism versus the Rule of Law

The importance of the rule of law for Thatcherism explains also its opposition to socialism. For socialism requires, at least to a large degree, government by fiat that makes it impossible for individuals to retain their independence and run their own lives because they are governed by arbitrary commands rather than rules.

Of course, arbitrariness can never be wholly eradicated from government. Because political decisions cannot be deduced from indisputable principles, they always contain an element of discretion and are thus to some degree inescapably arbitrary. But in some decisions, such as those made by a judge, the area of discretion is narrowly defined. The more remote a decision is from the rule that authorized it and the more indefinite the rule, the larger and more amorphous becomes the area of discretion, and hence the more room for arbitrariness.

Under socialism, the room for arbitrariness is greatly enlarged because the government does not merely establish the framework within which industries, hospitals, or schools manage themselves. When such institutions are nationalized, the government does the managing. As a result, the discretion exercised by a socialist government bears no resemblance to the discretion exercised by a judge. A socialist economy can be kept going only by a continuous stream of promiscuous interventions. Insofar as a socialist government issues rules for the management of enterprises, they must authorize broad discretion to be exercised by remote officers. As a result, it becomes impossible to establish whether their decisions are duly authorized. For the most part, many officers of a socialist government are obliged to command the performance of narrowly specified duties. And the ordinary citizen cannot escape being affected by their commands.

Only where the government tries not to act as a manager, only where the government's authority extends over a clearly limited area, can the rule of law truly prevail. Then most people can go through life without ever coming into direct contact with the procedures or officers of the law. For rules of law, in the strict sense, stipulate conditions to be observed by individuals if and when they choose to engage in certain activities. Contract law, for instance, defines the conditions for making agreements which can be defended at law. It does not require anyone ever to make a contract. Criminal law defines behaviour that constitutes an offence; it does not oblige anyone to commit an offence.

Although Thatcherism accepts the necessity, which no government can escape, for making some laws which are really commands, such as tax laws, it opposes their proliferation because that would endanger the rule of law. That is the ultimate ground for the Thatcherite opposition to socialism, and for its own commitment to the 'paradigm shift' and its preference for a market economy.

What distinguishes a market economy, from the standpoint of the traditional British morality, is that, instead of requiring a stream of governmental orders, it integrates economic activities through free exchanges among buyers and sellers of goods and services. It leaves individuals free to move and to choose among a variety of independent organizations or individuals. What ensures that goods and services are bought and sold at 'fair' prices is that all buyers and sellers are subject to competition from others trying to acquire or to sell the same or similar things or substitutes for them. None can succeed unless he strikes a mutually satisfactory bargain with someone out to sell or buy what he wants or has to offer. The efficiency at which a market economy aims is the most economical way of supplying the things that people desire. The entrepreneur is valued because, by mediating between consumers and sellers of goods and services, he promotes the satisfaction of wants. That a market economy is also the most effective way of achieving economic growth is, from this standpoint, a welcome bonus but not its basic virtue.

It is important to notice, moreover, that while regard for the rule of law explains the Thatcherite commitment to a market economy and the competition it entails, that commitment in turn can only be implemented by promoting the rule of law. For free exchanges and competition do not spring up of their own accord. A market economy presupposes a legal framework which both facilitates and regulates the transactions between buyers and sellers. The legal framework has to ensure above all that the transactions are truly voluntary so as to prevent competition from turning into a zero-sum game, where one party wins at the expense of another. If the transactions in a market economy are genuinely voluntary, everyone gains. For properly regulated economic competition consists of mutually satisfactory exchanges among equals.

The Thatcherite commitment to a market economy does not then assume that human beings are aggressive combatants locked in a struggle for power. It assumes rather that they are possessors of creative intelligence which enables them to associate with others in an unlimited variety of ways. And because a market economy is a creature of law, Thatcherism could, without self-contradiction, both aim at the 'paradigm shift' and introduce laws which require the government to 'intervene' in new ways.

All this adds up to an unfamiliar conception of government because it denies that a government is an armoury from which thunderbolts issue forth to repress evil, or a forum where advocates of competing interests do what they can for their clients, or a dispenser of gratuities and benefits. Instead, a government is regarded here as a council of the whole community that has been given the right by its subjects to decide what conditions need to be maintained in order to preserve a congenial form of communal life. Its subjects think of themselves as self-moving, rational makers of their own lives, who wish to work and live together without losing their independence. The ultimate test of its justice is not whether it increases wealth or education, but whether its manner of governing respects the personality of all members of the community, secures them against intimidation by those who do not practice such respect, and permits a multitude of associations whereby power is diffused. It is in keeping with this conception of government to consider whether public efforts should be made to assist those who are unable to look after themselves. But deliberation about such measures is obliged to recognize that such assistance can be provided in a great variety of ways, some of which have yet to be discovered. This conception of government is the precise meaning of the freedom on which the British have prided themselves and which Thatcherism aimed to restore.

The morality postulated by Thatcherism explains its distinctive understanding of government. But no particular programme of action can be deduced from it. On the contrary, it obliges its adherents to recognize that what should be done here and now has to be decided by those acquainted with the circumstances. That is why Thatcherism is neither a theory nor an ideology but a practical response to a particular diagnosis of what was required in Britain at a particular time. Both the diagnosis and the response were made in the light of a certain way of understanding the human world which has been identified here as a morality that prevailed in Britain before the twentieth century. But as that understanding operated entirely unselfconsciously, the rhetoric of Thatcherism often drew on the language of a very different and conflicting morality, the only language in common usage, thus promoting confusion about the nature of Thatcherism.

After Thatcherism?

In all the battles fought by Thatcherism however, there was no direct confrontation between the traditional British morality and the foreign antagonist. Mrs Thatcher was so pre-eminent in the governments that she led because she alone sensed that something of the sort was at issue. But as her insight was inchoate and wholly unselfconscious, she could not communicate it even to her most loyal followers. Thus the old morality remained, as it had been, a faint melody that many yearned to hear more distinctly.

Instead of reviving the British morality that had inspired it, Thatcherism succeeded in providing an attractive new tune for the usurper. Old socialists learnt to chant in praise of 'a social market economy'. Everyone rejoiced that the battle between socialism and free enterprise was over. And the line between the parties again became blurred. As a result, for the immediate future, whichever party is in power, the major changes made by Thatcherism are not likely to be reversed.

Nevertheless, the issue that Thatcherism had brought to life did not disappear. The battle was merely relocated. Whether the morality, which had for centuries made Britain a model of how to combine freedom with order, would be strengthened or would wither away now rested on whether the European Community would be transformed into a supra-national state which would put an end to the independence of Britain. That British individualism never took root on the Continent has been regularly recognized since the seventeenth century by foreign visitors to Britain. On the Continent, individualism has generally been equated with conflict and disorder, from which it followed that without reducing multiplicity to unity and variety to uniformity, there could be no order or peace. The dominance of this view in Continental countries explains the greater readiness of their leaders to board M. Delors' train heading toward ever greater uniformity and unification. It took the British Labour Party some years to realize that, as socialists, they belonged on that train. But by the time of the Maastricht meeting of the European heads of government in December 1991, Labour's old passion for building great bureaucratic monoliths had been firmly refocused on restoring through Brussels, Strasbourg and The Hague what Thatcherism had destroyed in Britain, although stalwarts like Peter Shore continued to support the Eurosceptics.

Given the connection between Thatcherism and a distinctive British morality, it was dramatically appropriate that Mrs Thatcher's downfall should have been provoked by her intransigence in defending the independence of Britain. Nevertheless, it must also be acknowledged that, British and practical though it is, Thatcherism contains a message of universal significance. It is this message, more than the association of Thatcherism with the defeat of socialism, that may account for the continued and widespread interest in Thatcherism. For the morality on which it has unwittingly relied offers an answer to the moral confusion that is now agitating the whole of the Western world.

Not only countries deprived by the fall of communism of their past certainties are thus afflicted. The difficulty arises from the combination of a devotion to securing freedom for individuals to shape their lives as they choose with a loss of loyalty to any variety of the classical morality that might once have directed their efforts. All the pipelines to absolute truth, which civilized men have been ingeniously discovering since ancient times, appear to have disintegrated. While the virtues of democracy, liberty, tolerance, altruism, human rights, etc. are everywhere celebrated, there is no undisputed ground for holding them sacred or even ascertaining their meaning. As a result, we are being told on every side that the traditional verities have been reduced to metaphysical absurdities, and that there is no firm distinction between true and false, right and wrong, beautiful and ugly. The new liberated man must be left to decide for himself and wholly by himself how he will live, what he will believe and hold to be valuable. In short, we are being urged to embrace nihilism, qualified only by the dictum that there is but one sin – inflicting pain, from which it follows that it is evil to insist that children should be made to learn that $2 + 2 = 4$.

Thatcherism, as we have seen, postulates a very different outlook. But the British morality, which ultimately justifies it, lays no claim to absolute truth. It is not based on any of the 'metaphysical absurdities' associated with the classical moralities of Platonism, Aristotelianism, Kantianism, or Marxism. And yet it could hardly be further from nihilism, as those who have castigated Mrs Thatcher for her confident leadership have rightly recognized. What distinguishes the British morality is that, though untainted by nihilism, it is a sceptical morality because it lays no claim to be based on truths beyond human questioning. It rests rather on a commitment – to a particular understanding of the human world, an understanding that is recognized to have been made by human beings. That is not, however, anything like the commitment of a nihilist, plucked at will out of the air. It is rather a commitment to an understanding of the human condition that has been found congenial by those who have for centuries enjoyed living the kind of life which has given rise to that understanding and been shaped by it.

We are thus obliged to conclude that the most curious thing about Thatcherism is that, addressed as it was to immediate practical concerns, nurtured by economists, and based on a quintessentially British outlook, yet it carries to the world at large a moral message. The message is that there is available a way of understanding the human world that does not require us to be either metaphysical dogmatists or nihilists, that offers no blueprints for what should be done in Britain or elsewhere, but that nevertheless enables us to discover within the historical world made by human beings firm criteria for distinguishing civilization from barbarism.

Reference Notes

Prologue

1. *Daily Telegraph* [hereafter simply *Telegraph*], 20 February 1984.
2. *Telegraph*, 9 March 1984
3. *Telegraph*, 20 March 1984
4. *The Times* [hereafter simply *Times*], 10 October 1988
5. *Times*, 29 July 1989
6. *Sunday Times*, 27 August 1989
7. *Telegraph*, 14 October 1989
8. *Spectator*, 4 October 1989
9. *Sunday Times*, 10 September 1989
10. *Telegraph*, 27 October 1989
11. *Times*, 6 November 1989
12. *Sunday Times*, 12 November 1989
13. *Spectator*, 2 December 1989
14. *Sunday Telegraph*, 3 December 1989
15. *Times*, 30 November 1989
16. *Times*, 3 December 1990
17. *Times*, 6 December 1990
18. *Times*, 6 December 1989
19. *Spectator*, 14 April 1990
20. *Sunday Times*, 28 October 1990
21. *Sunday Telegraph*, 28 October 1990
22. *Sunday Times*, 28 October 1990
23. *Sunday Times*, 28 October 1990
24. *Independent*, 17 September 1990
25. *Sunday Times*, 28 October 1990
26. *Times*, 1 March 1990
27. *Guardian*, 22 November 1990
28. Young, *Guardian*, 22 November 1990

Chapter One

1. Peter Riddell, *The Thatcher Government* (Oxford: Blackwell, 1985), p. 59
2. Ferdinand Mount in *The National Interest*, no 14, Winter 1988–9, p. 15
3. Robert Skidelsky (ed.), *Thatcherism* (Oxford: Blackwell, 1989), p. 2
4. Hugo Young, *One of Us* (London: Macmillan, 1989), pp. 321, 526
5. Ibid., pp. 140, 532, 140, 415
6. Cf. Ted Honderich, *Conservatism* (London: Hamish Hamilton, 1990)
7. Gordon Brown, *Where There is Greed—Margaret Thatcher and the*

354

Betrayal of Britain's Future
(Edinburgh: Mainstream
Publishing, 1989), pp. 94, 102
8. Peregrine Worsthorne, quoted
in Hugo Young, op. cit., p. 536
9. Hugo Young, op. cit., p. 536
10. Cf. Ted Honderich, op. cit.
11. Andrew Gamble: *The Free
Economy and the Strong State:
The Politics of Thatcherism*
(London: Macmillan, 1989),
pp. 223, 171, 232. Cf. also A.
Gamble, 'The Political
Economy of Freedom', in Ruth
Levitas (ed.), *The Ideology of the
New Right* (Cambridge Policy
Press, 1986); A. Gamble,
'Thatcherism and Conservative
Politics' in Stuart Hall and
Martin Jacques (eds), *The Politics
of Thatcherism* (London:
Lawrence and Wishart, 1983)
12. A. Gamble, *The Free Economy
and the Strong State*, op. cit.,
pp. 183, 191
13. Hugo Young, op. cit., pp. 533,
537
14. Ibid., p. 536
15. Gordon Brown, op. cit., p. 3
16. Hugo Young, op. cit., p. 508;
Peter Jenkins, *Mrs Thatcher's
Revolution* (London: Jonathan
Cape, 1989), pp. 84, 85
17. Ibid.
18. David Marquand, 'The
Continuing Relevance of
Socialism' in R. Skidelsky, ed,
Thatcherism (Oxford: Blackwell
1989) pp. 164-5
19. Hugo Young, op. cit., pp. 539,
538, 521
20. Ibid., pp. 543, 412
21. Peter Jenkins, op. cit., pp. 154,
66-8, 379
22. David Marquand, op. cit.
23. Peter Jenkins, op. cit.
24. David Marquand, op. cit.,
pp. 164-5, 166-7
25. Peter Jenkins, op. cit., pp. 375,
379; Kenneth Minogue, 'The
Emergence of the New Right',
in R. Skidelsky, op. cit.
26. David Marquand, op. cit.,
pp. 169-70, 171-2
27. Cf. Gordon Brown, op. cit.

Chapter Three

1. Lord Hinchinbroke, *Full Speed
Ahead—Essays in Tory Reform*,
(London: 1944) p. 72
2. Quintin Hogg, *One Year's Work*
(London: Hirst and Blackett,
1944), pp. 77, 44
3. *Onlooker*, August 1944, p. 6;
November 1944, p. 7
4. Harold Macmillan, *Tides of
Fortune, 1945-55* (London:
Macmillan, 1969), p. 34
5. R. A. Butler, *The Art of the
Possible* (London: Hamish
Hamilton, 1971), p. 126
6. *Tory Challenge*, November 1947,
p. 1
7. *Onlooker*, February 1945, p. 3
8. *Spectator*, 25 March 1949
9. *Spectator*, 14 April 1950
10. Peter Jenkins, *Mrs Thatcher's
Revolution* (London: Jonathan
Cape, 1987), p. 3

11. Alistair Horne, *Macmillan* (London: Macmillan, 1988), Vol I, pp. 107–8, 109

12. Harold Macmillan, *Winds of Change, 1914–1939* (London: Macmillan, 1966), pp. 223–4

13. *Crossbow*, No 1, 1957, No 2, 1958; No 5, 1958

14. *Crossbow*, No 5, 1958, pp. 9, 59, 1, 59

15. F. W. S. Craig (ed.), *British General Election Manifestos, 1918–66* (Chichester: Political Reference Publications, 1970), p. 189

16. Quintin Hogg, 'Introduction', *Prospect for Capitalism* (London: CPC, 1960), p. 8

17. Harold Macmillan, *Pointing the Way* (London: Macmillan, 1972), p. 15

18. *Conservatism 1945–50* (London: CPC, October 1950), p. 106

19. Ibid., pp. 56, 58, 30

20. Ibid., pp. 27, 63

21. Ibid., pp. 39, 38

22. Ibid., p. 28

23. Ibid., pp. 34, 57

24. Ibid., p. 60

25. Ibid., pp. 34, 16

26. Ibid., pp. 32, 48

27. Ibid., pp. 55, 76

28. Ibid., pp. 2, 40

29. Ibid., p. 40

30. Ibid., pp. 67, 53

31. Ibid., pp. 20, 8, 7

32. Ibid., pp. 3, 2

33. Ibid., p. 57

34. Julian Critchley, 'The Old Men', *Spectator*, 20 July 1962

35. Leading article, *Spectator*, 20 June 1962

36. Angus Maude, 'Party Paleontology', *Spectator*, 15 March 1963

37. T. E. Utley, 'Answering Utopia', *Spectator*, 11 October 1973

38. T. E. Utley, 'Eleven Years of Tory Rule', *Spectator*, 10 May 1963

39. T. E. Utley, 'Answering Utopia', *Spectator*, 11 October 1973

40. *Crossbow*, 17, 1961, p. 5; *Crossbow*, 16, 1961, p. 6

41. David Howell, *Efficiency and Beyond* (London: CPC, 1965), p. 9; cf. Timothy Raison, *Conflict and Conservatism* (London: CPC, 1965)

42. Russell Lewis, *A Bonfire of Restrictions* (London: CPC, 1965), p. 3

43. Nigel Lawson, 'The need for a national policy', *Conservatism Today* (London: CPC, 1966), p. 53

44. David Howell, 'Towards Stability', *Conservatism Today* (London: CPC, 1966), p. 43

45. *Crossbow*, 41, 1967, p. 5

46. Iain Macleod, *The Target for the Tory Party, A Fresh Approach* (London: CPC, 1965), p. 78

47. J. Enoch Powell, *A Nation Not Afraid–The Thinking of Enoch Powell*, ed. John Wood (London: B. T. Batsford, 1965), pp. 26, 27

48. J. Enoch Powell, *Freedom and Reality*, ed. John Wood (London: B. T. Batsford, 1969), pp. 1, 3

49. J. Enoch Powell, *A Nation Not Afraid*, op. cit., p. 26

50. Ibid., pp. 75, 76, 77

51. J. Enoch Powell, *Freedom and Reality*, op. cit., p. 13

52. Ibid., pp. 74, 79–80

53. J. Enoch Powell, *A Nation Not Afraid*, op. cit., p 102

54. Ibid., p. 90
55. J. Enoch Powell, *Freedom and Reality*, op. cit., p. 13
56. J. Enoch Powell, *A Nation Not Afraid*, op. cit., p. 126
57. J. Enoch Powell, *Freedom and Reality*, op. cit., pp. 58–59
58. J. Enoch Powell, *A Nation Not Afraid*, op. cit., pp. 132–3
59. Ibid., p. 132
60. J. Enoch Powell, *Freedom and Reality*, op. cit., p. 55
61. Keith Joseph, *Stranded on the Middle Ground* (London: CPS, 1976), pp. 20, 21

62. Morison Halcrow, *Keith Joseph* (London: Macmillan, 1989), p. 83
63. Keith Joseph, *Monetarism is Not Enough* (London: CPS, 1976), pp. 19, 11, 12
64. Angus Maude (ed.), *The Right Approach to the Economy* (London: CPC, 1977), pp. 5, 47, 17, 7, 11
65. Ibid., p. 44
66. Ibid., p. 51

Chapter Four

1. 'The Rise and Fall of a Myth' in Rhodes Boyson (ed.), *Goodbye to Nationalisation* (London: Churchill Press, 1971)
2. *Why Privatise?*, (London: Conservative Political Centre, 1983)
3. Jean Loyrette, 'Remarques sur le Problème des Denationalisations', UNIR Conference, May 1985

4. John Moore, 'The Success of Privatisation', speech, London, 17 July 1985
5. *The Value of Ownership* (London: Conservative Political Centre, 1986)
6. Ibid.
7. Alfred Sherman, 'The Crisis Calls for a Minister of Denationalisation' (London: Aims of Industry, 1980)

Chapter Five

1. Cf. *Independent*, 12 October 1989
2. Keith Joseph, *Monetarism is Not Enough* (London: CPS, 1976), p. 186
3. Jock Bruce-Gardyne, *Mrs Thatcher's First Administration* (London: Macmillan, 1984), p. 58

4. Ibid.
5. Martin Holmes, *The First Thatcher Government* (Falmer, Sussex: Wheatsheaf Books, 1985), p. 55
6. William Keegan, *Mr Lawson's Gamble* (London: Hodder and Stoughton, 1989), pp. 61–3, p. 65

7. Tim Congdon, *Monetarism Lost* (London: CPS 1985), pp. 13–17
8. W. Keegan, op. cit., pp. 176, 172–5
9. Tim Congdon, op. cit., pp. 27–35, 33
10. W. Keegan, op. cit., p. 219
11. Keith Joseph, *Reversing the Trend: A Critical Reappraisal of Conservative Economic and Social Policies* (London: CPS, 1975) p. 31
12. Keith Joseph, *Monetarism is Not Enough*, op. cit., p. 6

Chapter Six

1. Ian Gilmour, *Britain Can Work* (Oxford: Martin Robertson, 1983), pp. 190, 191–2
2. Ibid., pp. 193, 192, 195
3. *Weekend World*, ITV, 10 September 1972
4. T. E. Utley, *A Tory Seer*, ed. Charles Moore and Simon Heffer (London: Hamish Hamilton, 1989), p. 113
5. Enoch Powell, *One Nation Not Afraid*, ed. John Wood (London: Batsford, 1965), p. 133
6. Michael Oakeshott, *Rationalism in Politics* (London: Methuen, 1962), p. 45
7. T. E. Utley, op. cit., p. 147
8. Arthur Shenfield, *What Right to Strike* (London: IEA, 1986)
9. Ibid., p. 30
10. Enoch Powell, *A Nation Not Afraid*, op. cit., pp. 121–2
11. Michael Oakeshott, *Rationalism in Politics*, op. cit., pp. 45, 53–4
12. *Sunday Times*, 14 October 1990
13. Conservative Party Conference, 9 October 1984
14. *Nepsava*, 14 May 1985
15. *Times*, 12 September 1989
16. T. E. Utley, *A Tory Seer*, op. cit., p. 113
17. *Telegraph*, 1 May 1991
18. Leader in *Sunday Telegraph*, 28 October 1990
19. *Sunday Telegraph*, 3 February 1980

Chapter Seven

1. J. Redlich and F. W. Hirst, *Local Government in England* (London, 1903), II, 9
2. Sidney and Beatrice Webb, *English Local Government from the Revolution to the Municipal Corporations Act* (London: Longman, 1906–29), IV, 353–5
3. Ibid.
4. Alex Henney, *Inside Local Government* (London: Sinclair Browne, 1984), p. 156

5. Bryan Keith-Lucas and Peter G. Richards, *A History of Local Government in the Twentieth Century* (London: Allen and Unwin, 1978), p. 36

6. A. Henney, op. cit., p. 27

7. W. H. Greenleaf, *The British Political Tradition*, Vol III: *A Much Governed Nation* (London: Methuen, 1987), pp. 93-4

8. K. Newton and T. Karvan, *The Politics of Local Expenditure* (Basingstoke and London: Macmillan Education, 1985), p. 15

9. A. Henney, op. cit., pp. 159, 160

10. Robert Bacon and Walter Ellis, *Britain's Economic Problem: Too Few Producers* (London: Macmillan, 1978)

11. Michael Heseltine, *Where There's A Will* (London: Hutchinson, 1987), p. 40

12. *Hansard*, 22 December 1976, Col 740

13. John Cunningham, speech to Association of Metropolitan Authorities, 24 October 1986

14. Stewart Lansley, Sue Goss, Christian Wolmar, *Councils in Conflict—The Rise and Fall of the Municipal Left* (London and Basingstoke: Macmillan, 1989), p. 107

15. Richard Crossman, *The Diaries of a Cabinet Minister*, Vol I: *Minister of Housing 1964–6* (London: Hamish Hamilton, 1975), pp. 230, 81, 450, 24, 66

16. Ibid., p. 341

17. A. Henney, op. cit., pp. 183, 189

18. S. Lansley et al., op. cit., pp. 66, 68

19. *Today*, 13 January 1987

20. *Western Daily Press*, 29 August 1986

21. John Carvel, *Citizen Ken* (Chatto, 1984), pp. 201–9; Peter Gerard Pearse and Nigel Matheson, *Ken Livingstone or 'The End of Civilisation As We Know It', A Selection of Quotes, Quips and Quirks* (Proteus Books, 1982)

22. K. Ascher, *The Politics of Privatisation* (London: Macmillan Education, 1987), p. 218

23. S. Lansley et al., op. cit., p. 116

24. B. Keith-Lucas and P. G. Richards, op. cit., p. 75

25. Ibid., p. 69

26. S. Lansley et al., op. cit., p. 16

27. Ibid., p. 10

28. *Tribune*, 19 July 1985

29. S. Lansley et al., op. cit., pp. 205, 193

30. Paul Beresford, *Good Council Guide* (London: CPS, 1987), p. 22

31. K. Ascher, op. cit., pp. 238, 27

32. Nicholas Ridley, *The Local Right* (London: CPS, 1988), p. 27

33. Peter Malpas and Alan Murie (London: Macmillan Education, 1987), pp. 99

34. Gerry Stoker, *The Politics of Local Government* (London and Basingstoke: Macmillan Education, 1988), p. 179; cf. also K. Ascher, 'The Politics of administrative opposition–council house sales and the right to buy', *Local Government Studies* vol. 9, no 2

35. M. Heseltine, op. cit., pp. 145–6

36. *Tribune*, 21 December 1984

37. *Labour Herald*, 8 February 1985

38. *Tribune*, 21 December 1984
39. *Islington Gazette*, 7 June 1985
40. *Daily Telegraph*, 6 July 1985
41. *Sunday Times*, 12 April 1987
42. *Sunday Times*, 23 November 1986
43. *Daily Telegraph*, 11 May 1990
44. Nicholas Ridley, speech at Bournemouth, 8 October 1986
45. Nicholas Ridley, speech to Conservative Central Council, Torquay, 20 March 1987
46. *Daily Telegraph*, 26 March 1990
47. Ibid.
48. Speech to his constituency, September 1980, reported in *Sunday Times*, 29 July 1990
49. *Independent*, 8 April 1990
50. *Sunday Times*, 24 June 1990—Statement by Mrs Thatcher at Tory Women's Conference in London

51. *Times*, 17 March 1990
52. *Telegraph*, 10 April 1990
53. *Spectator*, 28 April 1990
54. *Independent*, 4 May 1990
55. *Times*, 19 June 1990
56. *Daily Telegraph*, 6 March 1990
57. S. Lansley et al., op. cit., p. 198
58. Ibid., pp. 197–8
59. Ibid., pp. 198, 171, 195, 118
60. G. Stoker, op. cit., p. 214
61. S Lansley et al., op. cit., pp. 177–8
62. Ibid., pp. 200, 203
63. Ibid., pp. 178, 200
64. *Telegraph*, 24 October 1988
65. S. Lansley et al., op. cit., p. 117
66. *Independent*, 19 April 1990
67. *Sunday Times*, 13 May 1990
68. *Telegraph*, 21 May 1990
69. *Telegraph*, 1 October 1990

Chapter Eight

1. Social Services Committee First Report, Session 1987–8, *Resourcing the National Health Service: Short Term Issues* (London: HMSO, 1988, H.C. 264)
2. Speech by John Hoare, London, 23 September 1987
3. Harry Eckstein, *The English Health Service* (Cambridge, Mass.: Harvard University Press, 1959), p. 161
4. *A National Health Service*, HMSO, Comd 6502, 1944, p. 6
5. Cf. Arthur Seldon, *Capitalism* (Oxford: Blackwell, 1990), pp. 262ff; David Green, *Working*

Class Patients and the Medical Establishment (London: Temple Smith Tower, 1985)
6. *Hansard*, 5th Series, Vol 422, 30 April 1946, Col 66
7. *Fabian Essays* (London: Allen & Unwin, 1948), p. 54
8. *Independent*, 3 November 1990
9. Ray Whitney, *National Health Crisis* (London: Shepheard Walwyn Ltd, 1988), p. 12
10. *Sunday Times*, 30 November 1986
11. Enoch Powell, *A New Look at Medicine and Politics* (London: Pitman Medical Publishing Co Ltd, 1966), p. 16

12. David Willetts, *Guardian*, 1 February 1989
13. *Times*, 1 November 1989
14. 'Evidence to the government internal review of the National Health Service', *British Medical Journal*, Vol 296, 14 May 1988, pp. 1411–3
15. *Independent*, 3 November 1990
16. Ibid.
17. R. Klein, op. cit., p. 206
18. Ibid., pp. 201, 195, 193
19. David Green, *The NHS Reforms* (London: IEA, 1990), pp. 1, 3
20. Ibid., p. 5
21. Ibid., p. 21
22. Ibid., pp. 12, 13

Chapter Nine

1. Caroline Cox and John Marks, *The Right to Learn* (London: Centre for Policy Studies, 1982), p. 79
2. Terry Ellis, Jackie McWhirter, Dorothy McDolgan and Brian Haddow, *William Tyndale: The Teacher's Story* (London: Writers and Readers Publishing Cooperative, 1976), p. 171
3. Cf. *The Trend of Reading Standards*, National Foundation for Education Research, March 1972
4. *Daily Mail*, 18 October 1976
5. Interview with Professor Sig Prais
6. *Sunday Telegraph*, 9 December 1990
7. *Independent*, 30 June 1990
8. *Telegraph*, 13 April 1987
9. *Telegraph*, 24 April 1990
10. Interview with Kenneth Baker
11. *Telegraph*, 7 September 1989
12. *Telegraph*, 19 August 1989
13. *Sunday Telegraph*, 30 December 1990
14. *Times*, 3 December 1990
15. *Independent*, 29 July 1988
16. *Telegraph*, 12 October 1989
17. *Sunday Telegraph*, 5 March 1989
18. *Times*, 21 August 1986
19. *Times*, 14 August 1986
20. *Sunday Telegraph*, 12 March 1990
21. Letter, *Sunday Telegraph*, 21 March 1990
22. Letter, *Telegraph*, 19 July 1986
23. Nigel Collins, 'MSC and the Education of Young People', *Political Quarterly*, Vol 57, No 3, 1986
24. *Times*, 28 March 1990
25. 20 July 1984
26. *Sunday Times*, 29 July 1990
27. *Telegraph*, 17 September 1990
28. *Independent*, 22 October 1990
29. *Times*, 22 October 1990
30. Interview, *Sunday Telegraph*, 15 April 1990
31. Noel Malcolm, *Spectator*, 21 April 1990
32. Interview, *Sunday Telegraph*, 15 April 1990
33. *Telegraph*, 29 March 1990
34. *Telegraph*, 24 August 1989
35. *Telegraph*, 20 April 1990
36. *Telegraph*, 7 January 1990
37. *Sunday Telegraph*, 12 April 1987
38. *Sunday Times*, 22 July 1990

39. *Sunday Times*, 22 April 1990
40. *Times*, 10 July 1990
41. *Times*, 10 July 1990
42. Noel Malcolm, *Spectator*, 21 April 1990
43. *Times Literary Supplement*, 8 May 1987
44. *Croham Report*, February 1987
45. Ibid., para 2.49
46. Ibid., para 2.43
47. Ibid., para 4.4.4
48. Ibid., para 5.10
49. Ibid., para 5.14
50. Ibid., para 6.12.iii
51. Ibid., paras 4.6 and 4.11
52. Cmd. 114, p. iv
53. Ibid., para 2.13
54. Ibid., para 4.43
55. House of Commons Debate, 19 July 1988, col 988
56. *Times Higher Education Supplement*, 14 October 1986
57. Elie Kedourie, *Perestroika in the Universities* (London: IEA Health and Welfare Unit, 1989), p. 29
58. House of Lords Debate, 12 April 1989, pp. 302–3
59. CVCP Press Briefing, 1 July 1988
60. Elie Kedourie, op. cit., p. 84
61. House of Commons Debate, 19 July 1988, col 1025
62. Enoch Powell, review of Michael Oakeshott, *The Voice of Liberal Learning*, in *Independent*, 9 March 1989
63. *Sunday Times*, 21 February 1988
64. *Spectator*, 10 June 1990
65. Elie Kedourie, op. cit., p. 23
66. House of Lords Debate, 18 April 1988, col 1292
67. Elie Kedourie, op. cit., p. 9
68. Ibid., p. 26
69. Ibid., pp. 29–30, 21
70. Ibid., p. 44

Chapter Ten

1. *Hansard*, vol 888, p. 314
2. *Hansard*, Fifth Series, Vol 796, col 1221
3. Cmnd. 4715, p. 8
4. *Hansard*, Fifth Series, Vol 823, Col 1311
5. *Hansard*, Fifth Series, Vol 840, Col 627
6. Interview, *Europa*, in *The Campaign Guide 1977* (London: Conservative Research Department, 1977), p. 610
7. *The Right Approach* (London: Conservative Central Office, 1976), p. 67
8. *The Campaign Guide*, 1977, op. cit., p. 605
9. 1979 *Conservative Election Manifesto*, p. 293
10. Ibid., p. 293
11. *Winston Churchill Memorial Lecture*, Luxembourg, 18 October 1979
12. *Daily Express*, 27 June 1984; *Daily Mail*, 27 June 1984
13. *Daily Mail*, 27 June 1984
14. Leader, *Daily Express*, 27 June 1984
15. *Times*, 27 June 1984
16. *Labour Manifesto*, 1983, p. 328
17. *Conservative Manifesto*, 1983, p. 302
18. *Question Time*, BBC1, 28 April 1983

19. *Hansard*, Sixth Series, Vol 96, Col 325
20. *Hansard*, Sixth Series, Vol 96, Col 388
21. *The Campaign Guide*, 1987, op. cit., p. 522
22. *DTEU*, Article 42
23. Ibid., Articles 23, 38
24. Ibid., Articles 63, 64, 65, 69
25. Ibid., Article 82
26. *Times*, 20 June 1990
27. *Times*, 7 July 1988
28. *Independent*, 10 June 1990
29. *Independent*, 13 June 1989
30. *Telegraph*, 10 November 1989
31. *Telegraph*, 5 December 1989
32. *Sunday Telegraph*, 19 November 1989
33. *Times*, 2 November 1989
34. *Independent*, 18 November 1989
35. *Sunday Times*, 10 December 1989
36. *Hansard*, Delors Committee Report, EEC Report, 18 December 1989
37. *Telegraph*, 14 December 1989
38. *Spectator*, 21 July 1990
39. *Times*, 25 October 1988
40. *Sunday Times*, 11 February 1990
41. *Independent*, 30 October 1989
42. *Sunday Times*, 29 October 1989
43. Peter Jenkins, *Independent*, 11 December 1989
44. *Times*, 11 December 1989
45. *Independent*, 11 December 1989
46. *Sunday Times*, 10 December 1989
47. Ferdinand Mount, *Telegraph*, 27 April 1990
48. *Sunday Times*, 15 April 1990
49. *Times*, 21 June 1990
50. *Independent*, 26 June 1990
51. *Times*, 23 April 1990
52. *Telegraph*, 20 August 1990
53. *Times*, 24 July 1990
54. Ibid., 17 September 1990
55. *Times*, 17 September 1990
56. *Times*, 17 September 1990
57. *Telegraph*, 30 October 1990
58. *Times*, 30 October 1990
59. *Today, Daily Mirror, Daily Mail*, 30 October 1990

Chapter Eleven

1. *Times*, 11 April 1989
2. Ibid.
3. *Telegraph*, 14 April 1989
4. Margaret Thatcher, *The Revival of Britain* (ed. A. B. Cooke) (London: Aurum Press, 1989), p. 187
5. *Times*, 25 May 1990
6. Ibid.
7. *Telegraph*, 25 May 1990
8. *Times*, 17 April 1991
9. *Telegraph*, 17 April 1991
10. Interview with Brian Walden, *Sunday Times*, 8 May 1991
11. The Rt. Revd Ronald Bowlby, Bishop of Southwark, and the Revd Michael Newman, Principal of the National Children's Home, *Independent*, 9 April 1988
12. *Sunday Telegraph*, 10 January 1985
13. *Times*, 15 October 1988
14. *Sunday Telegraph*, 10 January 1988
15. *Statesman*, 3 June 1983
16. Brian Walden, *Sunday Times*, 8 May 1988

17. Graham Turner, *Sunday Telegraph*, 10 January 1988. For a wide-ranging and profound portrait of the intellectual attitudes antagonistic to Thatcherism see Noel Annan's *Our Age* (London: Fontana, 1991)

18. Interview, Brian Walden, *Sunday Times*, 8 May 1988
19. *Spectator*, 2 December 1989
20. St Augustine, *City of God* (London: Penguin, 1976), p. 866

Chapter Twelve

1. *Times*, 17 October 1985
2. *Times*, 9 January 1986

3. *Times*, 31 October 1986
4. *Times*, 25 July 1988

INDEX

Index

376 *Index*

The Politics of the Judiciary
Fourth Edition

J. A. G. Griffith

The furore caused by the initial publication of this book – described by the *Guardian* as 'an instant classic' – made front-page news in *The Times*. Since the third edition appeared much has happened – particularly concerning censorship of the media and freedom of speech, miscarriages of justice and police accountability, immigration policy, and labour injunctions – to reinforce Professor Griffith's controversial thesis that, given our legal system as it is now composed, the judiciary cannot act neutrally but must act politically. He shows, by examining specific cases, how the senior judiciary, constrained by their own self-imposed limitations, frequently fail sensibly to interpret the public interest.

'It is the achievement of Professor Griffith's book to lift the debate to an altogether better level . . . He has, in effect, thrown down the gauntlet to any believer in the neutrality of the judiciary, or in its independence from government.'
                                        Michael Zander, *Guardian*

'Presents in detail, cogently and without hysteria, a controversial view.   *The Times*

'A masterly analysis of the role of the judiciary . . . We are being warned: informatively, intelligently, forcefully.'   *New Society*

Fontana Press

The Rise and Fall of British Naval Mastery

Third Edition

Paul Kennedy

By the author of *The Rise and Fall of the Great Powers*

Paul Kennedy's *Rise and Fall of the Great Powers* became a critically acclaimed international bestseller, and provided a focus for the intellectual debate about the fate of empires in a shifting world-order which raged late in the 1980s. This book – first published in 1976 but furnished with a postscript which extends the analysis to the most recent events in British naval history, including the Falklands War – displays the verve, lucidity and abundant insight which characterized that book, and with which Kennedy's many readers are so familiar. Kennedy traces the ebb and flow of Britain's maritime strength from the time of the Tudors down to our own day, placing the fortunes of the Royal Navy firmly in the context of prevailing political and economic conditions, both national and international.

'The rise and fall of British naval mastery is an ambitious subject, and Kennedy tackles it with the powerful combination of a lucid mind and a scholar's grasp of the sources . . . This is an excellent and stimulating synthesis and an exercise in total strategic history.'
Correlli Barnett, *New Society*

'Together with a lively literary style, Dr Kennedy possesses in abundance the insight, the perspective and the intellectual courage to draw broad conclusions about the development of the past.'
Michael Howard, *Sunday Times*

Fontana Press

Fontana History of England
General Editor: G. R. Elton

The Pursuit of Greatness
1900–1970

Robert Holland

When the twentieth century began, Britain was essentially a naval, Indian and colonial power enjoying 'splendid isolation' in world affairs. As it wore on, her imperial gaze gradually shifted from India to the Middle East, whilst at crucial junctures she sought also to play a more decisive role in continental Europe. Both these tendencies were to lead to great difficulties and occasional setbacks; the special relationship which developed with the United States was in part a means of compensating for the complications and risks which accrued elsewhere. The interaction between these European, imperial and American impulses in British policy-making is tellingly reconstructed here.

By the end of the twentieth century most Britons believed that their country's history during that century had been primarily a story of decline. It is Robert Holland's aim, in this incisive and sophisticated study, to grapple with the complexities generated by such images of 'rise and fall'. He charts the course of the grand compromise between Greatness overseas and Welfare at home, which successive British governments struggled to sustain. The language of greatness appealed to Britain's politicians and public alike, but both found the language of national modernization altogether more forbidding and divisive, only to see economic and social priorities, freshly rehabilitated, dictate the *lingua franca* of the radicalized British politics which was to emerge in the late 1970s.

Fontana Press

Thinking About Social Thinking
Escaping Deception, Resisting Self-deception
Second Edition

Antony Flew

Human beings are by far the most complicated objects within the known Universe; we are uniquely peculiar in that we can, and cannot but, make choices, and can, and often do, give reasons for those choices. Rationalizing human behaviour is our most compelling pastime, and temptations to deception and self-deception are endemic in this process; we are all disposed to offer and accept insufficient evidence and invalid argument when these seem to support conclusions which we merely *wish* were true. When our choices affect, or have pretensions to affect, the lives of others, we need to know how best to think clearly about out social thinking, how best to resist the allure of self-deception – how best to choose.

Everyone sceptical about or confused by the findings of the social sciences will appreciate Antony Flew's crisp analysis of the methodological flaws and systematic misunderstandings corrupting their study, teaching and application. *Thinking About Social Thinking* seeks to establish what can and cannot be learnt from such studies, indicating several instances where good work has been ignored, or much-needed work has yet to be done, because findings, or expected findings, prove, or would probably prove, unwelcome. Taking careful aim at the sometimes subtle and insidious falsehoods that permeate our social and political discourse, and distort our decisions, Flew issues a refreshing, impassioned warning against the perils of falling prey to complacently muddled thinking and false but comfortable conclusions.

Fontana Press

'My Style of Government'

The Thatcher Years

Nicholas Ridley

'The best inside job on the Thatcher years so far'   *Financial Times*

'I always admired her, but it was some time before I really understood the force of her character. It was her immense conviction about the rightness of certain basic ideas which carried through. She had at the same time an acute political understanding of the prides and prejudices of her fellow countrymen, many of which she shared. This combination of knowing instinctively how millions of people in the country would react, together with her iron determination to achieve something, or to stop something, but never to fudge, was all-powerful.'

Enlivened with revealing anecdotes, inside stories and considerable humour, Nicholas Ridley's book is nevertheless hard-hitting on the central issues on which Mrs Thatcher eventually foundered, and assesses candidly those whom she entrusted to carry out her aims, making an important contribution not only to the political history of the past twelve years but also to the debate on future Conservative Party policy.

'Ridley writes with passion and clarity'   *Independent*

'An important contribution to the story of Mrs Thatcher's rise and fall and a magnificent assessment of the Thatcher years'
                                          Norman Tebbit, *Evening Standard*

Fontana

The Crooked Timber of Humanity

Chapters in the History of Ideas

Isaiah Berlin

'Reading Isaiah Berlin is always exhilarating.'

Anthony Storr, *Independent on Sunday*

'Berlin's preoccupations are constant. His commitment is to individual and collective liberty and to moral and political pluralism. His writing an extended exploration of the conditions in which those ideals blossom and flourish or wither and perish. The eight essays collected here are all concerned with manifestations of anti-rationalism: utopianism, fascism, romanticism and nationalism are all passed in magisterial review. To read them is to sit at an unlit window and see the landscape of European thought illuminated by a spectacular display of fireworks.'

Ian McIntyre, *Independent*

'To read Isaiah Berlin is above all to listen to a voice, effervescent, quizzical, often self-mocking, but always full of gaiety and amusement. These essays remind the reader on every page of the many thousands of listeners over the decades for whom that voice has brought the drama and passion and imaginative depth of the intellectual tradition to which they belong unforgettably alive.'

John Dunn, *Times Literary Supplement*

Fontana Press